Henry Horwood

A manual of the practice of conveyancing

Showing the present practice relating to the daily routine of conveyancing in solicitors' offices

Henry Horwood

A manual of the practice of conveyancing

Showing the present practice relating to the daily routine of conveyancing in solicitors' offices

ISBN/EAN: 9783337146795

Printed in Europe, USA, Canada, Australia, Japan

Cover: Foto ©ninafisch / pixelio.de

More available books at **www.hansebooks.com**

A

MANUAL

OF THE

PRACTICE OF CONVEYANCING,

SHOWING

THE PRESENT PRACTICE
RELATING TO THE DAILY ROUTINE OF CONVEYANCING
IN SOLICITORS' OFFICES;

TO WHICH ARE ADDED

Concise Common Forms and Precedents in Conveyancing;—

CONDITIONS OF SALE; CONVEYANCES; AND ALL OTHER
ASSURANCES IN CONSTANT USE.

THIRD EDITION,
REVISED AND CONSIDERABLY ENLARGED.

By G. W. GREENWOOD, Solicitor,

AND

HENRY HORWOOD.

LONDON:
STEVENS, SONS, AND HAYNES,
Law Booksellers and Publishers,
26, BELL YARD, LINCOLN'S INN.

1865.

LONDON:
PRINTED BY C. ROWORTH AND SONS,
BELL YARD, TEMPLE BAR.

PREFACE

TO

THE THIRD EDITION.

In again appearing before the profession I tender them my best thanks for the manner in which they received the Second Edition of my Book.

Since that Edition was published great and important alterations have been made in the practice of Conveyancing, the last of which is destined at some future period to work a revolution in that branch of practice.

I have endeavoured to bring down the practice to the present time, and trust my efforts will be successful.

As in the beginning of 1858 so at the end of 1864, skill and ability are unnoticed in the taxation of costs, and he who can put the greatest number of words in a document, even although those words may consist of mere rubbish, fares better than he who by superior skill prepares a concise Conveyance, such as a Purchaser may read and understand. Can any one, therefore, be surprised that the best of our Precedents are still incumbered with a mass of verbiage that is a scandal to the science of Conveyancing?

89, Chancery Lane, February, 1865.

PREFACE

TO

THE SECOND EDITION.

THE favourable reception accorded by the profession to this Manual, as evidenced by the rapid sale of the first Edition, has laid me under a deep and pleasing obligation.

I avail myself of the call for a fresh Edition to show my sense of such obligation by endeavouring to render the present volume much more perfect and useful than the previous one. How well I have succeeded I must, of course, leave to the judgment of others.

I have added some other heads of Conveyancing Practice, which are of equal importance to those contained in the former Edition, namely, Composition Deeds and Arrangements with Creditors; Disclaimers, and Deeds of Copartnership; and have introduced much new and, I think, pertinent matter throughout the Treatise: I have also greatly extended the Precedents, besides classifying and making a separate Index to them.

To the gentlemen who reviewed the Book on its publication I tender my best thanks, for the kind spirit in which they noticed my maiden effort.

In the Precedents I have aimed at being as concise as is consistent with carrying out the objects of the deeds and the intentions of the parties to them. Many deeds even at present are so redundant of senseless language, so clogged and incumbered with what is both useless and troublesome, that we can scarcely feel surprise at the recent urgent demand by unprofessional persons for a General Registry; but so long as the present unsatisfactory mode of remuneration for Conveyancing business exists, so long will the evil alluded to exist with it. I trust, however, that the last barrier to a great improvement in the system of Conveyancing will be soon removed, by allowing professional men to charge for a document, not according to the number of words contained in it, but to the amount of skill brought to bear in the preparation of it.

FEBRUARY, 1858.

PREFACE

TO

THE FIRST EDITION.

In bringing before the profession an experience of many years in the practice of Conveyancing, my principal endeavour has been to produce such a Book as may be of service to Articled and other Clerks in the profession, who may sometimes feel the want of a simple guide to enable them to perform, with comparative ease and credit to themselves, such portions of Conveyancing business as may be intrusted to them. I need hardly say, that I have no intention of intruding my experience on those members of the profession who are now in practice, or the numerous gentlemen engaged in the profession, who, instead of requiring help of this description, could afford help and assistance to others, much better than I have done. This Book is not intended to be anything more than a Manual for those who, from want of experience, feel some difficulty, either at the commencement or during the progress of ordinary Conveyancing business. I have endeavoured to make the Book so simple, that a Solicitor may with confidence intrust small matters of business to Articled and other Clerks to proceed upon, and submit to him from time to time. Whether I am deceived in my expectations as to the utility of my performance, or as to my own capacity in undertaking it, I must leave others to judge; in writing it I have not trespassed on the preserves of others in any one particular; but have contented myself with a simple statement of the strictly practical part of Conveyancing as followed at the present day.

London, Feb. 1856.

TABLE OF CONTENTS.

TREATISE.

	PAGE
On Agreements	1
Sales	5
Purchases	20
Mortgages	38
Leases	54
Copyholds	67
Copartnership Deeds	80
Composition Deeds, Assignments for benefit of Creditors, &c.	86
Settlements	90
Disentailing Deeds, and Deeds executed by Married Women	103
Wills	107
As to obtaining Probate of Wills or Letters of Administration	115
Legacy and Succession Duties	117
Disclaimer	120

PRECEDENTS.

ACKNOWLEDGMENT.

1. On Deed to be inrolled in Chancery 125

ADVERTISEMENT.

2. For Creditors under 22 & 23 Vict. c. 35 125

AFFIDAVITS.

3. Of due Execution of Bill of Sale 126
4. Verifying Notice of Dissolution of Partnership.. 127

AGREEMENTS.

5. For Purchase of Leasehold Premises and Stock in Trade of a Lace Manufacturer, the Value of the Stock to be paid by Bills 127
6. For Sale and Purchase of a Freehold Estate by Private Contract 131

	PAGE
7. For Sale of Freeholds	133
8. For Sale of Ship	134
9. For Lease of a House	136
10. For Underlease of a Piece of Garden Ground	137
11. From Year to Year of Agricultural Land	138
12. For letting a House for Three Years	139
13. Under Seal between a Brewer and his Manager	140
14. Of Reference where no Action brought	143
15. Of Reference where Action brought	144
16. For a Mortgage	145
17. For releasing an Annuity charged on Real Estate	148

APPOINTMENTS.

18. Of Gamekeeper	150
19. Of Money under a Power and Surrender of two sixth Parts thereof, with Power to revoke the Appointment made as to one sixth Part	151
20. Of new Trustee	156
21. Of new Trustee, by Indorsement	158

APPRENTICESHIP.

22. Indenture of	159
23. Proviso to be inserted in Indenture of, if necessary	160

ASSIGNMENTS.

24. Of Leaseholds by Indorsement	161
25. Of Leaseholds by Mortgagor and Mortgagee	162
26. Of Leaseholds by a separate Deed	166
27. Of Leaseholds by a Mortgagee under his Power of Sale	168
28. Of Reversionary Interest in a Sum of Stock	171
29. Of the Goodwill of the Business of a Clock and Watch Maker, and the Clock-winding connected therewith	175
30. Of Debts	177
31. For the benefit of Creditors	180

ATTORNMENT.

32. Of Tenant	183

BILL OF SALE.

33. Bill of Sale conditional	183

BONDS.

34. From the Manager of a Brewery and his Sureties	187
35. Accompanying Marriage Settlement for securing £1,000 to Wife if she survives Husband, or dies leaving Issue, with the Interest to her for Life	188
36. Common Money	189
37. Defeasance to, conditioned for replacing a Sum of Stock, and the Payment of Annual Sums in lieu of Dividends	190

COMPOSITION DEEDS.

		PAGE
38.	Composition Deed	191
39.	Ditto	192
40.	Ditto	193
41.	Ditto	194
42.	Form of Assent to	197
43.	Ditto	197

CONDITIONS OF SALE.

44. Of Freehold Property in Lots, where an unexceptionable Title can be produced.. .. 198
45. Of Property held under an Underlease, where it is left to the Auctioneer to determine at the Time of Sale whether the Property is to be sold in more than one Lot 202
46. Of Leasehold Property in Lots by a Mortgagee, with special Stipulations .. 204
47. Of Freehold and Leasehold Property, and a Freehold Rent-charge sold in Lots at a Sale, with special Stipulations .. 206
48. Of Property under a Decree of the Court of Chancery.. .. 209
49. Of a Reversionary Interest in Money in the Funds 212
50. Where Property is held on an Underlease 213
51. If Title not marketable 214
52. Of Freehold Ground Rents 214
53. To be used where Land originally acquired by a Parish .. 216

CONFIRMATION.

54. Of a Deed to which either a Widow or a Spinster was a Party, but who married before she executed the Conveyance .. 217

CONVEYANCES.

55. Of Freehold by Appointment and Grant, with Covenant to produce Deeds 218
56. Of a Plot of Land by Vendor on lotting out a Field for Building Purposes 221
57. Of Freeholds in the City of London in Mortgage to the Trustees of a Loan Society 222
58. By a Mortgagee under his Power of Sale 225
59. Of Land for Burial Ground under the Powers of 43 Geo. 3, c. 108 226
60. Of Freeholds and Covenant to surrender Copyholds 227
61. Of Charity Property under direction of Charity Commissioners 229
62. Of Life Interest in Real Estate 230
63. By Clerk of Peace to Trustees of Settlement 231

COVENANT.

64. That Infant shall execute Deed on attaining Twenty-one .. 234

COPYHOLDS.

	PAGE
65. Surrender of Copyholds (absolute)	234
66. Deed of Covenants for Title to accompany same	236
67. Conditional Surrender of Copyholds	237
68. Deed of Covenant to accompany same	238
69. Power of Attorney to surrender Copyholds	239
70. Disclaimer by Trustees of Copyholds that only one of them may take Admittance	240
71. Deed of Enfranchisement with Grant of Common Rights	241
72. Warrant to enter Satisfaction on Conditional Surrender	244
73. Surrender of Copyholds to the Trustees of a Settlement	244

DEEDS OF COVENANT.

74. By Purchasers of Land set out for Building where it is intended the Buildings shall be uniform	245
75. Not to resort to certain Estates to raise Judgment Debts and to indemnify	248
76. To produce Deeds	251
77. Not to throw any Rubbish into the River or within Limits, and to prevent others from doing so	253

DECLARATION.

78. Of the existence of a Person who had given a Power of Attorney at the time of the Attorney exercising the Power	257

DISCLAIMERS.

[*Vide* COPYHOLDS, page 240.]

79. Of Trusts under Will	257
80. Ditto (Short Form)	259

DISENTAILING DEED.

81. By Tenant in Tail, with the consent of the Protector, to bar Entail of Freeholds	259

DISTRINGAS.

82. Affidavit to obtain Distringas on Stock	261
83. Notice to the Bank of England	262

ENFRANCHISEMENTS.

[*See* COPYHOLDS, page 241.]

GRANT.

84. In Fee of a Plot of Land subject to a Yearly Rent-charge	263
85. Of a Yearly Rent-charge	267
86. Of a Right of Road	268
87. Special Grant of Right of Road to Railway	269
88. Covenants and Proviso relating to the said Grants of Rights of Way	270
89. Instructions to be sent to a Non-professional Person with a Deed for Signature	271

LEASES.

		PAGE
90.	Of Public House and Premises	272
91.	Of Land for Building Purposes	276
92.	Of a House	282
93.	Covenant for Production of Original Lease contained in an Underlease	285
94.	Arbitration Clause in Lease	285
95.	Clause suspending Rent during Fire	286
96.	Exception out of Lease of Water from Well	286
97.	Licence by Lessor to Lessee to permit Sale by Auction on Premises	287
98.	Notice to Quit	288
99.	Clause restrictive as to Assignment, but not to be unreasonably withheld	288
100.	Proviso to determine Lease at option of either Party at end of first Seven or Fourteen Years	289
101.	Proviso in Lease requiring Lessee to give up any Part of demised Premises on receiving Notice from Lessor	290
102.	Proviso to be inserted in Mining Lease, providing for Reduction of Rent if Faults met with	291
103.	Proviso in Lease authorizing Lessor to dispose of Part of demised Land on allowing abatement or expending Money received	292
104.	Notice to Lessee to abate Nuisance	293
105.	Surrender of Lease by Indorsement	294
106.	Waiver by Lessor of past Breaches of Covenant by a Lessee	295
107.	Licence by Lessor to assign Lease	295

MEMORIALS.

108.	Of a Lease for Registration	296
109.	Of Conveyance	296
110.	Of an Assignment	297
111.	Of a Mortgage	297
112.	Memorandum to be indorsed on the Memorial where Deed and Memorial executed in the Country	298
113.	Of an Indorsed Deed	298

MORTGAGES.

114.	Of Freeholds to a Building Society	299
115.	Of Leaseholds to a Building Society	302
116.	Another Form of Power of Distress by Mortgagor	306
117.	Another Form of Power in Mortgage Deed for Mortgagee to distrain for Interest in Arrear when Property in possession of Mortgagor	306
118.	Mortgage of Leaseholds for a Sum certain and further Advances	307
119.	Mortgage of Leaseholds for a Sum certain	311

	PAGE
120. Of a Pecuniary Legacy	315
and Notice to Trustees	317
121. Of Freehold Houses to one Mortgagee	318
122. Of Freehold Houses to two Mortgagees	322
123. Further Charge (by separate Deed)	326
124. Further Charge (by Indorsement)	328
125. Reconveyance of Freeholds	329
126. Re-assignment of Leaseholds	331
127. Transfer of Mortgage on intended Marriage to Trustees of Settlement (Concise Form)	332
128. Transfer of Mortgage, with concurrence of Mortgagor	334
129. Transfer of Mortgage, with further Advance	338
130. Release of Equity of Redemption, by Indorsement	340
131. Proviso that Mortgagor, being a Solicitor, shall have his Costs	341
132. Proviso in Mortgage for Money to remain for a Term certain	341
133. Form of Recital when Mortgage paid off, but no Reconveyance taken	342
134. Notice of Sale by Mortgagee	342
135. Form of Undertaking by or on behalf of intending Mortgagor before Title investigated	343
136. Release by Mortgagee in Fee of Part of Hereditaments subject to Mortgage	343

NOTICES.

137. To Quit, from Landlord to Tenant	344
138. To Quit, from Tenant to Landlord	345
139. To Quit, and for Double Rent	345
140. To Railway Company from Claimant, requiring Compensation as Occupier under 68th Section of "The Lands Clauses Consolidation Act, 1864"	346
141. To Railway Company from Claimant, requiring Compensation as Owner under 68th Section of the last-mentioned Act	347
142. By Mortgagee to Tenant to pay Rent to him	349
143. By second Mortgagee to first	349

PARTITION.

144. Partition Deed by Tenants in Common	350

PARTNERSHIP.

145. Deed of Copartnership between two Traders, with usual Clauses	351
146. Deed of Dissolution of Partnership	363
146a. Notice of Dissolution of Partnership	366

POWERS OF ATTORNEY.

147. Under Tithe Commutation Act	367
148. Under Inclosure Act	367

	PAGE
149. To recover a Debt	367
150. From a Brewer to his Manager	368
151. By an Executor about to leave England	371
152. By a Person going to reside Abroad	375

RECITALS.

153. Of Payment of Succession Duty in Conveyance	377
154. Of Agreement for Sale	377
155. Ditto	377
156. Of Contract for Sale	378
157. Of Lease	378
158. Of Conveyance to Uses to bar Dower	378
159. Of Assignment	379
160. Of Mesne Assignments	379
161. Of Purchase Agreement of Leaseholds	379
162. Of a Mortgage	380
163. Of Agreement for Sale subject to [Incumbrances and] a Right of Re-purchase	380
164. Of Contract for Sale of Lands, and that no Conveyance made	381
165. Of Sub-Contract	381
166. Another Form of Ditto	381
167. Of Agreement to make new Conveyance and to join in confirming same	381
168. Another Recital in Confirmation Deed	382
169. Of Agreement by Persons interested in Purchase-Money to join in Conveyance	382
170. Of Agreement by Heir to effectuate Ancestor's Contract by joining in Conveyance	383
171. Of Agreement on Marriage to convey Copyholds and Leaseholds, and to pay off Mortgage out of Wife's Personalty—Husband to be entitled to Residue	383
172. Of Codicils not affecting Devise of Realty	383
173. Of no Devise of Mortgage or Trust Estates	384
174. Of Contract for Sale of Mortgage Debt	384
175. Of Contract for Licence to use Invention	384
176. Of Death of old and Appointment of new Trustees	384
177. Of Revocation of Appointment of Executor and Appointment of Substitute	385
178. Of Agreement by Executor to assent to Legacy	385
179. That Trust Property put up for Sale but bought in	385
180. Of Letters of Administration	385
181. Of Limited Administration	386
182. Of Purchase by Agent	386
183. Of Appointment of new Trustees	386
184. Of Tenancy by Curtesy	386
185. Of Death of Mortgagee Intestate as to Mortgaged Estate	387
186. Of Death of Surviving Trustee Intestate as to Trust Estates	387
187. Of further Charge	387

xvi   TABLE OF CONTENTS.

	PAGE
188. Of further Charge by Indorsement	387
189. Of Transfer of Mortgage	388
190. Of Erection of Buildings since Conveyance	389
191. Of Policy of Assurance for Life	389

RELEASES.

192. To Executors by a Residuary Legatee 389
193. Of Trusts created by Marriage Settlement of a Sum of Money 391
194. Of Charges on Real Estate 394

REQUEST.

195. By Cestuis que Trust to Trustees to sell out Stock for a Mortgage 395

SETTLEMENTS.

196. (On Marriage) of Real Estate 396
197. (Ditto) of Personalty 398
198. Proviso to be inserted in Settlement of Equity of Redemption 402

TESTIMONIUM.

199. To Instrument executed by Attorney 402

WILLS.

200. Of a Person making various Devises and Bequests, and giving Residue of Property to his Children 403
201. Of a Person giving all his Property to his Wife and appointing her Executrix 404
202. Codicil appointing new Trustee and Executor in room of one deceased, and giving an additional Legacy 404
203. Bequest of Furniture to Wife for Life and Widowhood, with directions as to Inventory 405
204. Bequest to Trustees upon Trust for Daughter to her separate Use, and afterwards for her Children 406
205. Devise of Trust Estates 407
206. Clause to be inserted in a Will prohibiting any Party claiming thereunder from disputing it 407
Conveyancing Charges 408

INDEX TO TREATISE 411
INDEX TO THE PRECEDENTS 425

ADDENDA ET ERRATA.

Page 30.—12th line from top, *omit* " Qy. Was D. married?"

Page 31.—4th line from bottom, *omit* the third requisition altogether.

Page 34.—*Lechmere* v. *Brotheridge* overruled by *Taylor* v. *Meades*, 13 Weekly Rep. 394, which decides that a feme covert, having an equitable estate in fee settled to her separate use, may dispose of it as if she were a feme sole by deed or will, without a deed acknowledged, and not the less so that a specific power of appointment in a particular way over the property is given her by the instrument settling it to her separate use.

Page 106.—24th line from top, *add* after "acknowledged" "but see *Taylor* v. *Meades*, 13 Weekly Rep. 394."

THE
PRACTICE OF CONVEYANCING.

AGREEMENTS.

An agreement is often treated as a very simple document, and is sometimes prepared by the parties to it, and at other times by those whose experience is insufficient to guard against the numerous questions likely to arise in carrying it into effect. It is, however, of as much importance as any subsequent assurance which may have to be prepared under it, because the agreement is the basis of all future operations, and when it is signed it cannot be departed from without the consent of all parties to it, a consent that can seldom be obtained. Nothing but experience can teach the necessity of exercising great care in the preparation of an agreement, and nothing sooner indicates professional knowledge and ability than a well-drawn agreement. It must not be too readily inferred, from what is before stated, that an agreement, when signed, can be departed from, even with the consent of all parties to it; for it may happen that, after signing it, some of them may die, leaving persons who are not *sui juris;* this, therefore, should be always borne in mind in the preparation or perusal of an agreement. If the framer of the document performs his duty correctly none of the parties will be able to withdraw from it without the consent of the others, and, at the same time, he will have guarded against the numerous alterations of circumstances likely to happen between the signing and the carrying into execution of the document he has prepared; in addition to this he will also have the satisfaction of giving effect to his client's intentions, and whatever turn the matter afterwards may take, he can always refer to the agreement as a landmark in enforcing or defending the rights of his client. In order to prepare an agreement properly, the subject-matter of it should be previously arranged in the mind of the draftsman, so that he may have a clear conception of the object in view, and the manner in which it is intended to be carried out. By adopting this course he will save himself considerable trouble, and also frame a creditable document. A precedent is seldom of much assistance in preparing an agreement, except by enabling the draftsman to form some idea of the manner in which it should be framed; the outline he may easily find, but the filling up, which is manifestly the most important part of the work, must be done by himself. In preparing agreements, the adoption of the style in some of the precedents, namely, setting out the subject-matter in numbered paragraphs, may be of service in cases where it becomes necessary, in the course of correspondence, to refer to some particular clause; it also saves needless repetition in the commencement of the different portions of the document. Should it be necessary to embrace several distinct matters in one agreement, the most scientific way will be to exhaust one matter before commencing another, and this will save much trouble in any subsequent reference to the agreement. A very good illustration of a special agreement is that embodied in the first precedent, and you will be seldom called upon to prepare one of a more complicated nature. In the agreement alluded to, it will be perceived that three distinct and separate matters, all forming part of one transaction, have to be carried out. This form is added in order to show at a glance how desirable it is to make every branch of the agreement complete in itself, and so avoid the necessity of continual references from one part of it to another. In the event of your not being concerned for both parties, then, after drawing the agreement, you will fair copy and forward it to the solicitor on the other side for approval; and, as soon as the draft has been finally settled between him and yourself, you will engross one part and he will engross the other, it being his privilege to engross the part to be signed by his client. After your engrossment has been signed by your client, you will make an appointment with the solicitor on the other side to exchange the parts signed by your respective clients; and, after this is done (which, in strictness, should be done at your office, but this is seldom insisted on), you will proceed to carry the stipulations embodied in the document into effect.

It is better to have a written agreement, even when you are acting for both parties; indeed a written agreement should never be dispensed with, it saves many difficulties that might otherwise arise during the progress of the business, and you will find in the course of practice that these difficulties will arise even where both parties are desirous of carrying out what they consider the understanding originally come to; so seldom is it that persons having opposite interests, however honestly disposed, will not differ as to the meaning or effect of a prior verbal arrangement. If you are acting on behalf of both parties, and the case is not one of magnitude or importance, it will generally be sufficient to write out the instructions in the presence of, and get them signed by, both parties; as should any doubt be afterwards entertained as to what has been agreed on, it will be set at rest on referring to the instructions with the signatures attached thereto.

An agreement under hand only (not being an agreement for a lease) requires a 6*d.* stamp, if under fifteen folios, and an extra 6*d.* for every additional fifteen folios; few agreements, however, contain more than fifteen folios, if concisely prepared. If written on unstamped paper, always bear in mind that not more than fourteen days after the date of the agreement is allowed for getting the stamp affixed, and it can only be done afterwards on payment of a penalty. Should the agreement be under seal, which must be the case where a company is a party to it, or where it is intended the heirs shall be bound, the proper stamp will be 35*s.* if under thirty folios, and every extra fifteen folios will require a 10*s.* stamp. In this case the time allowed for stamping the agreement is the same as any ordinary deed, namely, two months.

In commencing an agreement not under seal, it is quite

unnecessary to follow a form still in use in many offices; namely, "an agreement, &c., whereby the said A. B. doth hereby for himself, his heirs, executors and administrators agree," &c. Now the greater part of this is mere verbiage, as the heirs of a person cannot be bound by an instrument not under seal, and executors and administrators are bound without being named. If A. agrees to do an act and dies before the act be done, his executors or administrators are bound to do it, notwithstanding they are not named in the instrument creating the obligation: the only exception to this is where it is expressly stated that the obligation shall be personal only and not extend to the representatives of the person bound. Such a form as that just mentioned does no credit to the framer of it. The proper way is never to introduce words in documents that have no meaning. A profusion of words incumbers a document and answers no useful purpose. The golden rule is to express your meaning with clearness and brevity, to insert all that should be inserted, and to leave nothing to be inferred that ought to be expressed.

The forms of agreements which are given in the precedents are intended both as a guide to the manner of framing this description of document and also as precedents for use on any particular occasion, and from these you will have little difficulty in preparing others.

Before concluding this branch of the subject it may be advisable to mention that, with respect to an equitable interest in property, an agreement only is sufficient to transfer it from the seller to the purchaser; it is, however, very unusual to rely on the agreement alone; and the purchaser of an equitable interest may insist on having it transferred by the same description of assurance as is used in the transfer of a legal interest; and this appears to be the more proper course, inasmuch as the agreement invariably contemplates the doing of some further act by the parties, and although as matter of law it may be unnecessary that such act should be done, yet it is safer to do it as at some future time questions and doubts may arise whether it was or not done, besides leaving the matter in an unsatisfactory state. It is, therefore, advisable in such a case to have the agreement carried into effect in the usual way, by taking a transfer of the equitable interest in the same manner as if it were a legal interest.

In dealing with the interests of married women in real estate, provision must be made in the agreement as to the expense of acknowledging the conveyance if it be not intended that the vendor is to do all that is necessary at his own expense. It is not an uncommon practice at the present day for a vendor to stipulate for a certain sum clear, in which case his solicitor must take care to express the intention distinctly, otherwise the vendor may be called upon to pay costs which he had intended to throw upon the purchaser.

SALES.

On receiving instructions to put property up for sale by public auction, you will, if the matter is left entirely to you, consider what auctioneer should be employed. In some cases the vendor will name the auctioneer, in others he will leave the matter in your hands, in which case it is as well to bear in mind that with respect to large estates an auctioneer of repute and standing is likely to realize more than one less known to the public. Having fixed upon the auctioneer you will see and instruct him upon the matter, and (if a London auctioneer be employed) he will obtain all necessary particulars, and in some cases insert a preliminary advertisement that the property is in the market. He will also prepare and forward to you the particulars of sale, in order that you may peruse and settle them; if, however, the auctioneer is in practice in the country, you will insert the advertisement and prepare the particulars of sale, there being a difference in this respect between town and country practice. In preparing or settling particulars of sale great care should be exercised, as a misdescription may be taken advantage of by an unwilling purchaser to get rid of the contract. For instance, suppose property is described as being held under a lease, when it is in fact held under a sub-lease, a Court of Equity will not decree specific performance (*Brumfit* v. *Martin*, 30 Law Times, 98).

Before attempting to settle either particulars or conditions of sale, it would be advisable to read that part of Sugden or Dart "On the Law of Vendors and Purchasers" which relates to this branch of the subject. Having carefully settled the particulars, then proceed to draw the conditions of sale, but before you can do this properly, you must make yourself acquainted with the title; the best way of doing this, if you have no abstract, is to make an analysis of the deeds; this need only be very short, as your principal object is to satisfy yourself that the vendor can convey both the legal and the equitable estate, and to prevent a purchaser raising objections upon other parts of the title, which may be difficult or expensive to dispose of. The minor points in the title will invariably be covered by the general conditions used on almost every sale.

Should the estate be a large one, or the title complicated, it may be advisable to prepare an abstract and lay it before counsel with instructions to prepare the conditions of sale, as in this and many other cases, where the estate to be sold is an extensive one or the title very much complicated, it will be far better, and in the end less expensive, to give a fee to counsel to settle the conditions, than to take the responsibility of so doing upon yourself, it being next to impossible for any one in an attorney's office, even if he felt that he possessed the requisite knowledge, engaged in various matters of business and liable to frequent interruptions, to bestow the amount of care and attention required in settling conditions for the sale of a large estate, with a complicated and difficult title.

Having settled the particulars and conditions of sale, make a fair copy thereof, and either forward it to the auctioneers to be printed, or send it to your own printers. When you get the proof, carefully examine it in order to see that it is correct. Having examined and altered the proof where necessary, you will either return it to the auctioneer, or to the printer. Having obtained a sufficient number of copies, the auctioneer will forward some to the various inns and other places for distribution; he will also prepare and have bills posted in the neighbourhood of the property.

It is not the practice for country solicitors to have the conditions of sale printed and annexed to the particulars, the latter only being printed and distributed, and the conditions written out and read at the sale, as many copies being made as there are lots to be sold. Why such a difference between London and country practice should exist I cannot say; but the more preferable mode appears to be, to have both particulars and conditions printed, in order that an intending purchaser may know not only what is about to be sold, but also the conditions upon which he is to purchase, without hearing such conditions read for the first time among the noise and confusion of the sale room.

Where a large estate, or several fields or closes of land are intended to be sold, it is advisable to annex a plan to the particulars of sale, in order that the situation of the property and its advantages may be seen at a glance. And if an attractive-looking residence is on the land, it may also be advisable to have a lithographed drawing of it attached to the particulars. Should you and the auctioneer decide upon having a plan, he will cause it to be prepared and forward it to you with the draft particulars of sale, as before mentioned.

It is not within the scope of this work to point out what should or should not be stated in the particulars or conditions of sale, as so much depends upon the title. I may, however, say that you cannot state too plainly and distinctly in the particulars the nature and tenure of the property and the burdens thereon, and, in fact, everything that a man intending to purchase ought to be made acquainted with, and care should be taken to provide both against misrepresentation and misdescription, either of which might prevent the vendor from enforcing the contract. In the conditions of sale, equal clearness and distinctness are requisite in stating upon what terms the property is to be disposed of, and what the purchaser is and what he is not to be at liberty to require.

The cases on the subject are extremely numerous, in fact, too numerous to be carefully read and considered; they are, however, referred to in Sugden or Dart "On the Law of Vendors and Purchasers," one of which books should find a place in your library. The law upon this subject generally is by no means difficult to comprehend, and may be summed up thus: If the particulars of sale fully and accurately describe the estate and the tenure, so that a person of ordinary intelligence may not fail in discovering what is intended to be sold, there will be little fear of any objection being maintained; and if the conditions fairly state the points as to which you intend to restrict the purchaser, (and I need not remind you that in common honesty these points ought to be fairly stated,) he will very seldom be advised to resist the completion of the matter.

The day of sale having arrived, you will proceed to the place of sale to answer any question that may be put, either as to the property, the conditions, or otherwise. The auctioneer will get through this part of the business, and you will seldom be called on to interfere. An intending purchaser will sometimes ask questions about the title, and you must be guided by the circumstances of the case as to the course of proceeding.; if you give an answer to any question, do so readily and candidly, as you will find it far better not to give an answer at all than to answer in a manner calculated to show that your object is to conceal as much as possible.

Should the property be purchased, the auctioneer will see that the purchase contract, at the end of the conditions, is signed by the purchaser; and, if in London, he will also receive the deposit. In country sales the deposit is generally received by the vendor's solicitor, and not by the auctioneer. It may save trouble and delay if you ask the purchaser for the name of his solicitor, in order that you may forward the abstract to him at once; but, as in the hurry of the sale this may be forgotten, it will be found useful to put at the foot of the purchase contract these or similar words—" Abstract to be sent to —— ;" in which case the auctioneer or yourself, as the case may be, in obtaining the purchaser's signature to the contract, will make the necessary inquiry of him; and as this course saves any misconception as to your object, I should recommend its adoption.

It may happen that you are instructed to prepare a contract, to carry into effect the sale of property agreed upon by your client. Such contract is always drawn by the vendor's solicitor, he generally having the title deeds in his possession, and knowing more about the title and the property than the purchaser's solicitor does; the latter, in the majority of cases, understanding very little about the matter until after he has received the draft contract.

In order to prepare the contract properly, you will require the names and addresses of the vendor and purchaser, the description of the property, the price to be paid, the commencement and state of the title, the time for completing the purchase, whether any rights or interests are to be reserved to the vendor, and any other stipulations upon which the sale is to be made. Having obtained this information, you will prepare and forward a draft contract to the purchaser or his solicitor; and after he has perused it, and you and he have disposed of all debateable points, he will have one part fair copied and you another, and you will each get your copy signed by your client; and then, having compared both parts, exchange the one for the other. It is not necessary that both parties should sign each part of the contract, it is quite sufficient if signed by the party against whom you may have to enforce it.

The sale, whether by public auction or private contract, having progressed thus far, you will prepare and make a fair copy of the abstract of title, or, should you have laid an abstract before counsel prior to the sale, it will only be necessary to make a copy thereof. In either case the copy will be forwarded by you to the solicitor named by the purchaser, or, if he has not named a solicitor, to the purchaser himself at his address in the purchase contract; and, unless the abstract is delivered by a clerk or messenger, you should request an acknowledgment of its receipt, in order that you may know with greater certainty the time within which the purchaser, according to the conditions of sale, will be bound to forward his requisitions on the title. After the receipt of the abstract, the purchaser's solicitor will make an appointment with you for comparing it with the title deeds; this will be done at your office if the deeds are in your possession, but if they are not (which will be the case if your client is a mortgagor or cestui que trust), they must be examined at the place where they may happen to be. Unless, however, bound by the conditions of sale, a purchaser cannot be compelled to incur the expense of his solicitor running about the country from place to place to compare the deeds with the abstract, as a purchaser is justified in presuming that the deeds will be found at the office of the vendor's solicitor, or, at all events, within a reasonable distance therefrom, and this should always be borne in mind on preparing conditions of sale in cases where the title deeds are not in your client's possession.

On comparing the abstract of title with the deeds, it is the practice, in London, for the purchaser's solicitor to take with him a clerk to read the abstract, although the practice formerly was, and still is in many parts of the country, for a clerk in the office of the vendor's solicitor to read the abstract. You will have the deeds ready at the time appointed, and should, if practicable, be at hand in case any inquiry should arise on any part of the title. The abstract, having been compared with the deeds, will be perused by the purchaser's solicitor, who will send you the requisitions (if any) on the title, which, if forwarded within the time limited by the conditions, you will prepare to answer, and in doing so you will be guided by the conditions of sale. In some cases you may find it necessary to lay the requisitions, with a copy of the abstract, before counsel; but this can only arise in cases where the title is very much complicated. It may be useful to mention that the usual and most convenient plan is to copy the requisitions on brief or foolscap paper, half margin, and to write the answers opposite to the requisitions, and then to make a copy of the whole and forward it to the purchaser's solicitor. A great mistake is often made by vendor's solicitors in answering requisitions, which puts the purchaser's solicitor to much trouble, e. g., the purchaser's solicitor asks for particulars of the birth, marriage or burial of a certain person. The vendor's solicitor turns to the conditions of sale, and discovers that all certificates are to be obtained by and at the expense of the purchaser, and then proceeds either to inform the purchaser's solicitor of the fact, or that such certificates can be obtained at the expense of the purchaser. Now this is not such an answer as the purchaser has a right to demand; for, in the first place, the certificate should have been set out in the abstract, as it is quite as much a matter of title as any of the proceedings shown on the abstract, and in all well-drawn abstracts this is done; and, in the next place, although the purchaser is to obtain the certificate and pay for it, he is entitled to call upon the vendor for information as to where it may be obtained, in order that he may procure it himself. This mode of answering requisitions is frequently a source of much trouble to a purchaser's solicitor, and is hardly courteous conduct on the part of the vendor's solicitor.

The requisitions having been disposed of, you will receive from the purchaser's solicitor the draft conveyance for approval. This you will peruse on behalf of the parties for whom you are concerned, and should there be any for whom you are not acting, you will forward the draft to their respective solicitors for approval. After it has been approved on behalf of all parties, you will return it to the purchaser's solicitor; but however great the number of solicitors concerned, the vendor's solicitor is the medium of all communications between the respective solicitors.

In perusing the draft it is necessary to see that all recitals of documents and statements of facts are correct, that the person on whose behalf you are perusing the draft is not parting with any more of his property or any greater interest therein than he has contracted for; that any reservations intended to be inserted on his behalf are correctly inserted; that any liabilities which the purchaser is to take upon himself are set out in the draft, and that your client does not enter into covenants of a more extensive character than he can be required to do. It will be no part of your duty to alter the form of any recitals or statements in the draft, provided they are correct in substance, as the purchaser's solicitor may prepare his draft in any form he pleases, if the form he uses does not prejudice your client; and should he think proper to make the draft unnecessarily long, you are not justified in reducing it, in order that it may be in accordance with the forms generally used by you, or your own notions of conveyancing.

The covenants usually entered into by a vendor are the following:—

If a trustee or mortgagee, he covenants only that he has not done any act to incumber.

If the owner of the estate and having the legal fee vested in himself, he covenants that (notwithstanding any act by him, &c.) he has good right to convey free from incumbrances, and for further assurance, at the costs of the purchaser.

If the equitable owner of the estate, or beneficially interested in the purchase-money, his covenants extend to the acts of those in whom the legal estate is vested.

These covenants are entered into where the vendor is himself the purchaser of the estate (I use the word purchaser in its common acceptation), but should he take the estate as heir-at-law or under a settlement, whether voluntary or otherwise, or a will, his covenants extend to the acts of his ancestor or the person making the will or settlement, as the case may be.

All these covenants are more or less qualified, and therein contradistinguished from covenants for title given by a mortgagor, which are absolute.

As to the covenants a purchaser can require, you should read either Sugden or Dart "On the Law of Vendors and Purchasers," in either of which books you will find collected all the law on the subject.

The draft being finally approved by all the solicitors concerned, and returned by you to the purchaser's solicitor, will be engrossed by him and forwarded to you with the engrossment for examination; and after you have compared it with your own copy of the draft, you will send the draft and engrossment to the other solicitors (if any) who have approved it, in order that it may be examined by them; and this will be a convenient time for getting the deed executed by those (if any) who are merely consenting or nominal parties to it, as the solicitors who have approved the draft on behalf of such parties will, on your asking them to do so, readily get the deed executed while in their hands. After the engrossment has been examined, it will be returned to you and kept until an appointment is made for the completion of the business. This appointment is usually made by the purchaser's solicitor. You will bear in mind that the completion of a purchase always takes place at the office of the vendor's solicitor, unless the property be in mortgage, in which case the completion will be at the office of the mortgagee's solicitor, the rule being that "the money follows the deeds." On receiving an appointment, you will arrange for the attendance of such of the parties interested as have not previously executed the deed. Respecting the completion, the chief points necessary to call your attention to are—to have the interest (if any payable) calculated, deducting the income tax in all cases except on a sale under the direction of the Court of Chancery, in which case the income tax is never deducted, (but the purchaser may apply for the deduction when the money is paid out of Court, *Bebb* v. *Bunny*, 1 Kay & J. 216). The deeds, if to be given up to the purchaser, are put in order according to date, so that his solicitor may easily check them with the abstract; and should the sale of the property have been by public auction and a deposit paid to the auctioneer, you will also take a written authority from the purchaser or his solicitor to the auctioneer, to hand over the deposit to you or your client. Some solicitors require the purchaser or his solicitor to sign a schedule of the deeds handed over to him, but it is rather unusual and appears scarcely necessary.

In the majority of cases your duty will now cease, but

others may arise in which you may have some difficulties; for instance, the purchaser's solicitor may insist upon being furnished with abstracts of documents referred to in the abstract of title, but not abstracted in chief, or may require the title to be carried further back; or on certain requisitions being answered or more satisfactorily answered; or he may insist on other covenants being entered into than those he can require, or object to pay any interest on the purchase-money at the time of completing the purchase.

Your course of proceeding in all or any of these cases will be guided by the circumstances of each particular case. The conditions of sale or contract (if any) should be carefully perused by you, in order to see if you are obliged to satisfy the purchaser's demands; but if the sale has been made by private contract, without any condition as to title, then you must refer to the books before mentioned, in order to see how far the purchaser is justified in insisting on what he asks for, or you may take the opinion of a conveyancer on the matter. This course, however, will only be necessary where you are doubtful as to the purchaser's right; but in such a case it ought to be resorted to, as should *you* be doubtful, how can you expect to convince the purchaser's solicitor that *he* is wrong? Again, the delay and expense that will be occasioned by a long correspondence will be more unpalatable to your client than the fee to counsel for his advice.

The most difficult question to deal with is that relating to interest on the purchase-money; the solicitors of the vendor and purchaser can seldom agree as to which of them may have caused the delay in the completion of the matter. The cases on the subject are somewhat contradictory and do not lay down any clear rule by which you may act. It appears, however, that where the conditions of sale state that interest shall be paid, if "from any cause whatever" the purchase is not completed by a certain day, the purchaser must make out a strong case in order to succeed in his objection to pay interest, and must show that the delay has been wilfully caused by the vendor's solicitor; but in order to succeed even on this point he must show that the delay has been considerable; the delay of a few days from time to time during the proceeding of the business will certainly not be considered wilful delay. A very good case on the subject is *Bannerman v. Clark* (26 Law J., Ch. 77), where the prior cases are referred to. Another leading case on the point is *De Visme v. De Visme* (decided by the late Lord Cottenham), 1 Mac. & G. 336; 1 Hall & T. 408.

In some cases your client will have agreed to sell an estate without having obtained professional assistance, and you will generally find that he has signed what is termed "an open contract," the meaning of which is, that he has made no stipulations with the purchaser as to the title or evidence of title he may require, or in fact inserted anything on the subject. Both tact and judgment are required in these cases, and some consideration will be necessary before you furnish the abstract of title to the purchaser's solicitor, as although in some cases a sixty or even a forty years' title is considered sufficient, yet this must always depend on the manner in which the title is commenced. The principal point here is to decide what you shall make your root of title. If you commence with a will, the purchaser may require evidence of seisin by the testator, and this you may not be able to procure. The best deed to commence an abstract with is a mortgage, as it is a safe presumption that the title was investigated and approved on behalf of the mortgagee before he advanced his money. If you can commence your title with a mortgage or conveyance sixty years' back that will do, and in most cases a clear forty years' title will, and in fact ought, to be sufficient. You will also bear in mind that, under an "open contract," the purchaser is not only entitled to have a safe holding title but can require a strictly marketable one; and although to non-professional minds there may not appear any difference between these descriptions of title, yet to a professional man the difference is very great. A person may have a safe holding title from having for twenty years enjoyed property adversely against persons not under disability; but this would not in equity be considered a marketable title:

the general rule of that Court being that a vendor must deduce a sixty years' title; doubtless, in some cases, a forty years' title would be sufficient, but these cases are exceptions.

Under an open contract the purchaser can insist, and in most cases does insist, on having every question on the title cleared up and every information furnished at the expense of the vendor; again, he may require possession of the title deeds, or, if they are not in the vendor's possession or relate to a larger estate than that contracted to be sold, he is entitled to attested copies, with a legal covenant for production of the deeds, and for all this the vendor must pay the costs. If it should happen that no time is named for completion, then the purchaser is in equity entitled to the rents and profits from the date of the contract, as that is a complete conversion in equity, and the vendor is entitled to interest on the purchase-money at 4*l.* per cent. per annum from the same date until completion. If a time be fixed for completion and the purchase is not then completed, the purchaser takes the rents and profits from that time, paying the vendor interest on the purchase-money at 4*l.* per cent. per annum, unless the delay in the completion has arisen on the part of the vendor, and the purchase-money has been lying idle with notice to the vendor of that fact.

If the property contracted to be sold should be burnt down pending completion (it having been insured by the vendor), the purchaser is not entitled to the benefit of the insurance in the absence of an express stipulation to that effect in the contract (*Poole* v. *Adams*, 12 Weekly Rep. 683).

Whatever may be the nature of the contract, the vendor cannot be required, if a trustee or mortgagee, to enter into any covenant other than that he has not done any act to incumber, and if the owner of the estate or beneficially interested in the purchase-money, he will enter into precisely the same covenants as if he had sold under conditions of sale, as conditions of sale seldom define the covenants to be entered into by the vendor; I have more than once made use of the words, "the owner of the estate or beneficially entitled to the purchase-money." My meaning is this: it sometimes happens that a trustee under a will, with power to sell, enters into a contract to sell the estate, and on examining the will, it is found not to contain the usual clause making the trustee's receipt a good discharge to purchasers, and it may not be one of those cases where a Court of Equity considers that the testator must of necessity have intended his trustee to have the power of giving receipts. In this case (unless it falls within the 23 & 24 Vict. c. 145, s. 29, presently mentioned), the person entitled to the produce of the estate is required to join in the conveyance, and enter into covenants for title, which extend not only to the acts of himself, but also to the acts of his testator and trustee. Where trustees sell under conditions of sale, a clause is inserted providing for this difficulty, by stating that the parties beneficially entitled to the estate shall not be required to join in the conveyance.

Where railway companies take land under the compulsory powers of the Lands Clauses Consolidation Act, 1845, the whole of the vendor's costs are thrown upon the company under sect. 82 of that act, and also the cost of investing the purchase-money when paid into Court, as in the case of parties incapacitated to convey, and as to what these costs are, see *Re Hampstead Junction Railway Company* (12 Weekly Rep. 100). It sometimes happens that the vendor dies before the conveyance to the company is executed, leaving an infant heir; in this case, the company is not bound to pay the costs of getting the estate out of the infant. See Dart on "Vendors and Purchasers," where all the cases are collected on this and other points frequently arising on a company taking land under their compulsory powers.

If the vendor is a lessee or assignee holding under a lease, which contains a covenant not to assign without the lessor's consent, it is incumbent on him and not on the purchaser to obtain the lessor's license, unless otherwise expressed in the contract (*Lloyd* v. *Crispe*, 5 Taunt. 249; *Mason* v. *Corder*, 7 Taunt. 9).

While on this point, I may call your attention to the 6th section of the Act to further amend the Law of Property (23 & 24 Vict. c. 38), which practically reverses *Dumpor's case* (4 Coke's Reports), and enacts, that the waiver of the benefit of any covenant by a lessor shall be good for that turn only, and not be considered a general waiver. Also to the act 23 & 24 Vict. c. 145 (An Act to give to Trustees, Mortgagees and Others, certain Powers now commonly inserted in Settlements, Mortgages and Wills), ss. 1, 2, 3, of which greatly extend the power of selling property over which they have a power of sale; and sect. 11 and the following sections enable a mortgagee to sell in certain events, although no power of sale be comprised in the mortgage deed; but it must be observed, that the act only applies where any principal money is secured or charged by deed on any "hereditaments;" therefore, it would not apply where the mortgage is of chattels personal, e. g., policies of assurance, &c.

This act also contains (sect. 27) power to appoint new trustees, in cases where the instrument creating the trust gives no such power. This is one of the most useful provisions in the act.

There is also the 25 & 26 Vict. c. 53 (An Act to facilitate the Proof of Title to and the Conveyance of Real Estates), under which an indefeasible title may be obtained, and the 25 & 26 Vict. c. 67 (An Act for obtaining a Declaration of Title), under which a judicial declaration of title can be obtained, both of which acts should be carefully perused by you, in order that if an application be made to you by a client under either of them, you may be able to advise him on the subject.

The 9 Geo. II., intituled " An Act to restrain the Disposition of Land, whereby the same becomes Inalienable," and commonly called "The Mortmain Act," has been amended and improved by the 24 Vict. c. 9, and the 25 Vict. c. 17, both of which should be read, and the effect of the alterations carefully noted up. You should also make yourself acquainted with the Leases and Sales of Settled Estates Act (19 & 20

Vict. c. 120), and the Leases and Sales of Settled Estates Amendment Act (21 & 22 Vict. c. 77), as it may happen that you may be suddenly requested to advise upon those acts; and should you not previously have read them, or have only a very superficial knowledge of them, in all probability you will forget their contents, and it may be, their existence. At the most, you will have to turn to the acts in your client's presence, and fish out an answer to his question in the best way you can; whereas if you had carefully read the acts previously (and the two together are not very long), you would be able to turn to the very section required at almost a moment's notice.

There is another act of great importance to a vendor, namely, the Trustee Act, 1850 (13 & 14 Vict. c. 60), amended by the Trustee Extension Act, 1852 (15 & 16 Vict. c. 55), as under those acts an outstanding legal estate may be vested in a new trustee, or an order made vesting it in the vendor or purchaser at a comparatively small expense, and, what is still better, in a reasonably short space of time.

Before leaving this chapter, it may be well to call your attention to a species of document which is at the same time a conveyance and mortgage. I allude to the purchase of a coal-mine, where the consideration money is payable by instalments, and powers of distress and entry are given to secure payment of the instalments. This is very common throughout South Staffordshire, and I believe in other parts of the country.

The practice is, for the vendor's solicitor to prepare this document, and for his charges to be paid by the purchaser, except of course such charges as relate to the abstract and proving the title, which are borne by the vendor in the usual manner. Many practitioners considered that the powers of distress and entry given to secure payment of the instalments, took away from the instalments their character of unpaid purchase-money, and made them a species of rent, and therefore, like rent, subject to income tax. But it has now been decided that income tax cannot be deducted from the instalments, that, in fact, the instalments are unpaid purchase-money and not rent. (*Taylor v. Evans*, 25 L. J., Exch. 269; *Foley v. Fletcher*, 28 L. J., Exch. 100.)

PURCHASES.

Should you be professionally concerned for a purchaser, it will probably be in one of the following cases:—Your client will have bought property at a sale by auction, and will bring the conditions of sale and purchase contract to you; or he may bring the conditions of an intended sale to you, and ask your advice on the title to the property or to a particular lot, or he may have entered into what I have before spoken of as " an open contract:" or inform you that he has been treating for the purchase of an estate, and instruct you to peruse the draft contract on his behalf; or, lastly, he may have entered into a contract by letters. It may be convenient to mention here that two persons often correspond as to the sale and purchase of an estate, and although the correspondence may apparently be sufficient to form a complete contract, it may happen that either the vendor or purchaser in the last letter has referred to a formal contract to be prepared by his solicitor, or the expressions used by him may point to a more formal contract being entered into. In such a case there is abundant authority to show that you cannot throw overboard this reference to a more formal contract, and take the letters as forming in themselves a perfect and binding contract, inasmuch as the parties, or at least one of them, contemplated the terms being embodied in a formal manner, and his intention must be carried into effect.

In each of the cases above mentioned your course of proceeding will be different, and in order that I may make myself plainly understood, I will allude to them separately.

Should your client have purchased property at an auction, and bring the conditions of sale and purchase contract to you, your course will be a very simple one. You will, in the first place, write to the vendor's solicitor for an abstract of the title, and in the meantime diligently peruse the conditions of sale, in order to ascertain what title your client may require, and what restrictions as to title are imposed on him. You may find that a serious defect in the title is attempted to be covered by a loose condition, framed in such a manner that a non-professional man on reading it would be thrown off his guard, but yet apparently of sufficient stringency to cover the defect; in this case you will consider whether the condition is so framed that, by reading it, a man of ordinary intelligence may discover what is intended to be guarded against. If it is so framed, your client will be bound by it, whatever may be its effect; if, on the contrary, it is framed in an obscure manner, and with an evident intention to mislead a purchaser, or if so loosely framed that the meaning of it cannot be easily understood, a Court of Equity would probably refuse to decree a specific performance as against your client. It may be convenient here to allude to the clause now generally inserted in conditions of sale of leasehold property, namely, that the last receipt for ground rent shall be conclusive evidence of all the covenants in the lease having been performed up to the completion of the purchase. This condition properly applied is a very useful one in practice for both vendor and purchaser, inasmuch as if such a condition were not inserted, it would be your duty, as purchaser's solicitor, to make minute inquiries as to whether all the covenants in the lease had been duly observed and performed, and to take advantage of a breach of covenant, however unimportant it may be, a difficulty that can only be got over by a waiver of the breach by the lessor. On the other hand, the condition may have the effect of compelling your client to take a title that may be worth nothing; in fact, no title at all, owing to a prior breach of covenant, not relievable in equity, having been committed by the vendor.

The covenant to insure is that most frequently found to have been broken, and assuming such to be the case in the abstract before you, and that it must have been known to the vendor at the time of sale, it will be the safer plan, notwithstanding the conditions, to insist on his obtaining from the lessor a waiver of the breach. This is now an easy matter, as under the 22 & 23 Vict. c. 35, s. 1, a lessor may waive such a breach, without prejudice to his right to take advantage of a future breach. Under certain circumstances, the Common Law Procedure Act, 1860, will afford relief; but if neither of these courses be adopted, then, unless your client does not choose to take the title as it is, it is safer to rescind the contract, as it is doubtful if a Court of Equity would, under such circumstances, compel a purchaser to carry it into effect. In many instances a purchaser, whatever may be the state of the title, is so eager to become the owner of the property, that he will pay but slight attention to any caution you may give him. If such a case arises, take care to have some letter or writing, showing that you brought the objection to his notice, and that, with a full knowledge of the effect of it, he thought fit to waive it. As to whether a purchaser would be bound to complete, notwithstanding a breach of covenant by the vendor giving the lessor a right of re-entry, see *Howell* v. *Kightley* (25 L. J., Ch. 868), and as to where policy allowed to drop by vendor, after time named for completion and the contract not completed (*Palmer* v. *Goren*, 25 L. J., Ch. 841). See also the Acts 22 & 23 Vict. c. 35, s. 4, and the Common Law Procedure Act, 1860, sect. 2, for relief of lessees in certain cases from forfeiture on breach of covenant to insure.

Before leaving this branch of the subject, it may be as well to mention that the difficulty experienced by a vendor in selling, after a prior breach of covenant is attempted to be got over, is by inserting in the conditions the words "notwithstanding a prior breach of covenant may be shown:" and as words such as these are calculated to put the purchaser on inquiry, no doubt a Court of Equity would decree a specific performance, on the principle that if a man will be so blind or wilful as to purchase property under damaging conditions of sale, it is no part of the duty of a Court of Equity to help him. It will be sufficient for my purpose to draw your attention to the importance of carefully weighing in your mind the effect of the conditions under which your client has purchased, before you proceed to peruse the abstract of title, as, after some little experience, you will soon discover what sort of title you may expect to find, merely by reading the conditions of sale; and if they are of a stringent character, your vigilance will be excited when you proceed to peruse the abstract.

If your client has contracted to purchase leaseholds, you should either obtain some memorandum from the vendor with respect to the insurance money, or advise your client to insure immediately, as, if the property be burnt down before completion, the vendor will be entitled to the insurance money, and may compel the purchaser to pay the purchase-money; thus the vendor will be paid twice over, while your client gets nothing whatever for his money. (*Poole* v. *Adams*, 12 Weekly Rep. 683.)

Your client may bring the conditions of an intended sale, and request you to advise him thereon; that is, he wishes to know whether he may safely purchase under them. In such case your duty will be similar to that above pointed out, with this difference, that in the one case your client will have bound himself by entering into the contract, and in the other he will not. You will proceed to carefully look over the conditions; and although your client will probably stop with you while you are doing so, do not, if I may so express myself, "lose your head." It is a very common practice in such cases for young men to glance slightly over the conditions and hand them to the purchaser, saying, "They appear all right," or using some similar expression; the fact being that, owing to their client's presence, or their own inability to discover what is really intended to be met by the conditions, they will not have given the matter the consideration it deserves. Another very common practice on the part of a young professional man is to strive to obtain a reputation for superior quickness and penetration, and although these qualities are very excellent ones, the reputation of possessing them ought not to be obtained at the expense of your client; for, however quick in perception you may be, you will find that many conditions of sale used at the present day require all the consideration you can give them before you are able to form a correct opinion as to their meaning. Suppose, for instance, that your client, relying on your representation, that he can demand a fair title under the conditions of sale, becomes a purchaser, and a defect afterwards appears which has been successfully guarded against by the conditions, and which a man of fair experience ought to have foreseen. You may be placed in a very awkward position, and at the least lose your client, in addition to which you may have to compensate him for his loss. It is far better, in the case I am now contemplating, that, finding from the general tendency of the conditions, some defect in the title is attempted to be covered, to inform your client thereof, and if, notwithstanding, he still desires to purchase, propose to accompany him to the place of sale, and when there put such questions to the auctioneer or the vendor's solicitor with respect to the particular objection as you may deem advisable. From the answers you receive (although they, of course, will not vary the terms of the conditions), you will be able to advise your client what course he had better adopt; and should he in such a case be a trustee, the proper course will be to advise him at once not to purchase, unless the ambiguous condition is struck out or modified.

If your client informs you that he has entered into an open contract for the purchase of an estate (the nature of which contract I have before explained), you will apply to the vendor's solicitor for an abstract of title, and after obtaining it you must be careful in seeing that a marketable title is furnished, bearing in mind the distinction that exists between a marketable and a safe holding title. Under an open contract, the expense of everything your client may be entitled to must be borne by the vendor. I need hardly remind you that an open contract is the most advantageous one a purchaser can enter into, and the most disadvantageous to the vendor, the whole expense of proving the title having to be borne by the latter. As to what title you should require to be shown under such a contract, and as to what evidence is necessary to support it, you cannot do better than carefully refer to Sugden or Dart on the "Law of Vendors and Purchasers."

We will now suppose that your client informs you he has verbally agreed to purchase an estate, and that he wishes you to do what is needful, in such a case you will write to the vendor asking him to instruct his solicitor to send you the draft of the proposed contract for perusal on behalf of the purchaser; as before stated it is the practice of the vendor's solicitor to prepare the contract, he being of course acquainted with the title and the stipulations necessary to protect his client. When you receive the draft, if you have not previously been fully instructed, go through it with your client, in order to see that the amount of purchase-money, the situation and extent of the property, the burdens upon it, and the time of completion are correctly described; this is for your client's consideration. Your duty is to advise him as to the nature and effect of the clauses you find inserted in the draft. In many instances these clauses will be similar to those in ordinary conditions of sale, but this is unfair to the purchaser, as there is a material difference between purchasing an estate at an auction and purchasing one by private contract: in the former case a purchaser knows the terms under which he is buying and is sometimes content to purchase even under stringent conditions, either in the hope that he may make a good bargain, or because he has taken a fancy to the property; but in the latter case there is no chance of getting a bargain, the terms as to price being agreed upon between the vendor and purchaser with their eyes open, and as generally the latter is compelled to give the full market value of the property he has a perfect right to require a marketable title to be shown at the vendor's expense; in other words, as the vendor gets the value of the property, he ought not to be allowed to throw upon the purchaser any part of the expense of deducing a good title. In this case, however, as in many others, you may find that some tact is required on your part: the vendor may be an over-reaching man and your client may not, but, on the contrary, he may be so desirous of becoming the purchaser of the property that he may not feel disposed to pay much attention to your objections to the contract. Your course under such circumstances is a clear one; lay before your client (in writing if practicable) the consequences of his entering into such a contract, and explain to him fully the meaning of the clauses in it. If he elects, notwithstanding your advice to become the purchaser on such terms, he is at perfect liberty to do so; he runs the risk and incurs the expense; you will content yourself with having performed your duty, and the matter will proceed.

I have before pointed out all you will require to know with respect to the preparation and completion of the contract.

Contract by Letters.—Should your client inform you that he has entered into a contract by means of letters you will attentively peruse the correspondence in order to see whether a contract has been entered into, or whether a more formal contract be pointed to, as to which see *Honeyman* v. *Marryatt* (26 Law J., Ch. 619); *Ridgway* v. *Wharton* (5 Weekly Rep. 804). If you are satisfied that the letters form a contract, you will proceed to ascertain what conditions are inserted in the correspondence as to title or evidence of title and completion. You are of course aware that a contract by means of letters requires two things; namely, an offer and an acceptance. If an offer is clogged with a particular condition, and an answer is returned accepting the offer but rejecting the condition, that alone will not form a contract; or if an offer be made and an answer is returned accepting the offer, under certain conditions, that alone is not a contract, although in both cases it would be if a third letter was sent simply accepting the offer. In any case of this description you cannot do better than refer to Sugden or Dart on the "Law of Vendors and Purchasers," which in matters of sale or purchase will be your vade mecum.

I will now assume that everything has been done respecting the contract, that it is complete, and that the abstract of title has been forwarded to you by the vendor's solicitor. The first point requiring your attention will be the time limited (if any) by the contract or conditions of sale for sending in requisitions on the title, although it ought not to make any difference with respect to your course of proceeding in this dorsed on the back of it, and also insert the reference at the foot of the deed in the abstract, if not already done; and should the property be subject to the operation of the Bedford Level Drainage Acts, see that the requisites of those acts have been complied with. Also, where any succession duty is payable, take care to call for evidence of its having been paid, and if this be not produced make a note in the margin to that effect, so that the matter may be cleared before completion.

Having compared the abstract with the deeds and got back to your office, proceed to examine the stamps which you have marked in the margin of the abstract, so as to see if they are correct; after which, if you can rely upon your possessing a sufficient knowledge of conveyancing, peruse the abstract and prepare the necessary requisitions.

I have found it the simplest course in perusing an abstract to take a sheet of paper with a broad margin and insert the date of the deed in the margin, and on the opposite side put such part of the deed as is necessary to show the devolution of the title and any special clauses or stipulations. It may sometimes be convenient to keep the devolution of the legal and equitable estates separate. This will depend on the title; but it is always the best course in perusing an abstract to show the devolution of the title to any attendant term of years on a separate sheet of paper. All this may be done very briefly; it is only necessary to make a note in the margin opposite any particular clause or matter, in order that your attention may be readily called to it afterwards, as perhaps the next or a subsequent deed may have the effect of disposing of the point; and should this be so, insert a note in the margin under the defect you had previously noted, and thus, as you proceed, you will be able to get rid of many of the queries you may have found it necessary to raise, and those which are not cleared up will form the requisitions on the title. Of course, although you only insert the principal parts of the deed in the paper before you, you will carefully read over the whole of the deed in the abstract, so as to discover what objections it may be necessary to raise to any part of it. Take the following as an instance of the title to two houses on Ludgate Hill, Nos. 1 and 2, and the manner of perusing the abstract:—

1st Jan. 1800.	Conveyance from A. to B. in fee, of two houses on the north side of Ludgate Hill, occupied by X. and Y.
Qy. Evidence of identity with property purchased.	
1st Jan. 1810.	Mortgage from B. to C. in fee of some premises. To secure 1,000*l*.
1st Jan. 1820.	Death of B. intestate, leaving D. his heir at law.
Qy. Evidence of intestacy and heirship.	
1st Jan. 1830.	Conveyance from D. and E. (described as heir at law to C.) and F. (described as executor to C.) to G. in fee. Mortgage paid off.
Qy. Was D. married?	
Qy. Evidence of heirship of E.	
Qy. Abstract probate of will, and as to any devise of trust estates.	

Now in each of these cases you will first satisfy yourself that the deeds are nothing more than what you state them to be; for instance, that the first deed is a simple conveyance in fee to B., and should this be so, you may dismiss that deed, merely requiring evidence that the two houses therein described are the same as those contracted to be sold, namely, Nos. 1 and 2, and so proceed until you get to the end of the abstract. It may sometimes be necessary to insert in your synopsis the effect of a recital, or some provision in the deed; this will depend on the nature of the deed. If the mortgage to B. had been for a term, and the term had afterwards been kept distinct from the fee, then it would simplify the matter to take a separate sheet of paper and commence with the mortgage to C., so as to keep the term separate from the inheritance.

Should you not feel competent to peruse the abstract, or should it be very long and intricate, or any doubtful questions arise on it, or the property be of great value, your best course will be to lay it before counsel <u>with instructions to peruse it and draw the necessary requisitions</u>. The abstract will be accompanied by the conditions of sale or contract, and anything else you may think it necessary to send. Counsel's opinion in this case will enable you to prepare the requisitions on the title, and here you will perceive how necessary it is to carefully peruse the abstract with the deeds, otherwise your conveyancer will, and indeed cannot help raising a multitude of trifling questions as to whether a particular date or description be correctly stated, or as to the execution of a will or deed, or as to the correctness of a recital, and you can only satisfy him on this head by again referring to the deeds, thus incurring additional trouble and expense, besides putting yourself under an obligation to the vendor's solicitor, as, having once produced the deeds to you, it is hardly fair to put his client to the expense of your again referring to them for information which you might and ought to have obtained when they were first produced to you.

The usual and most convenient mode of copying requisitions on title is on foolscap paper, doubling it in half margin, writing your queries on the left hand, and reserving the right hand for the replies, thus:—

"Queries and Requisitions on the Title to two Freehold Messuages, Nos. 1 & 2, Ludgate Hill, in the City of London.

1. Evidence must be given of the identity of the two houses described in the deed of 1st Jan. 1800, with the property purchased.

2. Evidence must be given of the intestacy of B., and of the heirship of D. and E. respectively.

3. Was D. married at the date of the conveyance to G., and, if so, is his wife living?"

And so on until you have exhausted the requisitions.

Having obtained the vendor's replies to your requisitions on the title, it will be for you to consider whether they are satisfactory. This is a duty of almost equal importance to the perusal of the abstract, and sometimes more so, as there may be greater difficulty in deciding whether an answer is sufficient, than in raising the question. If you have any doubt as to the course to be pursued, you should, whether the abstract was or was not in the first place laid before counsel, place all the papers before him and take his opinion. If, however, you are not in doubt, then you will proceed either to send further requisitions to the vendor's solicitor, or to prepare the conveyance.

By raising only such questions as are of real importance, you will save yourself much trouble, and your client much expense. You may find it necessary sometimes to consult your client as to whether he will press for a more satisfactory answer to a particular requisition (when the vendor's solicitor has declined or expressed his inability to give any further information), or whether he will waive it and complete the purchase; but this will only arise in cases where you are not restricted in requiring a more satisfactory answer, and not often in those cases.

In preparing the conveyance, you will be guided by the state of the title as appearing on the abstract, for instance, should the last document in the abstract be a conveyance to the vendor in fee, you may either dispense with any recital, or state shortly, in the usual form, that the vendor is seised in fee of the premises intended to be conveyed; inasmuch as the prior title shows the vendor to be seised in fee, there can be no necessity, neither can it answer any useful purpose, to recite the last or any of the prior deeds in the conveyance to the purchaser. If the last deed on the abstract be a conveyance to the vendor, to uses to bar dower (a form now seldom seen owing to the operation of the Dower Act), it is customary to recite such deed, as the conveyance to your client will, in such a case, be in a different form.

With respect to the parties to the conveyance, should the vendor be seised in fee simple, it will be necessary only to make him (and his wife if living and married before 1834) the party of the one part, and the purchaser of the other part, unless the purchaser was married before 1834, and his wife be living, in which case you will insert the name of a third party, as a trustee to bar the inchoate right of dower in the wife. It will not be necessary to make the dower trustee in the conveyance to the vendor a party to your deed, as the power of appointment invariably reserved under that form of conveyance, and which is as invariably exercised, is alone sufficient to pass the estate, and the granting part which follows is subsidiary to the appointment. Should the estate be in mortgage, it will be necessary to make the mortgagee a party to your conveyance, and to recite the mortgage deed. In every case you must be guided by the state of the title, as to whom you will make parties, and the documents and statements necessary to be recited and stated. If you find by the abstract that the whole legal and equitable estates are vested in the vendor, it is manifest that none but he (and his wife if entitled to dower) need join in the conveyance. If the estate be mortgaged, then the mortgagee must join; and if any other persons appear by the abstract to have an interest in the property, then those persons, whoever they may be, must join in the conveyance.

It sometimes happens that a judgment creditor is induced to give up his charge upon part of an estate contracted to be sold, and if this should be so in the case before you, he must be made a party to the deed, and the particulars of the judgment and his consent to release the estate therefrom should be recited. Before the 22 & 23 Vict. c. 35, the judgment creditor would merely covenant not to resort to the estate conveyed for satisfaction of his judgment debt, because a release of part of the hereditaments affected by the judgment was at law a release of the whole, and in equity such a covenant was considered an effectual release; but now he will join in the granting part of the deed, as, under the 11th section of the above act, the release from a judgment of part of the hereditaments charged therewith is not to affect the validity of the judgment as to the hereditaments remaining unreleased, or as to any other property not specifically released. A creditor who has registered his judgment, even although the sale be made under a decree of the Court of Chancery, is a necessary party to the conveyance, or, at all events, you can require the vendor to get satisfaction entered on the judgment, unless the judgment creditor may have been made a party to the suit, which is very seldom the case (*Knight* v. *Pocock*, 30 L. T. 126).

Where devisees in trust, with power to sell and give receipts for purchase-money, are the vendors, the parties beneficially entitled will, as a rule, not be necessary parties to the conveyance, inasmuch as in such cases the trustees can make a title without them; indeed, it seems difficult now to conceive any case where the joinder of the parties beneficially interested will be necessary, as the 29th section of the 23 & 24 Vict. c. 145, enacts, that the receipts in writing of any trustees or trustee for any money payable to them or him, by reason or in the exercise of any trusts or powers reposed or vested in them or him, shall be sufficient discharges, &c. This seems to do away altogether with the ordinary objection as to the power of trustees to give receipts, and to leave the question as to the application of the purchase-money to be decided afterwards between the trustees and the parties beneficially interested, instead of, as formerly, between the trustees and the purchaser.

It may happen that the vendor is a married woman, and as the law respecting a married woman entitled to real estate is peculiar, it may be better to state it rather fully. It appears to be as follows:—

1. A married woman cannot pass the legal estate, whether settled to her separate use or not, unless the formalities prescribed by the Act for the Abolition of Fines and Recoveries are complied with.

2. A married woman cannot dispose of an equitable fee simple estate, given to her separate use, unless by a deed acknowledged (*Lechmere* v. *Brotheridge*, 11 Weekly Rep. 814).

3. A married woman may dispose of an equitable life

interest in real estate given to her for her separate use (and which she is not restrained from anticipating), and also of her absolute interest in personalty (whether in possession or reversion), without a deed acknowledged (*Lechmere* v. *Brotheridge*).

A wife, even with the consent of her husband, cannot make an assignment of her reversionary interest in personalty that will be binding on her in the event of her surviving her husband, unless her interest accrued after the 31st December, 1857, and the deed is acknowledged, and all the other formalities prescribed by the Fines and Recoveries Abolition Act are observed, and the wife is not restrained from anticipation by the deed or will under which she claims. (See 20 & 21 Vict. c. 57.)

Should you have any doubts as to the proper persons to make parties to the conveyance, which is very likely to be the case when dealing with large estates or estates that have been frequently dealt with, the more prudent course will be to hand all the papers to counsel and instruct him to prepare the conveyance.

I may here mention that, although the greatest accuracy should be observed in the description of the parties to the deed, a misnomer will not be a fatal objection, if the party can be identified (*Janes* v. *Whitbread*, 17 L. T. 78).

The draft having been prepared, a fair copy of it should be made and forwarded to the vendor's solicitor for approval, and after he has approved it on behalf of his own clients, he will forward it for approval to the solicitors of any of the parties to the draft for whom he may not be professionally concerned, and return it to you when it has been approved on behalf of all parties. On receiving back the draft, go carefully through it, in order to see what alterations have been made therein; and should any important alteration have been made, you will consider how it affects the draft, or how far you are obliged to submit to it; and in such a case, if the draft has been prepared by counsel, it should be laid before him to advise on the alterations, the framer of the draft being the most competent person to advise on the effect of any alterations therein. As to how far the vendor's solicitor is justified in insisting on alterations he may have made in the frame of the draft, or in any objection he may make to the mode in which the purchaser thinks fit to have the property conveyed, see *Clark* v. *May* (22 L. J., Ch. 382).

In cases where trustees are parties to the deed, you will sometimes meet with great pertinacity on the part of their solicitors in insisting on qualifying words being inserted in the operative part of the deed, such as the following:—" As far as they lawfully can or may, but not further or otherwise, and without warranty of title." Now, these words at the present day have no meaning at all, as trustees cannot convey more than they are authorized to do by the power which they exercise, and as they never enter into any more extensive covenant than that they have not done any act to incumber, it seems clear those qualifying words are not required, and are quite unnecessary. See the observations of the Master of the Rolls in *Calvert* v. *Sebright* (15 Beav. 156). And with respect to the word "grant" creating a warranty, an eminent conveyancer, half a century ago, stated his opinion that it would not have that operation; and to make the matter more clear, the 8 & 9 Vict. c. 106, expressly enacts, that the word "grant" shall not have the effect of creating any warranty of title. When, however, a solicitor acting for a trustee is disposed to insist on qualifying words being inserted, the better plan is to let them remain, as they are quite harmless, and the point is not worth a long discussion, although it is a pity that men of narrow understandings should have it in their power to incumber a well-drawn draft by useless and unmeaning words.

In case you modify or strike out any of the alterations that have been made in the draft as prepared by you, it should be again forwarded to the vendor's solicitor, as it is not regular to alter a draft (except for the purpose of reducing it in length to save stamp duty) after it has been approved by the vendor's solicitor, without submitting the alterations for his approval. After the draft conveyance has been finally approved, it will be engrossed by you, and the draft and engrossment sent to the vendor's solicitor for examination, and he will also get it examined by any other solicitor concerned in the matter. On sending the draft to the stationer for engrossment, it is better to mark on it the particulars of the stamps on which it is to be engrossed, in order to avoid the possibility, if the deed be engrossed on unstamped parchment, of its being put away and forgotten to be stamped until too late. Never instruct your stationer to engross the deed "on proper stamps," as it is unfair to him and may cause you some annoyance and expense if you forget, on receiving the engrossment, to examine the correctness of the stamps; and as you must, or, at all events, ought to, examine them, it is at least quite as easy to do this before the draft is sent for engrossment as after. A law stationer is by no means expected to be in a position to know what stamps should be affixed on any but the most simple documents.

On forwarding the draft and engrossment to the vendor's solicitor you may, if you are in a position to do so, appoint a time for the completion of the business. This appointment, so far as you are concerned, will be made with the vendor's solicitor (unless some other office is named in the conditions of sale), and he will arrange as to the place of completion, and inform you accordingly.

Before the completion of the matter you should satisfy yourself that no succession duty is payable in respect of the property, or if succession duty be payable, then the vendor's solicitor must either produce the receipt or procure a certificate from Somerset House, certifying that all duty has been paid. You must also search for judgments, crown debts, lis pendens and annuities, at the office for that purpose in Rolls Gardens, Chancery Lane, against the vendor and such other persons as may have any interest in the property dealt with; but as to judgments against a mortgagee, see *Greaves* v. *Wilson* (28 Law J., Ch. 103; and 18 Vict. c. 15, s. 11); and as to the search now necessary for judgments, see the Act to further amend the Law of Property, 22 & 23 Vict. c. 38, ss. 1, 2; and the 27 & 28 Vict. c. 112; and should the property be in Middlesex or Yorkshire, the register office for the county in which the property is situate must be also searched, in order to discover if any deeds affecting the property have been executed which do not appear on the abstract. These searches should be made as near the completion of the matter as possible; but where the searches are likely to take up much time they may be made at an earlier stage of the business, and another search made from the foot of the prior search immediately before attending to complete the matter. Should you discover a charge or incumbrance of any description of which you had not been apprised, inform the vendor's solicitor of the fact, and require its removal before the completion.

In cases where a married woman is a party to the deed it must be acknowledged by her pursuant to the Act for the Abolition of Fines and Recoveries, and the course necessary to be followed on such occasion will appear in a subsequent part of this book, and should the property be in Middlesex or Yorkshire, a memorial of the deed will have to be registered. At the time and place appointed for completion you will attend with your client and pay the money and take the deeds; if the property be leasehold, you will also require the policy of insurance and last receipt for premium to be handed over, and the last receipt for ground rent should be inspected by you. You will also satisfy yourself as to the rates and taxes having been paid up to the time appointed for completion, but it is more usual to accept the undertaking of the vendor's solicitor to clear up all rates and taxes to that day.

MORTGAGES.

It is scarcely necessary to mention here that a mortgage is a security given by one person to another to secure the repayment of a sum of money, or that almost every description of property and all interests therein may be the subject of a mortgage.

If you are professionally concerned for a mortgagor the observations I have added under the head "vendors," as far as regards the abstract and completion of the matter, will equally apply here; and, on the other hand, if your client is the mortgagee, the course of proceeding on your part will be similar to that of a purchase with this important difference, that a mortgagee is never subject to any restrictions as to title or evidence of title, or the time when the matter is to be completed; there is also this further difference, that a willing purchaser will often waive many points on the title through a wish to get what he has purchased; he may require a few extra acres to make his lands lie in a ring fence, or he may want a particular house either for occupation or for removal in order to improve a view; but in the case of a mortgage none of these circumstances can arise, a mortgagee lends his money on a particular security and expects to have it back again, and, therefore, if there is any doubt as to the title, or as to obtaining the evidence necessary to establish it, you should never advise your client to advance his money until such doubts are removed. If, however, your doubts resolve themselves merely into a question of expense hereafter in case a sale should have to be resorted to by the mortgagee, then you will consider how far the value of the property will be sufficient to pay for this extra expense; for if your client has a marketable title, and is amply covered by the value of the property mortgaged, he will be safe in making the advance. It is also important to see how far you can rely on the covenant of the mortgagor to repay the money, although this should not be taken into consideration until you are satisfied as to the value of the security and the title to it. The covenant of a responsible man is at all times of some value; if, therefore, you are satisfied with the mortgagor's responsibility, you will be justified in abating some of the rigour that you would otherwise exercise.

In the allusion here to the value of property "marketable value" is meant, in other words, the amount likely to be realized by a forced sale of the property. It often happens that property in mortgage consisting of mills, manufactories, furnaces, mines, &c. may be of considerable value, but yet unmarketable in times of commercial depression, and in such a case as this, however anxious the mortgagee may be to realize his security, he cannot do so unless the mortgagor be a man of substance, and can be reached under his covenant for repayment of the money. As there are various descriptions of mortgages, it may be of service if the principal are here stated, and a few remarks made on each. They are as follows:—

Mortgage of freehold land (this is the highest class of mortgage).
„ freehold houses.
„ copyhold land or houses.
„ leasehold houses..
„ freehold or leasehold mills, manufactories, mines, &c.
„ life interests.
„ reversions.
„ policies of assurance.
„ furniture, stock in trade, &c.

With respect to the first, viz., mortgages of freehold land, and in this I may include freehold ground rents (which if in a good locality form an unexceptionable security), your client will be quite safe in advancing to the extent of two-thirds of the value as certified by a respectable surveyor, as experience proves that commercial depression exercises very little influence on this class of property, unless it be to raise the price, many people at such times being more anxious to invest their money in something secure and tangible than at times when trade is buoyant.

With respect to freehold houses, and indeed house property of any tenure, locality is the principal consideration, and if that is good, the tenant responsible, the property held on lease, and the state of repair satisfactory, then freehold houses form a very good investment, although you should not recommend the advance of much more than one-half the value of the property.

Copyhold houses or land where the fine on death or alienation is certain, that is, nominal, form an investment of little less value than freehold; but in manors where the fine on admittance is arbitrary, that is, at a rough estimation, two years' annual value, then in estimating the value of the property, the amount of the fine must be taken into consideration, as every person admitted must pay a fine, and consequently a purchaser would give so much less for the property.

Leasehold houses are never looked upon with so much favour as freehold, unless situated in a first-class position. In advising your client on a leasehold security, many things require to be taken into consideration, namely, the amount of ground rent reserved by the lease, the nature of the covenants in the lease (some of which may be very onerous and may not have been duly performed), and the great depreciation of value experienced by this class of property in a time of commercial depression, unless it happens to be situate in a first-class neighbourhood, or have other corresponding advantages.

You may sometimes have to advise a client as to his advancing money on leasehold ground rents, or, as they are generally termed, " improved rents." These rents arise in this way : a person holds a house under a lease for, say 90 years, at a rental of 5l. per annum; he grants an underlease of this house for the whole of his term, less a few days, at a rent of, say 45l. Here the improved rental is 40l. per annum. In a case like this, precisely the same questions will arise for your consideration, as to covenants, &c., as in the case of a leasehold house offered as a security; but if you can satisfy yourself on these points, and the rents reserved by the underlease should be sufficiently below the rack rent of the property, then improved ground rents will form a better security than any other description of leasehold property.

The next head, freehold or leasehold mills, manufactories, mines, &c., will require your very serious consideration before advising your client to advance his money. I am aware that in mining and manufacturing districts owners of this class of property do not, in prosperous times, find much difficulty in raising money upon it; but this chiefly arises from the fact of the lender having it constantly before his eyes, and in many cases from the personal knowledge he has of the borrower and the value of the security. In advising as to a mortgage of this description of property, you will take into consideration the value of the building, steam boiler, machinery, gearing, &c., as estimated by a competent person, and also the responsibility of the borrower; and even if you find everything satisfactory, not more than one-half of the value should, as a rule, be advanced, because the mortgagor, being in possession, if he becomes bankrupt, only such of the machinery, working gear, &c., as may be affixed to the freehold can be claimed by the mortgagee, and the rest of this part of the security would go to the assignees. It has been decided that in these cases the mortgagee can claim what may be known as "trade fixtures," and everything not comprised in that term can be claimed by the assignees of the mortgagor. Now, in such a case as this, some difficulty would be found, and some delay arise, in disposing of the remainder, especially in times of depression of trade. In all mortgages of this or any other description, where chattels form part of the property comprised in the mortgage, the security, or a copy of it (of course, in practice it is always the latter) must be filed pursuant to the Bills of Sale Act, 17 & 18 Vict. c. 36, hereafter referred to, otherwise the mortgage as to such chattels would be void as against an execution creditor and the other persons mentioned in the act, but the filing the mortgage, or a copy of it, does not give any greater security to the mortgagee, in the event of the mortgagor becoming bankrupt, than he had before the passing of the act. Where freeholds are comprised in a deed, together with fixtures attached to the freehold, the deed need not be registered under the Bills of Sale Act (*Waterfall* v. *Penistone*, 4 Weekly Rep. 726; *Mather* v. *Foster*, 25 L. J., Ch. 361).

Under no circumstances, not even although the instrument under which they are empowered to advance money extends to this description of property (a very rare occurrence), ought trustees to be advised to make advances on it. Their position is very different to that of an ordinary lender, who, for the sake of obtaining a high rate of interest, will sometimes be content to incur a little risk as to his security, but trustees ought only to look at the value and nature of the security, and the certainty of being able to realize at any time; for, whatever may be the amount of interest obtained, it will not be taken into consideration in favour of the trustees, in the event of the security proving insufficient, and a loss accruing to the trust estate.

Life interests are seldom taken as securities for money, unless by insurance offices or professed money lenders, and when taken, the mortgagor is always required to effect an insurance on his life to secure the repayment of the mortgage money, a life interest in itself being only of value for securing payment of the interest on the money and the premiums on the policy of assurance. The principal is secured by the policy.

There are many disadvantages in this description of security. The mortgagor may do some act to avoid the policy, or it may be necessary to call in the money during his lifetime, in which case difficulty may be experienced in finding a purchaser. If your client is seeking an investment for his money, and does not make the obtaining a high rate of interest his primary consideration, you will never advise him to accept this kind of security.

A reversion in any description of property is also a very undesirable security, owing to there being no fund available for payment of the interest until the reversion falls into possession. Of course a vested reversion is here meant, as a contingent reversion is never thought of as a security for money about to be advanced, unless accompanied by a policy of assurance, and even then it is a desperate kind of security. Reversionary interests are always of a certain value, which can easily be ascertained by taking the opinion of an actuary. The character and responsibility of the mortgagor in a security of this nature is the most important consideration, as it enhances its value; but even if that is unexceptionable, the security is not a desirable one, and a prudent man, wishing to secure an investment for which a transfer can speedily be obtained, or the property realized in the market, should hesitate before he accepts a reversion as a security.

A policy of assurance, considered as a security, ranks still lower than a reversion. There is not only no means of paying the interest on the mortgage money, but there has also to be provided from some source the annual premiums on the policy, without punctually paying which the whole security vanishes. If these can be guaranteed by the covenant of a third person, the security is thereby improved, but is still undesirable. You may ascertain the value of a policy of assurance at any time by applying to the actuary of the company, who, for a small fee, will give you the office value, which increases every year the policy is kept up. This kind of security is generally taken in cases where the borrower is previously indebted to the mortgagee, in which case he takes an assignment of the policy, as the best or only security he can obtain.

Lastly, comes a mortgage of household furniture, stock in trade, &c. This can in no case be recommended to an intended mortgagee, as there is very little more than the personal character of the mortgagor to depend upon; for instance, he might sell the property comprised in the security, and put the money in his pocket, and it has been decided that he is not criminally liable for so doing, as he does not come within the Fraudulent Trustee Act. Next, the mortgagee is always under the liability of the goods being distrained upon by the landlord for rent in arrear, and if the mortgagor should become bankrupt while in possession, the chattels would pass to his assignees, as being in his order and disposition. This description of mortgage is generally taken to secure money already due, or which may become due on a trading account between the mortgagor and mortgagee. The security is bad at the best, but it is absolutely worthless as against third parties, unless a copy of it be filed within twenty-one days after its execution at the Queen's Bench Office. (See 17 & 18 Vict. c. 36.)

The foregoing remarks are principally applicable to the case of a mortgagee seeking to advance money belonging to himself; but where your clients are trustees, too much caution cannot be exercised. In the first place, it must be borne in mind that the strict duty of a trustee is to place the trust money in the Three per Cent. Consolidated Stock. In order, however, that a higher rate of interest may be obtained for the benefit of the cestui que trust, settlors and testators, almost invariably empower the trustees of the settlement or will to invest the money in any of the parliamentary stocks or public funds, or on mortgage of real or leasehold securities (the latter generally being limited to leasehold property not having less than a sixty years' unexpired term), and sometimes on the debentures or stock of any incorporated company paying a dividend that the trustees may deem well established and sound. Now, if your client be a trustee under such a power as this, and copyhold property is offered as security, it will be comprised within the words " real property," and therefore you can inform him that he is authorized to advance the trust money on copyhold property. If a leasehold security be offered, you will take care to see that it has a sixty years' unexpired term. If a security on debentures or stock, you must see that the debentures are issued properly, and that the stock is stock and not shares. In all these cases, if a trustee does not exceed his power as to the nature of the security, and does not advance more than a prudent and careful man would advance in dealing with his own money under similar circumstances, he will be protected in what he has done by a Court of Equity; but, as before observed, too much caution cannot be exercised when investing trust money, and in no case should the security be entertained until the valuation of an experienced surveyor has been obtained.

I have gone very fully into the question of the value of property submitted to a mortgagee, because a solicitor often has to form and give an opinion on the matter; but it should be borne in mind that it is no part of an attorney's duty to look to the value of a proposed security, unless that duty be specially cast upon him (*Brembridge* v. *Massey*, 32 L. T. 108).

The title to the property offered as security having been satisfactorily proved, you will proceed either to prepare the draft mortgage, or send instructions to counsel for that purpose. The draft, when prepared or settled, will be fair copied and sent by you to the solicitor of the mortgagor for perusal by him. He takes a copy of it in the usual manner, and, after approving the draft, returns it to you for engrossment. The principal difference between a conveyance and a mortgage are these—in the former you recite the agreement for sale or purchase, and the vendor, after conveying the property, enters into qualified covenants for title only; whereas in a mortgage you recite the agreement for the advance, then follows the conveyance of the property, then the proviso for redemption on repayment of the money, the covenant by the mortgagor to repay the money and interest on a given day, the power to the mortgagee to sell if not then paid, making his receipts good discharges to the purchaser (but as to this, see the act presently alluded to), lastly, absolute covenants for title by the mortgagor. If house property forms a part of the security, the mortgagor covenants to insure, and if leaseholds are included, the mortgagor, in addition to such a covenant, enters into a covenant to pay the rent reserved by, and to perform the covenants contained in, the lease under which the property is held.

Although at one time the contrary opinion was entertained, it is now settled that trustees, if raising money under a power to mortgage, are authorized to give the mortgagee a power of sale in case of default in repayment of the money (*Russell* v. *Plaice*, 18 Beav. 21; *S. C.*, 18 Jur. 254; but see the observations of Vice-Chancellor Kindersley in *Clarke* v. *The Royal Panopticon Society*, 5 Weekly Rep. 332).

Having engrossed the deed you will forward the draft and engrossment to the mortgagor's solicitor for examination, and arrange with him for an appointment at your office to complete the matter (the completion of a mortgage being invariably at the office of the mortgagee's solicitor), and then proceed to make the same searches for judgments, &c., and also at the register office (if the property is in a register county), as in the case of a purchase.

You should also ascertain whether any succession duty is payable, and if not paid require the mortgagor's solicitor to prepare and pass an account before completion, so that he may hand to you the official receipt for the duty, in order that your client may put it with the title deeds forming the security.

At the time appointed the mortgagor will execute the mortgage deed; and should his wife have been made a party in order to bar her right to dower, she will also execute and acknowledge the deed in the usual manner. After which you will see that all the deeds are handed over to you, for which, if required, you will sign a schedule and acknowledgment by the mortgagee that he holds them in that character (although this is now seldom required), obtain the amount of your costs from the mortgagor, or, which is usually the case, deduct them from the mortgage money (in the case of a mortgage the mortgagee does not pay any part of your costs), and complete the matter. If the property is in Middlesex or Yorkshire the deed must be registered, and if it comprises chattels of any description (except in the case of machinery, fixtures, &c. comprised in a mortgage of the freehold), a copy of it must be filed under the Bills of Sale Act. Occasionally the mortgagee's solicitor charges a procuration fee for finding the money, but this is not much adopted at the present day; and it should be borne in mind that if a procuration fee be charged, the preliminary attendances on obtaining the money, satisfying the mortgagee as to the security, &c., and many other items cannot be charged, as they are all covered by the procuration fee. The fairest way is not to charge a procuration fee, but to include in your bill of costs fair charges for the work you have done.

In case freehold and copyhold property form the security to your client it will be necessary to prepare a surrender of the copyhold property, and recite it in the draft mortgage; and the covenants for title in this case will require some slight alteration in order to comprise both tenures. If copyhold property alone be mortgaged you will prepare the surrender, and also a further deed, which will recite the application for the advance, the surrender and the agreement by the mortgagor to enter into the covenants thereinafter contained.

The witnessing part will contain the covenant for repayment, then will follow the proviso for redemption, the power of sale in case of default, and the covenants for title, and, if the security consists of house property, a covenant to insure.

It will be advisable in all cases to have the draft of this surrender perused by the steward of the manor before it is engrossed, otherwise he may make such alterations as may necessitate a new engrossment; few stewards will tolerate any surrender but such as complies with their accustomed form. After the surrender has been approved by the steward and the mortgagor's solicitor, you will make an appointment with both for all parties to attend at the steward's office to pass the surrender. There will be no necessity, and it is unusual at that time, for the mortgagee to take admittance. He can at any time procure admittance, if he should have occasion to sell the property; and, if he is paid off by the mortgagor, it is only necessary for the mortgagee to sign a warrant to the steward to enter satisfaction on the mortgage, and the mortgagor becomes in the same position as before the mortgage. Whereas, if the mortgagee were admitted tenant at the time of the surrender, there would be the expense of this admittance, and, on the mortgage being paid off, the additional expense of another surrender by the mortgagee and the admittance of the mortgagor. In such a case the hardship on the mortgagor is the greater, because the admittance of the mortgagee, at the time of completing the mortgage, does not give him the smallest additional security, and is generally taken through inadvertence. Should it be inconvenient for the mortgagor to surrender personally, his solicitor will procure a power of attorney from him to a third person, usually his solicitor, empowering him to make the surrender; but he should consult you before this is done, as a mortgagee is not bound to accept a surrender by attorney, although it is not often objected to.

It is perhaps scarcely necessary to mention, that, since the abolition of the acts of parliament respecting usury, any amount of interest may be reserved on any description of property, and there is now no restriction whatever on this head. The law wisely leaving it to the parties interested to make their own contracts.

When a mortgagor wishes to pay off his mortgage, his solicitor prepares and forwards to the solicitor of the mortgagee a draft of the reconveyance or reassignment for perusal, it being the practice for the mortgagor's solicitor to prepare this draft. If you are the solicitor for the mortgagee you will peruse the draft in the usual manner, keep a copy of it, and then return it to the mortgagor's solicitor for engrossment. He will afterwards forward to you the draft and engrossment for examination, or, if the reconveyance or reassignment be by indorsement on the original mortgage (a very common and convenient practice), he will request you to engross the document on the mortgage deed (for which you will be entitled to the usual charge of 8*d*. per folio). The mortgagor's solicitor will then appoint a time for attending at your office to pay the principal and interest money and your costs, and take away the deeds. The same observations that I have before made respecting a schedule apply here. I never could see the necessity for one.

As to mortgagee's costs on mortgagor paying off the mortgage, it may be observed that, if in consequence of the death of the mortgagee any additional expense is occasioned, the mortgagor must pay it, but otherwise if the mortgagee has settled the mortgage money. In the first-mentioned case the extra expense would not have been occasioned by any act of the mortgagee; but, in the other case, if a mortgagee chooses for his own convenience to settle the mortgage money, it cannot be expected that the mortgagor should bear the extra expense occasioned by so doing, and in this case such extra expense must be borne by the mortgagee.

The mortgagee may during the continuance of the security become lunatic or die, leaving an infant heir, in which cases great trouble and expense are incurred in obtaining a reconveyance. As to who pays the costs incurred by the lunacy of the mortgagee, see *In the matter of Sophia Wheeler a Lunatic* (reported 1 De Gex, Mac. & Gor. 134; *S. C.*, 20 L. T.

57; *Hawkins* v. *Perry* (15 L. J., Ch. 656); but where a mortgagee dies leaving an infant heir, the mortgagor must bear the costs of all proceedings necessary to obtain the reconveyance of the legal estate.

. If you find it necessary to exercise the power of sale in the mortgage deed, your course of proceeding will be similar to that before pointed out under the head of "Sales:" and after the purchase-money has been received you will, in the first place, deduct thereout the costs of and incidental to the sale; in the next place, pay the mortgagee his principal and interest, and any monies he may have properly paid for insurance or otherwise, and the balance will be paid to the mortgagor. In arriving at this balance, it should be borne in mind that the mortgagor must pay the expense of an abortive sale (*Sutton* v. *Rawlings,* 18 L. J. (N. S.) Ch. 249); and also of an action of ejectment brought by mortgagee to recover possession (*Owen* v. *Crouch,* 5 Weekly Rep. 545), but not the costs of an unsuccessful suit for specific performance of a contract for sale by the mortgagee (*Peers* v. *Seeley,* 15 Beav. 209). Should the mortgagee have been served with a notice by a second mortgagee of the property, you will inspect his security, and if you find it correct, the balance of purchase-money, or so much thereof as may be required, will be paid to such second mortgagee, and any residue to the mortgagor. In such a case as this, however, it would be the preferable course before parting with the money to the second mortgagee to inform the mortgagor of your intention to do so, and if he assents, or returns no answer to your notice, you will be quite safe in paying the money.

In some cases it may happen, that after the sale of the mortgaged property has been completed the mortgagor cannot be found, or he may be dead, and it may not be known who are his representatives, or several claimants may appear, each one requiring you to pay the surplus in your hands to him, or he may be living and may have given you notice not to pay the surplus to a subsequent mortgagee. In any of these cases, if no satisfactory arrangement can be come to, your better course will be to advise your client to pay the surplus in his hands into the Court of Chancery, under the Trustee Relief Acts (10 & 11 Vict. c. 96, and 12 & 13 Vict. c. 74), and let the claimants satisfy the Court as to their claims. You will be justified in adopting this course, and will have relieved your client from all responsibility with respect to the money; you may deduct your charges in the matter out of the fund before paying it into Court, and the costs of the mortgagee's appearance, on the petition to take the money out of Court, will come out of the fund. No undue haste need be shown by the mortgagee in paying the money into Court under the above acts, as it has been decided that a mortgagee, selling under a power of sale and retaining the surplus purchase-money unproductive in consequence of disputes between subsequent incumbrancers, is not chargeable with interest on such surplus (*Matthison* v. *Clark*, 4 Weekly Rep. 30).

In acting on behalf of a person having money to advance on mortgage, you must take care, in cases where you are not also employed by the mortgagor, on a security being offered, to obtain the written undertaking of the mortgagor or his solicitor to pay your charges in case the negotiation goes off on a matter of title, or on any other point except the default of your client; as, unless you arm yourself with this undertaking, neither you nor your client can recover your costs from the intended mortgagor, if the mortgage should go off (see *Melbourne* v. *Cottrell*, 29 L. T. 293); and this is practically losing them altogether, as your client will by no means expect to pay them.

By an act intituled "An Act to further amend the Law of Property and to relieve Trustees" (23 & 24 Vict. c. 35, s. 14), a trustee may, under certain circumstances, raise money by mortgage of the estate for the purpose of paying debts, legacies or specific monies, notwithstanding the want of an express power in the will. And under the 16th section of the act, executors are empowered, under the same circumstances as are set out in the 14th section, to raise money by mortgage for the purposes aforesaid, where the testator shall not have devised the hereditaments in the manner pointed out in the 14th section.

If you are instructed to sell under a power of sale in a mortgage deed, but which contains no power of giving receipts, the 23rd section of the above act will probably meet the case, and will be found of great utility.

Also, by an act intituled "An Act to give to Trustees, Mortgagees and Others, certain Powers, now commonly inserted in Settlements, Mortgages and Wills" (23 & 24 Vict. c. 145), under sect. 9, money required for the purposes of equality of exchange authorized by that act, and for renewal of leases, may be raised by a mortgage of the hereditaments to be received in exchange, or contained in the renewed lease (as the case may be). Part 2 of that act applies to mortgages only, and was evidently intended to operate as a means of shortening mortgages. It has not, however, had that operation, and probably never will have; the clauses are too complicated, and the power of sale only comes into operation on the happening of certain events, which would render it of no use whatever to a mortgagee wishing for private reasons to obtain his money at once. This part of the act may have been of service in some few cases where the mortgage deed contained no power of sale; but with respect to mortgages created since its operation, as far as I can learn, it has been, and is likely to remain, a dead letter. The act also gives power to appoint a receiver to collect the rents of mortgaged property.

Transfers of mortgages are very frequent. A mortgagee amply secured, and receiving his interest punctually, may require his principal money for some purpose. The mortgagor may wish to continue the mortgage. The requirements of both are met by a transfer. A third party is sought for, and, when found, comes into the matter as transferee, that is, he consents to pay the mortgagee off, and take to his mortgage security. The business is carried out by a transfer of the mortgage.

A mortgagee can transfer his mortgage either with or

without the concurrence of the mortgagor, but in practice the former course is almost invariably adopted; first, because unless the mortgagor is an assenting party to the transfer the costs of it would have to be borne by the mortgagee (*Re Radcliffe*, 27 Law T. 61), and of course under ordinary circumstances, and where his security is ample, he would rather proceed to a sale or foreclosure of the property than be saddled with the expense of a transfer; and secondly, it is always advisable on the part of the transferee that the mortgagor should join in the deed, by which in effect a new mortgage is made from the mortgagor to the transferee with privity between them, and a new covenant for payment of the principal and interest is given.

You may happen to be concerned for all parties in a transfer; if so, the matter will be simple. When instructed you will learn whether a further sum is to be advanced to the mortgagor (as is often the case) or not, and will prepare your deed accordingly; make an appointment for the parties to attend at your office, calculate the amount of principal and interest due to the mortgagee, get the deed executed by him and the mortgagor, pay the mortgagee his money and get the amount of your charges from the mortgagor, who, as the business is done for his accommodation, will pay all the attendant expense.

If you act for the mortgagee but not for the transferee, the solicitor of the latter will probably apply to you for an abstract of the mortgagee's title which you under ordinary circumstances would prepare and send to him, although you are not bound to do so, nor indeed to do any act which possibly might prejudice the security of your client, but in most instances with respectable parties the abstract is furnished as a matter of course, because it generally happens that a personal interview has taken place; or the transferee's solicitor, on applying for the abstract, states that his client is about to pay off the first mortgagee.

If and when the solicitor of the transferee is satisfied about the title, he will send you the draft transfer to peruse on behalf of the mortgagee and mortgagor, or one of them, as the case may be, and you will accordingly peruse it, with a view to protecting the rights of whoever you may be concerned for, have the usual copy to keep made, and return the draft approved (with such alterations, if any, as you may deem proper) to the transferee's solicitor, who, when the draft is finally approved, will have it engrossed, and fix an appointment to settle the business at the office of the solicitor to the mortgagee, which the parties will attend, and the matter will be completed.

LEASES.

In preparing a lease you will in many cases be required to act on behalf of both parties, i. e. the lessor and lessee; and this you may with propriety do, your duty not being of such a conflicting character as it would be were you concerned for a vendor and purchaser, inasmuch as the lessor invariably fixes the terms on which the lease is to be granted, and also makes it a condition that his title shall not be called for, inquired into, or objected to by the lessee. I will first proceed in the assumption that you have received instructions to peruse a draft lease on behalf of an intended lessee. The first thing your attention will be directed to here is — to see that the premises are correctly described and that the covenants are not of a nature calculated to interfere with the full enjoyment of the property by the lessee, although in the majority of cases you will not be able to do more than obtain some slight modification of the objectionable covenants, and in others you will not be able to obtain any modification at all: it may happen that the person granting the lease is himself a lessee, in which case, as a matter of course, all the covenants and stipulations under which he holds the property will be repeated in the lease he is granting. Your course will be to turn to the written agreement, if there is any between the parties; and should no agreement have been entered into, it will be for the lessee, if you are unsuccessful in obtaining a modification of the objectionable covenants, to elect whether or not he will take the lease; and in assisting him to make his election you should explain fully to him the nature and probable operation of the covenants in question. If, however, the parties have entered into a prior agreement, then the terms of such agreement will guide you as to the course to be pursued. Should the agreement express that the lease is to contain ordinary covenants, or which is much the same thing should be silent as to the covenants to be inserted, then you will object to any but the ordinary covenants being inserted, these are to pay rent, rates and taxes (except land tax, sewers rate, and tithes or rent-charge in lieu of tithes), to repair during the term, and to yield up the premises in good repair at the end of the term, that the lessor may from time to time during the term enter on the premises to view the state of repairs thereof, and that the lessee will repair within a given time (usually three months after notice). Whether the agreement be to grant a lease to contain "ordinary" covenants or "usual" covenants, or contains no mention of covenants, or the agreement be only verbal, the above are the covenants that the lessor could insist upon. In a lease of agricultural property, granted under such an agreement, the covenants would be those usually inserted in leases of similar property in the neighbourhood, and probably even with respect to the lease of a house, to be granted under such circumstances, the locality would to a certain extent be taken into consideration, and a covenant not to use the premises as a shop, or for the carrying on any trade or business, would be considered a usual covenant to be inserted in a lease of a house in one of the principal streets at the west end of London. But it is clear the lessor could not require the lessee to enter into a covenant to insure the premises or not to assign or underlet without license, or to contribute towards planting and keeping in condition any inclosed piece of ground, or covenants of a similar nature.

With respect to the production of the lessor's title, where the agreement is silent as to it, the result of the decisions appear to be that the lessee cannot compel its production; but on the other hand the lessor cannot, if he refuses to furnish his title, compel a specific performance of the contract to take the lease.

It is hardly likely the lessee in an ordinary case would require the lessor to prove his title to grant the lease; but in some cases it may be the means of getting rid of an onerous agreement for a lease by calling for the production of the lessor's title, the lessor preferring rather to consent to the agreement being cancelled than to prove his title on such an occasion, and, as before stated, it appears he can only compel specific performance on proving his title.

The covenant frequently inserted in leases prohibiting the lessee from assigning or underletting or parting with the possession of the premises for the whole or any part of the term, without the written consent of the lessor, is very objectionable, and seriously affects the marketable value of the property. This covenant is unreasonable, inasmuch as its tendency is to restrain the lessee in the enjoyment of the property and the free alienation thereof, and ought never to be consented to in a lease of ground intended to be built upon. Take the case of a man having a field which other persons wish to erect buildings upon: this is neither more nor less than a sale of the property for so many years under certain conditions; but, instead of receiving the consideration money at once, the lessor prefers to reserve a yearly payment, and the understanding implied between the parties always is, that the one shall give up possession of the land to the other for a certain term at a ground rent on such other erecting buildings on the land and consenting to certain stipulations, the breach of any one of which will enable the lessor to recover possession of the property. The lessee ought to be unfettered as to his enjoyment of the property and the free disposal of it, and it is unfair on the part of the lessor to insist on the lessee obtaining his sanction before he can deal with it. It is clear that, by the erection of a house or other building on the land, the lessor is always sure of his ground rent, which bears but a small proportion to the annual value of the property; and the covenants in the lease will always enable the lessor to insist on the premises being kept in good repair and free from damage by fire, in order that at the end of the term he may enjoy the benefit of the outlay of the lessee.

This is all that he ought to ask for: but even should he wish to go a step further, the extent should be to require the lessee or assignee to furnish him with a copy of every assignment, within a given time after its execution, or, which is better still, to furnish the lessor with the date of the assignment and the name and address of the assignee, so that the lessor may know from time to time who is the tenant of the property. This is not an unreasonable request, and it leaves the lessee in the full, unrestrained enjoyment of the property.

If, however, the covenant not to assign be inserted, add at the end of it a proviso that the consent of the lessor to any assignment or underlease shall not be capriciously or unreasonably withheld, nor withheld at all to a responsible assignee, and this is the next best step to obtaining the total omission of the covenant.

In some cases the solicitor to the lessor will insert a covenant that all assignments and underleases shall be prepared by him. This is a most unfair and unjust covenant, inasmuch as it does not in any way add to the security of the lessor, and the only meaning intended by its insertion is to put costs in the solicitor's pocket. It is not very often, however, at the present day, that such a covenant as this is inserted; but where it is inserted it is binding, and a breach of it would cause a forfeiture of the lease.

The costs of the lease, as well on the part of the lessor as the lessee, must be paid by the latter, unless there is an agreement to the contrary; but the costs of the lessor's solicitor, respecting the negotiations for granting the lease, or, in the case of copyhold property, the steward's fees for granting a licence to demise, do not form any part of these costs. As against the lessee, the costs of the lessor's solicitor should, in the absence of any agreement to the contrary, commence with "instructions for lease," and include all the costs incurred by the lessor in respect of the lease, up to the completion of the matter. If a plan is made and referred to in the lease, the lessee must pay the costs of it.

The draft lease is always prepared by the solicitor of the lessor, and he forwards it to the solicitor of the lessee for perusal. On receiving the draft, you should, as acting for the lessee (unless you are already satisfied that the premises, the rent, the duration of the lease, and the covenants are according to the instructions you have received from your client), make an appointment with him for reading through the draft; or, if he lives at a distance, you may send it to him for perusal. In either case you will call his attention to any covenants or stipulations you may think objectionable, and inform him whether they can be insisted on by the lessor, and take his instructions accordingly.

If the lease in question is of coal or iron mines, you will, unless there is an express stipulation to the contrary, be careful in inserting a provision for cesser of rent, in case the mine is exhausted, or becomes unworkable during the term. This is not an unfrequent case. Your client may have formed an erroneous opinion as to the quantity of coal or ironstone or other mineral to be obtained, or the mine may become filled with water, and this may arise from various causes, or become otherwise unworkable. Now, in leases of this description of property, there is invariably a minimum rent reserved, and the ordinary reddendum clause would bind the lessee to pay such rent, notwithstanding the mines had become exhausted or unworkable until the expiration of the term granted by the lease ; and this would be so although the lessee could establish his inability to reap one farthing benefit from the lease. You may consult the cases of *Marquis of Bute* v. *Thompson* (13 Mees. & Wels. 487), *Milne* v. *Taylor* (16 L. T. 172), and *Jowett* v. *Spencer* (1 Exch. 647), on this head with great advantage. These are cases at law, but there is no relief for the lessee in equity ; (*Morris* v. *Smith*, 3 Doug. 279; *Ridgway* v. *Sneyd*, 24 L. T. 58; and *Mellor* v. *Duke of Devonshire*, 22 L. J., Ch. 210.) This is a matter of such a serious nature in mining leases, that it excites one's surprise how professional men residing in the neighbourhood and advising the lessee can omit to provide for it; but that such omission very frequently takes place, the above cases and numerous others which lessees, finding they can have no relief, are obliged to submit to in the best manner they may, sufficiently prove.

The proviso to be inserted on the part of the lessee should be to the effect, that in case the mine should become exhausted or unworkable at a profit to the lessee, at any time during the term, he should have power to determine the lease on giving six months' notice to the lessor of his desire to do so.

Having perused the lease and made such alterations as you may deem advisable, you will return it to the lessor's solicitor, and after you and he have finally approved of the draft, he will engross it and forward it to you for examination; but, unless so expressed in the agreement (if any), the lessor cannot require a counterpart of the lease to be executed at the expense of the lessee: he may require the lessee to execute a counterpart, but it must be at his own expense, and if the agreement states that the lease is to be prepared by the lessor's solicitor, and that the lessee shall execute a counterpart thereof, and pay the costs of the lease and counterpart, then, although it is not always the practice to do so, I think the lessee's solicitor is entitled to engross the counterpart of the lease, and forward it to the lessor's solicitor for examination, as although the latter prepares the lease as a matter of right, yet, so long as the counterpart is executed by the lessee and handed to the lessor, he gets what the agreement binds the lessee to give him. If you choose to adopt this course, you can have the counterpart engrossed from your own copy of the draft lease, but you ought in fairness to give the lessor's solicitor notice of your intention to engross the counterpart, on returning to him the draft lease. With respect to the completion of the matter, you may either arrange for a meeting with the lessor and lessee at the office of the solicitor for the former, or the lease and counterpart may be previously executed, and an appointment made by you or the lessor's solicitor for exchanging the counterpart for the lease, and this is the more usual course.

On exchanging the lease and counterpart, you should see

that the lease is properly executed and attested, and hand to the lessor's solicitor the amount of his charges. The better plan is to request him to send his costs to you at the same time that he forwards the engrossment of the lease, in order to enable you to examine them before the appointment for completing the matter, as, in case the lessor and lessee are present at the completion, it is as unpleasant for you as for the lessor's solicitor to have any dispute about his charges, notwithstanding you may feel it necessary to perform your duty in objecting to some of the items in his bill of costs.

If the lease comprises property in Middlesex or Yorkshire, but does not exceed twenty-one years, or reserves a rack rent (i. e., the full value of the premises to let), it will not require registering, but if for more than twenty-one years, and at a nominal rent, as in the case of building leases, or when a consideration is paid, it must be registered. A lease, conveyance, or assignment of property situate in the city of London does not require to be registered, the city of London not being within the scope of the act establishing the registry for the county of Middlesex.

It is no part of the duty of the lessor's solicitor to register the lease, the registration or putting it on record is for the lessee's security, and it cannot by any means benefit or injure the lessor, whether registered or not. In this case, therefore, you will prepare a memorial of the lease, and get it signed by your client, at the same time putting an extra seal on and obtaining the execution of the lease by him. But if you have had an intimation that the lessor will be present at the time of completing the matter, you can take a memorial of the lease with you, and get it executed by him, and this will avoid the necessity of the lease being executed by your client.

I will now make a few observations as to your duty when professionally concerned for a person about to grant a lease. If the property is very small, or both parties are content to leave the business in your hands, there will be no necessity to prepare any formal agreement; but in all other cases a preliminary agreement should be prepared. This agreement should be prepared with care, as sometimes the lessee repents of his bargain before the lease is granted, and will then use every exertion to get out of his contract. It may be useful to mention here the principal points to be attended to.

Should your client hold all or any part of the premises under a lease, he can only grant an underlease, and the best course will be to read the covenants in the original lease to the person intending to take such underlease, and then express in the agreement that the underlease is to contain similar covenants to those in the lease under which the lessor holds the property; and it may be advisable to state in the agreement that such lease has been previously read over to the lessee, after which it will only be necessary to state shortly what other covenants (if any) are to be inserted. If your client is the freeholder, it becomes necessary to insert in the agreement the terms on which the lease is to be granted, and in preparing an agreement of this nature, general words or expressions should not be used, as you will soon discover that they do not bear the meaning you intend them to do; make particular inquiry of your client whether the lessee is to be restricted from carrying on any particular trades or businesses, or any trade or business at all on the premises, whether he is to be restricted from having any sale of household furniture or other things thereon, whether he is to be restricted from assigning or parting with the lease or the possession of the premises for the whole or any part of the term, without the license of the lessor, and also as to any other special covenants it may be necessary to insert, as all these should be concisely mentioned in the agreement, and this may be done and the agreement still comprised within reasonable limits. Should the intended lease be for building purposes, it will be necessary to insert stipulations as to making roads, sewers, pavements, &c., and for the lessee's fencing off the demised land from the other land of the lessor within a given time. If, on the other hand, it is an agricultural lease, or a lease of a house with farming land attached, it will be necessary to state in the agreement the manner in which the lessee is to use the land, and also as to the state of cultivation, &c.; but whatever may be the nature of the property, take care, unless the parties agree to the contrary, to stipulate in the agreement that the lessee shall pay the land tax, sewers rate, tithes, or rentcharges in lieu of tithes, and all other rates, taxes, charges, and assessments whatsoever, as, if this be omitted, the lessee may possibly, and in some cases successfully, resist being made liable to the payment of the three first-mentioned charges. As to whether he is bound to pay land tax and sewers rate without express mention will depend altogether on the wording of the agreement. You will find all the cases collected and commented on in Platt " On Leases," and Woodfall's " Landlord and Tenant." Unless the lessee binds himself expressly to pay tithes, or the rentcharge in lieu thereof, the lessor probably could not compel him to pay it, but the safest course is to express concisely in the agreement what the lessee is and what he is not to do, and to leave as little as possible to be gathered from inference or implication. A clause should also be inserted that the lease and a counterpart thereof shall be prepared and engrossed by the lessor's solicitor, and the expenses thereof and also of the agreement shall be paid by the lessee. This will prevent the lessee's solicitor from claiming to engross the counterpart. If it is necessary to register the lease, it should be left to the lessee's solicitor, it being done for the security of his client only.

The agreement being prepared, you will make a fair copy thereof and forward it to the solicitor of the lessee for perusal, he will return it to you approved, and either with or without having altered it. When it has been finally settled, you will engross one part and get it signed by your client, and the lessee's solicitor will engross another part and get it signed by his client, after which you will make an appointment for exchanging your part for his. Strictly speaking, this should take place at your office, but it is a point seldom insisted on, and it is really of trifling importance whether you wait on him or he on you.

The agreement having been exchanged, you will proceed to prepare the draft lease, the stipulations to be inserted in which will be regulated by the agreement previously entered into. These stipulations, however, will have to be clothed in appropriate and legal language as concisely but as clearly as practicable. Should the lease be of a house, there will be little difficulty in preparing the draft, as the covenants generally entered into by the lessee are to pay rent, rates, and taxes (specifying land tax, sewers rates, and tithes, or rent-charges in lieu thereof, if any), to repair and keep in repair during the term, and to yield up in good repair at the end of the term, to insure in the names of the lessor and lessee, not carry on any particular trade, or any trade or business of any description on the premises; not to assign or part with the possession of the premises without the license of the lessor, and any other special stipulations that it may be considered necessary or advisable to insert. If the lease is of agricultural or mining property or of manufacturing premises, the covenants will be of an entirely different nature. Some very good precedents of leases of this description of property are given in Platt " On Leases," or Bythewood or Davidson " On Conveyancing ;" but it will not be safe to rely entirely on those precedents, as both in agricultural and mining districts the customs vary considerably, and that which in one county would be a very appropriate form of lease, would in another be quite the contrary; and although the agreement (if any) may be decisive as to the nature of the covenants and stipulations to be inserted, it will afford you no information as to carrying it into effect in a businesslike and creditable manner.

Having now pointed out the care and attention that will be required in cases of this nature, I will proceed to other matters connected with the draft you may be called upon to prepare.

Should the property be in mortgage, you must bear in mind that the mortgagor alone cannot make a lease binding on the mortgagee, although in such a case the lease would be binding upon the mortgagor by estoppel; but the case of *Wilton* v. *Dunn* (15 Jur. 1104) decides that a lessee claiming under a lease granted by a mortgagor, after the execution of the mortgage, will be protected in paying rent to the mortgagor until he receives notice from the mortgagee to pay the rent to him; and even if he has received such notice, but has not actually paid the rent to the mortgagee, the receipt of such notice will be no answer to an action by the mortgagor for the rent. The proper course is to make both the mortgagor and mortgagee parties to the lease. The mortgagee, by direction of the mortgagor, will demise, and the mortgagor will demise and confirm the property to the lessee. The rent will be reserved generally in this form: "Yielding and paying therefor yearly during the said term hereby granted the rent or sum of £   ," as the law will carry the rent to the party for the time being entitled to the property, it being unnecessary to mention in the reddendum the name of the person to whom the rent is to be paid.

A lease is sometimes granted under a power, in which case you may either recite the power or prepare the lease in the common form. It is of little importance which course you adopt, although, if the lease is a valuable one or of extensive property, it is usual to shortly recite the power and make the lessor grant, &c. (following the words of the power) in pursuance thereof; but, in any case, you must strictly follow the conditions under which the person empowered to grant the lease is enabled to do so.

You may be called upon to advise a mortgagee in possession, as to what power he possesses of granting a lease of property comprised in the mortgage deed, in the absence of any express authority given him by the deed. Your advice here will depend altogether upon the circumstances of the case. Properly speaking, a mortgagee has no power to grant a lease, although if the lease granted by him be a beneficial one to the estate and for an ordinary term, and such as a prudent man would grant if the property were his own, it would probably be supported in equity; and I should not hesitate in advising a mortgagee to adopt this course if it were the only one by which he could make the property productive. If the mortgage deed contains an express power enabling the mortgagee to grant leases, it will only be necessary for you to see whether the lease proposed to be granted is within the terms of the power. It is very seldom this power is found in mortgages of small properties; but in a mortgage of a large property it should never be omitted.

The ordinary and usual clauses in leases have already been referred to. The extraordinary clauses must depend on the circumstances of the case, and the nature of the property. In any case, the treatises I have referred to will show what covenants you should insert if your own experience, or the instructions of the lessor, are not sufficient for the purpose.

Having prepared the draft lease, make a fair copy of it; and if you are not concerned for both parties, send it to the solicitor of the lessee for perusal. He will return it to you, and if no alterations are made, or none that you can fairly object to, your next step will be to engross the lease. Sometimes a long correspondence and several interviews take place before the draft lease is finally settled.

The draft lease having been engrossed, together with a counterpart thereof, you will forward the draft and engrossment to the lessee's solicitor; but if there is no agreement, or if it is silent as to who is to engross the counterpart, the lessee's solicitor may claim to do this, although it is not unsually done.

After comparing the engrossment with the draft lease, the lessee's solicitor will return it to you for execution; and if he has, under the circumstances I have mentioned, engrossed the counterpart, he will forward such engrossment to you at the same time, in which case you will compare it with the draft, and return it to him for execution by the lessee. Your costs relating to the transaction should be forwarded to the lessee's solicitor about this time, in order that he may have an opportunity of examining them, and, if necessary, obtain the amount from his client. After you have obtained the execution of the lease by the lessor, make an appointment with the lessee's solicitor for the completion of the matter at your office. At this meeting, you will exchange the lease for the counterpart, after having seen that it is duly executed and attested. The lessee's solicitor will hand you the amount of your costs, and the matter will be completed.

The above remarks will apply to leases of freehold and leasehold property; but with respect to copyhold property it will, as a rule, be necessary to obtain a licence from the lord of the manor before the lease is executed, as the grant of a lease by a copyhold tenant, without previously obtaining a licence from the lord of the manor, may be a forfeiture of the copyhold. In this case, it will only be necessary for you to write to the steward of the manor for a licence informing him the names of the parties, the property to be demised, and the term to be granted, and he will forward you a licence to grant the lease, for which he will charge a fee, and a small fine will also generally become payable to the lord. These fines and fees, if not otherwise provided for by the agreement, must be paid by the lessor.

It will be advisable for the lessee's solicitor to inquire what interest the lord has in the manor, because should he only have a partial interest, i. e., be tenant for life without express power to grant licences to demise, the licence by him will only exist so long as his interest exists; in other words, if the lord be a tenant for life without power to grant licences to demise, and he should grant a licence to demise for twenty-one years, and live only seven years after the date of the lease, it will be necessary to obtain a new licence from the remainderman on his coming into possession.

A licence to demise for more than a year is necessary in most cases; but there are a few exceptions: for instance, in the manor of Highbury, in the county of Middlesex, a copyholder may grant a lease for twenty-one years without licence (*Rawstone* v. *Bentley*, 4 Brown's C. C. 515); and in the manors of Stepney and Hackney, a copyholder may grant a lease for thirty-one years and four months in possession without a licence, so that the lease be presented to the homage, and entered on the court rolls at the first or second court after making it (Scriven on Copyhold, 3rd ed., p. 544).

The 19 & 20 Vict. c. 120, enables the Court of Chancery

to authorize a lease of property in settlement upon certain conditions, mentioned in the 2nd section of that act; and the court, under sect. 7, may either approve of particular leases, or make an order vesting powers of leasing either in the existing trustees of the settlement or in any other persons. All applications to the court under this act are to be by petition to the court in a summary way (see sect. 16).

The orders of the Court of Chancery of the 15th November, 1856, show what is necessary to be done in seeking to obtain the privileges given by this act.

COPYHOLDS.

It appears somewhat like an anomaly in the latter half of the 19th century to find property in this country which is neither freehold nor leasehold, nor transferable direct from one party to another, but by the medium of a gentleman called a steward (usually the family solicitor of the lord of the manor), that such property is held by the purchaser by the tenure of a rod at the will of the lord according to the custom of the manor, and that the usual mode of transfer is by means of a surrender to the steward in this wise. The vendor and purchaser and their respective solicitors meet together at the office of the steward of the manor, when the following ludicrous scene takes place:—The vendor takes in his hand a ruler, or a walking-stick, or an umbrella, and repeats after the steward, " I, A. B., in consideration of &c., surrender such and such property (naming it) to the lord of the manor to the use of C. D., in token whereof I deliver you this rod," whereupon he gravely hands to the steward the walking-stick or umbrella. It is now the steward's duty to take the active part, and accordingly he says to the purchaser (holding out, as he speaks, the walking-stick or umbrella), " I, So-and-so, in the name of the lord of the manor, do admit you tenant of such and such property, this day surrendered to your use by A. B., in token whereof I deliver you this rod," and accordingly he hands the umbrella or walking-stick to the purchaser, who ipso facto becomes seised in fee, according to the custom of the manor of the property he has bought. The purchaser thinks all this uncommonly droll, and rather likes it than otherwise; but his eyes presently become very considerably opened—he wants to grant a lease of the whole or a portion of the property, or to cut timber growing upon, or dig valuable mines which may lie under his property; but if he were rash enough to do this without first obtaining the consent of the lord of the manor and paying certain fines and fees, his property would be absolutely forfeited to the lord, who could eject him therefrom as easily as a lessor could eject a lessee for breach of covenant. Or, supposing the purchaser does not think fit to lay out his money in keeping his property in repair, but prefers to let it remain out of repair, it is also a cause of forfeiture, and the lord of the manor may seize it. The more the copyholder expends upon his property the greater the benefit to the lord: for instance, a piece of land in a manor where the fine is arbitrary may be worth 20s. per annum; in this case, on admittance, the lord of the manor at the utmost could demand as a fine the sum of 2l. Upon this land the copyholder may erect buildings worth 100l. per annum. Immediately after he finds that if he sells the property the purchaser must pay on admittance, or, if he dies without having sold the property, his heir or devisee must pay on admittance, to the lord of the manor 200l. instead of 2l. as before, and that, not because of any exertions or outlay on the part of the lord, but solely because of the exertions and expense of the owner of the property. Such a tenure, to say the least of it, savours greatly of absurdity, and it is astonishing, in these days of railways and general progress, to find its existence; it should, so far as this country is concerned, have disappeared with the mammoth and the elk.

Notwithstanding many acts have been passed of late years for the abolition of copyhold tenure, there is much copyhold property in this country, the practice respecting which, although by no means difficult to master, is less understood than that relating to any other branch of conveyancing. As there can be no doubt that for some years to come a knowledge of this practice will be necessary, I will endeavour to explain it as clearly and concisely as possible.

Suppose, therefore, that your client has purchased an estate of copyhold tenure, it is of no consequence for the present purpose whether he has purchased by public auction or private contract: on receiving the abstract, you will perceive what manor the property is part of; and on afterwards examining the abstract of title with the copies of court roll, at the office of the vendor's solicitor, in the usual manner, you will learn from those copies the name of the steward of the manor. It will be necessary to make an appointment with him, to compare the abstract with the court rolls, i. e., to search the court rolls, in order that you may discover whether the abstract contains particulars of every act that has been done respecting the title since the period of its commencement on the abstract. This part of your duty is of equal importance to that of searching at the register office, on the purchase of an estate situate in a register county, as the court rolls are the only means of discovering what dealings have taken place respecting the property in question. If on searching the rolls you find the property has been dealt with in any manner inconsistent with the abstract of title, you will point that out to the vendor's solicitor, and require him to amend the abstract accordingly.

Having finished the examination of the court rolls, you will probably find it necessary to make inquiries of the steward respecting the customs of the manor. For instance, the abstract may show that A. B. was admitted tenant as heir of C. D., or that a recovery has been suffered, or a surrender made and admission taken thereon, in order to bar a recovery. Now, in any of these cases, it will depend on the custom of the manor whether or not a good title be shown. In the first-mentioned case you will inquire of the steward the usual course of descent in the manor, whether according to the common law or otherwise, for in some manors the eldest son is heir, in others the youngest, following the custom of lands of borough English tenure. Sometimes the custom carries the property to the second son, and sometimes to all the sons, according to the custom of gavelkind. It is manifestly, therefore, of great importance to make these inquiries of the steward, as the title may depend upon a particular person being properly admitted: for, although the eldest son may have been admitted as heir-at-law, yet if, according to the custom of the manor, the youngest or second son is the heir, such admittance gives no title to the eldest son; it is simply of no force whatever. In the case secondly mentioned, viz., the barring of an entail, it will be necessary to inquire of the steward whether it has been perfected according to the custom of the manor. In some manors a recovery was formerly suffered at the Copyhold Court in precisely the same manner as in the superior courts, while in others an entail was barred by forfeiture and regrant, or by a new surrender and admittance; and in any dealing with copyhold property, and any question arising on the title to it, before the 3 & 4 Vict. c. 74, it will still be necessary to make these inquiries.

Since the above act, legal estates tail in copyholds can be barred only by surrender, but equitable estates tail may be barred either by surrender or deed (sect. 50). The provisions with respect to the protector apply to copyholds, and the consent of the protector may be given by deed entered on the court rolls of the manor, or personally to the person taking the surrender of the tenant in tail (sects. 51 & 52).

Should an equitable tenant in tail bar the entail by deed, such deed must be entered on the court rolls of the manor, but need not be enrolled (sects. 53 & 54).

It is not uncommon for a purchaser's solicitor to refrain from making these inquiries, under the impression that the steward would always have taken care to see that the right person was admitted; but this is by no means the case, as it must be remembered that the steward is bound to admit any person showing a colorable title; and in some few manors it is the custom to admit any person who will pay the fine and fees, the steward knowing that the mere fact of admission gives no title whatever. The safer and more proper course is to make these inquiries of the steward. There is yet a further inquiry you should make, and that is as to dower or freebench, as it is termed when applied to lands of copyhold tenure. This only arises by special custom, and varies in different manors. You should learn whether the widow of a copyholder can claim dower out of land of which the husband was seised at any time during the coverture, or only out of land of which he died seised. This freebench is a serious matter, as in most manors it entitles the wife to one-half, and in others to the whole estate during her life.

These preliminary inquiries having been satisfactorily disposed of, you will forward the requisitions on the title (if any) to the vendor's solicitor, and proceed thereon in the same manner as on a purchase of any other description of property. While on this subject it may be useful to call your attention to the importance of having all the copies of court roll (which are, in fact, the copyholder's title deeds) satisfactorily accounted for. It sometimes happens that the vendor has not all the copies of court roll in his possession, and can give no account of their absence; in such a case it will be prudent to decline completing the matter until a satisfactory explanation has been given of the missing copies; for, should they have been deposited as security for an advance of money, it would make a good equitable mortgage. See *Whitbread* v. *Jordan* (1 You. & Coll. 303). If you find that the vendor cannot account for the copies of court roll not being in his possession, and you have no notice of their having been deposited, and nothing appears on the court rolls in the nature of a charge on the property, and that, after making every inquiry a prudent man ought to make, you can discover nothing to lead to the supposition that they have been deposited by way of security, your client would probably be safe in completing the matter. The circumstances of every case of this nature must influence the advice you give your client, and your own course of action. Should the vendor have been in possession for some years, and be a responsible man, or if the earlier part only of the copies of court roll are missing, there cannot be much risk in completing. It may sometimes happen that the missing copies are with the steward. I have known several cases of this nature, and there are few stewards who have not in their possession many copies of court roll which have never been asked for, and doubtless many purchases have been completed without any inquiry, or, if any inquiry has been made, without any satisfactory explanation as to the custody of the missing copies. This is, however, a matter of much more importance than it is sometimes thought, and I would recommend you always to keep on the safe side with respect to these copies of court roll.

The purchase will proceed in much the same manner as a purchase of any other description of property; but as soon as the time arrives for the preparation of the necessary assurances for carrying the contract into effect, a widely different course of practice becomes necessary. Instead of preparing a draft conveyance or assignment, you will prepare a draft surrender of the property—a surrender being the only instrument that has any operation on copyhold property—and as a surrender cannot contain any covenants or other stipulations in the nature of covenants, it is usual to prepare a deed to bear even date with the surrender, containing, in the case of a sale, the usual recitals and vendor's covenants for title, and in the case of a mortgage the recitals, mortgagor's covenants for title, &c., and power of sale, and this is the most proper course; the surrender being nothing more than an instrument whereby the vendor or mortgagor divests himself of the legal estate in the property, and the use limited by the surrender is the direction to the lord of the manor to admit the person in whose favour the surrender is made.

With respect to copyhold property settled on a marriage or otherwise, the court rolls seldom show anything more than a surrender by A. to B., and B.'s admittance. The trusts on which the property are to be held, and the numerous provisions usually contained in settlements, are generally declared by a separate document. Many stewards of manors will not allow any trusts whatever to appear in the surrender; others are not so strict. It is, however, not usual to declare the trusts in the surrender, but by means of a separate document.

It was formerly the practice to execute this separate document, or deed of covenants, as it is generally called, first, whereby the vendor or mortgagor covenanted to surrender the property at the next copyhold court or out of court; but as surrenders are now much more frequently passed out of court than in court, the usual and more correct course is to pass the surrender first, and to recite it in the deed bearing even date, as in this latter case the covenants run with the land; but it is doubtful if they would do so in the former case, in consequence of the legal estate not being vested in the covenantee at the time the deed of covenants was executed.

When the drafts of the surrender and deed of covenants are prepared, you will copy and forward them to the vendor's or mortgagor's solicitor in the usual manner; but after he has returned to you the draft surrender approved, it will be advisable to forward it to the steward of the manor for his approval, as some stewards are very particular with respect to the form of surrender they adopt; and as a steward is not compelled to take a surrender in a form materially different to the one usually followed in the manor, some delay may be occasioned. The form of surrender, however, is similar in most manors.

Should the steward approve of the draft surrender, he will return it to you for engrossment, after which you will engross it and the deed of covenants, and forward them to the vendor's solicitor for examination, and he will make an appointment with the steward to take the surrender. This appointment should be at the steward's office, but, if more convenient to be taken elsewhere, he will seldom insist on its being taken at his office, as the extra fee charged by him for the attendance elsewhere will compensate him for his trouble.

Where freehold and copyhold property are purchased together, the freehold portion will be conveyed in the same manner as in an ordinary case, and the only difference in the form of the draft will be that the surrender must be recited and the covenants made to extend to both descriptions of property, and in this case you are required by the Stamp Act to apportion the ad valorem duty on the purchase money: for instance, if freehold and copyhold property are purchased for 1,000*l.*, then you must apportion so much for the freehold and so much for the copyhold, and stamp the conveyance and surrender accordingly. This apportionment may be in any manner you think fit.

Where freehold and copyhold property are sold together, the purchaser can require the vendor to distinguish the boundaries of the copyhold land, and to state which part is freehold and which copyhold, unless there is a stipulation to the contrary (*Cross* v. *Lawrence*, 9 Hare, 462; *Dawson* v. *Brinkman*, 3 Mac. & Gor. 53). If, therefore, you are instructed by a client to sell freehold and copyhold property, which have been held together for a long period, you should insert a stipulation restricting the purchaser's right to have the boundaries of each distinguished.

An appointment having been made with the steward for taking the surrender, either at his office or elsewhere, you will make the usual searches as to judgments, &c., and inquire as to succession duty (if any) payable, and if all be satisfactory, you will, either with or without your client according to circumstances, attend the place of completion. The vendor will either personally or by attorney (although a purchaser is not obliged to accept a surrender by attorney), surrender the property into the hands of the lord of the manor, by the acceptance of his steward, and pay all arrears of quit rent up to the time of passing the surrender, or such other time (if any) as may be named in the contract or conditions of sale; also all rates, taxes, and other outgoings, in the same manner as on the completion of a conveyance. This completes the business on the vendor's part, and it now only remains for the purchaser to take admittance to the property surrendered to his use.

It may be useful to mention here, that in cases where the steward lives at a distance from the place where the matter is to be completed, it is usual to write to him for a deputation to take the surrender. On giving him short particulars of the property, with the names of the vendor and purchaser, he will forward you or the vendor's solicitor the deputation, which merely consists of a letter authorizing you or him to take the surrender. It does not require any stamp or any other formality. For this deputation the vendor must pay, as it is usually obtained for his convenience. The usual fee is one guinea.

The admittance may be taken either at the time of passing the surrender (if the surrender is taken by the steward) or at any time afterwards, and either at a copyhold court or anywhere else. If your client is not present at the completion, you can take admittance as his attorney without any power of attorney or authority from your client. After the admittance, which simply consists in the steward handing you a rule or stick, or some other symbol, accompanied by these or similar words—" The lord of this manor, by me his steward, admits you tenant to the premises this day surrendered to your use by A. B., in token whereof I deliver you this rod ;" the whole ceremony is concluded. It is not usual in the case of a mortgage of copyhold property for the mortgagee to take admittance immediately after the surrender. He can take admittance at any time, and generally does when he finds it necessary to take possession of the property, to receive the rents and profits, or to sell it under his power of sale. It is quite optional with the mortgagee, whether he takes admittance immediately or not. Should he wish to do so, or should you think it necessary that he should do so, he is quite at liberty to be admitted; but it is seldom done, as, in case the mortgagee is admitted, he must re-surrender to the mortgagor on being repaid his mortgage money, and this saddles the mortgagor with the fines and fees on two admittances and a surrender, which in some manors will amount to a large sum; whereas if the mortgagee had not taken admittance, it would only have been necessary for him, on receiving his mortgage money, to give a written authority to the steward of the manor to enter satisfaction on the court rolls of all monies due under the conditional surrender having been paid, on receiving which the steward enters the satisfaction on the court roll, and the matter is at an end.

After the surrender has been perfected, the steward will take it with him; or, should it have been taken by deputation, it must be forwarded to him, in order that he may enter it on the court rolls. It is the best plan on all these occasions to ask the steward whether it is his practice to keep the surrender. You will find that it is the practice to do so in nineteen manors out of twenty, but there are stewards who do not. It is not of much practical importance whether he does so or not, as he will forward you a copy of the entry on the court roll, which is sufficient evidence of the transaction. If an admittance has taken place on the surrender, the copy of court roll will comprise both the surrender and admittance. It is the practice to pay the steward's fees at the time of passing the surrender, and, unless there is an express agreement to the contrary, the purchaser always pays for both the surrender and admittance, as the two together form the conveyance of the property. It is advisable to bear in mind that the customs in two manors out of three (or, what is practically the same thing, the steward will claim it as a custom,) authorizes the steward to charge for preparing the surrender, notwithstanding you may have prepared it yourself, and this has been decided to be a reasonable custom. Knowing this, some practitioners send instructions to the steward to prepare the surrender, instead of preparing it themselves; but the better plan is to prepare it yourself, as, having the abstract before you, you know more about the parties necessary to concur in the surrender than the steward. You may also think it advisable to have a new description of the property; but in this case the steward will invariably insist on the old description appearing on the surrender as well as the new one, and considering the loose description of property found on the court rolls, there can be no doubt that, unless the old description appears as well as the new one, it would be almost impossible on a subsequent sale to identify the one with the other.

The inaccuracy of the description of property on the court rolls is so well known, that, even in the absence of any stipulation as to identity, a vendor cannot be required to identify the property contracted to be sold with the description of it on the court rolls, but he must show that the property has been actually held under such a description (*Long* v. *Collier*, 4 Russ. 267).

The fine payable to the lord on admission varies in different manors: in some it is certain, that is, a nominal sum, seldom or never varying; in others it is arbitrary, and the fine is generally payable both on death and alienation.

In some manors heriots become due on the death of a copyhold tenant. The custom here again varies, and is sometimes one thing and sometimes another, but generally it is the best live beast. The heriot is usually compounded for, and a sum of money paid to the lord in lieu thereof.

In the case of tenants in common, a heriot is due on the death of each; but when all the property becomes again vested in one individual, only one heriot can be demanded.

In the case of an arbitrary fine, the law allows no more to be demanded by the lord than two years' improved annual value of the property, that is, where the custom has fixed it at that amount. In some manors the custom has fixed the fine at two years on death and one year and a half on alienation. The steward will always give you any information on this head. Where more than one person is admitted in joint tenancy, the fine is increased: thus, suppose four persons to be admitted as joint tenants, the first would pay a full fine, i.e., either two years' improved annual value or one year and a half, as the case may be; the second would pay half that amount; the third, one-fourth; and the fourth, one-eighth; all these added together would make the fine: but in the case of coparceners, however many, only one fine is payable.

Tenants in common are admitted severally, and pay one fine between them, and on the death of either, his heir or devisee pays another fine, and the same on the admittance of a purchaser from one of the tenants in common; but immediately on the whole property becoming vested again in one person, only one fine is payable (see *Garland* v. *Jekyll*, 2 Bing. 273; *Holloway* v. *Berkeley*, 1 Barn. & Cres. 2).

The steward may demand payment of his fees before admittance, and may refuse to admit until they are paid. The lord, however, has not the same right, as the fine is not due until after admittance, and therefore the steward cannot refuse to admit unless the fine be first paid. It is seldom that stewards insist on their right of requiring payment of their fees before admittance.

Should the steward refuse to admit a claimant, either on the ground of the fine not being first paid or on any other insufficient ground, your remedy is by application to the Court of Queen's Bench, for a mandamus to compel admittance. If you have to resort to this course, you will find every information for conducting the matter in any of the Common Law Books of Practice.

The above will, doubtless, enable you to satisfactorily conduct all ordinary proceedings with respect to copyhold property, the principal difference between that and freehold property being the intervention of the steward and the court rolls; the former is the instrument through which any dealings with the copyhold property must be made, and the latter the record of all proceedings respecting transactions relating to property in the manor.

Where copyhold property is taken by a railway company, it is not necessary or usual to have any surrender. The property is under the 95th section of the Lands Clauses Consolidation Act, 1845, conveyed by deed, as in the case of freehold; and, on payment of the steward's fees, he is to enter it on the court rolls, when it is to have the same effect as if the land had been of freehold tenure; but, until enfranchisement, the lands will continue subject to the same fines, &c., as before. Sect. 96 compels the company to enfranchise the copyhold land taken by them within a certain time. Sect. 97 applies to refractory lords of manors and to those who cannot show a good title; and sect. 98 applies to an apportionment of the quit rent, where all the copyholder's land is not taken by the company.

In the case of an enfranchisement of copyhold property, i. e., turning it into freehold, the title of the lord of the manor should (unless there is some stipulation to the contrary) be called for by you, and inspected in the usual manner, in order to see if he has power to enfranchise. He may be tenant for life of the manor, with power to enfranchise; or the manor may be in settlement, and the trustees under the settlement have power to enfranchise. In either of those cases the title should be inspected by you on behalf of your client; and in carrying out the enfranchisement, the terms of the power must be strictly followed. Should the lord be tenant for life, without power to enfranchise, he can, under the authority of the 4 & 5 Vict. c. 35, with the consent of the copyhold commissioners, enfranchise the property: however, in this case they must be parties to the deed.

The act of parliament above named has been explained and amended by two other acts, namely, the 6 & 7 Vict. c. 23, and the 7 & 8 Vict. c. 55. But the most important acts on this subject are the 15 & 16 Vict. c. 51, the short title of which is "The Copyhold Act, 1852," and which incorporates all the before-mentioned acts, besides making most important alterations respecting the enfranchisement of copyhold property; and "The Copyhold Act, 1858," 21 & 22 Vict. c. 94. The other acts apply to voluntary enfranchisements, and were chiefly intended to apply to cases where the lord of a manor was under disability; but copyhold tenure generally being found to be a burthen, other legislation became necessary, and "The Copyhold Act, 1852," became law. (This act is explained and amended by the 16 & 17 Vict. c. 57.) Under these acts either the lord or tenant can compel enfranchisement, and the mode in which it is to be done is pointed out in the 2nd section.

There are one or two useful little works on enfranchisement, which can be obtained by applying to any law bookseller.

In the case of an enfranchisement, where the title is clear, and the aid of the Copyhold Commissioners is not required, it is the practice for the steward to prepare the necessary deed, and to forward it to you, as the copyholder's solicitor, for perusal. Your duty will be to see that the lord has power to enfranchise, that the property is correctly described, and that proper covenants for title and a covenant for production of the title deeds are inserted, an enfranchisement being, in fact, a purchase of the freehold.

The Copyhold Act, 1852, has an express provision to the effect that, notwithstanding the enfranchisement, the copyholder shall have the same right of common as he had before (see sect. 45).

It will be necessary to search for judgments, &c., against the lord of the manor, and if the manor is situate in a register county, to search the register for incumbrances, for a manor is within the Registry Acts, although copyhold property held of such manor is not.

In case you should be concerned for a copyholder seeking to enfranchise, and a difficulty should arise between you and the steward as to the proper amount of compensation for fines and fees, your better course will be to carry it into effect through the Copyhold Commissioners; or, if you prefer in the first place, to enfranchise through the Commissioners, you need only send or write to the Copyhold Commission in St. James's Square, for their printed instructions and a list of forms, and these will be immediately supplied you. After reading the printed instructions, you will find no difficulty in doing what is necessary to carry out the enfranchisement. I have found from experience that generally it is cheaper for the copyholder to enfranchise through the medium of the Copyhold Commissioners, and for his solicitor to begin with them in the first place, than to open a communication with the steward of the manor, who, as a matter of course, wishes to procure as much as possible for his lord in the shape of compensation for fines, and as much as possible for himself in the shape of compensation for fees.

COPARTNERSHIP DEEDS.

In some few cases persons join together for the purpose of carrying on a trade or business without any written document being previously executed: but as this invariably leads to much difficulty and confusion at or before the termination of the copartnership, it is always the safest course to have a proper document prepared, in order that the position of the partners and their interests in the concern may be defined.

If you are concerned for all the parties intending to enter into copartnership you will only have to prepare the necessary deed in order to carry their intentions into effect, for which purpose you should take down the names and descriptions of the parties, the time at which the partnership is to commence, the duration thereof, the amount of capital, and the manner in which it is to be brought in, and whether any partner is to bring in any goods or stock as part of his capital: whether all or which of the partners are to give their whole time and attention to the business, and any other matters which the parties may wish to have inserted beyond what are to be found in the usual and common clauses of a copartnership deed. If you have used some little care in obtaining accurate and full instructions, you will not find much difficulty in preparing the draft of an ordinary deed of copartnership. When prepared and fair copied, you will either send the draft to one of the partners with instructions for him to read it over and afterwards to hand it to the others, or you will arrange for them to meet at your office for the purpose of having the draft read over and settled. You ought never to take the responsibility of engrossing the draft until it has been approved by all the partners.

After the draft has been finally agreed upon, you will have it engrossed (I have found it much more convenient in practice to have long deeds and particularly copartnership deeds engrossed on parchment folded bookwise), and then make an appointment for the parties to execute the deed. This can be a matter of previous arrangement. Sometimes the deed is executed at your office and sometimes at the counting-house or place of business of the firm. You will consult the convenience and wishes of your clients in the matter.

After the deed has been executed the partners will either keep it at their place of business or request you to keep it for them for the purpose of general reference, if the latter, a plain copy should be made for the use of the partners to be kept by them at their place of business.

Thus far in an ordinary matter where you are acting in behalf of all parties; but in some cases you may be concerned for a person about to join another in partnership, or for a firm about to admit a new partner, or for such new partner. In the case first put it will be a matter of prior arrangement between you and the solicitor on the other side as to which of you shall prepare the deed; the most usual and most equitable arrangement is for both your bills of costs to be added together and paid by the clients equally, and for you and the other solicitor afterwards to divide the profit on the whole business; in this case it becomes quite a matter of indifference whether you or he prepare the deed, but if he is an older practitioner than yourself, it will be a graceful act on your part to offer to prepare the deed, and I would strongly recommend you to prepare it for the sake of practice. These deeds are awkward matters to handle unless you have had some previous experience, and one cannot begin too soon to obtain all the experience he can, as no amount of theory can compensate for a deficiency in practical knowledge, and in copartnership deeds a good deal of practical knowledge is necessary.

The solicitor who prepares the draft will forward a copy of it to the other solicitor concerned for his perusal, and afterwards the engrossment for examination in the usual manner; and when this has been done an appointment will be made at one of your offices, (in making this appointment you will consider the convenience of your clients,) for all parties to meet for the purpose of executing the deed. A copartnership deed is generally executed by all the parties together, although, of course, this is not necessary.

If you are concerned for a firm about to admit a new partner, he will probably wish his own solicitor to look after his interests in the transaction. In this case you will, as a matter of right, prepare the deed, and forward a copy thereof to the incoming partner's solicitor for his perusal, and when all points have been settled and you have engrossed the draft, both draft and engrossment will be sent to him for examination.

The appointment to execute the deed will be either at your

office or at your client's place of business. In a case of this description the general rule is, that your clients pay your charges, and the incoming partner will pay the charges of his own solicitor.

If, on the other hand, you are acting for the new partner instead of the firm, your position will be reversed, and you will on receiving the draft either forward it to your client or get him to call on you for the purpose of going through it with him. After perusing the draft it will be returned by you to the solicitor who prepared it, and when you and he have settled all points in-dispute, he will forward you the draft and engrossment for execution, and either at the same time or afterwards an appointment for you and your client to attend and complete the business. In this case you will charge your own client with your costs.

These matters generally proceed without much difficulty after the preliminaries are arranged, and, as mentioned before, if you exercise sufficient care in obtaining full instructions in the first place, you will get through the business without inconvenience.

The best selection of partnership deeds is contained in the 7th volume of Bythewood's Conveyancing, by Sweet. You will there find almost every form of deed which can be required.

A deed of copartnership requires to be stamped with a 35s. stamp.

A dissolution of partnership may take place either on a total giving up of the business by the partners, or on the death of one partner, or on one partner retiring from the firm. In the case first mentioned, whether you are acting for one or both partners, the course before suggested as to the preparation of the copartnership deed will equally apply here. If, on the other hand, the dissolution is only a partial one, and is confined to a partner retiring from the firm, and you are concerned for the firm, you will prepare the deed of dissolution, and send it to the solicitor of the retiring partner for his perusal, and afterwards the engrossment for examination and execution, as in such a case it is seldom that the parties meet on the completion of the business; after which you and the other solicitor will meet together and complete the matter. In this case your client pays your costs, and the solicitor of the retiring partner looks to his own client for his charges.

If, however, you are acting for the retiring partner, then it will be for you to peruse the draft and examine the engrossment, and perform the duties above pointed out, as being done by the retiring partner's solicitor, and you will charge your client with your costs in the matter.

If the dissolution of the copartnership is by death, then for whichever party you may be concerned you will turn to the deed of copartnership (and here I may mention that if you are advising the representatives of a deceased partner, and do not happen to have a copy of the deed, you will obtain one from the solicitor of the surviving partner), in order to see its provisions in the event of the death of one of the partners. In some cases the deed provides that, in the event of one partner dying during the continuance of the copartnership, his representatives shall assign all their interest in the concern to the surviving partner, and that he shall give a bond to such representatives for the deceased partner's share of capital in the concern, and in a proportionate share of profits, or a given sum in lieu of profits, for the current year. In other cases it goes further, and provides, in addition, that the surviving partner shall pay an annuity to the representatives of the deceased partner for a given period. The usual course is for the solicitor of the surviving partner to prepare the assignment from the representatives of the deceased partner, and for their solicitor to prepare all bonds or other securities which may be provided for by the partnership deed for securing the share of capital or the annuity, or both, as the case may be. If both the share of capital and an annuity are to be paid, it will be better to have separate bonds. The share of capital is generally provided to be paid by instalments, but the current year's share of profits, or the given sum to be paid in lieu of profits, is invariably provided to be paid on the execution of the necessary assignment and bonds. With respect to the costs of these documents, the copartnership deed generally provides for them; but if it should contain no provision in this respect, the practice is for the surviving partner to pay his own solicitor's charges for preparing the deed of assignment, and the costs on both sides of the preparation and execution of the necessary bonds; but the charges of the solicitor of the representatives for perusing and completing the assignment by his clients are generally paid by them.

Whether you are concerned for the one side or the other, the before-mentioned observations as to preparing, perusing, engrossing, and completing the matter, will equally apply here.

Should you be concerned for a partner retiring from the concern, then the solicitor of the continuing partners will prepare the deed of dissolution and assignment of such partner's share. This dissolution is, of course, confined to the retiring partner. You will refer to the deed of copartnership, for the purpose of ascertaining what your client becomes entitled to on his retirement; or it may be a matter of arrangement between the parties; at all events, in the absence of any arrangement to the contrary, the observations as to the preparation of the necessary documents on the death of a partner, and the payment of the costs occasioned thereby, will apply here.

After a dissolution of the partnership by effluxion of time or consent, notice should be inserted in the "Gazette" and other newspapers, in order that any person who had been in the habit of dealing with the firm may not be in a position, after the dissolution, to say that any subsequent dealings were entered into and credit given on the faith of the retiring member continuing to belong to the copartnership. This is very important, and, if you are acting for a retiring partner, you should always take care that it is done.

COMPOSITION DEEDS, ASSIGNMENTS FOR BENEFIT OF CREDITORS, &c.

Occasionally you may be applied to for advice respecting a person unable to meet his engagements, and where it is not wished that he should be made a bankrupt or insolvent. In large concerns the debtor more usually pays a composition, either altogether or by certain instalments, and either secured or not by the guarantee of a third party; or it is arranged that the business shall be carried on under inspectorship. In small matters the debtor sometimes makes an assignment of all his estate and effects to one or two of his creditors, upon trust for them all rateably.

Assuming the case before you to be that of a trader carrying on a small business, and a composition cannot be guaranteed, your best course will be to prepare an assignment for the general benefit of his creditors. The best precedent you can have for such a deed is that given in the schedule to the Bankruptcy Act, 1861.

This deed is not an act of bankruptcy, unless a petition for adjudication be filed within three months from the execution thereof, provided such deed be executed by every trustee within fifteen days after its execution by the trader and the execution thereof by the trader, and by every trustee, be attested by an attorney or solicitor, and notice of the deed be given within one month after the execution thereof by such trader in the following manner : In case the trader resides in London or within forty miles thereof, in the "Gazette" and two London daily newspapers; and in case he does not reside within forty miles of London, then in the "Gazette," one London newspaper and one provincial paper, published near to the trader's residence, such notice to contain the date of execution of the deed, and the name and place of abode respectively of every such trustee and attorney (vide 12 & 13 Vict. c. 106, s. 68, "The Bankruptcy Law Consolidation Act").

This deed must be registered under the 194th section of the Bankruptcy Act, 1861, otherwise it cannot be pleaded in bar to an action, even although the deed may contain a release, and the creditor bringing such action may have executed the deed (*Hodgson* v. *Wightman*, 32 L. J. (N. S.) Exch. 147).

After the execution of the deed you will proceed to inform the creditors of it by addressing circular letters to them individually, and get in the estate and divide it as early as practicable.

A deed of composition is of a different nature. This deed is executed in cases where a debtor being unable to pay his creditors in full, and his creditors wishing him to go on, have resolved to accept a composition in discharge of their claims, and to release the debtor from his liabilities. This composition is either paid down, or, more generally, secured by bills of exchange, drawn by a third party on and accepted by the debtor, and payable at certain months after date.

The deed in this case recites the fact of the debtor being indebted, and, being unable to pay his creditors in full, that they had agreed to accept a composition on their debts, and that bills of exchange for securing the composition had been given or deposited for all the creditors. The debtor then covenants that the money shall be paid or the bills duly met. The creditors on their part covenant not to sue the debtor if the composition is duly paid, and a clause for avoiding the deed is generally inserted in case a sufficient number of the creditors do not concur within a given time, and also a clause providing that creditors may execute the deed by attorney.

A deed of inspectorship is only resorted to in the case of large concerns, and where there is a feeling among the creditors in favour of the business being carried on under the inspectorship of two or three of their number. This deed recites the fact of the trader being indebted, and the agreement to allow him to carry on the business under inspection for a term. Then follows the grant of licence by the creditors to the debtor, allowing him for a certain term to carry on the business under inspection.

Provisions are generally made as to finding capital for carrying on the concern, and for the surplus profits to be appropriated from time to time toward paying off the creditors.

The debtor covenants to deliver statements from time to time to the inspectors, and act generally under their control. Various other provisions are contained in such a deed, forms of which you will find in almost any book of precedents, but before using them you should carefully read the cases that have been decided under the 192nd section of the Bankruptcy Act, 1861.

It must be borne in mind that the trustees under a deed of inspectorship and also the creditors may, in some cases, be held liable for all debts contracted during the time the business is so carried on: you should carefully consider the case of *Hickman* v. *Cox* (25 L. J., C. P. 277); *S. C.*, on appeal (6 Weekly Rep. 166), before proceeding to advise your clients or to prepare the deed, as it may influence you in determining under what style or name, and in what manner the business is to be carried on.

Under the 192nd section of the Bankruptcy Act, 1861, a new class of composition deeds was initiated, with the intention of affording increased facilities for the arrangement of claims and debts between debtors and creditors, and to save, as much as possible, the necessity for the intervention of the Bankruptcy Court, and its attendant expense in adjudicating an insolvent estate. But from the peculiar framing of the particular clauses of the act by which this object was sought to be attained, and the great difficulty experienced in arriving with any certainty at the intention of the legislature, in consequence of the conflicting and ambiguous nature of those clauses, the class of composition deeds, prepared in accordance with the provisions of the act, have been from the beginning and still continue (although very numerous) in a most unsettled, undefined and unsatisfactory state; and in neither the Bankruptcy Court nor the Common Law Courts has such an interpretation of the act, in relation to composition deeds, been yet given as may serve as a general landmark to guide professional men, and enable them to act with confidence in preparing the deeds, and taking the requisite steps for perfecting them in accordance with the provisions of the act. The following are a few among the numerous points which have been raised and submitted to judicial decision, viz. :—

1. A deed of arrangement under sect. 192 of the act must be on the face of it for the benefit of *all* the creditors, and not merely for those who execute it (*Walter* v. *Adcock*, 10 Weekly Rep. 542; 31 L. J., Bank. 92; *Ex parte Morgan*, 32 L. J., Bank. 15).

2. Such deed need not contain an assignment of all the debtor's property (*Ex parte Morgan; Re Woodhouse*, 11 Weekly Rep. 316; *Ex parte Cockburn*, 33 L. J., Chanc. 17; *Clapham* v. *Atkinson*, 33 L. J., Q. B. 81).

3. It must be assented to by a majority in number representing three-fourths in value of the *secured*, as well as unsecured creditors (*Ex parte Golden; In re Shettle*, 32 L. J., Bank. 37; *Turquand* v. *Moss*, 12 Weekly Rep. 960.)

4. A composition deed must contain a release of the estate of the debtor, otherwise it cannot be pleaded in bar to an action in respect of a debt for which a composition is payable under such deed (*Ipstone Park Iron Ore Company* v. *Pattinson*, 12 Weekly Rep. 344), and query, whether a deed could be framed with a covenant, making it so pleadable without rendering it void against non-assenting creditors (*S. C.*).

5. Such a deed, if duly executed and containing a release, may be pleaded in bar to an action by a non-assenting creditor (*Whitehead* v. *Porter*, 12 Weekly Rep. 742).

6. Every deed of arrangement between a debtor and the whole body of his creditors *must* be registered under the 194th section, whether it be framed under the provisions of sect. 192 or not (*Ex parte Morgan*, supra).

7. The production of the registrar's certificate of registration is primâ facie evidence that the conditions of the act have been complied with, but a creditor may produce evidence to show the contrary, and may require that the deed be examined to see that the necessary assents have been given (*Re Church*, 1 N. R. 86).

8. To render a deed of composition and release binding on

the minority of the creditors who have not executed or assented to or approved of it in writing, it is necessary that the non-assenting creditors should stand under the deed in the same situation and with the same advantages as the creditors forming the majority (*Ex parte Cockburn*, 12 Weekly Rep. 673).

9. The deed to be binding must be complete at the time it is registered, and it cannot be subsequently executed by any creditor who had not previously assented to or approved of it in writing (*Ex parte Cockburn*, supra).

A question regarding costs was recently decided by the Lord Chancellor in *Re M'Turk*. A composition deed had been executed in the form prescribed by the act, but before it was registered a petition for an adjudication in bankruptcy was presented against the debtor. The deed was subsequently registered, and thereupon the petition was dismissed. The petitioning creditor then applied for his costs to be paid out of the trust estate, but the Lord Chancellor said he had no jurisdiction. The bankruptcy was gone by the dismissal of the petition. He thought it was an omission in the act, but he could not supply the omission.

I have inserted in the precedents some forms of composition deeds under the act, which, as far as concerns the form, have been tested and decided to be sufficient. With regard to registration and other requirements to make the deed valid, I deem it better to refer you to the act itself than to incumber a small work like the present with it.

SETTLEMENTS.

There are various descriptions of settlements; namely, those executed before marriage and those executed after. Those made bonâ fide, and others for fraudulent purposes. I will as concisely as possible state the more prominent points of each, in order that your attention may be directed to them when the proper occasion arrives.

1st. Settlements executed in contemplation of marriage,

which may be divided into two parts, viz., settlements of real estate, and settlements of personal estate. With respect to the first, it is always desirable, after receiving instructions to prepare a marriage settlement, to look into the title, in order to see what is necessary to be done before the estate can be settled in the manner required. Take, for example, the case of an intended marriage of the heir of a family estate. You will generally find that the title was examined on the marriage of the parent, and if that be so, the settlement then executed will be the only document requiring your attention, and which you will find very much in the following form:—
Habendum to trustees: To the use of the trustees for a term of 500 or some other number of years, upon trust to secure pin money to the wife, and subject thereto to the use of the husband for life, remainder to trustees to secure the wife's jointure, remainder to trustees to secure the portions of younger children, remainder to the use of the first and other sons of the marriage in tail male, remainder to the first and other sons of the marriage in tail, general remainder to the first and other daughters in the same manner, with remainders over. There may be other terms created for various purposes, or the uses may be somewhat varied, but the above will be sufficient for our present purpose.

Now apply the above to the case supposed, that is, your receiving instructions to prepare a settlement, to be executed on the marriage of the eldest son of the settlor who has attained his majority, and the father and mother both living. In such a case as this, the first thing to be done will be to bar the entail created by the existing settlement, and this may be done by the father and eldest son executing a disentailing deed. This deed will be between the father of the first part, the son of the second part, and a nominee of the third part: it will recite the settlement, and that the eldest son has attained his majority; and then the father and son, in order to bar and destroy the estate tail created by the settlement and all other estates tail and vest the estate in manner thereinafter mentioned, will convey the estate to the party of the third part to such uses as the father and son may jointly appoint.

The new settlement will be by another deed, by which the father and son will appoint the estate to A. B. to the use of trustees for a term of, say, 1,000 years, remainder to the use that the son shall during the joint lives of his father and himself receive a certain annual sum, with powers of distress and entry for securing the same, remainder to the use that after the death of the father his widow, if living, may receive an annuity by way of jointure, with powers of distress and entry, remainder to the use of the father for life, remainder to the use of the son for life, remainder to the use of the trustees for, say, 500 years, remainder to the use of the first and other sons in tail male, and so on as in the former settlement, with an ultimate remainder to the use of the son in fee. Then the trusts of the terms which have been limited are declared. The first term is declared to be for securing the portions of the younger children of the father, the second for securing the portions of the younger children of the son, and if any other terms are limited, the trusts will be declared in a similar manner. Should, however, there have only been one son of the marriage, or the mother be dead, of course in the first case no term will be necessary for securing the portions of younger children by the father's marriage, and in the second case no provision will be necessary for securing the mother's jointure. The above illustration is given simply to draw your attention to what will be required in instructing counsel to prepare the settlement, as it is very seldom that such a settlement as the foregoing is prepared in a solicitor's office; neither is it expected of the solicitor that he should prepare it, although there is no reason why he should not do so if he feels himself competent to do it, and likes to undertake the trouble and responsibility.

Having formed in your own mind an outline of the intended settlement, you will not have much difficulty in preparing proper instructions to counsel. On receiving the draft from counsel, it will be necessary to go carefully through it, in order to see if it is prepared in accordance with the intentions of the parties. This should never be omitted, more especially as the instructions to counsel often consist of a copy of the existing settlement, and a statement of the particulars of the family and of the intended marriage. If the lady is represented by a separate solicitor, you will fair copy the draft and forward it to him for perusal, and afterwards to the solicitor of the trustees, if they are separately represented, and the same with respect to any other parties to the deed for whom you may not be concerned. It will be your province, as solicitor to the intended husband, to prepare the settlement; and if there be a settlement on the lady's part, which is often the case, it will be by a separate deed, which her solicitor will prepare and forward to you for perusal, and afterwards engross it and get it executed in the usual manner. Your own draft, having been finally approved, will be engrossed by you, and the engrossment and draft forwarded to the other solicitors concerned for examination, after which you will get it executed by the necessary parties.

Should the estate or any part of it be in a register county, the settlement must be registered in the same manner as any other deed.

If the property intended to be settled be a small freehold, leasehold, or copyhold estate, you will sometimes find that the object of the parties is to benefit the issue equally, and not, as in the case of a family estate, entail it. The better course, in a case of this nature, will be to convey the property to trustees upon trust, that the husband may receive the rents for life. This will give him ample power, and make him quite independent of the trustees as to the receipt of the rents and management of the property, as the difference between a trust to pay the rents and profits to a person for life and a trust that such person shall receive and take the rents and profits during his life is, that the first-mentioned trust gives the beneficiary no power over the property, while the second gives him every necessary power over the management of it. The settlement will then proceed as follows:—Upon trust after the death of the husband that the wife may receive the rents during her life, or if the other course is preferred, then that the trustees may pay the rents to the wife during her life; and after the death of the survivor of the husband and wife, upon such trusts as the husband and wife may jointly appoint; and in default of a joint appointment as the survivor may appoint, and in default of appointment by the survivor, and subject to any partial or incomplete appointment upon trust for the children as tenants in common, the issue of deceased children to take their parents' share, and in default of issue upon any other trusts the parties may wish to have inserted. You will take care to give either the husband or the trustees, and if the latter, then with the consent of the husband and wife during their joint lives, or of the survivor during his or her life, a power to grant leases and also a power to sell the property; and whenever a power to appoint among a class is given by any document, the hotchpot clause should be inserted. This clause is inserted for equalizing as much as possible the shares of the children, otherwise a child who claimed, say, one-third of the property under the appointment, would share with his brothers and sisters in the other two-thirds under the gift over in default of appointment, unless there were some special stipulations in the appointment under which he claimed, having the effect of barring him from making any further claim. In the case of a settlement such as we are now considering, if the property brought into the settlement belongs to the lady, the first life estate will be given to her and the ultimate remainder will be to her or her family.

The process of settling personal property is generally very simple, and after some little experience you will not have much difficulty in preparing such a settlement, although at all times you would be justified in resorting to counsel for his assistance.

In a settlement of personal property, say, of a sum of money possessed by one of the parties, it will only be necessary to recite that fact, and then the marriage that is contemplated, and that on the treaty for such marriage it was agreed that such sum of money should be handed over to the trustees upon the trusts thereinafter declared. You then proceed to declare that the trustees shall invest the money and stand possessed thereof and of the interest, dividends, and annual proceeds thereof upon the trusts thereinafter declared. These trusts will be referred to presently.

Should either of the parties be possessed of stock in the funds, you will recite that he or she, as the case may be, is possessed of so much stock lately standing in his or her name in the books of the Governor and Company of the Bank of England, then the intended marriage on the treaty for which it was agreed that the stock should be transferred into the names of the trustees upon the trusts, &c., as before. The declaration of trust in this case will authorize the trustees either to allow the stock to remain in its then state of investment or to sell it and invest the produce either in similar or other stocks or on mortgage, and the trusts will follow in the same manner as before. Other cases will be noticed hereafter.

The trusts are generally as follows:—If the property is the husband's, the first life estate is given to him, unless he is in business, and it is wished to preserve the income for the maintenance of the family in case of bankruptcy; but even this may be done and the life interest given to the husband, provided such life interest is made determinable on the bankruptcy or insolvency of the husband, and given over to the wife or to the trustees for the maintenance of the children on either of those events happening. If, on the other hand, the property is the wife's, the first life interest is given to her, unless the contrary is wished, which is seldom the case; and after the death of one the life interest is given to the other. Whenever a life interest is given to the wife, it should be for her separate use, free from the debts, control, or interference of her husband for the time being, and without power of anticipation. With respect to the separate use of the wife, and restraining her alienation of the income, and under what circumstances such restraint is binding on her, you cannot do better than carefully read the case of *Tullatt* v. *Armstrong* (1 Beav. 1; affirmed on appeal, 4 Myl. & Craig, 377). After the death of the survivor of the husband and wife, the fund will be held by the trustees upon trust for such one or more of the children of the marriage as the husband and wife shall jointly appoint, and in default of any joint appointment as the survivor shall appoint, and in default of such appointment upon trust for the children of the marriage equally, the issue of a deceased child taking the share their, his or her parent would have been entitled to if living. You will declare the interest of the sons to be a vested interest at twenty-one, and the daughters at twenty-one or marriage. Then follows the hotchpot clause, the effect of which has been already mentioned; and in default of any of the children taking a vested interest, then, if the property is the husband's, upon such trusts generally as he shall by deed or will appoint, and in default of appointment to his next of kin. If the property be the wife's, then upon trust as she shall by deed or will appoint, and, in default of appointment, to her next of kin. In either case, on the death of one without leaving issue of the marriage living to attain a vested interest, the husband or wife, as the case may be, may, by appointing the property to himself or herself by deed, obtain the absolute control over it. There formerly followed a provision authorizing the trustees to apply the annual income, or any part thereof, arising from the trust property, for the maintenance of any infant taking a vested or presumptive share of the capital; but now, since the 26th section of the 23 & 24 Vict. c. 145, it will be unnecessary to insert such a clause, but you should insert a clause enabling the trustees to apply a portion of the capital of the share of any such infant for his or her advancement or preferment in the world. This portion may either be limited, or, which is the preferable plan, if the trust fund is of small amount, may be left to the discretion of the trustees. The clause for advancement should apply to all infants, whether male or female, as in settlements of small property it is a provision very likely to be needed by females.

If the property be brought into the settlement by the wife a provision should be inserted, enabling her to settle some part of it on the children of a second marriage, or which is by far the better plan, instead of settling the property on the children of the marriage, settle it generally on the children of the wife; this will embrace all her children, and the justice of this is obvious; for, supposing there be only one child of the marriage and the husband die, and the wife marry again and have a large family, if the property be settled on the children of the first marriage, the one child will take all to the total exclusion of the others, although his claim to it would be no better than that of the other children.

In some cases a clause is inserted authorizing the trustees to lend a portion of the trust money to the husband, on his giving to the trustees his bond or other security for the repayment thereof. If you are instructed to insert such a clause (and I need scarcely say it should not be inserted without authority), you should declare in express terms that the trustees shall not be answerable or responsible for the loss of the whole or any part of the money so lent.

It will not be necessary to insert a clause declaring the receipts of the trustees good discharges for the trust money or any part thereof, for the 29th section of the 23 & 24 Vict. c. 145, will apply, and is in the same words that you would probably use.

For the same reason it will be unnecessary to insert a power to appoint new trustees, inasmuch as the same act gives a general clause framed to meet almost every case that may arise, and it will apply to every deed, will, or other instrument (see sect. 27).

It may be useful to state here the mode of vesting the settled property in the trustees. Stock or money invested in the public securities are transferred at the bank to the trustees, either by power of attorney or personally. If by power of attorney the power must be bespoke at the Bank of England one clear day before the day appointed for executing the settlement; and in this case the settlement and the power of attorney for transferring the stock will be executed together, and the transfer made immediately after. If, on the other hand, the transfer is made personally, it should be done immediately before the settlement is executed, and the trustees by the settlement, as before mentioned, will declare the trusts upon which the stock is to be held.

If the property intended to be settled consists of money

secured on mortgage, two deeds will be necessary, viz., an ordinary transfer of the mortgage to the trustees upon the trusts of the settlement, in which transfer will be inserted full power to give receipts for the mortgage money, in order to avoid the necessity of making the settlement part of the title to the property comprised in the mortgage; and the other deed will be the settlement, and this document will declare the trusts upon which the mortgage money is to be held by the trustees.

In cases where bonds or promissory notes are settled, one deed only is necessary, viz., the settlement. Should a bond be settled it will be assigned to the trustees by the settlement, in which case full power must be given to the trustees to use the name of the obligee to the bond to sue for and recover the monies secured thereby, a bond being what is called a "chose in action," in other words, something that is not in possession, the recovery whereof can only be enforced by an action or suit. But where promissory notes are settled they will simply be indorsed to the trustees, and the fact of their having been so indorsed will be recited in the settlement, a promissory note being, by the law of commerce, capable of transfer by indorsement. In this case the settlement proceeds to declare the trusts upon which the money secured by the promissory note is to be held; and, unless it is intended to call in the money immediately it is due, or the promissory note be payable upon demand, power must be given to the trustees to allow the money to remain on the promissory note, without being liable for any loss occasioned thereby, as it would be a breach of trust to allow the money to remain on the promissory note, even in a case where money so secured is part of the settled property.

Shares in railways, canals, or other companies are transferred by the ordinary and usual transfer, and the trusts upon which they are to be held are declared by the settlement.

In the case of household furniture, &c., it is assigned to the trustees and the trusts afterwards declared. The only way of securing this description of property against the liabilities of the husband, is to settle it upon trust for the separate use of the wife, free from the control or interference of the husband, or of his debts or engagements, and the settlement should give power to the trustees to insure the furniture from loss or damage by fire, or to sell it if the wife should so direct, or if she is not living, then if the trustees shall think fit to do so.

A settlement of chattels executed on marriage does not require to be registered as a bill of sale.

In some cases the subject of the settlement is a policy of assurance on the life of the husband. This should be assigned to the trustees upon trust after the money has been received, to invest it and apply the interest to the wife for life, with remainder to the children as before mentioned. The husband covenants to keep the policy on foot and not to do anything to invalidate it.

It would be useful in such a settlement as this to insert a clause that in case of the death of the wife in the lifetime of the husband, without leaving issue, who have attained a vested interest in the money secured by the policy, it should be lawful for the husband, if he should think fit, to permit the policy to drop, or to sell or assign it to the company.

With respect to a settlement executed after marriage, where no marriage articles have been executed previously to the marriage, the principal question will be whether the husband is or is not solvent. A man owing as much or nearly as much as he is worth cannot make a voluntary settlement binding on his creditors; but if a man owes to his creditors, say 500*l.*, and has property worth, say 2,000*l.*, then he might make a settlement after marriage binding on his creditors, provided he left sufficient in his hands to pay off his debts. The case of *Crabb* v. *Moxey* (21 Law Times, 99) is worthy of an attentive perusal on this point. In deciding that case the Vice-Chancellor said : " It is not sufficient, in order to set aside a voluntary settlement, to show that the settlor had at the time of executing the deed some debts; neither, on the other hand, is it necessary to prove that he was absolutely solvent. The question must always be whether the effect is such as to be injurious to the creditors." In that case an inquiry was granted as to the state of the settlor's property, and the amount of his debts at the date of the settlement.

A voluntary settlement is binding on the settlor, and all persons claiming under him; and the settlor cannot revoke the trusts of such settlement unless express power is therein reserved to him to do so; but if the property settled be freehold, copyhold or leasehold property, he can in effect revoke such trusts by conveying the property to a purchaser for valuable consideration; and even if the purchaser had notice of the settlement before entering into the contract, he could hold the property without being affected by the trusts of the settlement. All the cases on this subject will be found in Sugden on "Vendors and Purchasers."

Always bear in mind that there exists a rule respecting personal estate, somewhat analogous to the well-known rule in Shelley's Case, namely, that a gift to A., followed by a gift to the executors or administrators of A., is an absolute gift to A. This is well illustrated by the case of *Page* v. *Soper* (17 Jurist, 851; *S. C.*, 22 L. J., Ch. 1044), where funded property settled upon A. for life for her separate use, and after her decease to such persons as she should by will appoint, and, in default of appointment, for her executors or administrators, was declared to belong to A. absolutely. A serious mistake might easily be made through ignorance of the above rule.

With respect to the custody of the deeds, the following appears to be the rule and practice.

If the property settled be real estate, the tenant for life, having the legal estate, is entitled to the custody of the deeds, as it devolves upon him to defend the inheritance. If the legal estate be in trustees they hold the deeds. If the property is leasehold the trustee holds the deeds, and where there are more trustees than one they usually arrange among themselves which of them shall hold the deeds, or agree to deposit them with some solicitor or banker. There is seldom any difficulty on the point.

After executing a settlement of a policy of assurance or

reversionary interest, notice of the settlement should be given by the trustees to the assurance office, or to the trustees of the deed or will under which the reversionary interest was created, as the case may be. The neglect to do this is in itself a breach of trust; and should the settlor, owing to such neglect, effect a charge on the policy or reversionary interest, and the person in whose favour such charge was made should give notice to the assurance office or the trustees of the deed or will as before mentioned, before any notice is given by the trustees of the settlement, such trustees would be liable in equity to make good any loss occasioned by their neglect; but if the settlor were living and a party to a suit in equity, instituted by some of the objects of the settlement for the purpose of charging the trustees, the decree charging them would probably order the settlor to recoup the trustees. As, however, the settlor is seldom able to do this, or, which is the most frequent occurrence, no proceedings are taken against the trustees until after his death, you should always make it a point, in the case of a settlement of property of this description, to give immediate notice of the settlement to the necessary parties; and likewise, if money secured by a bond or covenant is settled, notice of the settlement should immediately be given to the obligor or covenantor.

It is advisable in every case where money in the funds forms part of the settled property to place a distringas on the stock immediately after the settlement is executed. This may be done either on the affidavit of the trustees or of any person taking a beneficial interest under the settlement, or on your own affidavit, and is a very simple process.

I have given in the precedents the form of affidavit required to be sworn in order to obtain the writ of distringas, which writ may be obtained at any law stationer's; and on taking the writ and the affidavit sworn (no office copy is required to be taken) to the Record and Writ Clerks' Office in Chancery Lane, the writ will be sealed and the affidavit filed. Then take the writ and a notice (similar to the form in the precedents) to Messrs. Freshfields, the solicitors to the Bank of England, and pay them 13$s.$ 4$d.$; and after this has been done, take the writ and notice to the Chief Accountant's office at the Bank of England, when the distringas will be placed on the stock. If the names of the persons holding the stock and the amount and description of the stock are correctly described, this distringas effectually prevents any dealing with the stock without notice; and in case it should become necessary to deal with the stock for the purposes of the settlement, the distringas can be speedily removed. For the purpose of removing a distringas on stock, you should present a petition at the office of the Secretary of the Rolls (the form of petition may be obtained at any law stationer's), and the order is drawn up on this petition as a matter of course, and can be obtained two days after the petition has been left with the Secretary. Take this order to the Bank Solicitors as before, and the distringas will be taken off the stock.

The whole cost of these proceedings is of trifling amount, but the security to the fund and to all parties concerned is incalculable.

Great difficulty and inconvenience having been found to arise from inability to dispose of settled property, where no power of sale was given in the instrument creating the trust, the 19 & 20 Vict. c. 120, was framed in order to meet cases of this description. Under this act the Court of Chancery may authorize sales of the whole or any parts of any settled estates or of any timber (not being ornamental timber) growing thereon (see sect. 11).

All applications under this act are to be commenced by petition in a summary way (see sect. 16).

The orders made by the Court of Chancery, regulating proceedings under this act, are dated the 15th November, 1856, and show what is necessary to be done in any proceeding thereunder.

DISENTAILING DEEDS AND DEEDS EXECUTED BY MARRIED WOMEN.

Thirty years ago the only mode of barring an entail was by fine or recovery. The latter was the more frequent mode of assurance, as it not only barred the entail, but all remainders over. The 3 & 4 Will. 4, c. 74, abolished fines and recoveries, and substituted a new mode of assurance, and one much better adapted to the modern and more simple system of conveyancing. Under the provisions of this act, an entail can be barred by a deed which must be enrolled in Chancery, within six months after its execution. There is no particular name attached to this deed, and for want of a better it is known as a disentailing deed.

If a tenant in tail in possession wishes to bar the entail, he can do so without the necessity of any other person concurring in the deed. He has merely to execute a deed between himself of the one part and A. B. of the other part, and declare that, in order to bar all estates, he grants the estate to A. B., to the use of himself in fee; if this deed be enrolled in Chancery within six months from its execution, the entail is at an end, and the former tenant in tail becomes as much tenant in fee simple as if the estate had been so vested in him in the first place. Now, take the case of a tenant in tail not in possession (i. e., the tenant for life is living), who wishes to bar the entail and all remainders over. In order to do this, he must procure the consent of such tenant for life, and this consent may be given either by the disentailing deed (in which case he will be made a party to it), or by a separate instrument; but even if the tenant for life will not give his consent, the tenant in tail is not prevented from barring the entail, although his power is limited, the effect being that his issue only is barred, and not the remainders over, and he has therefore what is called a base fee in the property; the deed in such a case having the same operation as a fine had before the passing of the act abolishing fines and recoveries.

We will now suppose that the tenant for life concurs in

the deed; in this case it is made between three parties, viz., tenant for life of the first part, tenant in tail of the second part, and A. B. (a nominee) of the third part. It usually recites the instrument creating the entail, and any facts necessary to show the title of the tenant in tail, his desire to bar the entail, and that the tenant for life had agreed to concur. The tenant in tail, with the consent of the tenant for life (testified, &c.), and in order to bar and extinguish the entail created by the recited assurance and all other entails in the property, and to limit the property in manner thereinafter mentioned, conveys the property to the party of the third part. Habendum to him and his heirs to such uses as may be necessary to carry into effect the intentions of the parties.

This deed must be enrolled in Chancery within six calendar months after its execution, and the entail and all remainders over will then be effectually barred. If you are concerned only for the tenant in tail, and a separate solicitor is concerned for the tenant for life, you will forward to his solicitor the draft of this deed for perusal, and afterwards the engrossment for examination in the usual manner.

No acknowledgment of a deed executed under the 3 & 4 Will. 4, c. 74, is necessary before enrolling it (sect. 73). After the deed has been duly executed, it must be taken to the Enrolment Office in Chancery Lane, where it will be enrolled, and handed back to you a few days after leaving it. Thus an entail may now be barred at a small expense and less difficulty, although before the passing of the act above referred to it was an expensive and troublesome process, and one requiring great experience to do effectually.

The same act also provides a new mode by which a married woman, whether the owner of, or having only an inchoate right of dower in, freehold property, can part with her interest therein. The practice formerly was for the husband and wife to levy a fine; but under the above act the husband and wife join in the conveyance, and after they have both executed it, the latter acknowledges the deed before a Judge, or two Commissioners appointed by the Court of Common Pleas to take acknowledgments of deeds by married women. The forms of certificates and affidavit used on this occasion may be obtained at any stationer's, but I prefer Messrs. Dunn & Duncan's, the law stationers in Fleet Street.

The act requires the deed to be executed by the husband before it can be acknowledged by the wife; but where it is the wife's estate, and the interest of the husband is only such as he takes by virtue of his marital right, and he is either a lunatic or abroad, not having been heard of for some time, and in some other cases enumerated in the act, the Court of Common Pleas will, on application being made to them for that purpose, dispense with the concurrence of the husband in the deed.

This application is made by motion, supported by an affidavit of the facts.

Under the act you have the option of taking the married woman either before a Judge, or two Commissioners authorized to take acknowledgments of deeds by married women for the county in which the property is situate; but in London the acknowledgment is generally taken before a Judge, on account of the fees being much less than those paid to two Commissioners.

Before the day appointed for the completion of the business you should call at the Judge's chambers, and inquire which Judge will be at chambers on that day. Having obtained the name of the Judge, fill up the certificate of acknowledgment accordingly. The lady, accompanied by her solicitor, proceeds to the Judge's chambers, and acknowledges the deed, after which the Judge signs the certificate, and also the memorandum indorsed on the deed. The solicitor then makes the affidavit as to the identity of the lady, and as to her being of full age, &c., and this is usually sworn before the Judge's clerk. The certificate and affidavit are afterwards left at the proper office in Lancaster Place, Strand, and a small fee paid, and, on inquiring a few days after, a certified copy will be handed to you.

In the country the acknowledgment is taken by two Commissioners, one of whom only may be a solicitor engaged in the transaction. The appointment with the Commissioners having been made, they will attend at your office at the time appointed, take the acknowledgment, sign the memorandum on the back of the deed and the certificate, and one of them will make the affidavit. The certificate and affidavit are then sent to and left by the London agent, and a certified copy obtained as before pointed out.

Where a married woman is seised of, or interested in, freehold property to her separate use, whether for life only or in fee, and whether she has the legal or the equitable estate or both, provided she has a power of appointment, she can dispose of such property, without the concurrence of her husband; and whether the husband does or does not join in the conveyance of such property, the deed does not require to be acknowledged by the wife, inasmuch as, with respect to that property, she has the same right of disposition as a feme sole would have, but if she has not a power of appointment, her right of disposition is greatly restricted, although the property may be limited to her separate use. For instance, if she has the legal estate in the property, whether her interest be for life only or in fee, she cannot pass that interest unless by deed acknowledged; again, if her interest be only equitable, provided it be more than a mere estate for life, she cannot pass it, unless by deed acknowledged. If, however, her interest is an equitable life interest settled to her separate use, she alone can effectually dispose of it.

Until the passing of the 20 & 21 Vict. c. 57, a married woman could not in any manner or by any process dispose of a reversionary interest in personal property, unless settled upon her for her separate use. As no reason could be discovered why any difference should exist in this respect between real and personal property, the above act was passed, in order that both those descriptions of property might be placed on the same footing. It must, however, be borne in mind that the old law still continues in force as to all instruments made before the 31st day of December, 1857 (see sect. 1), and that even the new law does not extend to settlements made on the marriage of the feme covert (see sect. 4).

All deeds executed under this act must be executed by the husband and acknowledged by the wife, in the same manner as required by the 3 & 4 Will. 4, c. 74.

WILLS.

A prevalent, but most erroneous, impression prevails among non-professional persons that a will is a very simple document and easily prepared by almost any one, and the consequence is that agents, schoolmasters, and others quite incompetent, are frequently entrusted to prepare an instrument that above all others requires the greatest skill and legal knowledge. The reports show that, by far the greater number of cases have arisen in consequence of ill-drawn and obscure wills. Although the 7 Will. 4 & 1 Vict. c. 26, has set at rest a great many questions that previously were continually arising on wills, and which could only be decided by resorting to the aid of a court of equity, yet, the number of cases arising upon ill-drawn wills are very numerous, and can be only determined after much delay and expense, which, to a great extent, would be avoided, if they were prepared only by skilful and experienced persons.

On being instructed to make a will you should take down in writing full particulars respecting the testator's property, whether in possession, reversion, remainder or expectancy, and also the particulars of his family. After doing this, insert opposite each description of property the name and any necessary identification of the person to whom the testator intends to devise or bequeath it; and this should be continued until the whole property is disposed of. The following is an outline that may prove of assistance to you:—

Testator.	James Thompson, of 1, Cheapside, hatter.
Freehold messuage, 1, Cheapside, in occupation of Testator.	To son William Thompson, in fee, and 500*l*.

Stock in trade.	To be valued and taken by son William at his option (if taken, to be paid for with interest by quarterly instalments in three years): if not taken, to be sold by executors.
Freehold farm containing about 100 acres, at Twyford, Berks, let to John Jones as yearly tenant.	To son James Thompson for life, remainder to his issue as he may appoint, in default to his children equally: in default of issue, to testator's other children.
£100 cash, and an annuity of 50*l.* per annum out of farm, and another annuity of 50*l.* per annum out of messuage at Cheapside.	To his wife, she giving up her right of dower in freeholds.
£1,000	To daughter Sarah, to be settled on her and her issue.
£50	To shopman James Tomkins, if in testator's service at time of death.

And so proceed until you have disposed of all the specific devises and bequests the testator wishes to make, and then wind up as follows:—

Residue.	To sons William and James and daughter absolutely, as tenants in common.
Executors.	Son William and Simon Jackson, of 100, Watling Street, to each of whom a legacy of 100*l.* to be given.

With the above before you, you will not find much difficulty in the preparation of the will. Should the testator's property be very large, and the devises and bequests intricate and complicated, your safest course will be to lay instructions before counsel to prepare the will; and with such memoranda before you as the above, you will be in a position to give him every information he may require. When the will has been prepared, make a fair copy of it, and either send it to the testator to read over, or make an appointment and read it over to him yourself. The first course is preferable, as the testator will more readily remember any omission that may have been made, or any alteration he may wish, if he reads over the draft in his own way, than he would be able to do if you read it to him.

If the testator has any property in mortgage, and intends the person to whom such property is devised or bequeathed to take it subject to the mortgage, the best course will be to make the devise or bequest as if the property were not subject to the mortgage, as the 17 & 18 Vict. c. 113, has taken it out of the power of the devisee or legatee to require the mortgage to be paid off out of the testator's personal estate, unless a contrary intention appears in the will. If, therefore, the property is devised or bequeathed in the same manner as it would be were there no mortgage on it, the testator's wishes will be carried into effect, and the devisee or legatee, if he takes the property at all, must take it subject to the mortgage, as no contrary intention will appear in the will. But if the testator intends the property to be taken by the devisee or legatee free from the mortgage, then it must be so expressed in the will; and precisely the same care will be required in this case as was required before the passing of the above act, where it was intended that a devisee or legatee should take property subject to the mortgage upon it.

A devise of trust estates should in almost every case be inserted in a will. The clause is very short, and, if not required, can do no harm; while, on the contrary, if it should at any time be found necessary, it may save great trouble and expense. Of course, some little discretion must be exercised as to the insertion of this clause, as in the will of a person possessed of very little property, and who never remembers having been made trustee or advancing money on mortgage, it can scarcely be necessary.

You will sometimes find a testator desirous of appointing a great many trustees or executors to his will. This you should discourage, if possible, as it is seldom more than two or three will act, and the others must at some time execute a disclaimer of the trusts and a renunciation of the will—a proceeding that causes expense for no useful purpose. Two, or at the outside three, trustees or executors are sufficient for any case, and it will be found desirable to make the same persons both trustees and executors.

Sometimes it is advisable to have two or more sets of trustees, each set taking a particular property, with trusts attached to it. The necessity for this, however, only arises where an extensive property is intended to be dealt with, and the trusts of one part of it may be inconsistent with the trusts of another part. It certainly should not be recommended, unless absolutely unavoidable.

Should the testator be seised of copyhold property, which he intends to have sold by his trustees, you will be careful to give to the trustee a power only to sell the property, and by no means to devise it to them, as, if devised, they must take admittance to it, and pay the fine, which, if arbitrary, will amount to two years' improved annual value, and if there is more than one trustee admitted, the fine would be greatly increased. In case three trustees were acting, the fine would be two years' annual value for the first, say 100*l.*; one-half of this amount for the second, and one-fourth for the third; this would amount to 175*l.*, besides the steward's fees: whereas, if the will merely directed the trustees or executors to sell the copyhold property, the whole of this expense would be saved, as the persons taking the power would exercise it by deed in favour of the purchaser of the property, who thus would come in as a person claiming under the will, and take admittance accordingly, and pay the fine and fees due thereon.

I have added in the precedents the forms of one or two simple wills, and a few clauses which, I hope, may be found useful. The best precedent book for wills is Bythewood's "Conveyancing," by Sweet, title "Wills," where the clauses are arranged under distinct and separate heads, and almost everything that can be required will be found there. These precedents, however, should be carefully read and studied before a familiar use is made of them, otherwise, after preparing the will, you may find your clauses not quite consistent with each other, the consequences of which would often lead to a Chancery suit.

The draft, having been approved by the testator, will be fair copied on brief paper, and signed by him in the presence of two witnesses, who will sign their names in the presence of each other and in the presence of the testator, neither sealing nor publication being necessary. Care must be taken that neither of the witnesses nor their wives take any benefit under the will, otherwise such witness, although competent to prove the due execution of the will, would lose any benefi t intended to be given to him or his wife by it.

After the will has been signed and witnessed, seal it up and hand it to the testator, as most people like to keep their own wills; some, however, will prefer leaving it with you. The best course, when the testator is a man of property, is to engross two parts of the will, and let him sign them both, you keeping one part and the testator the other.

On receiving instructions to prove a will, you will obtain from the executor the particulars of all the personal property the testator died possessed of, and for this purpose you will find it useful to have the form of a residuary account before you, as it will assist your memory, and also the memory of the executor, as to the particulars of the estate of the deceased.

In estimating the amount under which the property is to be sworn for probate, no deduction must be made for any debts or payments of any description. For instance, suppose the personal estate of the testator to consist of 10,000*l*. in the funds, and nothing more, and his liabilities to amount to 9,900*l*., the probate must be sworn under 12,000*l*., and probate duty paid on that amount; but after passing the residuary account you may proceed to obtain a return of duty on the ground of debts, and your account would show that the proper stamp on the probate should be 2*l*., the property being under the value of 200*l*. In proceeding for a return of duty, you may be saved some trouble by bearing in mind that every receipt produced by you must be stamped and signed by the proper person, otherwise no deduction will be allowed on account of the money mentioned in such receipt.

Having estimated, as nearly as possible, the value of the personal estate of the testator at the time of his decease, you must fix upon the amount under which the probate is to be sworn; and, in some cases, you will find that you have a margin of one or two thousand pounds between the different amounts under which the probate may be sworn; in others, the value of the property will, within a few pounds, amount to the sum under which you intend to swear it; and should this be the case, your better course will be, unless you are very clear that nothing has been omitted, to take the next higher sum in the scale, and swear the probate under that, for it is frequently found afterwards that something was forgotten in estimating the value of the personalty; and although it may appear somewhat strange, there is less difficulty in getting a return of overpaid duty than in obtaining permission from the board of inland revenue to pay additional duty.

Having arrived at this point, your course will be very different to what it was formerly; for, instead of handing the business over to a proctor, you will now proceed to prove the will, and perform the duties heretofore as a matter of right done by him.

The new practice is regulated by the 20 & 21 Vict. c. 77, and the act commenced at such period, not earlier than the 1st January, 1858, as her Majesty might by order in council appoint. A court was established, to be called the Court of Probate, which has to deal with the grants of probates of wills, letters of administration, &c., and is to have the same jurisdiction throughout England as the Prerogative Court; but no suits for legacies or distribution were to be entertained by this court (sect. 23); the Court of Chancery therefore will still be the only court for matters of this description. Rules for regulating the practice of the new court have been issued, and where not provided for by the rules, the practice will be the same as formerly existed in the Prerogative Court (sects. 29 and 30). District registrars are appointed for certain cases, and a new system altogether is brought into action in dealings relating to this branch of the profession.

If you are professionally concerned for executors, remember that there are many acts he may do before proving the will; but as this is a very wide field, and not within the scope of this book, I cannot do better than refer you to Mr. Justice Williams's Book on the "Law of Executors and Administrators," which should find a place in your office.

You may be consulted by executors or trustees, as to whether they can safely proceed to administer the estate, or you may feel it to be your duty to inform them that it is doubtful whether they ought to proceed to do so without the assistance and protection of a court of equity. Questions of this nature will only arise when the will is of a complicated nature, or where the testator has been engaged in various mercantile transactions, or where great trouble and difficulty or responsibility is anticipated in the performance of the trusts of the will. Every case must rest on its own peculiar circumstances. It will be your duty to consider the matter carefully, and if you deem it proper you will advise your client to have the estate administered under the direction of a court of equity, which never refuses to assist a trustee seeking its aid; but, notwithstanding this, it is the paramount duty of a trustee or executor, after having accepted the trust, to perform it, if he can do so without involving himself in responsibility, or the estate in needless expense. A testator on making his will expects his trustees and executors to administer his estate in the best and least expensive manner they can, and by no means considers that, in order to escape trouble or imaginary responsibility, they will involve the estate in expensive litigation. Before, however, advising your client to seek the aid of a court of equity, you should as a matter of precaution take the opinion of counsel, although counsel will invariably recommend the estate being administered in Chancery; and indeed he cannot well do otherwise, for the question generally put to him is, "what is the safest course the trustees can take in administering the estate?" To which there can only be one answer, and that is, "by administering under the direction of the Court of Chancery." But, notwithstanding this, you will be placed in a much better position if you are fortified with the opinion of counsel on the propriety of such a step before filing the bill.

In paying legacies bequeathed by a will the legatee should sign the proper form of legacy receipt, which can be obtained at Somerset House, and in distributing the residue the safer course always is to take a release from the residuary legatees. Releases, however, are more generally prepared than there is any occasion for. The case of *King* v. *Mullins* (20 L. T. 178; *S. C.*, 1 Drew. 308) will afford you every information as to where, and under what circumstances, a release may be demanded.

On advising executors to give up possession of leasehold property of their testator to a legatee under the will you should refer carefully to the "Law of Property and Trustees Relief Amendment Act" (22 & 23 Vict. c. 35, s. 27), which defines the liability of executors or administrators in respect of rents, covenants and agreements; and sect. 28 defines the liability of an executor or administrator in respect of rents, &c., in conveyances or rent-charges.

You must also bear in mind the modern practice of advertising for creditors, &c., under sect. 29 of the same act, as this is a great protection to an executor or administrator.

Also that, if a trustee, executor or administrator does not want to file a bill in Chancery, but merely obtain advice or direction as to some particular clause in the will, it may be obtained by petition to any equity judge, or by summons at chambers (see sect. 30), but it should be taken rather by petition, with the assistance of counsel, than upon summons at chambers (*Re Trusts of Dennis's Will*, 35 Law T. 158).

The orders under this section are dated the 20th March, 1860, and the 9th sect. of the 23 & 24 Vict. c. 38, enacts that the petition or statement shall be signed by counsel.

It may be added, that trustees under the above 30th section cannot obtain the opinion of the court on questions of construction (*Re Mary Hooper's Estate*, 9 Weekly Rep. 729).

A will of real estate, situate in a register county, must be registered, but a will relating only to leasehold estate, wherever situate, need not be registered; it is often done, although quite unnecessary. The primary object of registration is notice, and as neither an executor nor a legatee can dispose of leaseholds without producing the probate or referring to the will, which would, of course, be inspected by the purchaser's solicitor; it seems difficult to comprehend what further publicity can be gained by registering the probate.

AS TO OBTAINING PROBATE OF WILLS OR LETTERS OF ADMINISTRATION.

The present practice for proving a will of a testator or procuring a grant of letters of administration to the personal estate of an intestate is as follows: In either case you will fill up the printed forms of affidavits, No. 1 being called "Oath of Executors (*or* Administrators)" which is filed in the Principal Registry of the Probate Court in London, or in some one of the district registries in the country, according as the application for the probate is made in town or country, and No. 2 being called "Affidavit for Commissioners of Inland Revenue." For probate you must have a probate copy of the will engrossed on parchment, which, for the principal registry, must be in engrossing hand, but for a district registry may be in ordinary round hand. You must then get both affidavits sworn by such of the executors who intend to prove, or by the administrator, as the case may be. These affidavits may be sworn in London at the Probate Court, or before any of the numerous commissioners appointed under the act to administer oaths in that court or in Chancery, and in the country at the district court, or before a country commissioner to administer oaths in Chancery.

The most convenient plan in either case is to get the affidavits sworn before a commissioner, and save the executors or administrators the time and trouble of attending at the registry. When the affidavits are sworn, take them, if for a grant of administration to an intestate's estate, but if for probate take also the original will and the engrossment of probate, and the proper stamps, to the clerk in whose division, according to the initial of the surname of the deceased, the matter will belong in the principal registry at Doctors' Commons, London, or to the office of the district registrar in the country, within whose district the deceased has died; and within a few days (if there is nothing to raise any impediment) the probate or letters of administration will be ready for delivery to you. In the country the most convenient way is to send the documents by post, registered, to the district registrar, with a request for probate or letters of administration as the case may require, and he will, by return of post, send you a receipt for the documents, and either then, or a few days afterwards, an account of fees, and inform you that on payment of them the probate or letters of administration are ready, and on receipt of the amount will forward them to you by post. The previous remarks apply to what is termed non-contentious business, that is, when no opposition or impediment is raised against the grant of probate or administration by any third parties; and when such is the case, the business is properly termed contentious, and commences with the entry of a caveat at the registry. In both contentious and non-contentious business, numerous peculiar and difficult points constantly arise, both as to practice and forms; and the work in most general use is that known as "Coote's Practice," with which you will be able to carry through business connected with probates and grants of administration, whether contentious, non-contentious, or otherwise.

You are doubtless aware that the Bank of England never, under any circumstances, take notice of trusts affecting stock; it frequently happens, therefore, that stock, standing in the name of a testator, does not belong to him beneficially, but as trustee, and in such case, if the stock is of large amount, it becomes a matter of considerable importance to save the probate duty which would be payable thereon.

The 48 Geo. III. c. 149, s. 37, applies to the cases where executors or administrators of a deceased trustee of government stock wish to exempt such stock from probate duty. The Bank of England require the provisions of that act to be strictly followed.

The form of affidavit required is given in the precedents, and will be found applicable in most cases.

If the deceased had any beneficial interest in the stock, state the particulars, and the value of such interest, and that the duty paid on the probate or letters of administration is sufficient to cover such value, and all the residue of the personal estate of the deceased, in respect of which such probate or letters of administration have been granted (following the words of the above-mentioned act).

Should the facts not be within the personal knowledge of the executor or administrator any other competent person may depose to them, in which case the executor or administrator must join and state that such deposition is true to the best of his knowledge, and also that he intends to apply the funds accordingly.

Engross the affidavit on a 2s. 6d. stamp. It can be sworn in England at the Record and Writ Clerks' Office, or before a commissioner to administer oaths in Chancery; in Ireland, before a master ordinary or extraordinary in Chancery; in Scotland, before a justice of the peace; and, out of the United Kingdom, before a magistrate, whose signature must be authenticated by a competent British authority.

LEGACY AND SUCCESSION DUTIES.

Part of the duty cast upon executors and trustees under wills, and administrators of the estates of intestates, is to pay all legacy duties, duty on residue and succession duty (if any) in respect of the property of their testator or intestate. A similar duty has also to be performed by either beneficiaries or trustees under deeds or other instruments, upon any succession arising to property under the Succession Duties Acts.

I will briefly point out the practice in these matters. With respect to all of them, the proper forms of legacy and annuity receipts, residuary accounts and succession accounts (there are several of the latter), can be obtained in London at the office of the Commissioners of Inland Revenue, Somerset House, and in the country from the stamp distributor of the district.

As to Legacy and Annuity Receipts and Residuary Accounts.—Fill up separate receipts on the printed forms according to the instructions on them for each legatee and annuitant, specifying whether the legacy is pecuniary or specific, if the latter, it is often necessary to get the value assessed by an appraiser, calculate and fill in the amount of duty. Do the same with the annuity receipts. If the legacy consists of stock in the government funds, you must calculate its value in money at the price at which the stock may be officially quoted, at or about the day on which you pass the accounts and pay the duty. In London take the accounts and duty to the Legacy Duty Office at Somerset House, where the clerk in the department will examine the former, and, if correct, will pass them, and you can then pay the duty, and get the proper stamps affixed. Should the account or receipts require any material alteration or amendment, you may have to take them away, and attend another day to pass them and pay the duty. In the country take the account and receipts with the total duty in cash as you have calculated it to the stamp distributor of the district, and take his official receipt for them. He will forward them to Somerset House, and in about a fortnight you will have the account and receipts back through him, either passed and completed, or with written queries and requirements by the clerk in London, which you must answer and return the accounts to London through the distributor, until the matter is completed.

The previous remarks apply to residuary accounts of personal property of testators and intestates, and legacy and annuity receipts to be prepared and passed, and the duties, in respect of them paid, by executors or administrators pursuant to the provisions of the Legacy Duties Acts. The preparing and passing these accounts, although not strictly forming any part of conveyancing business, is generally performed, as a matter of course, by the solicitor who acts for the executors or administrators in proving the will, or procuring a grant of letters of administration of the personal estate of the testator or intestate, as the case may be. The legacy and residuary accounts affecting only personalty a purchaser of real property is not in any way concerned with, or affected by them, but the case is different with regard to succession duty, about which I will now make a few remarks.

The passing of the 16 & 17 Vict. c. 51, commonly cited as "The Succession Duties Act," has cast an additional and important onus upon solicitors in numerous conveyancing matters, and affecting both real and personal property. By that act it is declared, that as regards the purchaser of any property within the scope of the act, both freehold and leasehold (the latter being declared real estate for the purposes of the act), and if the vendor, either beneficially or in a fiduciary character, derives the property as successor under a deed, will or other instrument upon the death of any person after the act came into operation (19th May, 1853) such property in the hands of the purchaser is liable to the succession duty, which will have accrued on such death, and he is entitled, before completing, to have official evidence that such duty has been paid, and a proper receipt given for it by the Board of Inland Revenue.

It is therefore necessary whether you are acting for a vendor on the sale of freehold or leasehold property, or are professionally concerned for beneficiaries, trustees, executors or administrators, that you should take care and ascertain whether any and what succession duty is payable in respect of real or personal estate, which may have in any manner devolved upon them, and proceed to prepare and pass the proper accounts and pay the duties. After the accounts are prepared in duplicate, in London you take them to the Succession Duty Office at

Somerset House and settle them with the clerk there, and pay the duties in another part of the building. In the country the business is transacted through the stamp distributor, but there is this difference between legacy and succession accounts, that the country distributor will not take any money on account of succession duty, until after the account has been examined and approved, and the duty assessed at Somerset House.

There are various forms of succession accounts, issued by the Commissioners of Inland Revenue, all of which can be readily obtained on application, except that which is used when for any particular reason it is wished to anticipate the time when duty would accrue, and have such duty commuted and paid forthwith, regarding which the Commissioners have a discretion, which they only exercise upon a written statement of the circumstances, and the reason for anticipating the time of payment. The legacy and succession duties are important matters, and numerous difficult and special questions constantly arise regarding them, and I would therefore recommend to you Mr. Thring's book on the "Succession Duty Act," and Mr. Trevor's on the "Legacy and Succession Duties Acts," as the most likely to meet the difficulties that may arise.

DISCLAIMER.

A disclaimer is a deed executed for the purpose of proving at all times that a person to whom property has been devised as a trustee declines to accept the trust, or take any interest under the will; in other words, he disclaims the estate devised to him by the will. Disclaimers are principally used in cases where trustees appointed by a will refuse to act in the trusts thereof. A verbal refusal to act is a sufficient disclaimer, and where a trustee has never acted or interfered in any way, it will be considered that, by his conduct, he has disclaimed any intention of ever interfering; but, notwithstanding this, a deed is generally executed in practice, as it is the best evidence that can possibly be obtained of the refusal to act on the part of the trustee.

This deed is very simple; it usually recites so much of the will as is necessary to show the devise to the trustee, and what property the deed is intended to act upon, and then the trustee proceeds to disclaim the estate devised, and all trusts and powers created by the will. The form in the precedents will give you an idea of the manner in which this document is generally prepared.

A disclaimer is often resorted to, and very usefully in the case of copyhold property held of a manor in which the fines are arbitrary. Now, if there are several trustees of a will, and all the trustees take admittance, the fine, as I have before pointed out [vide page 77], is very considerably increased; whereas, if all the trustees except one disclaim, then, on the admittance of that one, a single fine is payable; and it does not follow that the other trustees by executing the disclaimer are shut out from interfering in the trusts of the will, inasmuch as they merely disclaim, in order that the one trustee may take admittance to the property: it is true that he alone has the legal estate, but the other trustees are still necessary parties to any act done under the will, as in the execution of a power for instance; and the steward of a manor is bound to admit one trustee, where such a disclaimer has been executed, even although he knows that the others disclaimed their right to be admitted, merely to save the fine (*Wellesley* v. *Withers*, 24 L. J., Q. B. 134). He can, however, require the disclaimer to be entered on the court rolls, and, in practice, it is generally sent to him for that purpose with instructions for the admittance.

The disclaimer is prepared by the solicitor of the acting trustee, and paid for out of the testator's estate. It is very unusual for the disclaiming trustee to wish the draft to be sent to his own solicitor, and in such a case he ought to pay the costs of perusing the deed; but as I am not aware of any mode of compelling a trustee to execute a disclaimer, you must exercise your own discretion as to how far you will insist on the disclaiming trustee paying his own solicitor's costs. I know of no rule of practice on the point, and think the acting trustee would be justified in paying the costs.

Where a disclaimer relates to freehold property situate in Middlesex or Yorkshire, it should be registered.

A deed of disclaimer requires a 35s. stamp to be impressed on it.

PRECEDENTS.

PRECEDENTS.

ACKNOWLEDGMENT.

1.

Acknowledgment to be indorsed on Deed required to be inrolled in the Court of Chancery.

MEMORANDUM, that on the   day of   , 18 , this deed was duly acknowledged before me at   , in the county of   , by A. B., one of the parties to the same, who desired that the same may be inrolled in her Majesty's High Court of Chancery.

    , a commissioner to administer oaths in Chancery in England, *or*

    a London commissioner to administer oaths in Chancery.

ADVERTISEMENT.

2.

Advertisement for Creditors under the 22 & 23 Vict. c. 35, intituled "An Act to further amend the Law of Property and relieve Trustees" [*vide Treatise, page* 114].

A. B., deceased.

NOTICE is hereby given, that all creditors and other persons having any debt or claim upon or affecting the estate of A. B., late of   , who died on the   day of   , 18 , and whose will was proved in the Principal Registry of her Majesty's Court of Probate, on the   day of   , 18 , by C. D., of   (the relict of the deceased), and   , the executors thereof, are hereby required to send in the particulars of their claims to the said executors, at No.   , or to us the undersigned, their solicitors, on or before the day of , 18 , at the expiration of which time the said executors will proceed to distribute the assets of the said A. B., the testator, among the persons entitled thereto, having regard to the debts and claims only of which the said executors shall then have had notice; and the said executors will not be liable for the assets so distributed to any person of whose debt or claim they shall not have had notice at the time of such distribution.

Dated the day of , 18 .

, London, solicitors to the executors of the said A. B.

AFFIDAVITS.

3.

Of the due Execution of a Bill of Sale.

IN the Queen's Bench.

I, , of , in the county of , make oath and say, that the paper writing hereunto annexed and marked ( ) is a true copy of a bill of sale and of every schedule or inventory thereto annexed or therein referred to, and of every attestation of the execution thereof, and that the said bill of sale was made and given on the day it bears date, being the day of , in the year of our Lord one thousand eight hundred and sixty- , and that I was present and did see in the said bill of sale mentioned, and whose name is signed thereto, sign and execute the same on the said day of in the year aforesaid: and that the said resides at and is ; that the name set and subscribed as the witness attesting the due execution thereof is of my proper handwriting, and that I am the only attesting witness to the said bill of sale, and reside at and am .

Sworn at this . day of one thousand eight hundred and sixty- .

Before me

4.

Verifying Notice of Dissolution of Partnership.

I, G. H., of   , in the county of   , make oath and say, that I was present on the   day of   instant, and did see A. B., of &c., C. D. of &c., and E. F. of &c., severally sign the notice of dissolution of copartnership hereunto annexed, and that the names " A. B.," " C. D." and " E. F." severally set and subscribed, and now appearing at the foot of the said notice of dissolution, are of the several and respective handswriting of the said A. B., C. D. and E. F., and that the name " G. H." appearing as that of the witness to the signing by the said A. B., C. D. and E. F. of the said notice, is of my proper handwriting.

G. H.

Sworn at   , in the county of   , this   day of   , 18 , before me,   , a commissioner to administer oaths in Chancery in England.

AGREEMENTS.

5.

For the Purchase of Leasehold Premises and Stock in Trade of a Lace Manufacturer, the Value of the Stock to be paid by Bills.

AN AGREEMENT, made this   day of   18 , between A. B. of the one part, and C. D. of the other part, as follows, namely :—

1. The said A. B. agrees to sell, and the said C. D. agrees to accept, an assignment of all that warehouse, situate in the town of   with the appurtenances thereto belonging, as the same is held by the said A. B., under an indenture of lease for a term of twenty-one years, commencing at   , at and under the yearly rent of £   , and subject to the several covenants and conditions in the said indenture con-

tained on the part of the lessee, his executors, administrators and assigns, and now in the occupation of the said A. B., together with the warming apparatus and all and every the fixtures therein or thereto belonging (except fixtures belonging to the landlord): And also all those premises or factory of the said A. B., situate in the town of   aforesaid, with the appurtenances thereto belonging, as the same are held by the said A. B. under an indenture of lease for a term of twenty-one years, commencing at   , at and under the yearly rents therein mentioned, and subject to the several covenants and conditions in the said indenture contained on the part of the lessee, his executors, administrators and assigns, and now in the occupation of the said A. B., together with all and every the fixtures therein or thereto belonging (except fixtures belonging to the landlord): And also all that room at the said factory, and all those other rooms situate at   Street, in the town of   aforesaid, with the appurtenances, held by the said A. B. as a yearly tenant, at and under the respective yearly rents of £   and £   together with all and singular the fixtures therein or thereto belonging (except fixtures belonging to the landlord).

2. Each party shall on the signing this agreement appoint a valuer, or in case either party shall make default in so doing the other party may appoint two valuers; the two valuers, immediately after their appointment, shall name an umpire to decide between them in case of dispute; such two valuers or their umpire shall, on the   day of   next, proceed to fix and award the sum to be paid by the said C. D. to the said A. B. for the purchase of the said premises and fixtures, including therein the value of the several fixtures in and about those parts of the said premises, or of any adjoining premises of which the said A. B. is tenant at will, and the sum so fixed and awarded shall be final and conclusive.

3. The said purchase shall be completed and the purchase-money paid on the   day of   next; and in case default shall be made in the completion of the said purchase on that day, then and in such case interest shall be paid on the amount of the said purchase-money at and after the rate

of 5*l*. per cent. per annum, from the said   day of
next to the time the money shall be paid.

4. On the completion of the purchase the said C. D. shall be let into possession of the said premises, and entitled to the rents and profits thereof as from the   day of   next; all outgoings up to which time shall be paid by the said A. B.

5. The title to the said premises shall commence with the respective leases under which the same are held, and the said C. D. shall not call for the title of the lessors, nor make any objection whatever in respect thereto; and the production of the receipts for the payment of the rents in respect of the said premises up to the   day of   last shall be conclusive evidence of all the covenants in the said respective leases having been duly performed, notwithstanding any prior breach may be shown.

6. The said A. B. also agrees to sell, and the said C. D. agrees to purchase, upon the terms mentioned in the next paragraph of this agreement, all the 1,416 frames belonging to the said A. B.

7. The said C. D. shall on the completion of the purchase of the before-mentioned premises execute to the said A. B., his executors, administrators and assigns, a bond prepared by the solicitors of the said A. B., but at the expense of the said C. D., in a sufficient penalty conditioned for the payment to the said A. B. during his life, by quarterly payments of a yearly annuity of £   , the first quarterly payment to be made on the   day of   next, and for the payment to the wife of the said A. B., in case she shall survive him, during her life of a yearly annuity of £   : Provided always, that the said respective annuities, or any aliquot portion thereof respectively, shall be and be made redeemable by the purchase of a government annuity or other satisfactory annuity or security of like amount as the annuity or portion thereof redeemed.

8. In case it shall happen that the purchase of the premises mentioned in the first paragraph of this contract shall, through the neglect or default of the said C. D., not be completed on the   day of   next, then the said C. D. shall pay to the

said A. B. or his wife, as the case may be, the first quarterly payment of the said annuity on the   day of   next, and shall continue to make the said quarterly payments until the above-mentioned bond shall have been given.

9. The said A. B. also agrees to sell, and the said C. B. agrees to purchase, all the stock in trade, wares and merchandize of the said A. B., both manufactured and unmanufactured, at the price following, that is to say, the manufactured articles to be purchased at the sums specified in the regular list of prices of the said A. B., less five per cent. discount; and the unmanufactured articles, both in the warehouses and in the hands of the workmen, to be purchased at their net prime cost, to be fixed and ascertained by reference to the business books of the said A. B.

10. The said stock in trade, wares and merchandize shall be paid for, with interest, as follows, namely, interest shall begin to run in respect of such part of the purchase-money thereof as shall remain unpaid from and after the   day of   but not from any earlier period. The said C. D. shall, on the   day of   next, accept bills drawn by the said A. B. on him, and payable in manner following, that is to say, a bill payable six months after date for one-fourth part of the full amount or value of the said stock in trade, wares and merchandize, ascertained in the manner mentioned in the 9th paragraph of this contract; a bill payable nine months after date for 1,000*l*., and such further sum added thereto as three months' interest on the amount or value of the said stock in trade, wares and merchandize, ascertained as aforesaid, shall amount to, after deducting the aforesaid one-fourth part thereof so paid as aforesaid; a bill payable twelve months after date for 1,000*l*., and such further sum added thereto as three months' interest on the balance remaining of the said full amount or value shall amount to, after deducting the amounts so paid as aforesaid: a bill payable fifteen months after date for 1,000*l*., and such further sum added thereto as three months' interest on the balance then remaining of the said full amount or value shall amount to, after deducting the amounts so paid as aforesaid; and such further bills for 1,000*l*. each, payable at every succeeding three months, with

interest added thereto, calculated in manner aforesaid, as shall be requisite or necessary to make up the full amount or value of the said stock in trade, wares and merchandize. The stamps on all which said bills of exchange shall be paid for by the said C. D.

11. And for the due observance and performance of the stipulations and agreements herein contained on the part of the said C. D., his executors or administrators, he the said C. D. doth hereby bind himself, his executors and administrators, unto the said A. B., his executors and administrators, in the following sums, namely:—

For the performance of the agreement hereinbefore contained for the purchase of the said warehouse and factory in the sum of 500*l*.; for the performance of the agreement hereinbefore contained for purchase of the said frames in the sum of 2,000*l*.; for the performance of the agreement hereinbefore contained for purchase of the said stock in trade, wares and merchandize, in the sum of 2,000*l*.; all which said sums it is hereby declared and agreed shall be considered and taken as liquidated damages, and not by way of penalties. As witness the hands of the parties.

As to the last clause, vide *Kemble* v. *Farren*, 6 Bing. 141; *Reynolds* v. *Bridge*, 4 Weekly Rep. 640; and *Cass* v. *Thompson*, 5 Weekly Rep. 289.

6.

For the Sale and Purchase of a Freehold Estate by Private Contract.

AN AGREEMENT made the   day of   18 , between   and   (hereinafter called the vendors) of the one part, and   of   of the other part, as follows, namely:

1. The said vendors agree to sell and the said   agrees to purchase for the sum of £   , the fee simple and inheritance in possession of and in ALL   as the same are now in the occupation of   under an agreement bearing date the   day of   18 .

2. The said purchase shall be completed on the   day of

next, up to which time the vendors shall be entitled to the rents and profits of the said premises; but if from any cause whatever the purchase shall not be completed at that time, the said   shall thenceforth pay interest on the said sum of £   after the rate of five pounds per cent. per annum, until the said sum be paid.

3. The vendors shall deliver to the said   an abstract of their title to the property purchased, and such title shall commence with an award dated in April, 1804, under the   Inclosure Act, and the regularity of such award, and its validity in all respects, shall not be questioned, but considered as admitted by the said   , and he shall not be entitled to call for the production of the title of the lands in respect of which the allotments were so made, or to call for the production, or any copy of, or investigate or make any objection whatever in respect of any deed, instrument or document of title dated previous to the said award, whether the same is recited in or referred to in any subsequent deed, or otherwise appears on the abstract, and every recital or statement in any deed, will or other document, dated twenty years or upwards prior to the day of sale, shall be conclusive evidence of the fact or matter recited or stated, and all certificates, attested, official, or other copies or extracts from deeds, wills, awards and other documents, and all declarations or other evidence required for supporting the title or for verifying or perfecting the abstract or otherwise, and the production and inspection of all deeds and evidences not in the possession of the vendors, and to the production of which the said   may under these conditions be entitled, and the expense of deducing or proving the title to any outstanding term of years, and of any assignment or merger thereof, and all searches, travelling and other incidental expenses incurred in respect of the matters aforesaid, shall be got, made, procured and discharged by the said   .

4. The said   shall send to the office of the vendor's solicitors his objections and requisitions, if any, on the abstract within twenty-one days after the delivery of the abstract, and any further objections or requisitions within fourteen days after the delivery of the replies in respect of which they

are made, the title, except as so objected to, shall be considered accepted, and in this respect time shall be of the essence of the contract: if any objection or requisition be made which the vendors are unable to answer or comply with, they shall be at liberty, notwithstanding any previous negociation respecting such objection or requisition, to rescind the contract.

5. On payment of the purchase-money, the vendors shall execute a proper conveyance to the said   , but being only devisees in trust for sale, they shall not be required to enter into any covenants for title except separate covenants against incumbrances.

6. All deeds in the vendors' possession relating solely to the property sold will be delivered over to the said   on the completion of his purchase, but the vendors will retain the probate of their testator's will; and as to such deeds as are not in the vendor's possession, but for the production of which a covenant has been obtained, the said   shall be satisfied with such covenant, and shall make no objection thereto, nor be entitled to any other.

7.

For Sale of Freeholds.

AN AGREEMENT, made this   day of   18 , between A. B., of &c., of the one part, and C. D., of &c., of the other part, as follows, namely:—

1. The said A. B. agrees to sell and the said C. D. to purchase for the sum of £   the fee simple and inheritance in possession of and in ALL [*parcels*].

2. The purchase shall be completed on the   day of   next, when the said C. D. shall be let into possession or into the receipt of the rents and profits of the said premises, all outgoings up to that time being cleared by the said A. B.; and if from any cause (not being the fault of the said A. B.) the said purchase shall not be completed on the said   day of   , the said C. D. shall pay interest on the balance of purchase-money from that day until the actual payment thereof at the rate of 5*l*. per cent. per annum.

3. The title to the said premises shall commence with a conveyance dated the   day of   18 , and no earlier title shall be called for or objected to, and all certificates from registers and declarations which the said C. D. may require, whether for the purpose of title, identity or otherwise, shall be paid for by him; all recitals and statements in the said conveyance shall be deemed sufficient proof of the matters and facts therein recited or stated.

4. The said C. D. shall pay a deposit of £   on the signing hereof, and in case the said C. D. shall make a valid objection to the title which the said A. B. shall be unable to remove, it shall be lawful for him to put an end to this agreement by notice in writing to the said C. D. to that effect, in which case the said A. B. shall repay the said sum of £   , which shall be accepted by the said C. D. in full satisfaction of all claims in respect of this agreement. As witness the hands of the parties.

8.

For the Sale of a Ship.

MEMORANDUM OF AGREEMENT made this   day of   one thousand eight hundred and sixty   , between   .

The said   agree to buy and   agree to sell the   or vessel called the   built   of the measurement of   tons or thereabouts, now lying   for the sum of   to be paid as follows:—
and two guineas to the broker to bind the bargain; which said ship or vessel hath been duly registered pursuant to an act of Parliament for that purpose made and provided, and a copy of the certificate of such registry is as follows:—

"No.   This is to certify, that   having made and subscribed the declaration required by law, and having declared that   together with   sole owner (in the proportions specified on the back hereof) of the ship or vessel called the   , of   , which is of the burthen of   tons, and whereof   is master, and that the said ship or vessel was   , and   having certified to us that the said ship or vessel has   deck and   mast, that her length from the inner part of the main stem to the fore part of the stern post aloft is   , her breadth in midships is   , her depth in hold at midships is   , that she is rigged with a   bowsprit, is   sterned,   built, has   gallery and   head, that the framework and is   , and that she is   . And that the said subscribing owner having consented and agreed to the above description, and having caused sufficient security to be given as required by law, the said ship or vessel, called the   , has been duly registered at the port of   .

Certified under our hands at the Custom House, in the said port of , this   day of , in the year one thousand eight hundred and   .

Collector.
Comptroller.

Endorsed.

Names of the several owners within mentioned.	Number of sixty-fourth shares held by each owner.

On payment of the whole of the purchase-money as aforesaid, a legal bill or bills of sale shall be made out and executed to the purchaser or purchasers at his or their expense, and the said   with what belongs to her shall be delivered according to the inventory which has been exhibited, but the said inventory shall be made good as to quantity only. And the said   , together with   , her stores shall be taken with all faults, in the state and condition in which they now lie, without any allowance or abatement whatsoever, within one month from the date hereof. But in case any default shall be made by the purchaser or purchasers in the payment above mentioned, the money so paid in part shall be forfeited to the sole use of the present proprietor, and   shall be at full liberty to put up and sell the said   again, either by public or private sale, and the deficiency, if any, by such re-sale shall be made good by the said defaulting purchaser, who shall be responsible for risks of every description, subsequent to the present purchase, and for all charges that may be incurred in consequence of noncompliance with this agreement; and neither the said broker, nor any of the present proprietors, his or their heirs, executors, administrators or assigns, shall be anyways accountable or liable to be sued, either at law or equity, for the said money paid in part and forfeited as aforesaid.

The said ship is declared to be at the risk of the purchaser immediately after   put into possession of her.

As witness the hands of the parties the day and year above written.

Witness,

9.

For the Lease of a House.

AGREEMENT made this   day of   18 , between A. B., of &c., of the one part, and C. D., of &c., of the other part, as follows:—

1. The said A. B. agrees to grant, and the said C. D. to take, a lease of the messuage and premises, No.   in   street, as the same were late in the occupation of   for   years at £   per annum, payable quarterly.

2. The lease and a counterpart thereof shall be prepared and engrossed by the lessor's solicitor at the lessee's expense.

3. The lease shall contain the following covenants by the lessee, to pay rent, land tax, sewers and main drainage rates, and all other rates and taxes (property tax excepted), to keep the premises fully insured against fire in the sum of £   , in the usual manner, not to assign or underlet without lessor's consent, but such consent not to be capriciously or without reasonable cause withheld, to keep the premises in good repair, and so to yield them up, and also all other usual and proper covenants and provisions.

And particularly similar covenants in the lease under which the lessor holds the premises. As witness the hands of the parties.

10.

For an Underlease of a Piece of Garden Ground.

AN AGREEMENT made this   day of   18 , between A. B., of &c., of the one part, and C. D., of &c., of the other part: Whereas the said A. B., being possessed of a lease dated the   day of   18 , whereby a messuage or tenement with the garden and ground thereunto belonging, situate at   , were demised by R. S. and others to the said A. B., for   years, commencing the   day of   , and under the yearly rent of £   , did by an indenture of assignment bearing even date herewith assign the same to the said C. D. for the remainder of the said term of   years; and whereas it was upon the treaty for the said purchase agreed that the said C. D. should grant such underlease to the said A. B. of a part of the said leasehold premises as herein mentioned: Now the said C. D. doth hereby agree with the said A. B., that he the said C. D. will, at the request, costs and charges of the said A. B., execute unto him an underlease of all that small piece or parcel of ground on the   side of the garden demised by the said indenture of lease of the   day of   , as the same is now staked out and separated from the residue of the said garden ground, and now in the possession of the said A. B., and which said small piece or parcel of ground contains about   square yards, for the residue now unexpired of the said term of   years, except the last two days thereof, at and under the yearly rent of one peppercorn, if the same shall be demanded: and it is agreed that the said underlease shall contain such and the like covenants, provisoes and agreement as are contained in the said indenture of lease of the   day of   , so far as the same are applicable, but no further or otherwise, and the said A. B. agrees to execute a counterpart of the said indenture of underlease, and to pay the charges of the said lease and counterpart.

11.

From Year to Year of Agricultural Land.

AN AGREEMENT, made the   day of   18 , between S. D. of the one part, and G. W. of the other part, whereby the said S. D. agrees to let and doth let, and the said G. W. agrees to take and become tenant, of all [*parcels at length*] situate at   , and now in the occupation of the said G. W., from the   day of   last (from which time he has had the possession), for one year, and so from year to year, until such notice shall be given for determining the said term as hereinafter mentioned, at the yearly rent of £   , free from the land tax and all taxes and deductions whatsoever, by half-yearly payments (that is to say), on the   day of   and the   day of   in every year, the half-year's rent which became due on the 25th day of March last to be paid within ten days next after the date hereof, and the next half-yearly payment of rent to be made on the 29th day of September next: And the said G. W. agrees with the said S. D. that he the said G. W. will duly pay the said rent in the proportion and in manner aforesaid, and also the land-tax and all other rates, taxes, tithes, and rent-charge in lieu of tithes, and other outgoings whatsoever payable or to be paid for the said premises, or charged or to be charged on the landlord or tenant in respect thereof, and also that he will repair and keep in good and tenantable repair and condition the fences, hedges, gates, stiles and boundaries, and will scour out the ditches as often as the hedges shall be cut, and will not cut the hedges under seven years' growth, and will not cut, stock or injure the timber or timber-like trees, tellers, saplings or young trees, or trees likely to become timber, but use his best endeavours to preserve the same, and shall and will dung, manure and cultivate the land in a good and husbandlike manner, and not waste, destroy, impoverish or make barren the same, and will deliver up the same accordingly at the end or expiration of the said term: Provided always, that if the said rent, or any part thereof, shall be behind or unpaid by the space of twenty-one days, or if breach shall be made in all or any of the agreements aforesaid which on the part of the said G. H., his executors and administrators, are or ought to be observed and kept, then it shall be lawful for the said S. D., his heirs or assigns, to re-enter upon the said premises and repossess and enjoy the same, and remove the said G. W. and all other occupiers thereof: Provided always, that if the said S. D. shall be desirous that the said G. W. shall quit the said premises, or if the said G. W. shall be desirous of quitting the same, then one year's notice shall be given by either party to the other party, and until such notice shall be given this agreement shall be in full force.

In witness whereof the said parties have hereunto set their hands and seals. (L.s.)

[The above is a lease, and requires the same stamp as a lease would require].

12.

For Letting a House for Three Years.

AN AGREEMENT made the day of 18 , between A. B., of &c., of the one part, and C. D., of &c., of the other part, as follows :—

1. The said A. B. lets, and the said C. D. takes, as and from the date hereof, for the term of three years, all that messuage or dwelling-house known as No. 1, street, in the parish of , with the yard, garden, outbuildings and appurtenances thereto, (as the same were lately in the occupation of) at the yearly rent of £ .

2. The said C. D. shall pay the said rent quarterly, and the first quarter's payment shall be made on the day of , and shall also pay all rates, taxes and other outgoings whatsoever in respect of the said premises (except only the property tax and).

3. The said A. B. shall, during the said term, keep the said premises in tenantable repair and condition.

4. The said premises shall be used by the said C. D. as and for a private dwelling-house only, and no alteration shall be

made by him in the same, nor shall any trade or occupation whatsoever be carried on therein, nor shall the said C. D. allow any sale by auction to take place on the said premises.

As witness the hands and seals of the parties.

(L.S.)

[The above requires a lease stamp.]

13.

Under Seal between a Brewer and his Manager.

ARTICLES OF AGREEMENT made this   day of   , 18 , between J. B., of &c., of the one part, and J. H. B., of &c., of the other part: Whereas the said J. B. hath agreed to take the said J. H. B. as his clerk for the managing, superintending and conducting the trade or business of a brewer and as his receiver of the rents and profits of the messuages, cottages, lands, tenements and hereditaments of the said J. B. in the said county of   , on the terms hereinafter mentioned: Now these presents witness, that, in consideration of the covenants hereinafter contained on the part of the said J. B., he the said J. H. B. doth hereby for himself, his heirs, executors and administrators, covenant with the said J. B., his executors, administrators and assigns, in manner following (that is to say), that he the said J. H. B. shall and will henceforth from the date hereof become and continue the clerk of him the said J. B. in the aforesaid trade or business of a brewer, and as a receiver of the rents and profits of the messuages, cottages, lands, tenements and hereditaments of him the said J. B. in the said county of   , and shall and will give his whole time and attention to the said trade or business, and in the managing, conducting, superintending and improving the same to the utmost of his power and ability, and also shall and will do and perform all such services, acts, matters and things as he the said J. B. shall from time to time order, direct or appoint, and shall not nor will at any time or times hereafter, without the consent in writing of the said J. B., his executors or administrators, divulge or make known any of the trusts, secrets, accounts or dealings

of or relating to the said trade or business of him the said
J. B.; and also that he the said J. H. B. shall and will be
just and faithful to him the said J. B. in all his business,
dealings and transactions whatsoever; and also shall and will
give and render to the said J. B. a just and true account of
the same at all times when the same shall be required of
him; and also provide and keep such and so many books of
account as shall be necessary, wherein he shall fairly write
or cause to be written all monies received·and paid, and all
goods which shall be bought or received in, or sold or
delivered out upon credit or otherwise, and the rates and
prices at which the same shall be bought or received in or
sold or delivered out, and all matters, circumstances and
things necessary to manifest the state and condition of the
said trade; which said book or books of account shall
always be kept in some convenient place on the said premises
where the said trade shall from time to time be carried on,
and be at all times open to the inspection of the said J. B.,
or any person or persons appointed by him for that purpose:
And these presents further witness, that, in consideration of
the covenants herein contained on the part of the said
J. H. B., he the said J. B., for himself, his heirs, executors
and administrators, doth hereby covenant with the said
J. H. B., his executors and administrators, that he the said
J. B. shall and will yearly and every year, so long as the
said J. H. B. shall be in the service and employ of the said
J. B. (the said J. H. B. well and truly performing, fulfilling
and keeping all and singular the covenants and agreements
hereinbefore contained on his part), pay unto the said
J. H. B. by quarterly payments on the   day of   ,
the   day of   , the   day of   , and the
day of   , in every year, the clear yearly sum of £
sterling, without any deduction whatsoever, the first quarterly payment thereof to be made on the   day of
next; and also shall and will from and after the   day of
      next permit him the said J. H. B. to use and occupy
the dwelling-house and premises which are now in the
occupation of   , adjoining the brewery in   aforesaid,

free of rent and taxes; and also shall and will, at the costs and charges of the said J. B., find and provide for the said J. H. B. sufficient coals and beer which may be required by him the said J. H. B. for the use of himself and his family and domestic servants for the time being residing in the said dwelling-house and premises, to be used or consumed upon the said premises; and also shall and will, at the like costs and charges, not only find, provide, keep and maintain a cow near the said premises for the use of him the said J. H. B. and his family and domestic servants residing in the said house, but also a horse to be used by the said J. H. B. in and about the necessary journeys on business of the said trade: Provided always, and it is hereby agreed and declared between and by the parties hereto, that in case of the decease of either of them, or in case either of them shall be desirous to determine these presents, it shall be lawful for him so to do on giving to the other of them six calendar months' notice thereof in writing; and in case such notice shall be given as aforesaid, a proportionate part of the said yearly salary or sum of £   from the last quarterly day of payment thereof up to the time of the expiration of the said notice shall be paid by the said J. B., his executors or administrators, unto the said J. H. B.; and then and thereafter these presents and everything herein contained shall cease, determine and be absolutely void, but without prejudice to any right of action, claim or demand of or by either of them the said parties, for or by reason of any previous breach or non-performance by the other of the said parties of any of the covenants or agreements herein contained.

As witness the hands and seals of the parties.

Signed, sealed and }
delivered by } (L.S.)

[The above form may easily be adapted to any business. If if be under hand only, the reference to the heirs, executors and administrators may properly be omitted, vide "Treatise," page 4.]

14.
Of Reference where no Action brought.

AN AGREEMENT made &c., between A. B., of &c., of the one part, and C. D., of &c., of the other part: Whereas the said A. B. alleges that the messuages, land and outbuildings belonging to him, situate at &c., have been shaken, sunk and cracked through the mining operations of the said C. D., and also that the mines and minerals in, under and adjoining to the said messuages, land and outbuildings belonging to the said A. B., have been worked and taken by the said C. D., but which the said C. D. denies: Now these presents witness, that, in order to prevent proceedings being taken by either of the said parties, and to settle the questions in dispute between them, the said A. B. and C. D. have mutually agreed to refer the said questions and disputes to the arbitrament of E. F., of &c., upon the terms and in manner following :—

1. The said E. F. shall view the said messuages, land and outbuildings, and inspect any plans, and examine such witnesses upon oath as he shall think proper, and shall afterwards make his award in writing under his hand, by which he shall determine what (if any) damage has been caused to the said messuages, land and outbuildings through the mining operations of the said C. D., and assess any such damage accordingly, and what sum (if any) the said A. B. shall receive as the value of the minerals so alleged to be gotten, and shall fix the time and place, when and where the said C. D. shall pay the same to the said A. B., and such award shall be binding on the said A. B. and C. D.

2. The said A. B. and C. D. shall afford every facility to the said E. F. for conducting his said view and examination, and submit themselves for examination, and produce their plans at such time as the said E. F. shall require [but he shall not be attended by counsel or attornies].

3. The said E. F. shall publish his award on or before &c., or within such extended time not exceeding one calendar month after that day, as the said E. F. shall by writing under his hand appoint.

4. The expenses of and incidental to this agreement, and of the reference and of the award, shall be paid by such of the parties hereto in such manner, at such time and place, as the said E. F. shall appoint.

5. This submission may be made a rule of her Majesty's Court of Exchequer at Westminster at the instance of either party, and shall not be revoked by the death of either party before the publishing of the said award, and shall be deemed a reference within the meaning of the Common Law Procedure Act, 1854.

As witness, &c.

15.

Of Reference where Action brought.

An Agreement made this   day of   , 18 , between A. B., of &c., of the one part, and C. D., of &c., of the other part: Whereas on the   day of   , 18 , a writ was issued out of the Court of   , at Westminster, against the said C. D. at the suit of the said A. B., for recovering the sum of £   : And whereas the said C. D. claims a set-off to the said action, amounting to the sum of £   : Now these presents witness, that, in order to end all differences between them, the said A. B. and C. D. do hereby agree with each other as follows:—

1. The said action and set-off, and all other matters in difference between the said A. B. and C. D., shall be referred to E. F., of &c., who shall make his award under his hand on or before the   day of   next, or such further time as the said E. F. shall by writing indorsed hereon appoint, but not later than   months from the date hereof.

2. The said A. B. and C. D. respectively, and their respective witnesses, shall be examined on oath before the said arbitrator, and produce all books and papers in their possession.

3. The said A. B. shall, within seven days from this date, deliver to the said C. D. an account in writing of all the items of his claim; and within seven days after receipt thereof the said C. D. shall deliver to the said A. B. an

account in writing of all the items of his set-off, and in case of default by either party as aforesaid, the arbitrator shall be at liberty to proceed as if the party making such default had abandoned his claim or set-off, as the case may be.

4. If either party shall make default in attending any appointment made by the arbitrator, he shall be at liberty to proceed ex parte, and as fully and effectually as if such absent party were present.

5. The costs of the action shall abide the event of the award, and each party shall pay his own costs of this agreement, but the costs of the reference and award shall be in the discretion of the arbitrator.

As witness the hands of the parties.

———

16.

For a Mortgage.

AN AGREEMENT made this &c., between T. L., of &c., of the first part, G. H. L., of &c., of the second part, and E. G., of &c., of the third part: Whereas, under the will of H. L., late of &c., deceased, dated &c., the said T. L. alleges that he will, upon the attainment of the age of twenty-five years, become absolutely entitled for an estate in fee simple, free from incumbrances (except the annuities of &c., amounting in all to the yearly sum of 240*l.*) to an undivided moiety or half share of and in certain estates devised by the said will and therein described as all those the said testator's estates respectively called &c., situate in &c.: And whereas the said T. L. alleges that he is now of the age of twenty-three years: And whereas the said T. L. also alleges that the said G. H. L. is now of the age of twenty-one years, and that he will also become entitled to the other moiety of the same estates upon attaining the age of twenty-five years: And whereas the said T. L. has applied to the said E. G. for a loan of 12,000*l.* at interest at 5*l.* per cent. per annum, to be secured by a mortgage in fee of his undivided moiety in the said estates, devised by the will of the said T. L. the testator as aforesaid; and the said E. G. has agreed that upon the said T. L. satisfying him the said E. G., that the proposed security will be adequate in point of value, and deducing a good title to the aforesaid moiety, to lend the sum of 12,000*l.* to the said T. L., upon the security of a mortgage of the said moiety and of a policy of assurance to be effected if required in such office to such amount, and on such terms for indemnifying the said E. G. against loss in the event of the said T. L. dying under the age of twenty-five years, as the said E. G. shall reasonably require: And whereas the said G. H. L. has agreed to join in these presents in manner hereinafter appearing: Now, therefore, it is agreed between the said parties as follows:

1. The said T. L. shall forthwith, at his own expense, deduce and show a good title to an undivided moiety of the estates alleged to have been devised to him as aforesaid, to the satisfaction of the said E. G. or his solicitor, and also produce or procure such evidence of the value thereof as the said E. G. shall reasonably require.

2. When and as soon as the title of the said T. L. to the said moiety shall have been investigated and approved of on behalf of the said E. G., the said T. L. and all other necessary parties (except the said annuitants) shall, upon the request of the said E. G., but at the cost of the said T. L., convey the said moiety of the said estates to the use of the said E. G. in fee simple in possession, free from incumbrances (except the said annuities), by way of mortgage for securing the payment to him of the sum of 12,000*l.* with interest thereon, at the rate of 5*l.* per cent. per annum, from the day on which the same sum shall be advanced, and the said mortgage shall contain such power of sale, and such covenants and clauses as the solicitor of the said E. G. shall reasonably require, including a clause or clauses, proper and sufficient to charge the whole of the said annuities upon the mansion and lands whereof the said T. L. is seised in fee simple, free from incumbrances, and which are now in his own occupation at, &c., and upon the mill and premises at, &c., also occupied by him, and all other buildings to be erected on any part of the same premises, and upon all furniture, fixtures and effects which are or shall be in,

upon or about any part thereof during the continuance of the said mortgage security, with powers of entry and distress, and all other usual and necessary powers for enabling the said E. G., his executors, administrators or assigns, to hold the said moiety so to be mortgaged as aforesaid, freed and discharged from the said annuities and for exonerating not only the same moiety, but also (as between the said parties to these presents) the moiety of the said G. H. L. from the said annuities, and every of them, and every part thereof, and for indemnifying and protecting the said E. G., his executors, administrators and assigns, and the entirety of the said estates so devised by the said will as aforesaid during the continuance of the said mortgage security, from and against the said annuities, and every of them, and every part thereof.

3. If the said mortgage shall be completed, the said G. H. L. shall concur with the said T. L. in securing the interest of the said mortgage debt upon his moiety of the said estates.

4. If from any reasonable cause whatever the said mortgage shall not be completed, and the said deeds and assurances shall not be executed on or before the   day of   next, the said E. G. may, on or at any time after that day, and notwithstanding any subsequent negotiations, by a notice in writing sent to the said T. L. or his solicitor, rescind and abandon the proposed mortgage, and the said T. L. shall, whether the said mortgage shall be completed or not, pay or discharge all the costs incurred by the said E. G. in or about the negotiation for the said mortgage, and the preparation, engrossment and execution of the agreement, and the investigation of the title to the said estates, or in anywise incidental to the said mortgage.

5. The said T. L. shall, if required, at his own expense, effect an assurance on his life for indemnifying the said E. G. against all loss in the event of the death of the said T. L. under the age of twenty-five years, such assurance to be effected in the name of the said E. G. in such office for such sum, and upon such terms and conditions, as the said E. G. shall reasonably require, and the premiums paid or to be paid in

respect of such assurance shall be deducted from the amount of the proposed advance.

6. The said E. G. shall, on the completion of the said mortgage, advance and pay to the said T. L., or as he shall direct, the sum of 12,000*l*.

7. At any time after the said   day of   , but before the completion of the said mortgage, the said E. G. shall be at liberty to pay the said 12,000*l*., or any part thereof, into the   bank to a deposit account in his own name, but at the risk of the said T. L.; and from the date of such payment (unless there shall be a delay in completion arising through the default of the said E. G. or his solicitor), the said T. L. shall pay to the said E. G. interest on the said sum of 12,000*l*., or so much thereof as shall be so paid in, at the rate of 5*l*. per cent. per annum; but the said E. G. shall, in that case, account to the said T. L. for all sums (if any) which he may receive from the said bank by way of interest in respect of such deposit and the money so paid in, and the interest thereon shall be a charge on the moiety of the said T. L. under the said will.

8. In the meantime, and until the said mortgage shall be completed, the said share and interest of the said T. L. in the said estates devised by the said will as aforesaid shall be and remain a security to the said E. G., his executors, administrators and assigns, for all monies payable to him or them under this agreement, including all costs and expenses whatsoever incurred or to be incurred by the said E. G. in or about the premises.

As witness the hands of the parties.

17.

For releasing an Annuity charged on Real Estate.

AN AGREEMENT, made this   day of   , 18 , between A. B., of &c., of the one part, and C. D., of &c., of the other part: Whereas E. F., late of &c., deceased, by her will, dated &c.,

devised her estate called A., in &c., to the said A. B., his heirs and assigns, charged with the payment of the sum of 1*l*. per week to the said C. D., during her life, and which the testatrix bequeathed to the said C. D. accordingly: And whereas the said testatrix died on &c. without having revoked or altered her said will: And whereas the said A. B. is desirous of selling the said estate, and the said C. D. hath, at the request of the said A. B., agreed to join in the conveyance or conveyances thereof to the purchaser or purchasers, or to release the said estate from the said annuity in the manner and upon the terms hereinafter appearing: Now, therefore, it is hereby mutually agreed between the said parties hereto as follows, namely :—

1. The said C. D. will, when required by and at the costs in all things of the said A. B., and upon the said A. B. complying with the requirements contained in clause 2 of these presents, join in the conveyance or conveyances of the said estate to the purchaser or purchasers thereof, or release the said estate from the payment of the said annuity.

2. If the said C. D. shall execute such conveyance or conveyances or release as aforesaid, the said A. B. will, at his own costs in all things, concurrently with such execution as the said C. D. or her solicitor shall require, execute and give to the said C. D. his bond in the penal sum of &c., conditioned to be void on payment to the said C. D. during her life of the weekly sum of 1*l*., to commence and be computed from the date of the said bond; and will at the same time pay all arrears of the said annuity up to the date of the said bond; and will also at the same time deposit in the Bank of &c., at &c., in the names of G. H. and I. K., of &c., the sum of £   , as a further security for the due payment of such annuity.

3. The said sum of 450*l*., when deposited, shall, together with all interest thereon, remain in the said bank until default shall be made in payment of the said annuity, and thereupon the said G. H. and I. K., or the survivor of them, or the executors or administrators of such survivor, shall, at the request of the said C. D., either pay the said annuity and all

arrears thereout, or pay the arrears out of the interest thereof, if sufficient, and invest the said sum of 450*l.*, or a sufficient part thereof, in the purchase for the said C. D. of a Government annuity for the life of the said C. D. of 1*l.* per week, and pay the residue (if any) of the said sum of 450*l.* and interest (after deducting all expenses incurred by such payment or purchase as aforesaid) unto the said A. B., his executors, administrators or assigns.

4. The said sum of 450*l.* so to be deposited as aforesaid shall in no way prejudice the right of the said C. D. under the said bond, but the said bond and deposit shall be considered auxiliary and collateral to each other, and nothing herein contained shall prejudice the right of the said C. D. against the said estate, until the whole of the arrangement contemplated by these presents shall be fully carried out.

5. The costs and expenses incurred by the said C. D. of and incidental to the said arrangement, and the perusal and execution of these presents, and of any such conveyance or conveyances or release as aforesaid, and all other costs and expenses of and incidental to these presents and the release or extinguishment of the said annuity, shall be borne and paid by the said A. B.

As witness the hands of the parties.

APPOINTMENTS.

18.

Of Gamekeeper.

KNOW ALL MEN by these presents, that I, A. B., of &c., do hereby appoint C. D., of &c., to be my gamekeeper for my manor of &c., to look after, take care of, and preserve the game therein, with full power to take and kill any hare, pheasant, partridge, or other game in and upon my said manor, for his own use: And also to seize all such guns, dogs, ferrets, nets, and engines for killing and taking conies, hares, pheasants, partridges, or other game, as within the precincts of my said manor shall be used by any person or persons who by law is or are prohibited to keep or use the same : And also to do all other things belonging to the office of a gamekeeper, according to the several acts of Parliament now in force.

In witness, &c.

———

19.

Of Money under a Power and Surrender of two sixth parts thereof, with Power to revoke the Appointment made as to one sixth part.

THIS INDENTURE, made the   day of   , 18 , between E. H., of &c. (hereafter called E. H. the elder), of the first part; W. C., of &c., and Mary his wife (formerly M. H., spinster), E. H., of &c. (hereafter called E. H. the younger), W. R., of &c., and M. his wife (formerly M. H., spinster), J. H., of &c., and G. H., of &c., of the second part, and the said W. R. and M. his said wife, and the said G. H. of the third part: Whereas J. H., late of &c., duly made his will, dated the   day of   , 18 , and thereby devised unto J. M., his heirs, executors, administrators and assigns, all the common which he lately purchased on   , in the county of   , and all other his real estate and hereditaments whatsoever and wheresoever of which he was seised or anyways interested in or entitled unto, and of which he had the power of disposal, together with all the term or interest which he might have in his farm at   at the time of his decease, and also all his goods, chattels, monies, securities for money, credits and personal estate whatsoever, to hold to the said J. M., his heirs, executors, administrators and assigns, according to the nature or tenures thereof respectively, upon trust to pay to or permit and suffer his wife Elizabeth to take and receive out of the rents, interests and profits thereof, to her own sole use, one clear annuity or yearly rent-charge of £   during her natural life, and he did thereby charge and make chargeable the same estates, real and personal, accordingly; and he willed that his said wife should have the use and occupation of such and so many of his household goods

and furniture as she should think proper to take during her
natural life, not exceeding the value of £   , according to
an inventory and valuation thereof to be taken, and of all
other his personal estate after his decease, and subject as
aforesaid, and also subject to the payment of his debts,
funeral expenses and the charges of probate of his said will,
with all expenses incident to the execution thereof, upon
further trust of all his said real and personal estate as to
three equal undivided parts or shares (the whole into four
equal parts to be divided) of and in all the said trust estates
and effects, real and personal, for the use of his the said
testator's daughter M., wife of the said J. M., and of the said
testator's daughters M. H. and S. H., equally to be divided
among them and their respective heirs, executors, administrators and assigns, according to the natures or tenures thereof
respectively, as tenants in common; and as to the remaining
one fourth undivided part or share of the said trust estate
and effects, real and personal, upon further trust thereof, to
pay the rents, interests, dividends and profits, as the same
should come to hand and be received, to his the said testator's
daughter, the said E. H. the elder, from and after his decease,
during her natural life, or otherwise permit and suffer her to
receive the same from the person or persons liable to pay
such rents, interests, dividends and profits; and it was the
said testator's will that the said rents, interests, dividends and
profits so payable to his said daughter Elizabeth should not
be subject or liable to the debts, control, management, engagements or intermeddlings of any husband or husbands which
she might thereafter take, but her receipt and receipts for the
same alone from time to time, signed with her own proper
hand, whether covert or sole, and notwithstanding any future
coverture of hers, should be a good and sufficient discharge
and discharges to his said trustee or other person or persons
paying the same; and from and after the decease of his said
daughter E., upon further trust of all the said last-mentioned
one fourth part of the said estates, real and personal, so
limited for her use during her life as aforesaid, for such one
or more of her children then born and thereafter to be born

of her body and lawfully issuing, in such shares and proportions, manner and form, and for such estate or estates as the testator's said daughter E., whether covert or sole, and notwithstanding any future coverture of hers, by any deed or other instrument in writing, with or without power of revocation and new appointment, by her duly signed, sealed and delivered in the presence of and attested by two or more credible witnesses, or by her last will and testament in writing, or other writing in the nature of her last will and testament, by her duly signed, sealed and published in the presence of and attested by the like number and quality of witnesses, should give, devise, limit, direct or appoint the same, and for want of or in default of such gift, devise, limitation, direction or appointment, or so far as the same being made should not be a complete disposition of the said last-mentioned one fourth part of the said trust estates and effects, and subject thereto, upon such trusts as are in the said will now in recital declared of and concerning the same; and if it should be found necessary or proper for the purposes therein mentioned, or for the advancement of the said one fourth part of the said real estates remaining in trust for the use of his said daughter E. and her issue, to sell any part or parts thereof, and his said trustee, the said J. M., or his heirs, should approve thereof, the said testator thereby empowered him and them to sell any part or the whole of the said one fourth part or share of his said real estate and hereditaments accordingly, by public sale or private contract, and together or in parcels, for the best price or prices which could well be got for the same, and receive the purchase-money or monies, and after deducting thereout the expenses of such sale or sales, should and might invest the same again, as well as any other of the monies set apart for the use of his said daughter E. and her children as long as the same should remain in trust under that his will, either in Government or some other good security or securities, or in the purchase of other lands or hereditaments of equal or greater value, and take the security or securities, title or titles thereof, in his or their own name or names, upon the trusts thereinbefore specified respecting the said one fourth part or share of his said estates real and personal; and the said testator appointed the said J. M. and his said daughters E. and M. and S. executor and executrixes of his said will; and whereas the said testator died on the day of   , 18   , without having revoked or altered his said will, and the same was proved by the said J. M. in the Consistory Court of the Bishop of   [*or* in her Majesty's Court of Probate] on the   day of   in the same year; and whereas the said E. H. died many years ago, and all arrears of her annuity have been long since paid: and whereas all the debts, funeral and testamentary expenses of the said testator have been long since paid; and whereas the three fourth parts not settled to the benefit of the said E. H. the elder and her children, as aforesaid, of the real and personal estate of the said testator have been disposed of and accounted for to the persons entitled thereto under the said will, and the one fourth part by the will settled for the benefit of the said E. H. the elder hath been converted into money, pursuant to the trust or power in that behalf in the said will, and produced by such conversion the clear sum of £   , and that sum now remains in the hands of the said J. M.; and whereas the said E. H. the elder has six children now living, all of whom have attained the age of twenty-one years, namely, the said W. H., the said M. C., the said E. H. the younger, the said M. R., the said J. H. and the said G. H., and has not hitherto exercised the power of appointment limited to her by the said recited will; and whereas the said E. H. the elder is desirous of exercising in manner hereinafter appearing the said power of appointment given to her by the hereinbefore recited will; and, in consideration of an arrangement between her and the said W. C., and M. his wife and G. H., hath agreed to make such assignments and surrenders as are hereinafter contained: Now this indenture witnesseth, that for effectuating her said desire, and in exercise or execution of the said power or authority given to her the said E. H. the elder by the said will of the said J. H. and of every other power or authority in anywise enabling her in this behalf, she the said E. H. the elder

doth by this deed or instrument in writing signed, sealed and
delivered by her in the presence of the two credible persons
whose names are intended to be hereupon endorsed as witnesses
attesting the signing, sealing and delivery hereof by her the
said E. H. the elder, limit, direct or appoint that, from and
immediately after the signing, sealing and delivery of these
presents, the said sum of £   and the stock, funds and
securities whereon the same shall from time to time be invested, shall go, remain and be, and, subject to the life interest
of the said E. H. the elder, shall be held in trust for the said
W. H., the said M. C., the said E. H. the younger, the said
M. R., the said J. H. and the said G. H., their executors,
administrators and assigns, in equal shares and proportions:
And this indenture also witnesseth, that in pursuance of the
said agreement in this behalf and for the considerations aforesaid, and to the intent that the said M. C. may be entitled
immediately and in possession to the said one sixth part
hereinbefore appointed to her of and in the said sum of
£   , she the said E. H. the elder doth hereby assign and
surrender unto the said M. C., her executors, administrators
and assigns, all that the estate, right and interest to which
she the said E. H. the elder is entitled for her life of and in
the interest and annual produce of the said one equal sixth
part or share to which the said M. C., under or by virtue of
the appointment hereinbefore contained, became entitled expectant on the decease of the said E. H. the elder, of and in
the said sum of £   and the stocks, funds or securities
whereon the same shall from time to time be invested, to the
intent that the one sixth part hereinbefore appointed to the
said M. C. of the said sum of £   may forthwith become
and be vested in her in possession, and be held by the said
J. M., his executors, administrators or assigns, in trust for the
said M. C., her executors, administrators or assigns: And
this indenture also witnesseth, that, in further pursuance of
the said agreement in this behalf, and for the consideration
aforesaid, and to the intent that the said G. H. may be
entitled immediately in possession to the said one sixth part
hereinbefore appointed to him of and in the said sum of

£   , she the said E. H. the elder doth hereby assign and surrender unto the said G. H., his executors, administrators and assigns, all that the estate, right and interest to which the said E. H. the elder is entitled for her life, of and in the interest and annual produce of the said one equal sixth part or share to which the said G. H., under or by virtue of the appointment hereinbefore contained, became entitled expectant on the decease of the said E. H. the elder of and in the said sum of £   and the stocks, funds and securities whereon the same shall from time to time be invested, to the intent that the one sixth part hereinbefore appointed to the said G. H. of the said sum of £   may forthwith become and be vested in him in possession and be held by the said J. M., his executors, administrators or assigns, in trust for the said G. H , his executors, administrators or assigns: provided nevertheless, and it is hereby declared, that it shall be lawful for the said E. H. the elder at any time or times and from time to time, by any deed or instrument in writing to be by her duly signed, sealed and delivered in the presence of and attested by two or more credible witnesses, or by her last will and testament in writing duly executed and attested as required by law, absolutely to revoke, determine and make void, either wholly or in part, the appointment hereinbefore made in favour of the said W. H., and so far as any such revocation shall extend by the same or any other deed or instrument in writing or by her will or codicil, to be respectively executed and attested as aforesaid, to make any new or other appointment (consistent with the powers in that behalf in the said recited will) of the said sixth part or share hereinbefore appointed to the said W. H.

In witness, &c.

20.

Of New Trustee.

THIS INDENTURE, made, &c., between A. B., of &c., and C. D., of &c., of the one part, and E. F., of &c., of the other part: Whereas G. H, late of   deceased, by his will dated the   day of   18 , devised all [*set out parcels from the will*] unto and to the use of I. K. and the said A. B. and C. D., their heirs and assigns, upon the trusts therein expressed, several of which trusts are still subsisting, and appointed the said I. K., A. B. and C. D. executors of his said will; and the said testator declared, that if any of the trustees nominated in and by his said will, or to be appointed as thereinafter mentioned, should die (either before or after having acted in the trusts aforesaid), or any of them should decline [*recite in the past tense the power to appoint new trustees as set out in the will*] : and whereas the said testator died without having revoked or altered his said will, which was proved by the said executors on the   day of 18 , in the   Court of Probate : and whereas the said I. K. died on the   day of   18 , and was buried at   in the county of   : and whereas the said A. B. and C. D., in pursuance of the hereinbefore recited power in that behalf, have proposed to appoint the said E. F. to be a trustee of the said will in the place of the said I. K., and the said E. F. has consented to become such trustee : Now this indenture witnesseth, that, in consideration of the premises, they the said A. B. and C. D., in exercise of the power given to them by the hereinbefore recited will of the said G. H. and of every other power enabling them in that behalf, do hereby nominate and appoint the said E. F. to be a trustee in the place of the said I. K. deceased, for all the trusts and purposes and with all the powers and authorities expressed and contained in the said will of the said G. H., so far as the same are now subsisting and capable of taking effect; and the said E. F. doth hereby testify and declare his acceptance of the said trust : And this indenture also witnesseth, that, in consideration of the premises, they the said A. B. and C. D. do hereby grant unto the said E. F. and his heirs all the freehold hereditaments comprised in and devised by the said will of the said G. H. deceased, which are now vested in the said A. B. and C. D. by virtue of the said will, together with the appurtenances to the said hereditaments belonging, to hold the said hereditaments unto the said E. F. and his heirs, to the use of the said A. B., C. D. and E. F., their heirs and assigns, upon the trusts and for the intents and purposes, and under and subject to the provisions concerning the same, expressed and declared in and by the said will of the said G. H. or so much and so many of the same trusts, intents and purposes, powers, provisoes and declarations as are now subsisting and capable of taking effect.

Add covenant by A. B. and C. D. that they have not encumbered [*vide next* "Precedent"].

In witness, &c.

21.
Of New Trustee by Indorsement.

THIS INDENTURE, made the   day of   18 , between the within-named A. B. and the within-named C. D. of the one part, and G. H., of &c., of the other part: Whereas the within-named E. F. died on the   day of   18 , and was buried at   , and in consequence thereof the within-named A. B. and C. D. have proposed to appoint the said G. H. to be a trustee of the within-written indenture in the place of the said E. F., and the said G. H. has consented to become such trustee: Now this indenture witnesseth, that in consideration of the premises the said A. B. and C. D., by virtue and in execution of the power and authority given to them by the within-written indenture, and of all other powers enabling them in that behalf, do nominate and appoint the said G. H. to be a trustee in the place of the said E. F. deceased, for all the trusts and purposes and with all the powers and authorities expressed and contained in the within-written indenture, so far as the same are now subsisting and capable of taking effect; and the said G. H. doth hereby testify and declare his acceptance of the said trust: And this indenture also witnesseth, that, in consideration of the premises, they the said A. B. and C. D. do by these presents grant unto the said G. H. and his heirs the hereditaments mentioned and comprised in and assured by the within-written indenture, and which are now vested in the said

A. B. and C. D. under and by virtue thereof, to hold the same unto the said G. H. and his heirs, to the use of the said A. B., C. D. and G. H., their heirs and assigns, upon the trusts and for the intents and purposes, and under and subject to the provisions, of the within-written indenture, or such and so many of the same as are now subsisting and capable of taking effect: And each of them, the said A. B. and C. D. doth for himself, his heirs, executors and administrators, covenant with the said G. H., his heirs and assigns, that they the said covenantors respectively have not done, executed, or knowingly permitted any act, deed, or thing whereby the said hereditaments are or can be in any manner incumbered.

In witness, &c.

APPRENTICESHIP.

22.

Indenture of Apprenticeship.

THIS INDENTURE witnesseth, that   doth put himself apprentice to   to learn his art, and with him (after the manner of an apprentice) to serve from the   until the full end and term of   years from thence next following, to be fully complete and ended; during which term the said apprentice his said master faithfully shall serve; his secrets keep; his lawful demands everywhere gladly do. He shall do no damage to his said master, nor see it to be done of others, but shall forthwith give warning to his said master of the same. He shall not waste the goods of his said master, nor lend them unlawfully to any. He shall not contract matrimony within the said term. He shall not play at cards, dice, tables or any other unlawful games, whereby his said master may have any loss. With his own goods or others, during the said term, without licence of his said master, he shall neither buy nor sell. He shall not haunt taverns or playhouses, nor absent himself from his said master's service day or night unlawfully; but in all things as a faithful apprentice he shall behave himself towards his master, and all his, during the said term. He shall give a true and just account of his said master's goods, chattels and money committed to his charge, or which shall come to his hands, whenever required so to do by his said master. And the said   his said apprentice in the art of   which he useth, by the best means that he can, shall teach and instruct, or cause to be taught and instructed; finding unto his said apprentice sufficient meat, drink,   lodging and all other necessaries during the said term   : And for the true performance of all and every the said covenants and agreements, either of them the said parties bindeth himself unto the other by these presents.

In witness whereof the parties above named to these indentures have set their hands and seals, the   day of   18 .

Signed, sealed and delivered in
    the presence of   .

23.

Proviso to be inserted in Indentures of Apprenticeship, if necessary.

PROVIDED ALWAYS, and it is hereby agreed between the said parties, that in case the said apprentice shall at any time or times hereafter be wilfully guilty of disobedience or misconduct towards his said master or any of his family or servants, and his said master shall give notice thereof in writing to the said A. B. [*the person bound for the said apprentice*], then, if the said apprentice shall, after the said A. B. shall have received such notice at least twenty-four hours, again be wilfully guilty of the like or any other misconduct towards his said master, or any of his family or servants, it shall be lawful for his said master immediately wholly to discharge such apprentice from his said service, and it shall be lawful for him thenceforth, during the residue of the said term, wholly to refuse to maintain, instruct or receive his said apprentice, and he shall not be required to return any part of the said premium.

ASSIGNMENTS.

24.

Of Leaseholds by Indorsement.

THIS INDENTURE, made the   day of   18 , between the within-named A. B., of the one part, and C. D., of   , of the other part: Whereas the said C. D. has contracted with the said A. B. for the purchase of the premises comprised in the within-written indenture for the residue of the term of   years therein mentioned at the sum of £   : Now this indenture witnesseth, that, in consideration of £   sterling to the said A. B. paid by the said C. D. (the receipt whereof, and that the same is in full for the purchase of the premises hereinafter assigned, the said A. B. doth acknowledge and therefrom doth release the said C. D., his heirs, executors, administrators and assigns), he the said A. B. doth assign unto the said C. D., his executors, administrators and assigns, the premises comprised in and demised by the within-written indenture, with the appurtenances to the same belonging or in anywise appertaining, To hold the same unto the said C. D., his executors, administrators and assigns, henceforth for all the unexpired residue of the term of   years by the within-written indenture demised, subject to the payment of the yearly rent of £   by the same indenture reserved, and to the observance and performance of the covenants and agreements therein contained, and which by or on the part of the lessee or assignee of the said premises are to be observed and performed: And the said A. B. for himself, his heirs, executors and administrators, doth hereby covenant with the said C. D., his executors, administrators and assigns, that (notwithstanding any act or deed by the said A. B. done or executed to the contrary) the within-written indenture of lease is now valid and effectual, and that the rent thereby reserved, and the covenants and agreements therein contained by or on the part of the lessee of the said premises to be observed and performed, have been observed and performed up to the date hereof, and also that the said A. B. hath power to assign the said premises unto the said C. D., his executors, administrators and assigns in manner aforesaid, free from incumbrances; and further, that the said A. B., his executors and administrators, and all other persons whomsoever, now or at any time during the continuance of the said term lawfully claiming any estate or interest in or out of the said premises, will, at all times during the continuance of the said term, execute all such further acts and deeds for more perfectly assigning the same premises unto the said C. D., his executors, administrators and assigns, for the residue then to come of the said term, as by the said C. D., his executors, administrators or assigns, shall be reasonably required: And the said C. D. doth hereby for himself, his heirs, executors and administrators, covenant with the said A. B., his executors and administrators, that the said C. D., his executors, administrators or assigns, will, during the residue of the said term of   years, pay the yearly rent of £   reserved by and perform the covenants contained in the within-written indenture, and which from and after the   day of   are or ought to be paid or performed, and will at all times hereafter indemnify the said A. B., his heirs, executors and administrators, from and against the non-payment of the said rent and the non-performance of the said covenants or any of them.

In witness, &c.

25.

Of Leaseholds by Mortgagor and Mortgagee.

THIS INDENTURE, made the   day of   , 18 , between [*vendor*], of &c., of the first part, [*mortgagee*], of &c., of the second part, and [*purchaser*], of &c., of the third part:

Whereas by an indenture, dated the   day of   , 18 ,
and made between [*lessor*] of the one part, and [*lessee*] of the
other part, for the considerations therein mentioned, the said
[*lessor*] did demise unto the said [*lessee*], his executors, administrators and assigns, all [*here copy the parcels from the lease
verbatim*], with their rights, easements and appurtenances, To
hold the same unto the said [*lessee*], his executors, administrators and assigns, from Michaelmas-day then last, for the
term of ninety-nine years, at and under the yearly rent of
£   , and subject to the covenants and conditions therein
contained and on the part of the [*lessee*], his executors, administrators and assigns, to be observed and performed: and
whereas by divers mesnè assignments, and ultimately by an
indenture dated the   day of   , the premises comprised
in and demised by the hereinbefore-recited lease became vested
in [*mortgagor*] for all the residue of the said term, subject to
the covenants and agreements contained in the said recited
lease and on the lessee's part to be thenceforth performed:
And whereas by an indenture dated the   day of   ,
18 , made between the said [*vendor*] of the one part, and
the said [*mortgagee*] of the other part, in consideration of
£   sterling paid by the said [*mortgagee*] to the said [*vendor*]
he the said [*vendor*] did assign unto the said [*mortgagee*], his
executors, administrators and assigns, the premises demised
by the said indenture of lease, together with the two several
messuages or tenements thereon erected and built, and which
are now known and distinguished by the Nos.   and
   ,   Street aforesaid, and then or late in the occupation of   , with the rights, easements and appurtenances
thereto belonging, To hold the same unto the said A. B., his
executors, administrators and assigns, thenceforth for all the
residue of the said term of ninety-nine years granted by the
said indenture of lease, subject to a proviso in the same
indenture for re-assignment of the said premises on payment
by the said [*vendor*], his executors, administrators or assigns,
on or before the   day of   then next, unto the said
[*mortgagee*], his executors, administrators or assigns, of £
sterling, with interest for the same in the meantime at 5*l.*

per cent. per annum, without any deduction: and whereas the said [*vendor*] hath contracted with the said [*purchaser*] for the sale to him of the premises hereinbefore described for the residue of the term therein, subject to the payment of the rent reserved by and to the performance of the covenants contained in the hereinbefore-recited lease, but free from all other incumbrances, for the sum of £   : and whereas the said [*mortgagee*] hath agreed to join in these presents in manner hereinafter appearing: Now this indenture witnesseth, that in consideration of £   sterling to the said [*mortgagee*] paid by the said [*purchaser*] on the execution hereof, the receipt whereof and that the same is in full for all principal, interest and other monies due to him under the hereinbefore-recited mortgage, the said [*mortgagee*] doth hereby acknowledge and doth discharge the said [*purchaser*] therefrom; and also in consideration of £   by the said [*purchaser*] to the said [*vendor*], the receipt whereof the said [*vendor*] doth hereby acknowledge and doth declare the said sums of £   and £   to be in full for the purchase of the premises hereby assigned, He the said [*mortgagee*] at the request of the said [*vendor*] doth hereby assign, and the said [*vendor*] doth hereby assign unto the said [*purchaser*], his executors, administrators and assigns, all and singular the messuages or tenements, and all other the premises comprised in and demised by the hereinbefore-recited lease, To hold the said premises unto the said [*purchaser*], his executors, administrators and assigns, henceforth for all the residue of the term of ninety-nine years therein, subject to the payment of the rent of £   reserved by and to the performance of the covenants contained in the hereinbefore-recited lease, and which from and after the   day of   last are or ought to be paid, observed and performed; and the said [*mortgagee*] doth hereby for himself, his heirs, executors and administrators, covenant with the said [*purchaser*], his executors, administrators and assigns, that he the said [*mortgagee*] hath not made or executed or been party or privy to any act or deed whereby or by means whereof the premises hereby assigned are, can or may be in anywise charged, affected or incumbered: And the said [*vendor*] doth hereby for himself, his heirs, executors and administrators, covenant with the said [*purchaser*], his executors, administrators and assigns, that (notwithstanding any act or thing by the said [*vendor*] and the said [*mortgagee*] or either of them, or any person claiming through, under or in trust for them or either of them), the said lease is now a good and subsisting lease, unforfeited and unsurrendered, and in nowise become void or voidable; and that the rent thereby reserved, and the covenants therein contained, have been paid and performed up to the   day of   last; and also that the said [*vendor*] and [*mortgagee*], or one of them, now hath good right to assign the said premises for the term and in manner aforesaid, free from incumbrances; and also that he the said [*vendor*] and [*mortgagee*], and any person claiming as aforesaid, will at all times during the continuance of the said lease, at the request and costs of the said [*purchaser*], his executors, administrators or assigns, make and execute all such further and other deeds and assurances for better assuring the said premises unto the said [*purchaser*], his executors, administrators and assigns, for the term and in manner aforesaid, as the said [*purchaser*], his executors, administrators or assigns, shall reasonably require: And the said [*purchaser*] doth hereby for himself, his heirs, executors, administrators and assigns, covenant with the said [*vendor*], his executors and administrators, that he the said [*purchaser*], his executors, administrators or assigns, will at all times hereafter during the residue of the term for which the said premises are holden, pay the said rent of £   reserved by and perform the covenants contained in the hereinbefore-recited lease, and which from and after the   day of   last are or ought to be paid or performed; and will in the meantime keep indemnified the said [*vendor*], his heirs, executors and administrators, from and against the non-payment of the said rent, and the non-observance or non-performance of the said covenants or conditions, or any of them.

In witness, &c.

26.

Of Leaseholds.

THIS INDENTURE, made the   day of   , 18 , between [*vendor*], of &c., of the one part, and [*purchaser*], of &c., of the other part: Whereas by an indenture bearing date the   day of   , 18 , and made between [*lessor*] of the one part, and [*lessee*] of the other part, for the considerations therein mentioned the said [*lessor*] did demise unto the said [*lessee*], his executors, administrators and assigns, all [*here copy the parcels from the lease verbatim*], with their rights, easements and appurtenances, To hold the same unto the said [*lessee*], his executors, administrators and assigns, from Michaelmas-day then last, for the term of ninety-nine years, at and under the yearly rent of £   , and subject to the covenants therein contained and on the part of the [*lessee*], his executors, administrators and assigns, to be observed and performed: and whereas by virtue of divers assignments and other acts in the law, and ultimately by an indenture bearing date the   day of   , and made between A. B. of the one part, and the said [*vendor*] of the other part, the premises comprised in and demised by the hereinbefore-recited indenture have become vested in the said [*vendor*] for the residue of the said term of ninety-nine years therein, subject to the payment of the rent of £   reserved by and to the performance of the covenants and conditions contained in the said indenture and on the part of the lessee, his executors, administrators and assigns, to be observed and performed: and whereas the said [*vendor*] hath contracted with the said [*purchaser*] for the sale to him of the premises hereinbefore described and intended to be hereby assigned for the residue of the term therein, subject to the payment of the rent reserved by and to the performance of the covenants contained in the said lease, but free from all other incumbrances, for the sum of £   : Now this indenture witnesseth, that in consideration of £   sterling to the said [*vendor*] paid by the said [*purchaser*] on the execution hereof (the receipt whereof, and that the same is in full for the purchase of the said premises, the said [*vendor*] doth hereby acknowledge and declare), he the said [*vendor*] doth by these presents assign unto the said [*purchaser*], his executors, administrators and assigns, all and singular the messuages or tenements, and all other the premises comprised in and demised by the hereinbefore-recited lease, To hold the said premises unto the said [*purchaser*], his executors, administrators and assigns, henceforth for all the residue of the term of ninety-nine years therein, subject to the payment of the rent of £   reserved by and to the performance of the covenants contained in the hereinbefore-recited lease, and which from and after the   day of   last are or ought to be paid, observed and performed: And the said [*vendor*] doth hereby for himself, his heirs, executors and administrators, covenant with the said [*purchaser*], his executors, administrators and assigns, that (notwithstanding any act or thing by the said [*vendor*], or any person claiming through, under or in trust for him) the said lease is now a good, valid and subsisting lease, unforfeited and unsurrendered, and in nowise become void or voidable; and that the rent thereby reserved, and the covenants therein contained, have been paid, observed and performed up to the   day of   last; and also that the said [*vendor*] now hath good right to assign the said lease and the premises thereby demised for the term and in manner aforesaid, free from incumbrances; and also that the said [*vendor*], and any person claiming as aforesaid, will at all times during the continuance of the said lease, at the request and costs of the said [*purchaser*], his executors, administrators or assigns, make and execute all such further and other acts and assurances for further and better assuring the said premises unto the said [*purchaser*], his executors, administrators and assigns, for the term and in manner aforesaid, as the said [*purchaser*], his executors, administrators or assigns, shall reasonably require: And the said [*purchaser*] doth hereby for himself, his heirs, executors, administrators and assigns, covenant with the said [*vendor*], his executors and administrators, that he the said [*purchaser*], his executors, administrators or assigns, will, at all times hereafter during the residue of the term for which the said premises are holden, pay the rent of £   reserved by and observe and perform the covenants contained in the hereinbefore-recited lease, and which from and after the   day of   last are or ought to be paid, observed or performed; and will in the meantime keep indemnified the said [*vendor*], his heirs, executors and administrators, from and against the non-payment of the said rent, and the non-observance or non-performance of the said covenants, or any of them.

In witness, &c.

27.

Of Leaseholds by a Mortgagee under his Power of Sale.

THIS INDENTURE, made the   day of   , 18 , between A. B., of &c., of the one part, and C. D., of &c., of the other part: Whereas by an indenture bearing date the   day of   , 18 , made between [*lessor*] of the one part, and [*lessee*] of the other part, all [*parcels from lease*] were demised unto the said [*lessee*], his executors, administrators and assigns, from the   day of   then instant, for the term of   years, less five days then next, subject to the yearly rent of a peppercorn if demanded, and to the covenants therein contained and on the tenant or lessee's part to be observed and performed: and whereas by divers mesne assignments, and ultimately by an indenture bearing date the   day of   , the piece or parcel of ground with the two messuages thereon erected, and other the premises comprised in and demised by the hereinbefore-recited lease, became vested in [*mortgagor*] for all the residue of the said term of   years, less five days, subject to the observance and performance of the covenants contained in the said lease and on the lessee's part to be thenceforth performed: and whereas by an indenture bearing date the   day of   , 18 , made between the said [*mortgagor*] of the one part, and the said A. B. of the other part, in consideration of £   sterling paid by the said A. B. to the said [*mortgagor*], and also in order to secure to the said A. B. the repayment of such further sum or sums of money and interest as the said A. B. should at any time thereafter advance to the said [*mortgagor*], he the said [*mortgagor*] did assign unto the said A. B., his executors, administrators and assigns, the piece or parcel of ground comprised in and demised by the said indenture of lease, together with the two several messuages or tenements thereon erected and built, and which are now known and distinguished by the Nos.   and   ,   Street aforesaid, and then or late in the occupation of   , and all other the messuages and buildings erected and standing on the said piece or parcel of ground, and all other the premises comprised in and demised by the said indenture of lease, with the rights, easements and appurtenances thereto belonging, To hold the same unto the said A. B., his executors, administrators and assigns, thenceforth for all the residue of the said term of   years, less five days, granted by the said indenture of lease, subject to a proviso in the same indenture for re-assignment of the said premises on payment by the said [*mortgagor*], his executors, administrators or assigns, on or before the   day of   then next, unto the said A. B., his executors, administrators or assigns, of the sum of £   sterling, together with interest for the same in the meantime after the rate of 5*l*. per cent. per annum, and on demand of all such further sum or sums of money as the said A. B. should at any time thereafter advance to the said [*mortgagor*] without any deduction: And by the same indenture it was provided, that if default should be made in the performance of the proviso thereinbefore contained in any of its terms, it should be lawful for the said A. B., his executors, administrators or assigns, at any time thereafter, without any further consent on the part of the said [*mortgagor*], his executors, administrators or assigns, to sell the premises thereby assigned, or any part thereof, either together or in parcels, and either by public auction or private contract, and subject to such conditions of sale and generally in every respect as the said A. B., his executors, administrators or assigns, should deem fit, and upon such sale to assign the premises sold unto the purchaser or purchasers, his or their executors, administrators and assigns, or as he or they might require: And by the said indenture it was declared that every receipt which should be given by the said A. B., his executors, administrators or assigns, for any purchase or other monies to be derived from any such sale or sales or otherwise under the same indenture, should be an effectual discharge to the person or persons to whom such receipt or receipts should be given for the money therein acknowledged to be received: and whereas, by a memorandum bearing date the   day   , 18 , and indorsed on the last-recited indenture, the said [*mortgagor*] acknowledged to have received from the said A. B., on the security created by the said indenture, the further sum of £   : and whereas there is now due to the said A. B. under the hereinbefore-recited indenture the sum of £   , together with an arrear of interest thereon: and whereas the said A. B. hath contracted with the said C. D. for the sale to him of the said piece or parcel of ground, with the two messuages thereon erected, for the residue of the term therein, for £   : Now this indenture witnesseth, that in consideration of the sum of £   sterling paid by the said C. D. to the said A. B. (the receipt whereof is hereby acknowledged), he the said A. B. doth by these presents assign unto the said C. D., his executors, administrators and assigns, all that the piece or parcel of ground comprised in and demised by the hereinbefore-recited indenture of lease, together with the two several messuages or tenements erected and built on some part thereof, and which are known and distinguished by the Nos.   and   ,   Street aforesaid, the said messuages or tenements being in the occupation of   and   , and the piece of land in the rear thereof in the occupation of   , and all other the messuages or tenements and buildings erected and standing on the said piece or parcel of ground, with the rights, easements and appurtenances thereto belonging, To hold the said premises, with their appurtenances, unto the said C. D., his executors, administrators and assigns, from henceforth for all the residue of the said term of years, less five days, granted by the hereinbefore-recited indenture of lease, freed and absolutely discharged from all claims and demands in respect of the monies intended to be secured by the hereinbefore-recited indenture of the day of   , but subject nevertheless to the observance and performance of the covenants and agreements contained in the hereinbefore-recited lease, and which on the lessee's or assignee's part and behalf are and ought henceforth to be observed, fulfilled and kept: And the said A. B. doth hereby for himself, his heirs, executors and administrators, covenant with the said C. D., his executors, administrators and assigns, that he the said A. B. hath not made, executed or knowingly suffered or been party or privy to any act, deed, matter or thing whatsoever, whereby or by reason or means whereof the premises hereby assigned or any of them, or any part thereof, are, is or may be in anywise charged, affected or incumbered in title, estate, or otherwise howsoever.

In witness, &c.

28.

Of Reversionary Interest in a Sum of Stock.

THIS INDENTURE, made the   day of   18 , between A. B., of &c., widow, of the one part, and C. D., of &c., of the other part: Whereas E. F., late of   , deceased, made his will bearing date the   day of   18 , and thereby bequeathed unto H. I. and K. L. (whom he appointed executors of his will), their executors, administrators and assigns, his leasehold house called   and the fixtures, furniture, stock and effects therein at the time of his decease, and also his leasehold house, No.   in   Street, and all other his personal estate and effects whatsoever and wheresoever, upon the trusts following, (that is to say,) in case his trustees or trustee should not think fit to permit his wife to carry on the business of the said house in   Street, pursuant to the permission given to her in that behalf, or if she should decline so to carry on the same, then the said testator directed his said trustees or trustee with all convenient speed to sell and dispose of all and singular the said messuage or tenement, furniture and fixtures, stock or effects, and to stand possessed of the monies to arise from such sale upon the trusts thereinafter declared of and concerning his said residuary estate; and as to his house in   Street, upon trust to pay the net rents and profits thereof to his said wife so long as she should continue his widow; and as to all the residue of his estate and effects not thereinbefore disposed of, upon trust to convert into money such parts thereof as should be saleable, and collect and get in the residue, and to lay out and invest the monies to arise or be produced from and forming part of his residuary estate in some or one of the public stocks or funds of Great Britain, with full liberty to vary the securities as occasion might require, or they or he should see fit; and he directed his said trustees to pay the interest, dividends and annual produce thereof to his said wife during such time as she should continue his widow, and from and after the decease or second marriage of his said wife he directed his trustees to sell and dispose of his said messuage in   Street, and the furniture, fixtures and effects therein (in case the same should not have been previously sold), and also his said messuage in   Street; and he declared that his said trustees should stand possessed of the monies to be produced from such sales, and also the stocks or funds in which his residuary estate, and the monies arising from any sale of the said premises and effects in   Street, if sold during the widowhood of his said wife, should be invested, and all other his trust monies, upon trust to pay, assign and transfer the same unto the three children of his said wife by her former husband in the proportions following (viz.), three equal seventh parts thereof to   his executors or administrators, three other equal seventh parts thereof to   for her own separate use and benefit, and the remaining one equal seventh part thereof to the said A. B. for her own separate use and benefit, free from the control, debts or engagements of her husband; or in case of her death during the widowhood of his said wife, to such person or persons and in such shares and proportions as she the said A. B. should, notwithstanding coverture, by any deed to be executed by her in the presence of and to be attested by one or more witness or witnesses, or by her last will and testament, direct or appoint, give or bequeath the same; and the said testator thereby declared that the receipts of the said A. B. alone, notwithstanding coverture, should be an effectual discharge for the monies thereby given to her: and whereas the said E. F. died on the   day of   without having altered or revoked his said will, which on the   was duly proved by the said executors in her Majesty's Court of Probate: and whereas the leasehold messuages and premises in   Street, and   and all the stock, furniture and effects of which the said testator died possessed, or some part thereof, have been sold and disposed of by the said H. I. and K. L., and the proceeds thereof, and of all other his residuary estate, after payment of his debts, funeral and testamentary expenses, have been invested in the funds, and the same now consist of the sum of 1,768l., New £3 per Cent. Annuities, standing in the names of the said H. I. and K. L. in the books of the Governor and Company of the Bank of England: and whereas the widow of the said testator is still living, and is of the age of seventy years or thereabouts: and whereas the said A. B. caused the one seventh part or share to which she is entitled in reversion, expectant on the death of the said   , in the said sum of 1,768l., New £3 per Cent. Annuities, to be offered for sale by public auction at the auction mart in the city of London, on the   day of   last, under certain particulars and conditions of sale there produced; and at the said sale the said C. D. was the highest bidder for, and declared to be the purchaser of, the same for the sum of £   : Now this indenture witnesseth, that in order to effectuate the said sale, and in consideration of £   sterling to the said A. B. paid by the said C. D. on the execution of these presents, the receipt of which said sum of £   she the said A. B. doth hereby acknowledge, and doth hereby release the said C. D., his executors, administrators and assigns from the same, she the said A. B. doth hereby assign, and also appoint and confirm unto the said C. D., his executors, administrators and assigns, all that the one seventh part or share and other the part, share and interest to which she the said A. B. is entitled in reversion, expectant upon the decease of the said   the widow of the said E. F., of and in the said sum of 1,768*l*., New £3 per Cent. Annuities, and of and in all and singular the stocks, funds or securities in or upon which the same or any part thereof may from time to time be invested, and all the dividends, interest and income thereof from and after the decease of the said   , To have, receive and take the said part or share hereby appointed and assigned of and in the said sum of 1,768*l*., New £3 per Cent. Annuities, and other the money and premises hereinbefore mentioned, unto and by the said C. D., his executors, administrators and assigns, from henceforth absolutely, with full power and authority for the said C. D., his executors, administrators and assigns, at his or their costs and charges, as the attorney or attornies of the said A. B. or otherwise, to ask, demand, sue for, recover and receive, and give full and sufficient releases, acquittances and discharges for the said part or share, money and premises and every part thereof, and which receipt or receipts of the said C. D., his executors, administrators or assigns, for the said part or share, money and premises shall to all intents and purposes be a good and effectual acquittance and discharge to the trustee or trustees of the said will of the said E. F., or other the person or persons paying the same, for so much thereof as in such receipt or receipts shall be expressed to have been received: And the said A. B. doth hereby for herself, her heirs, executors and administrators, covenant with the said C. D., his executors, administrators and assigns, that notwithstanding any act, deed or thing whatsoever by her done, permitted or suffered to the contrary, she now hath in herself alone good right and absolute authority to assign the said part or share and premises hereby assigned or intended so to be in manner aforesaid, free from all incumbrances; and also that she the said A. B. and every other person claiming any title or interest of, in or to the said premises hereby assigned, through, under or in trust for her, will at all times hereafter, upon every reasonable request, and at the expense of the said C. D., his executors, administrators or assigns, do and execute, or procure to be done and executed, all such further and other lawful assurances as may be requisite or necessary for more effectually assigning the said premises unto the said C. D., his executors, administrators or assigns, or for enabling him or them to recover and receive the same, according to the true intent and meaning of these presents. In witness, &c.

[N.B.—In the above instance the assignor was a widow. If her husband had been living, he would not have been a necessary party to the deed, as the share was bequeathed to the assignor for her separate use. If, however, in such a case the husband be living and is willing to concur in the deed it is as well to procure his concurrence, in order that he may enter into the usual covenants, a married woman not being able to bind herself by a covenant except in equity, and then only so far as concerns her separate estate.

Notice of the deed should be given to the trustees immediately after its execution, and a distringas placed on the stock.]

29.

Of the Goodwill of the Business of a Clock and Watch Maker, and the Clock Winding connected therewith.

THIS INDENTURE, made the   day of   18 , between A. B., of &c., clock and watch maker, of the one part, and C. D., of &c., watch and chronometer maker, of the other part: Whereas the said A. B. has for some time past carried on the trade or business of a clock and watch maker, as well as the clock winding connected therewith, at   Street aforesaid, and he has also been and is now employed in winding the clocks of the several persons whose names appear in the Schedule hereunder written for the yearly remuneration appearing in the same Schedule: and whereas the said A. B. hath contracted with the said C. D. for the sale to him of the goodwill and custom of the said trade or business of a clock and watch maker as carried on by him, and the clock winding connected therewith, for the sum of £   , and the said A. B. has agreed to enter into the covenants hereinafter contained: Now this indenture witnesseth, that in consideration of £   sterling to the said A. B. paid by the said C. D. on the execution hereof, the receipt whereof the said A. B. doth hereby acknowledge, and therefrom doth discharge the said C. D., his executors, administrators and assigns, he the said A. B. doth hereby assign unto the said C. D., his executors, administrators and assigns, the goodwill and custom of the said business of a clock and watch maker, as carried on by the said A. B. at   Street aforesaid, together with the clock winding connected therewith, expressly including the winding and other business of the several persons whose names appear in the Schedule hereunder written, and all the interest of the said A. B. therein, To have, hold and enjoy the said goodwill, custom and premises hereby assigned unto the said C. D., his executors, administrators and assigns absolutely: And the said A. B. doth hereby for himself, his heirs, executors and administrators, covenant with the said C. D., his executors, administrators and assigns, that he the said A. B. now hath in himself good right to assign the said goodwill, custom and premises in manner aforesaid, and that the same shall be enjoyed by the said C. D., his executors, administrators and assigns, free from any interruption by the said A. B. or any person claiming through or under him, or by means of his acts or deeds; and also that he the said A. B. shall not nor will at any time or times, within the period of seven years from the date hereof, either by himself alone, or jointly with or as agent, journeyman or assistant for any person or persons whomsoever, either directly or indirectly, or upon any account or pretence whatsoever set up, exercise or carry on, or be employed in carrying on, the trade or business of a clock and watch maker, or the clock winding connected therewith, within ten miles from   Street aforesaid, and shall not nor will, either by himself, or by or with any other person or persons, do or cause to be done any wilful act or thing to the prejudice of the said trade or business of a clock and watch maker, and the clock winding connected therewith, hereby assigned, as hereafter carried on and conducted by the said C. D., his executors, administrators and assigns, but, on the contrary, shall and will to the utmost of his power endeavour to promote the interest of the said C. D. amongst the customers of the said A. B. and otherwise.

In witness, &c.

The Schedule referred to.

30.

Of Debts.

THIS INDENTURE, made the   day of   , 18 , between A. B., of &c., of the one part, and C. D., of &c., of the other part: Whereas the said A. B. hath for some time past carried on the business of   at   aforesaid, and in the course of such business the several persons whose names are mentioned in the Schedule hereunder written have become indebted to him in the several sums of money set opposite to their respective names in such Schedule, and he hath contracted with the said C. D. for the absolute sale of the same debts for the sum of £   : Now this indenture witnesseth, that, in consideration of £   to the said A. B. paid by the said C. D. on the execution hereof (the receipt whereof is hereby acknowledged), he the said A. B. doth hereby assign and transfer unto the said C. D., his executors, administrators and assigns, all and singular the several debts and sums of money mentioned in the Schedule hereunder written, which are now due and owing to the said A. B. from the several persons whose names are mentioned in the same Schedule, To have, receive and take the said debts and premises hereby assigned unto and by the said C. D., his executors, administrators and assigns, for his and their own absolute use and benefit; and the said A. B. doth hereby absolutely and irrevocably constitute and appoint the said C. D., his executors, administrators and assigns, the true and lawful attorney and attornies of him the said A. B., his executors or administrators, in his or their name or names or otherwise to receive, and, if the said C. D., his executors, administrators or assigns, shall deem it expedient so to do, to sue for and recover, the said debts and premises hereby assigned, or any of them; and, when the same respectively, or any part thereof respectively, shall be received, to give discharges for the same, and generally to perform all acts whatsoever which shall be requisite in order to give complete effect to the assignment hereby made, and to appoint a substitute or substitutes for all or any of the purposes aforesaid, and such substitution at pleasure to revoke; the said A. B. hereby ratifying and confirming, and agreeing to ratify and confirm, whatsoever his said attorney or attornies, or his or their substitute or substitutes, shall lawfully do in the premises: And the said A. B. doth hereby for himself, his heirs, executors and administrators, covenant with the said C. D., his executors, administrators and assigns, that the said several debts hereby assigned, or intended so to be, are now due and owing to him, and that he, his executors or administrators, will not at any time hereafter revoke the power or authority hereinbefore contained, or receive, compound for or discharge the said several debts, or any or either of them, or any part thereof respectively, or release or interfere with any action or suit which shall or may be commenced in his, their or either of their name or names, in pursuance of these presents, for the recovery of the same, without the consent in writing of the said C. D., his executors, administrators or assigns, but will at all times avow, justify and confirm all such matters and things, process and proceedings, as the said C. D., his executors, administrators or assigns, or any other person or persons by or through his or their direction or procurement, shall, in pursuance of the power hereinbefore contained, do, commence, bring or prosecute upon or by reason or means of the said debts and premises; and further, that he the said A. B., his executors and administrators, will at all times hereafter, on the request and at the costs of the sad C. D., his executors, administrators or assigns, make, do and execute all such further assignments, letters of attorney, acts, deeds, matters and things for the more effectually assigning and assuring unto the said C. D., his executors, administrators and assigns, the said several debts and premises, and enabling him or them to recover and receive the same respectively for his and their own absolute use and benefit in manner aforesaid, according to the true intent and meaning of these presents, as by the said C. D., his executors, administrators or assigns, shall be reasonably required: And the said C. D. doth hereby for himself, his heirs, executors and administrators, covenant with the said A. B., his executors and administrators, that he the said C. D., his executors, administrators or assigns, will at all times hereafter save harmless and keep indemnified the said A. B., his executors or administrators, from and against all losses, costs, charges, damages and expenses by reason of his or their name or names being used in any action, suit or other proceeding which shall or may be brought or instituted by the said C. D., his executors, administrators or assigns, or his or their substitute or substitutes, under or by virtue of the power or authority in that behalf hereinbefore contained, or otherwise by reason or in consequence of the same power or authority, or in relation thereunto.

In witness, &c.

The Schedule to which the above-written Indenture refers.

Name of Debtor.	Amount of Debt.	Name of Debtor.	Amount of Debt.

                                (L.S)   (L.S.)

Received on the day of the date of the above-written indenture of the above-named   , the sum of £   , being the consideration money above mentioned to be paid by him to me   . } £

Witness   .

Signed, sealed and delivered by the above-named   and   in the presence of   .

31.

For the Benefit of Creditors.

THIS INDENTURE, made the   day of   , 18 , between A. B., of &c., of the first part, C. D., of &c., and E. F., of &c., of the second part, and the creditors of the said A. B. of the third part: Whereas the said A. B. is indebted to the said parties hereto of the second and third parts in the several sums set opposite to their respective names in the Schedule hereinunder written, and being unable to satisfy the same in full has proposed and agreed to assign all his estate and effects unto the said C. D. and E. F. for the benefit of the creditors of the said A. B. in manner hereinafter mentioned: Now this indenture witnesseth, that, in consideration of the release hereinafter contained, he the said A. B. doth by these presents assign unto the said C. D. and E. F., their executors, administrators and assigns, all his real and personal estate and effects, whatsoever and wheresoever, To hold and receive the same, unto and by the said C. D. and E. F., their heirs, executors, administrators and assigns respectively, upon trust that they the said C. D. and E. F., or the survivor of them, his executors or administrators, or their or his assigns (hereinafter called the said trustees or trustee) do and shall, with all convenient speed, collect, get in, sell, dispose of and convert into money the said estate and effects, in such manner as to them or him shall seem most expedient, and stand possessed of the monies to be received by virtue of these presents, after paying thereout all costs, charges and expenses of proposing, preparing, engrossing and executing these presents, and carrying into effect the trusts hereby created, and incidental thereto, upon trust to pay and divide the same unto and among all and singular the creditors of the said A. B., rateably according to the amount of their respective debts; and the said A. B. doth hereby constitute and appoint the said trustees and trustee the true and lawful attornies and attorney of him the said A. B. to ask, demand, sue for, recover and receive all debts and sums of money owing to him on any account whatsoever, and all other the premises intended to be hereby assigned, and on payment and delivery thereof, or of any part thereof respectively, to sign and give proper receipts, acquittances and other discharges for the same respectively, and, on non-payment or non-delivery thereof respectively, to commence and prosecute any action, suit or other proceeding whatsoever for recovering and compelling payment and delivery thereof respectively, and also to adjust, liquidate and finally settle all actions, dealings and transactions whatsoever relating to the trust estate and premises, and for all or any of the purposes aforesaid to use the name of the said A. B.; and whatsoever the said attornies or attorney shall lawfully do or cause to be done in the premises, the said A. B. doth for himself, his heirs, executors and administrators, covenant with the said trustees or trustee to allow, ratify and confirm; and the said A. B. doth hereby for himself, his heirs, executors and administrators, covenant with the said C. D. and E. F., their executors and administrators, and also with each of the said several persons parties hereto of the third part, his and her executors and administrators, that he the said A. B. will, when requested by the said C. D. and E. F., or either of them, make out and fairly state in writing a true and exact account of all and singular his debts, credits, claims, demands, estate, property and effects, and of the several charges, outgoings, liens and incumbrances upon or affecting the same respectively, and deliver the same or a fair copy thereof unto each of them the said C. D. and E. F., and also will at all times hereafter, whenever required by the said trustees or trustee, use and employ his best endeavours, under and subject to their or his direction and advice, to collect and get in the estate, property, debts and effects of him the said A. B., and to perform and complete all contracts, engagements and orders undertaken and entered into by him for the purposes of these presents; and it is hereby declared, that every receipt of the said trustees and trustee for the time being for any money payable to them or him by virtue of these presents shall effectually discharge the person or persons paying the same from being obliged to see to the application thereof, or from being answerable or accountable for the misapplication or non-application thereof: provided always, that all questions relating to the said trust estate shall be decided according to English Bankrupt Law: And this indenture also witnesseth, that, for the considerations aforesaid, the said several creditors parties hereto of the second and third parts do, and each of them doth, acquit, release and for ever discharge the said A. B., his executors and administrators, of and from all and all manner of debts, sums of money, bills, bonds, notes, accounts, reckoning, judgments, executions, actions, suits, claims and demands whatsoever which the said releasing parties, or any or either of them, or their or any or either of their partner or partners, now have or hereafter may have against the said A. B., his executors or administrators, for or in respect of any debt, transaction, matter or thing up to the day of the date hereof.

In witness, &c.

The SCHEDULE above referred to.

This deed must be registered within twenty-eight days from its execution by the debtor, otherwise it cannot be pleaded as a defence to an action, even although the plaintiff may have executed it (*vide* " The Bankruptcy Act, 1861," and *Hodgson* v. *Wightman,* 11 Weekly Rep. 574).

ATTORNMENT OF TENANT.

32.

I THE undersigned A. B. do hereby attorn and become tenant to C. D. of the messuage, shop and premises at   in the county of   , now in my occupation: and I hereby agree to pay to him the weekly rent of 6s. for the same premises; and I have this day paid unto Mr. E. F., the agent of the said C. D., the sum of 6s., being the first week's payment of the said rent.

Witness my hand this   day of   18 .

BILL OF SALE.

33.

THIS INDENTURE, made the   day of   , 18 , between A. B., of &c., of the one part, and C. D., of &c., of the other part: Whereas the said A. B. is indebted to the said C. D. in the sum of £   , for the recovery whereof the said C. D. has threatened to commence immediate proceedings against the said A. B.; and whereas, in order to induce the said C. D. to forego such proceedings, the said A. B. hath proposed to execute the assurance hereby made, which the said C. D. has agreed to accept [*the recitals to be inserted here will of course vary according to the circumstances of the case. If the bill of sale is given for money advanced on its execution, no recitals will be necessary*]: Now this indenture witnesseth, that, in order to secure to the said C. D. the payment of the said sum of £   and interest thereon, he the said A. B. doth hereby assign unto the said C. D., his executors, administrators and assigns, all and every the goods, chattels, utensils, implements and things [which are particularly specified in the schedule hereunder written and] in, about or belonging to the messuage or dwelling-house and premises now in the occupation of the said A. B., situate at   aforesaid, To have, receive and take the premises hereby assigned unto the said C. D., his executors, administrators and assigns: and it is hereby declared, that this security shall extend to all chattels and effects which shall at any time, during the continuance thereof, be in or upon the before-mentioned premises, notwithstanding the same may not be in or upon the said premises at the date hereof, it being the understanding of the parties hereto that immediately any chattels or effects of the said A. B. shall be in or upon the said premises, such chattels and effects shall be subject to this security in the same manner as if they had been on the said premises at the date hereof (a): Provided nevertheless, that if the said A. B., his executors or administrators, shall pay unto the said C. D., his executors, administrators or assigns, the sum of £   , with interest thereon after the rate of 5*l.* per cent. per annum, on demand in writing under the hand of the said C. D., his executors, administrators or assigns, or his or their agent, given to the said A. B., his executors, administrators or assigns, or left at his or their last or usual place of abode in England, or at the said messuage or dwelling-house situate at   aforesaid, without any deduction, and observe and perform the covenants and provisions hereinafter contained on the part of the said A. B., his executors, administrators and assigns, these presents shall be void; and for more effectually securing to the said C. D., his executors, administrators and assigns, the payment of the said sum of £   and interest, the said A. B. doth hereby irrevocably appoint the said C. D., his executors and administrators, the true and lawful attorney and attornies of him the said A. B. in his or their name or names or otherwise, at any time or times hereafter, to sign, seal and deliver,

---

(a) The above clause is inserted in accordance with the Lord Chancellor's decision in *Reeve* v. *Whitmore*, 12 Weekly Rep. 113.

or at his or their option by gift or delivery, to make and perfect any assignment or transfer of any goods, chattels and effects not legally passing by virtue of these presents, and which the said A. B. shall before the passing of this security become beneficially possessed or entitled to or enabled to bind or affect, and all or any part of the interest of the said A. B. therein or thereto, and that whether the said goods, chattels and effects may be in or upon the before-mentioned premises or elsewhere: Provided always, that if default shall be made in payment of the said sum of £   and interest, contrary to the proviso hereinbefore contained, it shall be lawful for the said C. D., his executors, administrators and assigns, to receive and take into his or their absolute possession, and thenceforth to hold and enjoy, the premises hereby assigned, and to sell the same by public sale or private contract, for such price as can be reasonably gotten for the same, and to receive the monies to arise by such sale, and reimburse himself or themselves all expenses which he or they may incur in and about such sale, and also relating to the receipt and recovery of the said sum of £   and interest or otherwise in relation to the premises, and in the next place to reimburse himself and themselves the said sum of £
and the interest thereof, and such other sum as shall be due to him or them by virtue hereof, and to pay any surplus unto the said A. B., his executors, administrators or assigns; and the said A. B. doth by these presents irrevocably empower the said C. D., his executors, administrators and assigns, in person or by deputy, and with or without others, at any time or times to enter, and if necessary to break into, any dwelling-house for the time being belonging to or occupied or used by the said A. B., in which any property affected by this security shall be or reasonably supposed to be, and to inspect and take an inventory of or to remove or otherwise convert to the purposes of these presents all such property, and deal with the same in all respects as the said C. D., his executors, administrators or assigns, shall think proper; and it is hereby declared, that until default shall be made in pay-

ment of the said principal sum of £   and interest, contrary to the aforesaid proviso, it shall be lawful for the said A. B., his executors or administrators, to make use of (but not to remove from the premises) the premises hereby assigned without any hindrance by the said C. D., his executors, administrators or assigns; and the said A. B. doth hereby for himself, his heirs, executors and administrators, covenant with the said C. D., his executors and administrators, that the said A. B., his heirs, executors or administrators, will on demand in writing under the hand of the said C. D., his executors, administrators or assigns, or his or their agent, given or left as hereinbefore mentioned, pay unto him or them the sum of £   , with interest thereon after the rate of 5*l*. per centum per annum, without any deduction : and also that he the said A. B. hath not heretofore made, permitted or suffered, nor will at any time hereafter make, permit or suffer, any act, deed, matter or thing whereby or by means whereof the premises hereby assigned are or may be in anywise affected, incumbered or prejudicially affected; and also that he the said A. B., his executors or administrators, will, so long as any money shall remain due on this security, insure and keep insured the chattels and premises hereby assigned from damage by fire in some respectable insurance office in London or Westminster, in the name of the said C. D., his executors, administrators or assigns, in the sum of £   , and hand the policy for such insurance and the receipt for the current year's premium and duty to the said C. D., his executors, administrators or assigns, on demand; and that in default of the said policy being so effected or kept on foot as aforesaid, it shall be lawful for the said C. D., his executors, administrators and assigns, to effect or keep on foot the same, and all premiums and other expenses incurred by him or them in so doing shall be repaid on demand by the said A. B., his executors or administrators, and, until repayment, the same shall be a charge on the premises hereby assigned, and bear interest after the rate aforesaid; and also that the said A. B., his executors and administrators, will, during the continuance of this security, keep the chattels and premises hereby assigned in good repair and condition in all respects, and of as high a value at the least as at the time of the execution hereof.

In witness, &c.

BONDS.
34.
From the Manager of a Brewery and his Sureties.

KNOW all men by these presents, that we A. B., of &c., C. D., of &c., and E. F., of &c., are jointly and severally held and firmly bound unto G. H., of &c., brewer, in the penal sum of £   of lawful money of Great Britain, to be paid to the said G. H., his executors, administrators or assigns, or his or their lawful attorney or attornies, for which payment to be faithfully and truly made we bind ourselves jointly and each of us bindeth himself severally, and our and each of our heirs, executors and administrators, and every of them, firmly by these presents. Sealed with our respective seals. Dated this   day of   , 18   .

Whereas the above-named G. H. hath taken the above-named A. B. into his service, for the managing, superintending and conducting his trade or business of a brewer, and as his receiver of the rents and profits of the messuages, cottages, lands, tenements and hereditaments of him the said G. H. in the said county of   , and the above-bounden C. D. and E. F. have agreed to join with the said A. B. in the above-written bond or obligation for his fidelity in the said employ: Now the condition of the above-written bond or obligation is such that if the said A. B. do and shall from time to time and at all times, so long as he shall be in the service or employ of the said G. H., well, truly and faithfully account for, pay over and deliver unto him the said G. H., his executors, administrators, partners or assigns, or to such other person or persons as he or they shall direct, all and every the sum and sums of money, books, papers, matters and things of or belonging to the said G. H. which shall at any time and from time to time be received by or come to the hands of the said A. B., and also do and shall act and conduct himself at all times with fidelity, integrity and punctuality in and concerning the matters and things which shall or may be reposed in or entrusted to him as such manager and receiver as aforesaid, and do and shall return and make good any such monies, books, papers, matters or things as he may embezzle, take or misemploy within the space of seven days after he shall have been justly accused thereof, or in default thereof, if the said C. D. and E. F., or either of them, do and shall within the space of fourteen days after he or they shall have had notice in writing from the said G. H. of any such default, made due and sufficient repayment, restitution or compensation for the loss or damage which he the said G. H. shall have thereby sustained, then the above-written bond or obligation shall be void, otherwise the same shall remain in full force and effect.

Signed, sealed and delivered by
 the above-named   .

35.

Accompanying Marriage Settlement for securing £1,000 *to Wife if she survives Husband, or dies leaving Issue, with the Interest to her for Life.*

KNOW all men by these presents, that I [*husband*], of &c., am held and firmly bound to [*trustees*] in the sum of 2,000*l.* of lawful money of Great Britain, to be paid to the said [*trustees*], or to any two or one of them, or to their or his certain attorney, executors, administrators or assigns, for which payment to be well and truly made I bind myself, my heirs, executors and administrators, and every of them, firmly by these presents. Sealed with my seal. Dated this   day of , 18 .

Whereas a marriage hath been agreed upon, and is intended shortly to be had and solemnized between the said [*husband*] and [*wife*] of , spinster: and whereas, on the treaty for the said marriage, it was agreed for the consideration mentioned in a certain indenture already prepared and intended to bear even date herewith, and made between the said [*husband*] of the first part, the said [*wife*] of the second part, and the said [*trustees*] of the third part, that the said [*husband*] should enter into the above-written bond or obligation, with such condition thereto as is hereinafter contained: Now therefore the condition of the above-written bond or obligation is such, that if the above-bounden [*husband*] do and shall during the joint lives of himself and the said [*wife*] pay to the said [*trustees*], or the survivors or survivor of them, or the executors or administrators of such survivor, their or his assigns, the yearly sum of 50*l.* by equal half-yearly payments, without any deduction, on the   day of   , and the   day of   in every year (the first payment being made on the   day of   next); and if the executors or administrators of the said [*husband*] do and shall within six calendar months after his death, in case the said [*wife*] shall survive him or die in his lifetime leaving issue living at the time of the death of the said [*husband*], well and truly pay unto the said [*trustees*], or the survivors or survivor of them, or the executors or administrators of such survivor, their or his assigns, the sum of 1,000*l.*, without any deduction, then the above-written bond or obligation shall be void, or otherwise shall remain in full force and virtue.

36.

Common Money Bond.

KNOW all men by these presents, that we A. B., of &c., and C. D., of &c., are held and firmly bound to E. F., of &c., in the penal sum of £   sterling, to be paid to the said E. F., or to his certain attorney, executors, administrators or assigns, for which payment to be well and truly made we bind ourselves and each of us, our and each of our heirs, executors and administrators, and every of them, jointly and severally firmly by these presents. Sealed with our seals. Dated the day of , 18 .

The condition of the above-written bond or obligation is such, that if the above-bounden A. B. and C. D., or either of them, their or either of their heirs, executors or administrators shall, on demand, pay unto the said E. F., his executors, administrators or assigns, the sum of £   sterling, with interest for the same after the rate of £   per cent. per annum, without deduction, then the above-written bond or obligation shall be void, otherwise shall be and remain in full force and virtue.

Signed, sealed and delivered
  in the presence of   .   (L.S.)

37.

Defeasance to a Bond conditioned for replacing a Sum of Stock, and the Payment of Annual Sums in lieu of Dividends.

WHEREAS the above-bounden A. B. has requested the said C. D. to lend him the sum of £   stock of the £5 per Cent. Navy Annuities, transferable at the Bank of England, the said C. D. hath caused the same stock to be sold, and upon or immediately before the execution of the above-written obligation paid the produce thereof, amounting to the sum of £   , unto the above-bounden A. B., which he doth hereby acknowledge and admit, and it hath been agreed by and between the said A. B. and C. D. that the same or the like sum of £   stock in the said Navy £5 per Cent. Annuities shall be replaced and transferred to him the said C. D. at the time and in manner hereinafter mentioned: Now the condition of the above-bounden obligation is such, that if the above-bounden A. B., his heirs, executors or administrators, or any or either of them, shall and do on or before the   day of   next ensuing the date hereof, purchase the sum of £   stock of the £5 per Cent. Navy Annuities, transferable at the Bank of England, and transfer or cause the same to be transferred unto or into the name or names of the said C. D., or of his executors, administrators or assigns, or unto or into the name or names of such other person or persons as he or they shall direct or appoint, and well and truly pay or cause to be paid unto the said C. D., his executors, administrators or assigns, in lieu of the dividends thereof, such sum or sums of money as the said C. D., his executors, administrators or assigns, would have been entitled to receive as or for the dividends of the said sum of £   stock, £5 per Cent. Navy Annuities, in case the same had continued standing in his or their own name, for his or their proper use and benefit, at such time or times, in such shares or proportions, and in such manner, as the same dividends would have been payable to him or them in case the same had not been sold in manner aforesaid, then the above-written obligation to be void and of no effect, otherwise to be and remain in full force and virtue.

Composition Deeds.

38.

THIS INDENTURE, made the   day of   18 , between J. R. W. A., of &c., of the one part, and the undersigned creditors of the said J. R. W. A. of the other part : Whereas the said J. R. W. A. from divers causes is unable to pay us the said several creditors full 20s. in the pound : and whereas the said J. R. W. A. hath applied to us to receive and take a composition of 2s. 6d. in the pound in full satisfaction and discharge of our several and respective demands on him payable on the 9th day of March, 1863, which we the several creditors signing these presents have agreed to do, and being a majority in number representing three-fourths in value of the creditors of the said J. R. W. A. whose debts respectively amount to 10l. and upwards, have agreed to accept such composition as aforesaid, and in consideration thereof and on payment thereof, or whenever thereafter called on for the purpose, hereby severally undertake and agree to execute to the said J. R. W. A. a good and sufficient release in the law of our several and respective claims and demands on him. In witness, &c.

Held, that the above deed was in compliance with the 192nd section of the Bankruptcy Act, 1861, for following reasons:—

1. That it sufficiently appeared from the terms of the deed that it was intended to be for the benefit of all the creditors and not only of those who had signed it.

2. That as each creditor was only bound to release his claim after he had received the composition on his debt, he had a sufficient security for the payment of such composition.

3. That notwithstanding the case of *Tetley* v. *Taylor*, 1 E. & B. 521 (which was decided on the Bankrupt Law Consolidation Act of 1849), a cessio bonorum is not required to render a deed good under section 192 of the Bankruptcy Act, 1861. *Clapham* v. *Atkinson*, 12 Weekly Rep. 342.

───◆───

39.

THIS DEED, made the   day of   18 , between G. C. P., of &c., of the one part, and S. P., of &c., on behalf of and with the assent of the undersigned creditors of the said G. C. P., of the other part, Witnesseth that the said G. C. P. hereby conveys all his estate and effects to the said S. P., to be applied and administered for the said creditors in like manner as if the said G. C. P. had been at the date thereof duly adjudged bankrupt: and the creditors of the said G. C. P. assenting thereto, being fully satisfied that his estate will not realise more than 5*s.* in the pound, agree to accept the sum of 5*s.* in the pound in discharge of their respective debts, to be paid within twelve months from the date hereof: and the said G. C. P. doth hereby expressly declare that the whole of the debts owing by him and upon which the said composition will be payable do not exceed the sum of 2,100*l.*

MARTIN, B., said of the above deed, "With regard to the deed itself, so far from considering it void, I think it is the only good deed of the kind that has come before us, and that it has all the operation that such deeds were intended by the legislature to have."

[To make this deed complete, a short covenant to execute a release should be added, as in the last precedent (*Ipstones Park Company Limited* v. *Pattinson*, 12 Weekly Rep. 344.)]

40.

THIS INDENTURE, made the   day of   18 , between A. B., of &c. [trading under the style or firm of A. B. & Co.] of the one part, and all the creditors of the said A. B., of the other part: Whereas the said A. B. from divers causes is unable to pay his creditors 20s. in the pound : and whereas the said A. B. hath applied to his said creditors to receive and take a composition of 5s. in the pound, in full satisfaction and discharge of their several and respective debts, claims and demands on him, such composition to be payable on the 31st day of December next, which the several creditors executing these presents or in writing assenting thereto have agreed to do, and being a majority in number representing three-fourths in value of the creditors of the said A. B. whose debts respectively amount to 10*l*. and upwards, have agreed to accept such composition in full satisfaction as aforesaid, and in consideration thereof, and on payment thereof or whenever thereafter called upon for that purpose, hereby severally for themselves and their partners, and for their several executors, administrators and assigns, covenant with the said A. B., his executors and administrators, to execute to him the said A. B., his executors and administrators, a good and sufficient release in the law of all their several and respective debts, claims and demands on him. And in consideration of the covenant hereinbefore contained, the said A. B. doth hereby for himself, his executors and administrators, covenant with all his creditors to pay them the said composition of 5s. in the pound on their said several debts on the 31st day of

December next. In witness whereof the said parties to these presents have hereunto set their hands and seals the day and year first above written.

41.

This Indenture, made &c., between A. B., of &c., of the first part, C. D., of &c., and E. F., of &c., of the second part, and the several other persons whose names and seals are hereunto subscribed and set, who, with the said C. D. and E. F., are a majority in number, and represent three-fourths in value of the creditors of the said A. B. whose debts amount to 10*l*. and upwards, and concur in this deed on behalf of themselves and all others (if any) the creditors of the said A. B., of the third part : Whereas the said A. B. is indebted to divers persons in divers sums of money (*b*), and being unable to pay the same in full he some time since proposed to his creditors, and it was mutually agreed between the said A. B. and the said parties hereto of the second and third parts on behalf of themselves and all other (if any) the creditors of the said A. B., that the said A. B. should pay to or in trust for all his creditors and that they should accept from him a cash composition of 10*s*. in the pound on the full amount of their respective debts, and in part satisfaction thereof, and also that the said A. B. should enter into the covenant in that behalf hereinafter contained for payment of the balance or remainder of the said debts, but without interest, by such instalments, at such times and in such manner as is hereinafter expressed : and further, that in consideration of the premises the creditors should give to the said A. B. such release as is hereinafter contained : and whereas, in pursuance of the said arrangement, the said A. B. has paid to the said C. D. and E. F. (*c*) a composition or sum

---

(*b*) There should be a schedule to include the names and the amount of the debts of *all the creditors*, whether they execute or assent to this deed or not; but this schedule had better not be annexed to the deed lest the effect of the deed should be lost by the inadvertent omission of some creditor.

(*c*) Several deeds of this description have not been upheld, on the ground that they do not provide equally for all the creditors (executing and nonof 10s. in the pound on the amount of the several debts due to the creditors of the said A. B. to be paid to such creditors respectively on demand as hereinafter provided, as the said parties hereto of the second and third parts do hereby severally acknowledge: Now this indenture witnesseth, that, in further pursuance of the said arrangement and in consideration of the premises and of the release hereinafter contained, he the said A. B. doth hereby for himself, his heirs, executors and administrators, covenant with the said parties hereto of the second and third parts, and each and every of them, and each and every of their executors and administrators on behalf as well of themselves respectively as also of all other (if any) the creditors of the said A. B., that he the said A. B., his heirs, executors or administrators will pay to the said C. D. and E. F., or the survivor of them, or the executors or administrators of such survivor or other the trustees or trustee for the time being of these presents, the balance or remainder of the several debts due to the several creditors of the said A. B. without interest, by the several instalments and in manner hereinafter mentioned, that is to say, the sum of 2s. in the pound on the amount of the said debts respectively, on the   day of   , which will be in the year 1865, the like sum on the   day of   , which will be in the year 1866, the like sum on the   day of   , which will be in the year 1867, the like sum, which will be in the year 1868, and the like sum on the   day of   , which will be in the year 1869: and it is hereby agreed and declared between and by the parties to these presents, and in particular the said A. B. doth hereby for himself, his heirs, executors and administrators, covenant and declare with and to his several creditors and their respective executors and administrators, that the said C. D. and E. F., or the survivor of them, or the executors or administrators of such survivor, or other the trustees or trustee for the time being, shall and will tender and pay (*d*), to the several creditors of the said A. B. or their re-

executing); and in a recent case (*Ex parte Cockburn*, 3 New Rep. 227), the Lord Chancellor suggested such a provision as this might place all the creditors in as far as possible a position of equality, and so get over the difficulty.

(*d*) There should be a tender made to all creditors.

spective executors, administrators or assigns, whether parties to these presents or not, rateably and in proportion to the amount of their respective debts, as well the said composition of 10s. in the pound on their respective debts already received by the said C. D. and E. F. as aforesaid, as also the several further instalments or sums of money hereinbefore covenanted to be paid on the residue of the said debts as and when the same shall be received by the said C. D. and E. F., or the survivor of them, or the executors or administrators of such survivors or other the trustees or trustee for the time being of these presents, in pursuance of the covenant in that behalf hereinbefore contained, and, after making the several tenders or payments aforesaid, shall and may retain and pay to themselves (*e*), the said C. D. and E. F., or to their respective executors, administrators or assigns their proportion of the said composition and instalments respectively in respect of the debts due to them as aforesaid: And this indenture also witnesseth, that, in further pursuance of the said arrangement and in consideration of the premises and of the covenants hereinbefore contained, they the said parties hereto of the second and third parts, on behalf of themselves and all others (if any) the creditors of the said A. B., do and every of them doth hereby absolutely release and discharge the said A. B., his heirs, executors and administrators, and his and their estate and effects, of and from all and singular the debts or sums of money mentioned in the Schedule hereunder written, and of and from all other (if any) sums of money, bills, bonds, notes, accounts, reckonings, costs, charges, damages, expenses, claims and demands whatsoever, either at law or in equity, which the several creditors of the said A. B., or their or any of their partners respectively, or any other person or persons whom they or any of them respectively can bind by these presents, now have or otherwise can or may, or otherwise could or might, have, claim, challenge or demand of,

(*e*) I have postponed the right of the trustees to retain their debts till they have paid the other creditors, in order to avoid the suggestion that by the actual receipt of the money they are placed in a superior position to the other creditors. The trustees should of course be nominated by or with the concurrence of the creditors.

from or against the said A. B., his heirs, executors or administrators, or his or their estate or effects or any of them, for or by reason of any other matter, cause or thing whatsoever relating to the premises : provided always, and it is hereby agreed and declared, that nothing in these presents contained shall be construed to give to the parties hereto of the second and third parts respectively, any preference or right to priority of payment, in respect of their respective debts or any part thereof respectively over the other creditors (if any) of the said A. B.: provided also, and it is hereby further agreed and declared, that these presents are intended to be and shall (so far as lawfully may be) operate as a composition deed within the meaning of the provisions of the 192nd section of the Bankruptcy Act, 1861, in that behalf.

In witness, &c.

[NOTE.—The above deed was drawn by counsel in 1864, after thoroughly considering the effect of the prior decisions.]

42.

Form of Assent to a Composition Deed.

THE undersigned creditor of A. B., of , in the of [*merchant*] (trading under the style or firm of A. B. & Co.) hereby assent to and approve of a deed of composition, dated the day of , 1864, and made between the said A. B. of the one part and his creditors of the other part, whereby the said A. B. covenants to pay all his creditors a composition of 5s. in the pound on their debts, and in consideration thereof the said creditors covenant to release the said A. B. from their said debts. Dated this day of 1864.

43.

Another Form of Assent to a Composition Deed.

THE undersigned creditors of A. B., of &c. [*trading under the firm of " A. B. & Co."*] hereby assent to and approve of a deed of inspectorship, dated the day of , 1864, and made between the said A. B. (thereinafter called "the said debtor") of the first part, C. D., of &c., and E. F., of &c., (thereinafter called "the said inspectors") of the second part, and the several persons, companies and copartnership firms, who at the date thereof were respectively creditors of the said A. B., or who would be entitled to prove under an adjudication of bankruptcy against the said A. B., founded on a petition filed on the day of the date of the said deed, thereinafter called "the said creditors" of the third part, whereby the said debtor covenants to wind up his estate for the benefit of the said creditors under the direction of the said inspectors. Dated this   day of   , 1864.

Conditions of Sale.

44.

Of Freehold Property in Lots where an unexceptionable Title can be produced.

1. The highest bidder for each lot shall be the purchaser, and if any dispute shall arise between two or more bidders, the lot shall be immediately put up again at the last undisputed bidding.

2. The auctioneer shall fix the advance to be made on each bidding previous to commencing the sale, and no person shall retract his or her bidding.

3. Each purchaser shall immediately after the sale pay to the auctioneer a deposit of £   per cent. in part payment of the purchase money, and sign an agreement for payment of the remainder on the   day of   next at the office of Mr.   , solicitor for the vendor. Each purchaser will be entitled to possession on the completion of his purchase, and if from any cause whatever the completion of any purchase is delayed beyond the said   day of   next, the purchaser in such case shall pay interest upon the amount of his or her purchase money at the rate of £   per cent. per annum, until the completion of the purchase.

4. The vendor will within seven days from the day of sale,

at his own expense, make and deliver to the purchaser of each lot, on his requesting the same, an abstract of title to the property sold, and every recital or statement in a deed, will or other document of title, dated twenty years or upwards prior to the day of sale, shall be sufficient evidence of the instrument or matter recited or stated, and neither the production nor a covenant for the production of any such instrument shall be required, and the purchaser shall not require evidence of seisin of any testator named in the abstract.

5. The purchaser shall within ten days after the delivery of the abstract state in writing, and transmit to the office of the solicitors to the vendor, all his objections to and requisitions on the title shown by the abstract; in case no such statement shall be so delivered within such time, the purchaser shall be considered to have approved of and accepted the title, and in case of such statement being so delivered he shall be considered to have approved and accepted the title, except as mentioned in such statement, and any answer to any statement of objections to or requisitions on the title shall, within seven days from the delivery of such answer, be replied to by a statement in writing transmitted as aforesaid, and any such answer not so replied to within such time shall be considered satisfactory. And in case any purchaser shall take any objection or make any requisition, and the vendor shall be unable or unwilling to remove or comply with the same, the vendor shall be at liberty, notwithstanding any answers or requisitions, or any negotiations as to the same, by notice in writing from his solicitor, delivered to such purchaser or his solicitor, to annul and put an end to the contract for sale, and in such case the purchaser's deposit shall after such notice be returned in full satisfaction of all claims, and time shall in every instance be the essence of this condition.

6. The expense of the production and inspection of all deeds, evidences and writings relating to the title, and of all journeys incidental to such production or inspection, and of preparing, perusing, approving and executing all instruments required to be executed under the seventh condition, and of procuring, making and verifying all declarations, proofs,

official, attested or stamped or other copies of or extracts from acts of parliament, decrees, awards, registers, deeds, wills, probates, administrations or other documents and evidences, whether required for perfecting or verifying the abstract, or for the purpose of identifying the premises sold, or for any other purpose, whether provided for by these conditions or not, and all searches and applications for any such evidence and instruments, shall be paid by the purchasers.

7. Deeds and documents of title not relating exclusively to the property sold will not be given up, and purchasers shall be satisfied with having reasonably secured to them the production and delivery at their expense of copies of the deeds in the possession of the vendor, and as to any deeds or documents of title of which the vendor has not the possession, purchasers shall not require the same to be produced or comprised in the instrument to be executed as aforesaid.

8. If any misstatement, error or omission be discovered in this particular of sale, such error or misstatement is not to annul the sale, but a compensation shall be allowed or given by the vendor or purchaser, as the case may require.

9. If the purchaser shall object or fail to comply with any of the above conditions, the lot shall be resold, either by public auction or private contract, at such time and place, subject to such conditions, and in such manner in every respect as the vendor shall deem meet; and the deficiency in price (if any) which shall happen on such second sale, and all expenses attending the same, shall immediately be made good and paid by the purchaser on the first sale, in the manner mentioned in the third condition, and, in case of nonpayment, the whole or such part of the same as shall not be paid shall be recoverable as and for liquidated damages.

MEMORANDUM.

I   of   do hereby acknowledge myself to be the purchaser of lot   of the estate described in the within particulars of sale, at and for the sum of £   , and having paid   as a deposit and in part payment thereof, I hereby bind myself to complete the purchase of the said lot in every respect agreeably to the conditions of sale hereunto annexed.

Witness my hand this   day of   18   .

     £ s. d.
Amount of sale . . .   Purchaser.
Deposit . . . .

Balance to be paid

  As agent of the vendor, I hereby confirm the above sale and contract.
Witness   Auctioneers.
Abstract of title to be sent to   .

[*The following clause may be inserted where it is necessary to commence the title with a recent deed, in lieu of the* 6*th condition.*]

The title shall commence with indentures of lease and release of the   and   days of June, 18 , and the vendor shall not be required to produce or show, nor shall the purchaser be entitled to require or investigate, any earlier title than the said indentures, and all attested and other copies of or extracts from any deeds, wills, administrations or other documents whatsoever, and all certificates of marriage, baptisms and burials, and all evidence of heirship or intestacy, required by the purchaser for the verification of the abstract or otherwise, are to be made or procured at the expense in all respects of the purchaser, who shall also bear and pay all the expenses of registration or procuring any assignments or conveyances of any outstanding terms of years, or other outstanding legal estate or estates, including the expense of any administrations which may be necessary, and also the expenses of deducing and making out the title to such terms and estates respectively. The vendor shall not be required to produce the originals of any deeds not in his possession, notwithstanding it may appear that he is entitled to the benefit of a covenant entered into for the production thereof.

45.

Of Property held under an Underlease, where it is left to the Auctioneer to determine at the Time of Sale whether the Property is to be sold in more than one Lot.

1. THE highest bidder shall be the purchaser, and if any dispute arise between two or more bidders, the lot in dispute shall be put up again and resold.

2. No person shall advance less than £   at each bidding, nor retract his or her bidding.

3. The purchaser shall, immediately after the sale, pay into the hands of the auctioneer a deposit of £   per cent. in part payment of the purchase-money, and sign an agreement for completion of his or her purchase, and for payment of the remainder of the purchase-money on the   day of   next, with interest thereon at £   per cent. per annum, from the   day of   preceding until completion, at the office of   , when and where the purchase shall be completed, and the purchaser shall be let into possession of the premises, or into the receipt of the rents and profits thereof, as from the said   day of   , and all outgoings shall be cleared by the vendor to that day.

4. Within four days from the day of sale the vendor shall, at his own expense, deliver an abstract of his title to the purchaser or his or her solicitors; but no purchaser shall require the production of the lessor's title or any title prior to the underlease under which the property is held, or be at liberty to inquire into or make any objections to such prior title; notwithstanding any such title may be recited or noticed in such underlease; and the purchaser shall presume that the covenants contained in such underlease have been duly performed to the time of completion. And all objections to, or requisitions on, the title (if any) shall be made in writing, and delivered to the vendor's solicitors within ten days from the delivery of the abstract, or shall be considered as waived; and if any such objections or requisitions shall be made, which the vendor shall be unable or unwilling to remove, the

vendor shall be at liberty to rescind the contract and return the deposit money only, without interest, damages or costs. Upon payment of the remainder of the purchase-money, the vendor shall assign the premises to the purchaser, who shall, at his or her own expense, prepare the assignment. The vendor, being a mortgagee, shall not enter into any covenants except the usual one, that he has not done any act to incumber.

5. Should the property be sold in more than one lot, then the purchaser of the largest lot in value will, after the sale of all the lots, be entitled to the custody of all the documents in the hands of the vendor relating to the property purchased by him, but such purchaser shall enter into the usual covenants with the purchasers of the remainder of the lots for the production and furnishing copies of the said documents. If all the lots are not sold, the vendor will retain the said documents, and enter into the usual covenants for the production and furnishing copies thereof with the purchasers of such of the lots as shall have been sold; such covenants, nevertheless, to be determinable on the vendor parting with the said documents, and procuring the person to whom they shall be delivered to enter into the usual covenants for the production and furnishing copies thereof with the persons then entitled to the benefit of the vendor's covenants. The deeds containing any such covenants as aforesaid, whether original or substituted, shall be prepared by and at the expense of the covenantees.

6. If the purchaser shall neglect or refuse to comply with any of the above conditions, his or her deposit money shall be actually forfeited to the vendor, who shall be at liberty to re-sell the premises, and the deficiency (if any) occasioned by such second sale, together with all expenses attending the same, shall on demand be made good to the vendor by the purchaser at this sale; and in default shall be recoverable as liquidated damages.

Lastly. If any mistake or error whatever shall appear in the particulars of the property, such mistake or error shall not annul the sale, but a compensation or equivalent shall be given or taken, as the case may require, such compensation or equivalent to be ascertained by a reference in the usual way.

[*Here add the purchase contract, as at p.* 200.]

46.

Of Leasehold Property in Lots, by a Mortgagee, with special Stipulations.

[*The three first conditions may be taken from Precedent* 45, *p.* 202.]

4. THE abstract of the vendor's title to each lot will be delivered to each purchaser, or his solicitor, within seven days after the sale. The title to lot 1 shall commence with an indenture of lease dated the   day of   , and that to lot 2 with an indenture of lease dated the   day of   , and the purchaser of such lots respectively shall not be entitled to call for the production of, or to investigate, or make any objection to or requisition in respect of the title of the lessors respectively, or their right to grant such leases respectively; and it shall not be a ground of objection that the property comprised in lot 1 is held by the vendor under a derivative lease; and the production of a receipt for the last payment of rent accrued on each of the said lots respectively, previously to the completion of the purchase, shall be conclusive evidence that all the covenants and conditions in the said leases respectively have been respectively performed and observed up to the completion of the purchase of the said lots respectively.

5. The purchaser of each lot shall, within ten days after the delivery of the abstract of title, give the vendor, or his solicitor, a statement in writing of the objections or requisitions (if any) not precluded by these conditions to or on the title of the lot purchased by him, and every objection not taken and so communicated within such period shall be deemed waived, the title shall be deemed absolutely accepted and the purchaser precluded from objecting thereto. And if

any purchaser shall insist on any objection or requisition made within the time limited, which the vendor shall be unable or unwilling to remove or comply with, the vendor may, by notice in writing, to be given to such purchaser or his solicitor, at any time, notwithstanding any negotiation in respect of any objection or requisition, annul the sale, and the auctioneer shall thereupon return to such purchaser his deposit, but without any interest, costs or compensation whatever.

6. The leases of the property will be produced for inspection on the day of sale, and the purchaser or purchasers shall not afterwards refuse to perform his, her or their contract or contracts, on the ground of any covenants, stipulations, restrictions, conditions, matters or things therein respectively contained.

7. All extracts, attested, official or other copies of deeds, wills or other instruments, and all certificates, statutory or other declarations, and other documents which may be required either for the purpose of verifying the abstract, identifying the property of any persons or otherwise, are to be procured, made, furnished and obtained at the expense of the purchaser requiring the same.

8. Upon payment of the remainder of the purchase-money, pursuant to the third condition, the vendor will execute a proper assurance to the purchaser, such assurance to be tendered or left at the offices of the said   for execution by the vendor ten days at least before the said   day of   next.

9. The sale being made under powers of sale contained in two mortgage deeds, the purchaser shall not require the concurrence of any person interested in the equity of redemption, and shall not require any other covenants to be entered into than the usual covenant against incumbrances.

10. In case both lots shall be sold, the purchaser of the larger lot in value shall be entitled to the custody and possession of such of the title deeds as have reference to and include both of the said lots, and shall enter into a covenant for their production to the purchaser of the other lot; but in case

either lot shall remain unsold, such deeds shall remain in the custody of the vendor, who in that case shall enter into the usual defeasible covenant for the production of the same; and such covenant, and all substituted deeds of covenant, and all other deeds required for the assignment of the respective lots, shall be prepared by and at the expense of the purchasers.

Lastly. If any purchaser shall fail to comply with the above conditions, his deposit shall thereupon be forfeited to the vendor, and the vendor shall be at liberty to re-sell the lot bought by such purchaser, either by public auction or private contract, at such time and generally in such manner as the vendor shall think fit; and the deficiency in price (if any) which may happen on such second sale, and all costs and expenses attending the same, shall immediately after such second sale be made good and paid to the vendor by such defaulter at this present sale, and in case of nonpayment, the whole or such part of the deficiency and expenses as shall not be paid shall be recoverable by the vendor, as and for liquidated damages; and it shall not be necessary for the vendor to tender any assignment to the purchaser, and any profit at such second sale shall belong to the vendor.

[*The purchase contract may be taken from Precedent, p.* 200.]

47.

Of Freehold and Leasehold Property, and a Freehold Rent-charge, sold in Lots at a Sale, with special Stipulations.

[*The preliminary conditions can be taken from any of the foregoing Precedents.*]

THAT the title to all the freehold property shall commence with certain indentures of lease and release dated respectively the   and   days of   . The title to lot   shall commence with the will of   dated the   (by which will the rent-charge was created), and no earlier title shall be required; and the title to lot   shall commence with the lease under which it is held, and the purchaser of such lot shall not be entitled to the production of, or to inquire into, or on any ground to object to, the title of the lessors in such lease, whether appearing thereby to be freeholders or only leaseholders, nor shall any objection be taken, or any indemnity required, in consequence of such lot being, together with other property, subject to any superior or other ground rents or covenants; and the production of the last receipt for the rent reserved by the lease shall be deemed conclusive evidence of the satisfactory performance and observance of all the lessee's covenants in the leases up to the time of the completion of the purchase of such lot, and a waiver of all breaches of covenant (if any), and of all right of entry consequent upon any such breaches.

That upon payment of the balance of the purchase-money, [and the amount of the valuation of the fixtures,] at the time and place above mentioned, the vendor and mortgagee shall execute proper conveyances or assignments to the respective purchasers of the several lots purchased by them respectively, but such conveyances or assignments are to be prepared by and at the expense of the respective purchasers.

That every purchaser shall make his objections and requisitions (if any) in respect of the title to the lot or lots purchased by him, and send the same to the office of within fourteen days from the delivery of the abstract, and all objections and requisitions which shall not be made within the time specified shall be taken to be waived, and the abstract shall, as regards any objection or requisition, be considered perfect if it supply the information suggesting the same, although it may be otherwise defective; and in case any objection to or requisition on the title shall be made, on the part of any purchaser, with which the vendor may not be able or willing to comply, it shall be lawful for the vendor to rescind the contract (notwithstanding any conversation which may have passed between, or negotiation or correspondence with, the vendor and the purchaser, or their respective solicitors, with the view to the removal of such objection or requisition) by notice in writing to that effect to the purchaser, or his or her solicitor, and tendering to the purchaser, or his or her solicitor, his or her deposit money, without any interest, costs, damages or expenses, and such tender shall be accepted in full satisfaction of the same.

That no purchaser shall be entitled to call for the production of, or make any objection on account of the non-production of, any deeds or muniments of title of which the vendor shall produce attested copies.

That the recital of certain indentures of lease and release of the   and   days of   in an indenture of release of   shall be sufficient evidence of such indentures. No purchaser shall be entitled to call for the production of the same, or of any further or other evidence than such recital respecting the same indentures.

No objection shall be made by any purchaser of that part of the property now sold, which may be subject to leases or agreements granted or made by the vendor's testator, on account of such leases or agreements, or any of them, being liable to be defeated by reason of the mortgagee not having joined in the granting such leases or agreements, all of which will be delivered to the purchasers, but it shall be no objection to the title that any of such agreements are unstamped, nor shall the vendor be bound or compellable to stamp or cause the same to be impressed with the proper stamp duty.

[*The concluding conditions can be taken from the foregoing Precedents.*]

[N.B.—It may be here mentioned, that where property put up for sale is in mortgage, and not sold by the mortgagee under his power of sale, it is necessary in some part of the particulars or conditions of sale to give notice to the purchaser of the property being in mortgage; otherwise he could require the vendor either to get in the mortgage by a separate deed, or to pay any costs that may be occasioned by the extra length of his conveyance consequent upon the necessity of the recital of the mortgage in the conveyance, and of making the mortgagees parties to it.]

48.

Of Property under a Decree of the Court of Chancery.

1. THE highest bidder for each lot shall be the purchaser, and if any dispute shall arise between two or more bidders, the lot shall be immediately put up again at the last undisputed bidding.

2. The auctioneer shall fix the advance to be made on each bidding previous to commencing the sale, and no person shall retract his or her bidding.

3. The purchaser is at the time of sale to subscribe his name and address to his bidding, and the abstract of title, and all written notices, and communications and summonses, are to be deemed duly delivered to and served upon the purchaser by being left for him at such address, unless or until he is represented by a solicitor.

4. The chief clerk of the said judge will, after the sale, proceed to certify the result, and the   day of   at   of the clock at noon is appointed as the time at which the purchaser or purchasers may, if he or they shall think fit, attend by their solicitors at the chambers of the said judge at   in the county of Middlesex, to settle such certificate. The certificate will then be settled, and will in due course be signed and filed, and become binding without further notice or expense to the purchaser.

5. The vendor is, within three days after such certificate has become binding, to deliver to the purchaser or his solicitor an abstract of the title, commencing as to all the lots with the will of   dated   and established by a decree in chancery in   in a creditors' suit, under an order in which suit the estate was sold in   , and no purchaser shall require any other evidence of the seisin of the said testator than is to be collected or inferred from the abstracted documents, nor make any objection or requisition in respect of the earlier title, notwithstanding any notice thereof or reference thereto in the title abstracted; and the purchaser shall accept as sufficient evidence that   (who in   sold and con-

G.C.   P

veyed the premises to a purchaser in fee) was heir-at-law of   (letters of administration to whose effects were granted in   to   and the said   ) a document in the vendor's possession, purporting to be an affidavit of   (therein noticed to be the half-brother of the said   ), sworn before a master extraordinary in chancery in or about the same year; and every recital or statement in a deed, will or other document of title, dated twenty years or upwards prior to the day of sale, shall be sufficient evidence of the instrument or matter recited or stated; and neither the production nor a covenant for the production of any such instrument shall be required. The purchaser shall not require any further or other evidence relating to the suit of   *v.*   than a short statement, to be contained in the abstract, of the decree, certificate, and order of sale, and shall assume that such order is in all respects regular and binding. The purchaser of more than one lot shall be entitled to only one abstract, all the lots being held under the same title.

6. The purchaser is, under an order for that purpose to be obtained by him, or, in case of his neglect, by the vendor at the cost of the purchaser, upon application at the chambers of the said judge, to pay the amount of his purchase-money into the Bank of England, with the privity of the accountant-general of this court, to the credit of this cause, on or before the   day of   , and if the same is not so paid then the purchaser is to pay interest on his purchase-money at the rate of five pounds per cent. per annum from the said   day of   to the day on which the same is actually paid, and, upon payment of the purchase-money in manner aforesaid, the purchaser is to be entitled to possession, or to the rents and profits, as from the   day of   , down to which time all outgoings are to be paid by the vendor.

7. The purchaser shall, within twenty-one days after the delivery of the abstract, state in writing and transmit to the office of   , the solicitors to the vendor, all his objections to and requisitions on the title shown by the abstract; and in case no such statement shall be so delivered within such time, the purchaser shall be considered to have approved of

and accepted the title; and in case of such statement being so delivered, he shall be considered to have approved of and accepted the title except as mentioned in such statement, and any answer to any statement of objections to or requisitions on the title shall, within seven days from the delivery of such answer, be replied to by a statement in writing transmitted as aforesaid; and any such answer not so replied to within such time shall be considered satisfactory. And in case any purchaser shall take any objection or make any requisition, and the vendor shall be unable or unwilling to remove or comply with the same, or the purchaser shall not, within seven days, have stated in writing that he is satisfied with such answer (if any) as shall have been made thereto, the vendors shall be at liberty, with the approbation of the judge to whom the cause of   v.   stands referred, notwithstanding any answers or requisitions or any negotiation as to the same, by notice in writing from their solicitor delivered to such purchaser or his solicitor, to annul and put an end to the contract for sale; and in such case the purchaser shall not require any compensation whatever, and time shall in every instance be of the essence of this condition.

8. The expense of the production and inspection of all deeds, evidences and writings relating to the title, and the expense of all journeys incidental to such production or inspection, and the expense of preparing, perusing, approving and executing all instruments required to be executed under the ninth condition, and of procuring and making and verifying all declarations, proofs, official, attested or stamped or other copies of or extracts from acts of parliament, decrees, awards, registers, deeds, wills, probates, administrations or other documents and evidences, whether required for perfecting or verifying the abstract, or for the purpose of identifying the premises sold, or for any other purpose, whether provided for by these conditions or not, and all searches and applications for any such evidence and matters, and the registering of any instruments which the purchasers may require to be registered, shall be paid by the purchasers.

9. Deeds and documents of title not relating exclusively to

the property sold will not be given up, and purchasers shall be satisfied with having reasonably secured to them the production and delivery, at their expense, of copies of the deeds in the possession of the vendors; the instruments to be executed for that purpose being, in case of difference, in such form and between such parties as the said judge shall direct, the purchasers not requiring legal covenants, but being satisfied with the production and delivery of copies being reasonably secured to them in equity; and as to any deeds or documents of title of which the vendors have not the possession, purchasers shall not require the same to be produced or comprised in the instrument to be executed as aforesaid.

10. If any misstatement, error or omission be discovered in this particular of sale, such error or misstatement is not to annul the sale, but a compensation, to be settled by the said judge at chambers, shall be allowed or given by the vendors or purchaser as the case may require.

11. If the purchaser shall not pay his purchase-money at the time above specified, or at any other time which may be named in any order for that purpose, and in all other respects perform these conditions, an order may be made by the said judge, upon application at chambers, for the resale of the lot purchased by such purchaser, and for payment by the purchaser of the deficiency (if any) in the price which may be obtained upon such resale, and of the costs and expenses occasioned by such default.

[*These and the conditions immediately preceding will be found useful in many sales, as several of the clauses will frequently be found applicable.*]

49.

Of a Reversionary Interest in Money in the Funds.

[*The three first clauses will be as before.*]

4. The vendor shall at his own expense, within seven days from the day of sale, prepare and deliver to the purchaser an

abstract of title to the property purchased by him, consisting of a copy of so much of the will of   proved on the   day of   (an office copy of which will be produced at the sale) as relates to the property purchased by such purchaser. The purchaser shall be deemed to have full notice of the contents and effect of the will of the said   ; and the statements in the particulars as to the interest of the vendor, the nature of the investment, and the age of the person mentioned in the particulars (whether correct or not) shall be taken and accepted by the purchaser as accurate and correct in every respect, both in law and in fact, and no purchaser shall make any objection or requisition as to any of such statements, or as to the accuracy or correctness thereof.

5. The purchaser shall bear the expense of procuring all certificates of births, deaths and marriages, and all declarations and other evidence which he may require for the purpose of verifying the title to the abstract or otherwise, and of all searches, inquiries and journeys for the above purposes or any of them.

[*The remaining conditions can be taken from the former Precedents.*]

50.

Where Property is held on an Underlease.

THAT the property now offered for sale is subject along with other premises to the rent and covenants reserved and contained in the original demise of the entire premises, dated the   day of   , 18 , granted by A. B. to C. D. and others, but the purchaser shall not require any evidence of the discharge of the premises hereby offered for sale from the said rent and covenants, nor make any requisition or objection as to the same not being sufficiently secured by the other part of the premises charged therewith, neither shall the purchaser require any indemnity in respect of such rent and covenants, nor be entitled to any evidence as to whether the covenants comprised in such original lease have been observed and performed.

51.

If Title not marketable.

THAT if the counsel for the purchaser shall, on the examination of the title, be of opinion that a good title and conveyance cannot be made of the purchased premises within the time limited by the articles [*or* by these conditions] for carrying the same into execution [*or* for completing the said purchase], in that case the same articles [*or* these conditions] shall be at an end, and the purchaser shall be entitled to a return of the deposit, without interest or costs.

52.

Of Freehold Ground Rents.

1. THE highest bidder for each lot shall be the purchaser thereof, and if any dispute arise as to the last or highest bidding for any lot, the same is to be immediately put up again at some former bidding.

2. No person to advance less than 5*l.* on each bidding, nor retract any bidding.

3. Each purchaser is to pay to the auctioneer, at the time of sale, a deposit of 20*l.* per cent. in part payment of the purchase-money, and sign the subjoined agreement for payment of the remainder of such purchase-money, and for the completion of the purchase agreeably to these conditions, at the office of Mr.   , the vendor's solicitor, on the   of   next; and on such payment being made, each purchaser is to be entitled to the rents and profits of the lots purchased by him from that day; and if from any cause whatever, except the wilful default of the vendor, the completion of the purchase be delayed beyond the time specified, the purchaser is to pay interest from that time on the residue of his purchase-money, at the rate of 5*l.* per cent. per annum, until the time of actual completion, without making any claim for or being entitled to any compensation in respect of any such delay.

4. The title of the vendor to the several lots sold shall commence with a conveyance from   , dated   day of   : The purchaser shall not require the production of, or be entitled to investigate or object to, the prior title, notwithstanding there is a covenant for the production of title deeds of prior date. The vendor will within seven days from the day of sale deliver to the purchaser or his solicitor an abstract of his title to the lot or lots sold, commencing as aforesaid. No evidence shall be required for identifying any of the lots with the description, either general or particular, in any of the abstracted deeds or other documents or in the printed particulars. Any certificate or statutory declaration that may be required or necessary for making out or evidencing the vendor's title, and the obtaining all information relating thereto, are to be procured at the expense of the purchaser requiring the same.

5. All objections and requisitions (if any) to the title to be delivered in writing to the vendor's solicitors within ten days from the delivery of the abstract, and any replies to answers made thereto are to be furnished in writing within five days from the delivery of such answers, and all objections and requisitions not so delivered, or the answers to which shall not be replied to as aforesaid, are to be considered waived and the title accepted, although any negotiations may take place afterwards on the subject of such objections or requisitions (and time is to be deemed the essence of the contract); and if from any cause whatever the purchase be not completed agreeably to the conditions by the time specified, the vendor is then, or at any time afterwards, unless these conditions be expressly waived in writing, to be at liberty to annul the contract; and in such case the purchaser is to receive back his deposit money in full discharge of all claims and demands against the vendor.

6. On payment of the remainder of the purchase-money, the vendor will execute a proper conveyance to the purchaser of the lot or lots sold, subject to the existing lease or leases thereof, such conveyance to be prepared by the purchaser's solicitor at his expense, and the engrossment thereof with the

draft to be left at the office of the vendor's solicitor three days prior to the day named for completion. The vendor will retain the before-mentioned conveyance of the   day of   , and the conveyance to the purchaser shall contain a covenant on the part of the vendor to produce the same indenture to the purchaser, his heirs and assigns, such covenant to be determinable on the vendor parting with the said indenture, and procuring the person or persons to whom it shall be delivered to enter into at the purchaser's expense a like covenant with the person or persons who may then be entitled to the benefit of the vendor's covenant.

7. If any error, misstatement, or omission in the particulars shall be discovered, compensation shall be allowed or given by the vendor or purchaser, as the case may require; and such compensation shall be settled, regard being had to the amount of the purchase-money, by the auctioneer at the present sale.

LASTLY. If any purchaser neglect or refuse to observe or comply with these conditions, the deposit-money is to belong absolutely to the vendor, who may re-sell the property without previously tendering a conveyance of the lot or lots sold or giving any notice to such purchaser, and either by public auction or private contract, and subject to these or any altered particulars or conditions, as the vendor may think fit; and any deficiency on such re-sale, with all expenses attending the same, are to be made good by the purchaser at this sale, and recoverable by the vendor as liquidated damages without relief in equity.

53.

To be used where Land originally acquired by a Parish.

THAT in the year   the vendor bought the property, and now sells it subject to the following condition, namely, that it was acquired by the parish in or about the year   , in or by way of exchange for other parish property near   , given up by the parish. A statement of facts collected from the entries in the vestry and other parochial minute books, and from the court rolls of the manor of   , relating to the property, with a copy of the opinion of counsel thereon as to the power of the parish to sell the premises, may be seen by the purchaser before the sale, at the office of Messrs.   ; and a copy of such statement and opinion will be furnished to the purchaser if required, at his or her expense, but the purchaser must accept the title of the parish thereto without further investigation, and without requiring the vendor to give any further evidence or proof of title whatever, or proof of any statement contained in the case submitted to counsel as aforesaid; and the abstract of title to be furnished by the vendor shall commence with a conveyance from the guardians, churchwardens and overseers of the parish of   , dated the   day of   , and such shall be accepted as sufficient root of title to the premises, without it being incumbent on the vendor to abstract, produce, or verify any earlier muniments or facts of title whatever, recited or otherwise noticed or not in the abstracted documents, the purchaser being bound not to investigate or object to the earlier title.

———

CONFIRMATION.

54.

Of a Deed to which either a Widow or a Spinster was a Party, but who married before she executed the Conveyance.

THIS INDENTURE, made the   day of   , 18   , between A. B., of &c. [*husband*] and C. D. his wife, of the one part, and the within-named E. F. of the other part: Whereas since the preparation and engrossment of the within-written indenture and before the execution thereof by the within-named [*wife's maiden name*], the said [*wife's maiden name*] became the wife of the said [*husband*], and she hath, with his privity and consent, executed the same by her present name of [*wife's present name*], and she and the said [*husband*] have also agreed to execute these presents for the purposes hereinafter expressed: Now this indenture witnesseth, that in pursuance of the said agreement, and for the considerations within expressed, the said [*husband*] and [*wife's christian name*] his wife, do and each of them doth hereby ratify and confirm the within-written indenture and the respective grant, covenants and agreements therein expressed and declared, and agree to and with the said E. F., his heirs, executors and administrators, that the within-written indenture and every such grant, covenant or agreement shall, notwithstanding the aforesaid marriage, between the said [*husband*] and [*wife's christian name*] his wife, have the same or the like effect as if the same indenture had before such marriage, and with the privity and consent of the said [*husband*], been duly executed by the said [*wife's christian name*] his wife, by her then name of [*wife's maiden name*]. In witness, &c.

[N.B.—If this deed relates to freehold property it must be acknowledged by the wife.]

———

CONVEYANCES.

55.

Of Freehold by Appointment and Grant, with Covenant to produce Deeds.

THIS INDENTURE, made the   day of   18 , between [*vendor*] of the first part, [*purchaser*] of the second part, and [*trustee to bar dower*] of the third part: Whereas by an indenture dated the   day of   , 18 , and made between   of the first part, the said [*vendor*] of the second part, and [*trustee to bar dower*] of the third part, for the considerations therein mentioned, the hereditaments hereinafter described and granted were assured unto the said [*vendor*] and his heirs, to such uses and in such manner as the said [*vendor*] should appoint; and in default of appointment to the use of the said [*vendor*] and his assigns for life, with remainder to the use of the said [*trustee*], his executors and administrators during the life of the said [*vendor*], in trust for him and his assigns, with remainder to the use of the said [*vendor*], his heirs and assigns: and whereas the said [*vendor*] hath con-

tracted with the said [*purchaser*] for the sale to him of the said hereditaments, and the inheritance thereof in fee simple in possession, free from incumbrances, for the sum of £   :
Now this indenture witnesseth, that, in consideration of the sum of £   sterling to the said [*vendor*] paid by the said [*purchaser*] on the execution hereof, the receipt whereof, and that the same is in full for the purchase of the said hereditaments, the said [*vendor*] doth hereby acknowledge and declare, he the said [*vendor*], in exercise of all powers enabling him in this behalf, doth by these presents appoint, that all and singular the hereditaments hereinafter described and appointed shall from henceforth go, remain and be to the uses hereinafter declared concerning the same: And this indenture also witnesseth, that, for the considerations aforesaid, the said [*vendor*] doth grant and confirm unto the said [*purchaser*] and his heirs, all &c., together with all the easements and appurtenances thereto belonging or in anywise appertaining, To hold the said hereditaments unto the said [*purchaser*] and his heirs [to such uses and in such manner as the said [*purchaser*] shall by deed appoint; and in default of such appointment, to the use of the said [*purchaser*] and his assigns during his life; and after the determination of that estate by any means in his lifetime, to the use of the said [*trustee*], his executors and administrators, during the life of the said [*purchaser*], in trust for him and his assigns; and after the determination of the estate lastly hereinbefore limited], to the use of the said [*purchaser*], his heirs and assigns [and the said [*purchaser*] doth hereby declare that no widow whom he may leave shall be entitled to dower out of or in the said hereditaments]; and the said [*vendor*] doth hereby for himself, his heirs, executors and administrators, covenant with the said [*purchaser*], his heirs and assigns, that (notwithstanding any act or thing by him the said [*vendor*] to the contrary) he the said [*vendor*] now hath in himself full power and authority to appoint and grant the said hereditaments to the uses and in manner aforesaid, free from incumbrances; and also that he the said [*vendor*], and every person claiming as aforesaid any estate or interest in

the said hereditaments, will from time to time hereafter, at the request and costs of the said [*purchaser*], his heirs or assigns, execute or cause to be executed every such further assurance for better and more perfectly assuring the said hereditaments to the uses and in manner aforesaid, as the said [*purchaser*], his heirs and assigns, shall require: and also will from time to time, and at all times hereafter, upon the request and at the costs of the said [*purchaser*], his heirs or assigns, produce and show forth in England, as occasion may require, the deeds, evidences and writings specified in the schedule hereunder written, for the proof, manifestation or defence of the title of the said [*purchaser*], his heirs or assigns, to the said hereditaments; and will, upon the like request and costs, from time to time furnish to the said [*purchaser*], his heirs or assigns, true and attested copies or abstracts of or extracts from the said deeds, evidences and writings, and permit him and them to examine and compare the same with the originals; and also will, in the meantime, keep the same deeds, evidences and writings safe, whole and uncancelled (unless prevented from so doing by fire or other inevitable accident).

[*The following proviso for cesser of the covenant is sometimes added, but cannot be insisted upon by the vendor without express stipulation:*]

Provided always, that in case the said [*vendor*], his heirs or assigns, shall at any time hereafter sell and convey the remaining portion of the hereditaments to which the said deeds, evidences and writings relate as aforesaid, or any part thereof, and shall, at his or their expense, procure the purchaser thereof to enter into and execute a similar covenant with the said [*purchaser*], his heirs and assigns, to that herein contained, then and in such case the covenant hereinbefore contained for that purpose shall cease and be void.

In witness, &c.

56.

Of a Plot of Freehold Land by Vendor on lotting out a Field for Building Purposes.

THIS INDENTURE, made the   day of   , 18 , between A. B., of &c., of the one part, C. D., of &c., of the other part: Whereas the said A. B., being seised to him and his heirs, or otherwise well and sufficiently entitled to the inheritance in fee simple in possession of and in the hereditaments hereinafter described and granted, hath contracted with the said C. D. for the sale to him of the same hereditaments for the sum of £   : Now this indenture witnesseth, that, in consideration of £   sterling to the said A. B. paid by the said C. D. on the execution hereof (the receipt whereof the said A. B. doth hereby acknowledge and discharge the said C. D., his heirs, executors, administrators and assigns, therefrom), he the said A. B. doth hereby grant unto the said C. D. and his heirs the hereditaments described in the first schedule hereunder written and more particularly delineated on the plan hereupon appearing, To hold the said hereditaments unto and to the use of the said C. D., his heirs and assigns; and the said A. B. doth hereby for himself, his heirs, executors and administrators, covenant with the said C. D., his heirs and assigns, that, notwithstanding any act or deed by the said A. B. to the contrary, he hath good right and full power to grant the said hereditaments to the use of the said C. D., his heirs and assigns, free from incumbrances; and, moreover, that the said A. B., and any person claiming under or in trust for him any estate or interest in or out of the said hereditaments, will from time to time and at all times hereafter, at the expense of the person requiring the same, execute every such further assurance for better assuring the said hereditaments to the use of the said C. D., his heirs or assigns, as by him or them shall be reasonably required; and also will from time to time (unless prevented by fire or other inevitable accident) produce to the said C. D., his heirs and assigns, at his or their request and expense, and at such places in England as occasion shall require, for the manifestation and defence of his or their title to the hereditaments hereby granted, the deeds mentioned in the second schedule hereunder written, and at the like request and expense furnish to him or them attested or plain copies or abstracts of or extracts from the said deeds or any of them, and in the meantime keep the same deeds whole and uncancelled; [and the said C. D. doth hereby for himself, his heirs and assigns, covenant with the said A. B., his heirs and assigns, that any messuage or other building to be erected on the land hereby granted shall be set back six inches at the least, in order to provide for the projection of the necessary steps and windows and so and in such manner that the street in which the said messuage or other building may be erected may be of the clear width of twelve yards.]

In witness, &c.

The first Schedule referred to.

All that plot of land, &c.

The second Schedule referred to.

[*This will comprise the deeds covenanted to be produced.*]

57.

Of Freeholds in the City of London in Mortgage to the Trustees of a Loan Society.

THIS INDENTURE, made the   day of   , 18 , between [*vendor*] of the first part, [*mortgagees*] (trustees of the society established and enrolled under the Friendly Societies Acts, and hereinafter called the said trustees) of the second part, and [*purchaser*] of the third part: Whereas the said [*vendor*], being seised of or well and sufficiently entitled to the fee simple and inheritance in possession of and in the hereditaments hereinafter described, did by an indenture dated the   day of   , 18 , and made between the said [*vendor*] of the one part and the said trustees of the other part, in consideration of £   advanced by them to the said [*vendor*], demise unto the said trustees, their successors or assigns, the said hereditaments (and which in the indenture now being recited were by mistake called No. 4, instead of No. 5,   Street), with the appurtenances thereunto belonging, to hold the same unto the said trustees, their successors and assigns, for the term of five hundred years from the date thereof, subject to a proviso for redemption on payment by the said [*vendor*] to the said trustees, their successors or assigns, of £   , together with interest thereon at 5*l*. per cent. per annum by half-yearly payments in the manner therein mentioned: and whereas the said [*purchaser*] hath contracted with the said [*vendor*] for the purchase of the said hereditaments, with the appurtenances, and the inheritance thereof in fee simple in possession, free from incumbrances, for the sum of £   : and whereas there is now due to the said trustees, under and by virtue of the hereinbefore-recited indenture the sum of £   , all interest for the same having been paid up to the date hereof; and it has been agreed that the said sum of £   should be paid to the said trustees out of the said sum of £   : Now this indenture witnesseth, that, in consideration of £   sterling to the said trustees paid by the said [*purchaser*] on the execution hereof by the direction of the said [*vendor*], the receipt whereof, and that the same is in full for all principal, interest and other monies due to them on the hereinbefore-recited mortgage security, they the said trustees do hereby acknowledge and declare, and also in consideration of £   sterling to the said [*vendor*] paid by the said [*purchaser*] on the execution hereof, the receipt whereof, and that the said sums of £   and £   (making together the sum of £   ) are in full for the absolute purchase of the hereditaments hereinbefore mentioned and hereby conveyed he the said [*vendor*] doth hereby acknowledge and declare, and doth release the said [*purchaser*], his heirs, executors, administrators and assigns therefrom, they the said trustees, by the direction of the said [*vendor*], do and each of them doth assign, and he the said [*vendor*] doth grant unto the said [*purchaser*], his heirs and assigns, all that messuage or tenement situate and being No.   ,

Street, in the City of London, together with all rights, easements and appurtenances thereunto belonging or appertaining, or used, occupied or enjoyed therewith, To hold the said hereditaments, with their appurtenances, unto and to the use of the said [*purchaser*], his heirs and assigns. And each of them the said trustees doth hereby for himself, his heirs, executors and administrators, covenant with the said [*purchaser*], his heirs and assigns, that they the said trustees respectively have not at any time heretofore done or committed or been party or privy to any act or deed, whereby or by means whereof the said hereditaments can or may be in any manner incumbered or prejudicially affected: and the said [*vendor*] doth hereby for himself, his heirs, executors and administrators, covenant with the said [*purchaser*], his heirs and assigns, in manner following, that is to say, that notwithstanding any act or thing by the said [*vendor*], or the said trustees, or any person claiming through or under them, or any of them, made or done to the contrary, they the said trustees and the said [*vendor*], or some of them, have in themselves, or one of them now hath in himself, full power to grant the said hereditaments, with their appurtenances, unto and to the use of the said [*purchaser*], his heirs and assigns, free from incumbrances: and further, that he the said [*vendor*] and his heirs, and also the said trustees, their successors or assigns, and every other person claiming any estate or interest in or out of the said hereditaments, by, from or under them, or any of them, will from time to time and at all times hereafter, upon the request and at the costs of the said [*purchaser*], his heirs or assigns, do and execute every such further and other act and assurance for the further or more perfectly assuring the said hereditaments to the use of the said [*purchaser*], his heirs and assigns, as by him or them shall be reasonably required.

In witness, &c.

58.

By a Mortgagee under his Power of Sale.

THIS INDENTURE, made the   day of   , 18   , between A. B., of &c., of the one part, and C. D., of &c., of the other part: Whereas [*here insert such recital of the mortgagor's title as may be necessary, then recite the mortgage deed, setting out the powers of sale and receipt clause fully*]; and whereas the said sum of £   was not paid on the said   day of   , and the same still remains due to the said A. B. together with an arrear of interest thereon; and whereas the said A. B. hath contracted with the said C. D. for the sale to him of the hereditaments comprised in the said indenture of mortgage, and the fee simple and inheritance thereof in possession, free from incumbrances, for the sum of £   : Now this indenture witnesseth, that, in consideration of £   sterling to the said A. B. paid by the said C. D. on the execution hereof (the receipt whereof, and that the same is in full for the absolute purchase of the said hereditaments, the said A. B. doth hereby acknowledge and declare), he the said A. B. doth grant unto the said C. D. and his heirs, all [*parcels*], To hold the said hereditaments unto the said C. D. and his heirs (freed and absolutely discharged from the said sum of £   and all interest due in respect of the same, and all other monies intended to be secured by the hereinbefore-recited indenture of mortgage), to the use of the said C. D., his heirs and assigns: And the said A. B. doth hereby for himself, his heirs, executors and administrators, covenant with the said C. D., his heirs and assigns, that he the said A. B. hath not at any time heretofore made, done or executed any act or deed whereby or by reason or means whereof the said hereditaments or any part thereof are, is or can be in any manner incumbered or prejudicially affected.

In witness, &c.

59.

Of Land for Burial Ground under the Powers of 43 *Geo.* 3, *c.* 108.

THIS INDENTURE, made the   day of   18 , between [*donor*] of the first part, [*ordinary*] of the second part, and [*vicar*] of the third part: Whereas the said [*donor*] is seised of or entitled to the piece of ground hereinafter described and granted, with the appurtenances, for an estate of inheritance in fee simple in possession, free from incumbrances; and whereas the churchyard of or belonging to the vicarage of   and diocese of   is too small for the burial of the parishioners of the said vicarage; and whereas the said piece of ground adjoins to the churchyard of the said vicarage, and is convenient to be added thereto, and the said [*donor*] is desirous and, with the consent and approbation of the said [*ordinary*], as the ordinary of the said vicarage, hath proposed and intends to give and grant to and vest in the said vicar and his successors the said piece of ground, to be applied for the enlargement of the said churchyard, and for ever hereafter to be used as a burial ground for the parishioners of   aforesaid, pursuant to the statute made and passed in the forty-third year of the reign of his Majesty King George the Third (c. 108), intituled "An Act to promote the building, repairing or otherwise providing of Churches and Chapels, and of Houses for the Residence of Ministers, and the providing of Churchyards and Glebes:" Now this indenture witnesseth, that, in consideration of the premises, he the said [*donor*], by virtue and in pursuance and exercise of the power or authority given by the statute hereinbefore referred to, and of every other power or authority enabling him in this behalf, and with the consent and approbation of the said [*ordinary*] (testified by his being a party to and executing these presents), doth by this deed grant to and vest in the said [*vicar*] and his successors, vicars of   aforesaid, all that piece of land, part of a close called the churchyard piece, adjoining the churchyard of the said vicarage of   , and delineated on the map in the margin of these presents, and the fence whereof is thereon coloured blue and containing by admeasurement   , To hold the said piece of ground unto the said [*vicar*] and his successors, vicars of   aforesaid, for ever, as and for additional burial ground, and to be laid to the churchyard of the aforesaid vicarage for ever for the interment of the inhabitants of the aforesaid parish of   : And the said [*donor*] doth hereby for himself, his heirs, executors and administrators, covenant with the said [*vicar*] and his successors, vicars of   aforesaid, that he the said [*donor*], and every person having, or claiming, or who shall or may hereafter have or claim any estate or interest in or out of the said piece of ground, through, under or in trust for him, will from time to time, and at all times hereafter, upon every reasonable request and at the costs and charges of the said [*vicar*] and his successors, vicars of   aforesaid, make and execute such further acts and deeds for more satisfactorily conveying the said piece of ground unto and to the use of the said [*vicar*] and his successors, vicars of   aforesaid, for ever, for the use, trust, intent and purpose aforesaid, as by the said [*vicar*] and his successors, vicars of   aforesaid, shall be lawfully required. In witness whereof to these presents the said [*donor*] and [*vicar*] have set their hands and seals, and the said [*ordinary*] has set his hand and caused his episcopal seal to be affixed, the day and year first above written.

[*In the margin of the deed insert the following:*] Taken and acknowledged by the said [*donor*] at   in the county of   this   day of   18 , who desired that the same might be enrolled in the High Court of Chancery, before me,
     A London commissioner to administer
       oaths in chancery.

[*Or,* A commissioner to administer oaths in chancery
     in England.]

60.

Of Freeholds and Covenant to surrender Copyholds.

THIS INDENTURE, made &c., between A. B., of &c., of the one part, and C. D., of &c., of the other part: Whereas the said A. B. has agreed to sell to the said C. D. the freehold and copyhold hereditaments hereinafter described, for an estate in fee simple in possession, free from incumbrances, for the sum of £   : Now this indenture witnesseth, that, in consideration of the sum of £   (part of the said sum of £   agreed to be apportioned as the price of the said freehold hereditaments), paid by the said C. D. to the said A. B. on the execution hereof, the receipt whereof he doth acknowledge, and therefrom doth release the said C. D., his heirs, executors, administrators and assigns, he the said A. B. doth grant unto the said C. D. and his heirs, all &c. [*parcels*] together with all appurtenances to the said hereditaments and premises belonging or appertaining, To hold the said hereditaments unto and to the use of the said C. D., his heirs and assigns: And this indenture also witnesseth, that, in consideration of the sum of £   (residue of the said purchase-money) paid by the said C. D. to the said A. B. on the execution hereof, the receipt whereof he doth hereby acknowledge, and therefrom doth release the said C. D., his heirs, executors, administrators and assigns, he the said A. B. doth for himself, his heirs, executors and administrators covenant with the said C. D. and his heirs that he the said A. B., his heirs or assigns, will forthwith surrender into the hands of the lord of the manor of   in the county of   , all &c. [*parcels*] (to which hereditaments the said A. B. was on the   day of   18 , admitted tenant in fee simple in possession), to the use of the said C. D., his heirs and assigns, at the will of the lord according to the custom of the said manor, subject to the rents, suits and services therefore due and of right accustomed: And the said A. B. doth hereby for himself, his heirs, executors and administrators covenant with the said C. D. and his heirs that he the said A. B. hath power to convey and surrender the said freehold and copyhold hereditaments respectively in the manner and to the uses aforesaid free from incumbrances; and also that the said A. B. and his heirs, and all persons lawfully claiming any estate or interest in the said hereditaments through or under him, will at all times at the request and costs of the said C. D., his heirs or assigns, execute and do all such deeds and things for more effectually assuring the said hereditaments and every part thereof to the uses aforesaid, as the said C. D., his heirs or assigns, shall reasonably require. In witness, &c.

Note.—The better course is to surrender the copyholds before the deed is executed, and if this be done the deed should be thus varied. After the first recital go on: "And whereas the said A. B. has this day surrendered into the hands of the lord of the manor of   in the county of   all [*give a short description of the copyholds*] to the use of the said C. D., his heirs and assigns." Then resume with "Now," and continue to the end of the habendum of the freeholds; omit the covenant to surrender the copyholds; proceed with the covenants for title, making the vendor covenant that he "hath power to convey the said freehold hereditaments, and at the time of surrendering the said copyhold hereditaments had power to surrender the same to the uses aforesaid, according to the intent hereof and of the said surrender respectively, free from all incumbrances," and then resume with the covenant for further assurances, and go to the end as before.

The deed conveying the freeholds will only require an ad valorem stamp on the apportioned amount of purchase-money, and the surrender will require an ad valorem stamp on the residue of the purchase-money.

61.

Of Charity Property under direction of the Charity Commissioners.

THIS INDENTURE, made &c., between the trustees of the charity called "A. B.'s charity," [hereinafter called the vendors] of the one part, and C. D., of &c., of the other part: Whereas the vendors, being seised in fee of the hereditaments hereinafter described, lately agreed to sell the same to the said C. D. for the sum of £   , subject to the approval of the Charity Commissioners for England and

Wales; and whereas the said Charity Commissioners by an order under their common seal, dated &c., authorized the vendors within six calendar months from the date thereof to sell the said hereditaments for not less than the said sum of £   , and to execute all proper assurances for carrying the said sale into effect, and to give a conclusive discharge to the purchaser for the said purchase-money: Now this indenture witnesseth, that, by virtue of the said order, and in consideration of £   now paid by the said C. D. to the vendors (the receipt whereof is hereby acknowledged), the vendors do and each of them doth hereby grant unto the said C. D., his heirs and assigns, all &c. [*parcels*], with their rights and appurtenances, To hold the said hereditaments unto and to the use of the said C. D., his heirs and assigns; and each of them the said vendors, so far as relates to his own acts and deeds only, doth hereby for himself, his heirs, executors and administrators covenant with the said C. D., his heirs and assigns, that the vendors respectively have not done, or knowingly suffered, or been party or privy to, any deed or thing whereby the said hereditaments or any part thereof are, is or may be impeached, affected or incumbered in any manner howsoever.

In witness, &c.

62.

Of Life Interest in Real Estate.

THIS INDENTURE, made &c., 18 , between A. B., of &c., of the one part, and C. D., of &c., of the other part: Whereas J. S., late of &c., deceased, by his will dated &c., devised the hereditaments hereinafter described unto the said A. B. for her life with remainder over; and whereas the said testator died on &c. without having revoked or altered his said will, which was on &c. duly proved in &c.; and whereas the said A. B. has agreed to sell to the said C. D. for the sum of £   the said hereditaments hereinafter described for the remainder of the life of the said A. B.: Now this indenture witnesseth, that, in consideration of £   paid to the said A. B. by the said C. D. (the receipt whereof the said A. B. doth hereby acknowledge), she the said A. B. doth hereby grant unto the said C. D., his heirs and assigns, all &c. [*parcels*], To hold the said hereditaments unto and to the use of the said C. D , his heirs and assigns, during the remainder of the life of the said A. B. [Add covenants for right to grant " for the remainder of the life of the said A. B.," and for further assurance " during the life of the said A. B."]

In witness, &c.

63.

Conveyance by Clerk of the Peace to Trustees of a Settlement.

THIS INDENTURE, made &c., between A. B., of   , in the county of   , the clerk of the peace for the said county of   , of the first part; Sir C. D., of   in the county of   , knight, of the second part; and E. F., of   , in the county of   , and G. H., of   , in the county of   , of the third part: Whereas by an indenture dated the   day of   , 18 , and made between G. of the first part, the mayor, aldermen and burgesses of the borough of   aforesaid of the second part, H. of the third part, I. and K. of the fourth part, and the said A. B. of the fifth part, the hereditaments hereinafter described and assured were (with other hereditaments) assured unto and to the use of the said A. B., as such clerk of the peace aforesaid, and his successors and assigns for ever, in trust nevertheless for the justices of the peace of the county of   for the purposes of the said county; and whereas the said hereditaments are not required for the purposes of the said county; and whereas by an indenture dated the   day of   , 18 , made between O. P., since deceased (the late father of the said C. D.), and the said Sir C. D. of the first part, L. M. and the said G. H. of the second part, and Q. R. and S. T. of the third part, certain hereditaments now stand limited to the use of the said C. D. for his life; and it was thereby declared that it should be lawful for the said trustees at any time thereafter, at the request of the person who should for the time being be entitled under the indenture now in recital to the first estate of freehold in the hereditaments thereby settled, every such request to be signified by deed, to dispose of and convey the hereditaments thereby settled or any part thereof, by way of absolute sale in the manner therein mentioned, and that the said trustees should apply the monies to arise from any such sale in (among other purposes) the purchase of freehold hereditaments in fee simple in possession, to be situated in England or Wales or otherwise as therein mentioned, so that every such purchase were made with the consent in writing of the person entitled under the now reciting indenture to the first estate of freehold in the said settled estates, and that the said trustees should settle the hereditaments so to be purchased, to the same uses, upon the same trusts and subject to the same powers and provisoes as were in and by the now reciting indenture expressed concerning the hereditaments thereby settled in strict settlement, or as near thereto as the deaths of parties and other circumstances would admit; and whereas the said L. M. died on the   day of   , 18 , and by an indenture dated the   day of   , 18 , made between the said Sir C. D. of the first part, the said E. F. of the second part, the said G. H. of the third part, and Y. Z. of the fourth part, the said G. H. was (pursuant to a power for that purpose in the hereinbefore-recited settlement) appointed by the said Sir C. D. a trustee of the same indenture, in the place of the said L. M. deceased, jointly with the said E. F. for all the then subsisting purposes of such indenture; and all the hereditaments then subject thereto were duly vested in the said E. F. and G. H. upon the trusts thereof then subsisting; and whereas sales have been made by the trustees and trustee for the time being of portions of the said settled hereditaments pursuant to the powers contained in the said settlement; and whereas the said E. F. and G. H., as trustees of the said indenture of the   day of   , 18 , have, at the request of the said Sir C. D. (testified by his executing these presents), agreed with the said A. B., as such clerk of the peace for the county of   , for the purchase of the piece of land hereinafter described and the inheritance in fee simple in possession, free from incumbrances, at the sum of £   ; and whereas the said contract for sale and purchase of the hereditaments intended to be hereby assured was at the   sessions, 18 , for the said county of   , duly confirmed by the justices of the peace for the said county in general assembly: Now this indenture witnesseth, that, in consideration of the sum of £   sterling, upon the execution hereof paid to the said A. B. by the said E. F. and G. H. out of monies in their hands which have arisen from sales as aforesaid, with the consent of the said Sir C. D., testified by his execution hereof, the receipt whereof the said A. B. doth hereby acknowledge and from the same doth hereby release the said E. F. and G. H., their heirs, executors, administrators and assigns, he the said A. B., in pursuance of the power given to him by the 21 & 22 Vict. c. 92, doth grant unto the said E. F. and G. H. and their heirs all that &c., To hold the same unto the said E. F. and G. H. and their heirs, to such and the same uses, upon the same trusts and subject to the same powers and provisions as are in and by the hereinbefore-recited indenture of the   day of   , 18 , expressed and declared of and concerning the freehold hereditaments thereby limited, or as near thereto as the deaths of parties and other intervening circumstances will now admit. [Add covenants by A. B., for himself, his heirs, executors and administrators, with E. F. and G. H., that he has not incumbered, and by him for himself and his successors as clerks of the peace for the county of   , with E. F. and G. H., to produce and furnish copies of the thereinbefore-recited indenture of the   day of   , 18   (the conveyance to the said A. B. as such clerk of the peace.)]

In witness, &c.

[A certified copy of the justices' confirmation and approval of the sale should be obtained and annexed to the conveyance.]

64.

Covenant that Infant shall execute Deed on attaining Twenty-one.

AND THIS INDENTURE further witnesseth, that, for the considerations aforesaid, he the said A. B. doth for himself, his heirs, executors and administrators, further covenant with the said J. S., his heirs and assigns, that the said C. D., the son of the said A. B., will, at the request and costs of the said J. S., his heirs or assigns, sign, seal and deliver these presents when and so soon as the said C. D. shall have attained the age of twenty-one years, or at any time thereafter, within twelve calendar months after being thereunto required, and after this present indenture being duly tendered to him for that purpose; and also, that in case the said C. D. shall die without having attained the age of twenty-one years, or without having signed, sealed and delivered these presents, then the heir or heirs of the said C. D. (such heir or heirs being some one or more child or grandchild, children or grandchildren of the said A. B.) will at any time after such decease of the said C. D. as aforesaid, and whenever thereunto required by the said J. S., his heirs or assigns, and at the costs of the said J. S., his heirs or assigns, execute such further assurances for better assuring the said hereditaments to the use of the said J. S., his heirs and assigns, as by the said J. S., his heirs and assigns, shall be reasonably required.

COPYHOLDS.

65.

Surrender of Copyhold Hereditaments.

Manor of } BE IT REMEMBERED, that out of court on the day of , 18 , A. B., of &c., a copyhold tenant of this manor, and his wife came before steward of the said manor, and in consideration of £ sterling to the said A. B. paid by C. D. of &c., on the passing of this surrender (the receipt whereof the said A. B. doth hereby acknowledge, and from the same discharge the said C. D., his heirs, executors, administrators and assigns, and doth declare the same to be in full for the purchase of the hereditaments hereinafter described and surrendered), they the said A. B. and   his wife (the said   joining in this surrender, for the purpose of passing all her right or title to dower, and all other her interest whatsoever in, to or out of the said hereditaments, and being first examined by the said steward, separate and apart from her said husband, according to the custom of the said manor) did surrender into the hands of the lord of the said manor, by the hands and acceptance of the said steward, by the rod, according to the custom of the said manor, all [*parcels*], [together with full and free right for the said C. H., his heirs and assigns, and all other persons by his or their leave, on foot, and either with or without horses, carts or carriages, and for all other purposes for which a roadway can be used, over, upon or along the road or way leading out of and from the said piece or parcel of meadow or pasture land between certain premises in the occupation of   and others, and certain other premises in the occupation of   into the public road or way leading to   ], all which said hereditaments and premises hereby surrendered are holden of the manor of   and are situate, lying and being at   , in the parish of   , in the said county of Middlesex, together with the easements and appurtenances to the said hereditaments belonging or appertaining or appurtenant thereto, to the use of the said C. D., his heirs and assigns for ever, at the will of the lord, according to the custom of the said manor, by and under the suit and services, rents, fines and heriots therefore due and of right accustomed.

 Taken, together with the separate examination
  of the said   , the day and year aforesaid, by me,

          Steward.

66.

Deed of Covenants for Title to accompany such Surrender.

THIS INDENTURE, made the   day of   18 , between A. B. of the one part, and C. D. of the other part: Whereas the said A. B. agreed with the said C. D. for the sale to him of the hereditaments hereinafter described, with their appurtenances and the inheritance thereof in possession, according to the custom of the manor of which the same are holden, free from incumbrances, except the rents, fines, heriots, suits and services therefore due and of right accustomed, for the sum of £   , and upon the treaty for the said sale it was agreed that the said A. B. should enter into such covenants as are hereinafter contained; and whereas, in pursuance of the said agreement, the said A. B. and   his wife did out of court, immediately before the execution hereof, surrender into the hands of the lord of the manor of   by his steward, and according to the custom of the said manor, all [*parcels from surrender*], all which said hereditaments and premises are holden of the manor of   in the county of Middlesex, and are situate, lying and being at   in the parish of   in the said county, together with the appurtenances, to the use of the said C. D., his heirs and assigns, according to the custom of the said manor, and by and under the suits and services, rents, fines and heriots therefore due and of right accustomed: Now this indenture witnesseth, that, in consideration of the said sum of £   paid to the said A. B. by the said C. D. on the execution of the said surrender, he the said A. B. doth hereby for himself, his heirs, executors and administrators, covenant with the said C. D., his heirs and assigns, in manner following (that is to say), that, notwithstanding any act, deed or thing by the said A. B. made, done or executed or knowingly or willingly suffered to the contrary, the said A. B. and   his wife had at the time of making the said surrender in themselves, or one of them had in himself or herself, full power and authority to surrender the said hereditaments to the use of the said C. D., his heirs and assigns, according to the custom of the said manor and in manner aforesaid, free from incumbrances, but nevertheless under and subject to the rents, fines, heriots, suits and services therefore due and of right accustomed; and further, that the said A. B. and his heirs, and the said   his wife, and every other person claiming any estate or interest, either at law or in equity, in, to or out of the said hereditaments or any of them, under or in trust for the said A. B. or his heirs, or the said   his wife, will at all times hereafter, upon every reasonable request, by and at the costs of the said C. D., his heirs or assigns, make and execute, or cause to be made and executed, such further acts, surrenders and assurances for more perfectly surrendering and assuring the said hereditaments to the use of the said C. D., his heirs and assigns, according to the custom of the said manor, and under and subject to the rents, fines, heriots, suits and services therefore due and of right accustomed, as by the said C. D., his heirs or assigns, shall be reasonably required. In witness, &c.

67.

Conditional Surrender of Copyholds.

The Manor of } in the } the   day of   18   , A. B., of &c. (one of the customary tenants of the said manor) came before C. D., gentleman, steward of the said manor, and in consideration of £   sterling to the said A. B. paid by E. F. of &c., did surrender by the rod into the hands of the lord of the said manor, by the acceptance of the said steward, according to the custom of the said manor, all [*parcels*], together with all [trees, hedges, ditches, fences, ways, waters, watercourses, lights, easements, privileges, fixtures], rights, members and appurtenances to the said hereditaments belonging to the use of the said E. F., his heirs and assigns, at the will of the lord, according to the custom of the said manor, by the rents, customs and services therefore due and of right accustomed: provided always, that if the said A. B., his heirs, executors, administrators or assigns shall pay or cause to be paid to the said E. F., his executors, administrators or assigns the sum of £   together with interest for the same at the rate of £   per cent. per annum, on the   day of   without deduction, then this surrender shall be void, but otherwise shall remain in full force and virtue.

Taken and accepted the day and
year above written by me,

Steward of the said manor.

68.
Deed of Covenant to accompany such Surrender.

THIS INDENTURE, made the   day of   , 18 , between A. B., of &c., of the one part, and E. F., of &c., of the other part: Whereas the said A. B. did out of court, immediately before the execution hereof, in consideration of £   sterling to him paid by the said E. F., surrender into the hands of the lord of the manor of   , in the county of   , by his steward, according to the custom of the said manor, all [*parcels*], with their rights, easements and appurtenances, to the use of the said E. F., his heirs and assigns, by and under the rents, fines, heriots, suits and services therefore due and of right accustomed, but subject to a condition for making void the same on payment by the said A. B., his heirs, executors, administrators or assigns, unto the said E. F., his executors, administrators or assigns, of the sum of   , with interest thereon at £   per cent. per annum, on the   day of   next; and whereas on the treaty for the said advance it was agreed that the said A. B. should execute these presents in manner hereinafter appearing: Now this indenture witnesseth, that, in consideration of the premises, he the said A. B. doth hereby for himself, his heirs, executors and administrators, covenant with the said E. F., his executors and administrators, that he the said A. B., his executors or administrators, will pay unto the said E. F., his executors, administrators or assigns, the sum of £   with interest thereon, at £   per cent. per annum, on the   day of   next, without deduction; but in case default shall be made in payment of the said sum of £   or the interest thereon or any part thereof, on the said   day of   next, it shall be lawful for the said E. F., his executors, administrators or assigns, to sell [*here insert power of sale and receipt clause, and trusts of purchase-money, vide title "Mortgages"*]: And the said A. B. doth hereby for himself, his heirs, executors and administrators, covenant with the said E. F., his heirs and assigns, that he the said A. B. had in himself at the time of making the said surrender full power and authority to surrender the hereditaments therein comprised to the use of the said E. F., his heirs and assigns, according to the custom of the said manor and in manner aforesaid, free from incumbrances (except the rents, fines, heriots, suits and services therefore due and of right accustomed); and also, that the said A. B. and every other person whomsoever having or claiming any estate or interest in or to the said hereditaments will upon the request of the said E. F., his heirs or assigns, but at the costs of the said A. B., his heirs, executors or administrators, do and execute, or cause to be done and executed, every such further act, surrender and assurance for better assuring the said hereditaments to the use of the said E. F., his heirs and assigns, according to the custom of the said manor, and subject and in manner aforesaid, as by him or them shall be reasonably required. In witness, &c.

69.

Power of Attorney to surrender Copyholds.

KNOW ALL MEN by these presents, that I, A. B., of &c., one of the customary tenants of the manor of   , in the county of   , have constituted and appointed and by these presents do constitute and appoint C. D., of &c., and E. F., of &c., jointly and severally my true and lawful attornies or attorney for me and in my name forthwith, either in or out of court, and according to the custom of the said manor, to surrender into the hands of the lord of the said manor, according to the custom thereof, all [*parcels*], and to which said hereditaments I the said A. B. was admitted tenant at a court holden in and for the said manor on the   day of   , 18 , together with the appurtenances to the said hereditaments belonging, to the use of C. D., of &c., his heirs and assigns, according to the custom of the said manor.

In witness whereof I have hereunto set my hand and seal this   day of   , 18 .

———•———

70.

Disclaimer by Trustees of Copyhold Property, in order that One of their Number only may take Admittance.

THIS INDENTURE, made the   day of   , 18 , between [*disclaiming trustees*], of the one part, and [*continuing trustee*] of the other part : Whereas [*here recite will, death of testator and proof of will*]; and whereas no person hath since the decease of the said testator been admitted to the said copyhold hereditaments holden of the manors aforesaid, or any of them; and whereas the said [*disclaiming trustees*], and also the said [*continuing trustee*], are respectively desirous that the said copyhold hereditaments holden of the manors aforesaid should be vested in the said [*continuing trustee*] solely, to the intent that he alone may be admitted thereto, and for that purpose the said [*disclaiming trustees*] have respectively determined to execute the disclaimer and release hereinafter respectively contained : Now this indenture witnesseth, that, in pursuance of the said determination, they the said [*disclaiming trustees*] do by these presents absolutely and irrevocably disclaim all and singular the copyhold hereditaments devised by the said will of the said A. B., the testator, and holden respectively of the manors of   [except as to the said C. D. the power of appointment and the beneficial interest for her life respectively given to her by the said will]: And this indenture further witnesseth, that, in further pursuance of the said determination, they the said [*disclaiming trustees*] do and each of them doth hereby release unto the said [*continuing trustee*] and his heirs all and singular, if any, their right to be admitted, or other their right, estate and interest, if any, of and in the pieces or parcels of land or ground, messuages or tenements and hereditaments which the said A. B., the testator, held of the said manors of   , with the rights, members and appurtenances thereto belonging [except as to the said C. D. the power of appointment and beneficial interest for her life respectively given to her by the said will], to the intent that, by virtue of the said disclaimer and, if need be, of this present release, the right to be admitted to and to hold the said hereditaments and all and singular the premises may be vested in the said [*continuing trustee*], and his heirs, as sole tenant or tenants thereof, and according to the customs of the said manors respectively. In witness, &c.

[N.B.—As to the above disclaimer, vide *Lord Wellesley* v. *Withers*, 24 L. J., Q. B. 139; *S. C.*, 25 Law Times, 79.]

71.

Deed of Enfranchisement, with Grant of Common Rights.

THIS INDENTURE, made the   day of   , 18 , between A. B., of &c., lord of the manor of   , of the one part, and C. D., of &c., a copyhold tenant of the said manor, of the other part: Whereas the said A. B. is seised of or well and sufficiently entitled to the said manor of   for an estate of inheritance in fee simple in possession free from incumbrance; and whereas the said C. D. is seised to him and his heirs, according to the custom of the said manor, of and in the hereditaments hereinafter described, being part of the copyhold hereditaments of the said manor; and whereas the said C. D. hath contracted with the said A. B. for the enfranchisement of the said hereditaments for the sum of £   : Now this indenture witnesseth, that, in consideration of £   sterling to the said A. B. paid by the said C. D. on the execution hereof, the receipt whereof the said A. B. doth hereby acknowledge, and from the same doth discharge the said C. D., his heirs, executors, administrators and assigns, he the said A. B. doth by these presents grant unto the said C. D. and his heirs all [*parcels*], together with,

&c., to the said hereditaments belonging or in anywise appertaining or therewith used, occupied or enjoyed, or accepted, reputed, deemed, taken or known as part, parcel or member thereof, or any part thereof, To hold the said hereditaments unto the said C. D. and his heirs, to the use of the said C. D., his heirs and assigns, freed and absolutely acquitted, enfranchised and discharged of and from all and all manner of customary and other rents, fines, heriots, fealty, suit of court, forfeitures, duties, services or customs whatsoever, which according to the custom of the said manor of   the said hereditaments hereinbefore granted are or have been subject or liable to or charged with, or which would but for these presents be payable or to be done and performed for or in respect of the same hereditaments or any of them, or any part thereof: [And this indenture also witnesseth, that, for the considerations aforesaid, and in order to preserve to the said C. D., his heirs, and assigns, all such rights of common in, upon and over the waste lands of the said manor of

as he the said C. D., or any of his ancestors or predecessors, hath or have at any time heretofore used or enjoyed as belonging or appurtenant to the messuages, lands, tenements, hereditaments and premises hereinbefore described, notwithstanding the enfranchisement of the same respective premises, he the said A. B. doth by these presents grant unto the said C. D., his heirs and assigns for ever, all such commonage and right or title to common of what nature or kind soever, in, upon or over all or any of the wastes, commons and commonable lands of or belonging to the said manor of   as he the said C. D. immediately before the execution of these presents or as any of his ancestors or predecessors at any time heretofore held, possessed or enjoyed in respect of and as appurtenant or belonging to the said messuages, lands, tenements, hereditaments and premises hereby granted or intended so to be, and the freehold and inheritance of all such commonable rights as aforesaid, in as large, ample and beneficial a manner to all intents and purposes as he the said C. D., or any of his ancestors and predecessors, hath or have heretofore used and exercised all or any of the said rights or privileges, or as he or his customary heirs could or might have used and exercised the same if these presents had not been executed]; and the said A. B. for himself, his heirs, executors and administrators, doth hereby covenant with the said C. D., his heirs and assigns, in manner following (that is to say), that (for and notwithstanding any act, deed, matter or thing whatsoever by the said A. B., or any of his ancestors, made, done, committed, executed or wittingly suffered to the contrary) he the said A. B., at the time of the execution of these presents, hath in himself full power and authority to grant the said hereditaments with their appurtenances in manner aforesaid, free from incumbrances; and further, that he the said A. B. and his heirs, and all and every persons and person whomsoever having, or lawfully or equitably claiming or to claim, any estate or interest in, to or out of the said manor of   by, from, under or in trust for him or any of his ancestors, will at all times hereafter, upon the reasonable request and at the costs of the said C. D., his heirs or assigns, do and execute, or cause and procure to be done and executed, such further and other acts, deeds and assurances whatsoever for the further and more perfectly and absolutely enfranchising the said hereditaments, with their appurtenances, as by the said C. D., his heirs or assigns, shall be required. In witness, &c.

[N.B.—A covenant on the part of the lord of the manor for production of title-deeds should be added or taken by a separate document.

If there are no common rights in the manor, or if it is not intended to reserve common rights to the copyholder after the enfranchisement, the grant of common rights will of course be omitted.

If the copyholder was married before 1834, the limitations in the deed should be to uses to bar dower, instead of to him in fee as in the Precedent.]

72.

Warrant to enter Satisfaction on Conditional Surrender.

I, A. B., of &c., do authorize and require you or your lawful deputy for the time being to enter full satisfaction and discharge on the court rolls of the manor of   on and for a conditional surrender, dated the   day of   , made by C. D., of &c., of certain hereditaments in the said surrender, described to the use of me, my heirs and assigns, for securing to me the sum of £   in the manner therein mentioned. Dated the   day of   , 18 .   Witness   A. B.

To the steward of the manor of   .

73.

Surrender of Copyholds to the Trustees of a Settlement.

Manor of } BE IT REMEMBERED, that out of court on the   day of   , 18 , A. B., of &c., a copyhold tenant of this manor came before   , steward of the said manor, and in pursuance of a covenant contained in a certain indenture, dated the   day of   , 18 , made between &c. (being a settlement executed in contemplation of the marriage of the said A. B. with the said   ), did surrender into the hands of the lord of the said manor by the hands and acceptance of the said steward by the rod, according to the custom of the said manor, all [*parcels*] (which said hereditaments are holden of the manor of   in the county of   ), together with the easements and appurtenances to the said hereditaments belonging or appertaining or appurtenant thereto, to the use of the said   and   their heirs and assigns, at the will of the lord, according to the custom of the said manor, by and under the suit and services, rents, fines and heriots therefore due and of right accustomed [upon the trusts and subject to the provisions contained in and declared by the said indenture of the   day of   , 18 .]

NOTE.—If the steward does not object to the words within brackets, they had better be inserted; but some stewards will not allow a reference to any trusts to appear on the court rolls.

DEEDS OF COVENANT.

74.

By Purchasers of Land set out for Building, where it is intended the Buildings shall be uniform.

THIS INDENTURE, made the   day of   , 18 , between [*owner*], of the one part, and [*purchasers*] and the several other persons who should at any time hereafter execute this present indenture, of the other part: Whereas the said [*owner*] is seised in fee simple in possession of a piece or parcel of land containing   acres, situate at Ramsgate, on the South Cliff there, part of which he has laid out in separate lots or divisions for the erection of a row of houses thereon, intending to be called Nelson's Crescent, the form of the front building line of houses is delineated in a ground plan appearing in these presents, and contains, including the curve, 400 feet in front towards the south-east; and whereas, in order to preserve some degree of similarity and uniformity of appearance in such intended row of houses, the said [*owner*] has determined and proposed, and doth hereby expressly declare, that it shall be a general and indispensable condition of the sale of all or any part of the land intended to form such row, that the several proprietors of such land respectively for the time being shall observe and abide by the several stipulations and restrictions hereinafter contained or expressed in regard to the several houses to be erected thereon, and in all other particulars; and that the said [*owner*] and his heirs shall at all times observe the like stipulations and restrictions as to such of the lots or divisions of the same land as for the time being shall remain unsold by him or them; and whereas the said [*purchasers*] have severally agreed to purchase of the said [*owner*] lots   part of the said intended row, and appearing on the said plan, subject to the proposed stipulations and restrictions: Now this indenture witnesseth, that, in consideration of the premises and in pursuance of and in conformity to the conditions hereinbefore expressed of and for the sale of the several lots of land in the said row, and for effectuating, establishing and rendering perpetual the plan, design and purpose aforesaid, it is hereby mutually covenanted, declared and agreed by and between the said [*owner*], [*purchasers*] and the several other persons who shall at any time or times hereafter execute the same indenture (the respective times of the execution of the indenture by the several parties being expressed in the several attestations thereof), and each and every of them the said [*owner*], [*purchasers*] and the several other person or persons who should at any time or times execute this indenture, for himself and herself, for his or her heirs, executors and administrators, and for every of them, do hereby covenant with all and every the other and others of them, and with the several heirs, executors, administrators and assigns of all and every the others and other of them, mutually and reciprocally, in manner following (that is to say), that the front wall of every house in the said intended row shall be brought immediately up to, but shall not in any case project beyond, the building line as shown on the said plan; and also that none of the houses in the said intended row shall have bow windows of any sort; and also that the area in front of the said houses shall be of the width of five feet in the clear, and shall extend the whole length thereof, and that the forecourt in front of each house shall be surrounded by a uniform railing of iron or wood, which shall not extend beyond the height of four feet from the surface of the ground there; and also that the wall of partition between the several houses and the areas in front of the yard and garden behind such houses respectively shall be placed equally on the ground of the two proprietors of adjoining houses or ground, and shall at all times be considered as party-walls, and shall be built at the joint and equal expense of the two proprietors of the adjoining houses or ground; but if any of them shall be first and originally built at the sole expense of either of the proprietors of the adjoining houses or ground, then the proprietor who shall so first and originally build such walls shall build a brick party-wall nine inches thick, and at the height of seven feet from the surface of the ground from the front building ground throughout, and one half part of the expense thereof shall be paid to the proprietor who shall have so built the same, his or her heirs, executors or administrators, by the proprietor of the adjoining house or ground, his or her heirs, executors, administrators or assigns, within three calendar months after the proprietor of the adjoining house or ground shall begin to erect his or her house in the principal front; and also that the proprietor of such adjoining house or ground, his or her heirs, executors, administrators or assigns, shall also pay one half part of the expense of so much of the residue of the party-wall as he shall make use of and build to, within one calendar month after he shall make use of and build to the same, and the expense in both cases, if any difference shall arise thereon, shall be determined by admeasurement and value; and also that none of the proprietors of the houses or grounds in the said intended row shall lay any chalk or mould which shall be dug out of any of the lots of land appearing on the said plan, on the foot, horse or carriage way in front of the said row, or on the land lying between the said way and the edge of the sea cliff; and also that the piece or slip of land of the breadth of twenty-nine feet, intended to be mentioned in the conveyances to the several purchasers, beyond the area steps of entrance and forecourt, shall at all times hereafter remain open and unincumbered as and for a free foot, horse and carriage way in front of the said intended row, and shall be formed, made, maintained and kept repaired at the expense of the several proprietors of the said houses in the said row, in proportion to the extent of front towards the south-east of each respective house; and also that none of the proprietors of any of the lots for the time being shall at any time or times, or on any account or pretence whatsoever, erect or suffer to be erected on any of the several lots which shall respectively belong to them for the time being, or on any part of them, any public livery stables or public coach house, or use, exercise or carry on, or suffer to be used, exercised or carried on, through or on any part thereof, the trade or business of a   founder, tobacco pipe maker, common brewer, tallow chandler, soap boiler, distiller, innkeeper,   keeper, common ale-house keeper, brazier, working smith of any kind, butcher or slaughterman, or any other noxious or offensive trade or business whereby the neighbourhood might be in any respect endangered or annoyed, or burn or make, or suffer to be burnt or made, on any of the said lots, or on any part of them, any bricks or lime ; and also that no other building or buildings than good dwelling-house or dwelling-houses or lodging-houses shall be erected on the said lots or any of them.

In witness, &c.

[N.B.—The above is the form of the indenture in *Whatman* v. *Gibson*, 9 Sim. 196. An injunction will be granted to restrain a breach of the above deed ; but quære, an action will not lie against an assignee. In the different conveyances to the purchasers this indenture must be plainly referred to, so as to fix the different sub-purchasers with notice of it, otherwise the court will not interfere.]

75.

Not to resort to certain Estates to raise Judgment Debts and to indemnify.

THIS INDENTURE, made the   day of   , 18 , between A. B., of &c., and C. D., of &c., of the one part, and I. C., of &c., of the other part: Whereas a judgment was obtained by one C. L. against E. F., of &c., in the Court of Exchequer of Pleas at Westminster, on or about the   day of   , 18 , for the sum of £   and £   costs, and the same judgment was duly registered on or about the   day of   , 18 ; and whereas, by an indenture bearing date on or about the   day of   , 18 , and made between the said C. L. of the first part, the said E. F. of the second part, and the said A. B. and C. D. of the third part, for the valuable considerations therein mentioned, all that the said judgment for £ and interest, and also the said sum of £ so due for principal money thereon, and also all interest and costs due from the said E. F. to the said C. L. upon the same judgment, and all interest thenceforth to become due on the said judgment, were assigned unto the said A. B. and C. D., their executors, administrators and assigns absolutely; and whereas the said recited judgment is still subsisting; and whereas, by an indenture bearing date the day of , 18 , and made between the said E. F. of the one part, and the said I. C. of the other part, certain hereditaments, situate in the county of , were granted unto and to the use of the said I. C., his heirs and assigns, upon trust to carry out certain contracts for sale of the same estates and for other trusts and purposes in the same indenture particularly mentioned; and whereas, in order to obviate any objections which might be taken by the respective purchasers under the said contracts for sale, on the ground of the hereinbefore recited judgment being still subsisting, and for facilitating the completion of the said sales, the said A. B. and C. D. have agreed to enter into the covenant, agreement or stipulation hereinafter contained: Now this indenture witnesseth, that, in consideration of the premises, they the said A. B. and C. D. do hereby for themselves, their heirs, executors, administrators and assigns, and each of them doth hereby for himself, his heirs, executors, administrators and assigns, covenant with the said I. C., his heirs and assigns, that they the said A. B. and C. D. respectively, and their respective executors, administrators or assigns, or any or either of them, shall not nor will at any time or times hereafter cause, procure or knowingly permit or suffer any writ or writs of execution to be issued under or by virtue of the hereinbefore-recited judgment against the several messuages, lands, tenements, chief rents and other hereditaments and premises situate in the county of aforesaid, and of which the said E. F. was formerly seised and so contracted to be sold as aforesaid, and comprised in the said recited indenture of the day of , 18 , or any of them, or any part thereof, nor do, or cause, or procure or knowingly suffer to be done any other act, matter or thing whatsoever, whereby or by reason or means whereof the same several messuages, lands, tenements, chief rents and other hereditaments and premises shall or may be in anywise prejudicially affected by reason or means of the hereinbefore-recited judgment, or any writ or writs of execution to be issued under or by means thereof; and also that they the said A. B. and C. D., their heirs, executors, administrators and assigns, will at all times hereafter save, defend, keep harmless and indemnified the said I. C., his heirs and assigns, and all and every the purchaser and purchasers of the hereditaments comprised in the said last-mentioned indenture, or any part thereof, and his, their and each and every of their estates and effects, of, from and against all actions, suits, accounts, reckonings, costs, charges, claims and demands whatsoever, either at law or in equity, which the said A. B., C. D. and C. L., any or either of them, or their or any or either of their executors, administrators or assigns, or any other person or persons whomsoever, shall or may commence, prosecute, have, claim, challenge or demand against or upon the said I. C., his heirs or assigns, or any purchaser or purchasers under the contracts for sale of the said lands, hereditaments and premises in the county of   aforesaid, for or on account of the said recited judgment, or for or on account of any writ or writs of execution or any other proceeding that may be had, issued out or prosecuted by reason of the same judgment, or for or by reason of the said lands, hereditaments and premises so situate in the county of   as aforesaid, being seised under any writ or writs of execution, extent or other proceeding whatsoever, by reason or by virtue of the same judgment, and of and from all and all manner of losses, damages, costs, charges and expenses to be incurred, sustained or borne by the said I. C. or such purchaser or purchasers, his or their heirs, executors, administrators or assigns, by reason or in consequence of the said recited judgment or otherwise in relation to the premises: provided always, and it is hereby declared and agreed, that the covenant hereinbefore contained shall be considered as a covenant to stop them the said A. B. and C. D., their heirs, executors, administrators and assigns, from having recourse either in their or his own name or names, or in the name or names of the said C. L., his executors or administrators, or otherwise to all or any part or parts of the hereditaments so conveyed to the said I. C. in order to carry out the before-mentioned contracts for sale, and situate in the county of   aforesaid, for raising the said judgment debt or any part thereof or in relation thereto : provided always, that the said covenant (which is so entered into for the purpose of estopping the said A. B. and C. D., their heirs, executors, administrators and assigns as aforesaid) is not intended and accordingly shall not either at law or in equity be deemed or construed or taken to operate or enure as a release of the said judgment, which so far as regards all other property of the said E. F. is to be in full force.

In witness, &c.

76.

To produce Deeds.

THIS INDENTURE, made the   day of   , 18 , between A. B., of &c., of the one part, and C. D., of &c., of the other part: Whereas [*recite conveyance to C. D.*]; and whereas the several deeds mentioned in the schedule hereunder written are in the possession of the said A. B., and concern the title not only of the said messuage or tenement, farm and lands at   aforesaid, and the said one-third part of the said manor of   which were respectively the estate and inheritance of E. F. deceased, but also of certain lands and hereditaments situate at   in the county of Middlesex, formerly belonging to the said E. F., but recently purchased by the said A. B. from the trustees for sale thereof appointed by the said E. F.; and upon the treaty for such purchase it was agreed that the said several deeds should remain in the possession of the said A. B. upon his entering into the covenant hereinafter contained: Now this indenture witnesseth, that, in pursuance of the agreement in that behalf, he the said

A. B. for himself, his heirs, executors and administrators, doth hereby covenant with the said C. D., his heirs and assigns, that he the said A. B., his heirs or assigns, will at all times hereafter (unless prevented by casual fire or other inevitable accident), upon every reasonable request and at the cost of the said C. D., his heirs or assigns, produce and show forth, or procure to be produced and shown forth to the said C. D., his heirs or assigns, or to such person or persons as he or they shall require, or to his or their counsel, attornies, agents or solicitors, or to or before any court or courts of law or equity, or otherwise as occasion shall require, the several deeds mentioned and described in the schedule hereunder written, or any of them, whole and uncancelled; and at the like request and cost at all times hereafter, unless prevented as aforesaid, make and deliver to the said C. D., his heirs or assigns, fair, true and attested copies, abstracts or extracts from such several deeds, or any of them, and permit the same to be examined and verified with the originals either by the said C. D., his heirs or assigns, or any other person or persons whom he or they shall appoint for that purpose: [provided always, and it is hereby agreed and declared, that if the said A. B., his heirs or assigns, shall at any time hereafter sell and dispose of the said estate so purchased by him, and to which the said several deeds relate as aforesaid, or any part thereof, and shall and do procure the purchaser or purchasers thereof to enter into a like covenant to that which is hereinbefore contained with the said C. D., his heirs or assigns, for the production and delivery of copies of the said several deeds in manner aforesaid, then the covenant hereinbefore contained for that purpose shall from thenceforth cease and be void; and these presents shall, at the request of the said A. B., his heirs, executors or administrators, be delivered up to be cancelled.]

In witness, &c.

77.

Not to throw any Rubbish into the River   or within certain Limits, and to prevent others from doing so.

WHEREAS the several persons whose names and seals are hereunto respectively subscribed and affixed, hereinafter called the parties hereto or occupiers, are the owners of or are in the receipt of the rents and profits arising from or are otherwise interested in property situate on the banks of or contiguous to that part of the rivers   and   respectively, which, commencing as to the   at   , and as to the   at   , extends as to both to   below, all in the county of   : And whereas the said parties hereto for the purpose of preventing prejudice and injury to their property aforesaid by the deposit in or discharge into the said rivers within the limits aforesaid of any stones, clay, soil or ashes, dirt, rubbish or other refuse matter, or from obstructions or nuisances caused or created in the said rivers respectively, or either of them, have agreed to enter into the covenants hereinafter contained: Now this indenture witnesseth, that, in pursuance of the said agreement and in consideration of the premises, each of them the said parties hereto, so far as the covenants hereinafter contained are to be observed or performed by him, his heirs, executors or administrators, doth for himself, his heirs, executors and administrators covenant with the others of them the said parties hereto, their executors and administrators, and also with any two or any other greater number of the others of them the said parties hereto, their executors and administrators, and also with each of the others of them, the said parties hereto, his executors and administrators in manner following (that is to say), that they the said parties hereto will not at any time during the period of   years, commencing from the day of the date hereof, deposit or discharge any stones, clay, soil, ashes, dirt, rubbish or other refuse matter in or into the said rivers within the respective limits aforesaid, nor will at any time during the period aforesaid do or suffer to be done any act or thing whatsoever which may tend to the obstruction of the said rivers or either of them within the limits aforesaid, or which may be or become a nuisance, detriment or annoyance to any other of the said parties hereto, or whereby any one or more of them the said parties hereto may during the period aforesaid be prevented from enjoying the full benefit and advantage of the water of the said rivers respectively within the limits aforesaid or they the said parties hereto, or any of them, or the estate or effects of them may be in anywise prejudicially affected; and also that the said parties hereto respectively will at all times during the period aforesaid to the best of their respective ability prohibit and prevent any person or persons whomsoever from depositing or discharging any stones, clay, soil, ashes, dirt, rubbish or other refuse matter in or into the said rivers or either of them within the limits aforesaid, or from doing any act or thing whereby the supply of water to the said parties hereto respectively may be in anywise obstructed or lessened or whereby the estate or effects of them or any of them may be in anywise prejudicially affected; and also that the said parties hereto respectively, their respective heirs, executors and administrators will give all the aid and assistance in their respective power both by subscribing from time to time such sums of money not exceeding upon any one occasion the sum of £   , or by any other ways or means that may be considered most advisable by a majority of them the said parties hereto, or of the parties for the time being interested under these presents to be assembled at any meeting after due notice in writing have been given to them the said parties respectively or left at their respective usual or last known place of abode at least one week before the said meeting to or towards any proceeding at law or otherwise against any person or persons whomsoever who shall deposit or discharge any stones, clay, soil, ashes, dirt, rubbish or other refuse matter in or into the said rivers, or either of them within the limits aforesaid; and also will upon the determination and application of such majority as aforesaid do all such further or other lawful and reasonable acts, and also enter into such further deed or deeds, instrument or instruments that may be considered necessary for the further, better and more perfectly prohibiting or preventing the deposit or discharge of any stones, clay, soil, ashes, dirt, rubbish or other refuse matter in or into the said rivers, or either of them, within the limits aforesaid; and also for the further and more perfectly prohibiting or preventing any other person or persons from depositing or discharging any stones, clay, soil, ashes, dirt, rubbish or other refuse matter in or into the said rivers, or either of them within the limits aforesaid, or otherwise annoying or prejudicially affecting the said parties hereto, or any of them, their or either or any of their heirs, executors or administrators, or their or any of their estates or effects, by obstructing the course or lessening the quantity of the water of the said rivers, or either of them, within the limits aforesaid; and also all such other acts and things whatsoever as may be considered necessary or expedient by such majority as aforesaid; and also that each of them the said parties hereto, his executors and administrators, will from time to time and at all times during the period aforesaid defend and keep indemnified all and each of the others and other of them the said parties hereto, their and his executors and administrators, and their and his estate and effects, from and against all actions, suits, accounts, reckonings, costs, damages, claims and demands whatsoever either at law or in equity, which they or he may incur or sustain for or by reason or on account of their or his bringing, commencing or prosecuting and proceeding at law or otherwise under the terms or within the meaning of this indenture, and for the purpose of effectuating the same: provided always, that all monies that shall be required for the purpose of carrying these presents or anything herein contained or relating thereto into execution or effect shall, subject to the provision hereinafter contained, be contributed in equal shares and proportions by them the said parties hereto, their executors or administrators: provided always, that no one of them the said parties hereto, his heirs, executors or administrators shall be liable to pay any greater sum of money, or bear or be put unto any greater risk in proportion to the value of his property or interest than the other or others of them, their or his heirs, executors or administrators, unless it shall be declared or resolved otherwise by a majority of the parties hereto assembled at any meeting to be called as aforesaid: provided also, that no proceeding at law or otherwise shall be taken, commenced or prosecuted by any of the parties hereto, their or any of their heirs, executors or administrators, unless and until the party so taking, commencing or prosecuting the same shall have first obtained an authority in writing so to do signed by the majority present at a meeting to be called as aforesaid for the purpose of conferring or using such authority.

In witness, &c.

[Persons having a common interest may agree to unite in a defence, but the agreement must not go beyond the common object; and, therefore, an agreement by several owners and occupiers of land in a parish to concur in defending any suits that may be commenced against any of them by the present or any future rector for the tithes of articles covered by certain specified moduses or any other moduses, binding themselves not to compromise or settle, and not limited to their continuance in the parish or to any particular time, is illegal. *Stow* v. *Yea,* Jacob, 427.

Millowners bound themselves by a bond to stop their mills pursuant to resolutions passed by the majority (the object in fact being to prevent strikes by their workpeople). Held, that the bond was illegal at common law, as being contrary to public policy, and in restraint of trade, and of the free action of individuals, and was incapable of being enforced by action. [Query, whether the entering into such a bond is an indictable offence?] *Hilton* v. *Eckersley,* 4 Weekly Rep. 326.]

DECLARATION.

78.

Of the Existence of a Person who had given a Power of Attorney at the Time of the Attorney exercising the Power.

I,   of   , in the county of   , do solemnly and sincerely declare that on the   day of   , 18 , I saw A. B., of &c., as attorney of C. D., of &c., duly sign, seal and deliver a conveyance of hereditaments situate at   from   to , and that I was the attesting witness thereto; and I further declare that subsequently to the said A. B. signing, sealing and delivering the said deed I saw and conversed with the said C. D.; and I make this solemn declaration, conscientiously believing the same to be true, and by virtue of the provisions of an act made and passed in the fifth and sixth years of the reign of King William the Fourth, intituled " An Act to repeal an Act of the present Session of Parliament, intituled ' An Act for the more effectual Abolition of Oaths and Affirmations taken and made in various Departments of the State, and for the more entire Suppression of Voluntary and Extra-judicial Oaths and Affirmations, and to make other Provisions for the Abolition of unnecessary Oaths.' "

Declared at   , in the county of   , this   day of   , 18 , before me,
  A [London] Commissioner to administer
  Oaths in Chancery [in England].

DISCLAIMERS.

[*Vide* " *Copyholds*," *page* 240.]

79.

Of Trusts under Will.

To all to whom these presents shall come, A. B., of &c., sends greeting: Whereas C. D., late of &c., by his will, bearing date the   day of   , 18 , appointed the said A. B.

and E. F. trustees and executors thereof; and the said testator also appointed his wife and the said A. B. and E. F. guardians of his children so long as any of them should remain under the age of twenty-one years; and the said testator bequeathed his leasehold messuage and premises in   , wherein he then resided, for all his estate, term and interest therein, unto the said A. B. and E. F., their executors, administrators and assigns, upon the trusts therein mentioned; and the said testator devised and bequeathed unto the said A. B. and E. F., their heirs, executors, administrators and assigns, all and singular his freehold, leasehold and real estates, and the residue of his personal estate of what nature or kind soever or wheresoever, To hold the same unto and to the use of the said A. B. and E. F., their heirs, executors, administrators and assigns, according to the nature and qualities thereof respectively, upon the trusts therein mentioned; and whereas the said C. D. died on the   day of   , without having revoked or altered his said will, and the same was proved by the said E. F. alone on the   day of   in the Principal Registry of the Court of Probate, the said A. B. having first renounced probate thereof; and whereas the said A. B. has in nowise administered to the estate of the said testator nor acted or interfered in the execution of the trusts of the said will, or as guardian of the children of the said testator, and has declined to administer to the estate of the said testator, or to act or interfere in the execution of the trusts of the said will, or as guardian of the said children: Now these presents witness, that he the said A. B. hath renounced and disclaimed, and by these presents doth renounce and disclaim, all and singular the said leasehold messuage and premises in   , and all and singular the said testator's freehold, leasehold and real estate, and the residue of his personal estate, of what nature or kind soever or wheresoever, and all and singular other the real and personal estate and effects whatsoever given, devised or bequeathed by the said will, and all devises, bequests, legacies and benefits expressed to be made or given to him by the said will, and also the said office of trustee and executor of the said will and guardian of the children of the said testator, and all and singular the trusts, powers, authorities, rights and privileges whatsoever under the said will.

In witness, &c.

80.

Short Form.

To all to whom these presents shall come, A. B., of &c., sends greeting: Whereas C. D., late of &c., made his will, dated &c., and thereby appointed the said A. B. and T. S., of &c., executors, and devised and bequeathed all his real and personal estates unto the said A. B. and T. S., their heirs, executors, administrators and assigns, upon the trusts and for the intents and purposes therein mentioned; and whereas the said C. D. died on &c. without having revoked or altered his said will; and whereas the said A. B. has not acted in the trusts and executorship of the said will or accepted any of the devises or bequests thereby made to him jointly with the said T. S. or otherwise, and he is desirous of disclaiming the same in manner hereinafter appearing : Now this indenture witnesseth, that the said A. B. doth disclaim all the devises and bequests to him made, and all the trusts, powers and discretions reposed or vested in him in and by the said will, either jointly with the said T. S. or otherwise.

In witness, &c.

DISENTAILING DEED.

81.

By Tenant in Tail, with the Consent of the Protector, to bar Entail of Freeholds.

THIS INDENTURE, made the   day of   , 18 , between C. D., of &c. [*tenant in tail*] of the first part, E. F., of &c. [*protector*] of the second part, and G. H., of &c. [*releasee*] of the third part: Whereas by indentures of lease and release, dated respectively the   and   days of   , the release made between [*parties*], the hereditaments hereinafter mentioned and granted were limited and assured to the use of the said A. B. and his assigns for his life, without impeachment of waste, with remainder to the use of the said E. F. and his assigns for his life, without impeachment of waste, with remainder to the use of the said I. K. and his heirs during the lives of the said A. B. and E. F., and of the survivor of them, in trust for them, and to preserve contingent remainders, with remainder to the use of the first and other sons of the said E. F. on the body of the said L. M. begotten or to be begotten successively, according to their respective seniorities, in tail, with divers remainders over; and whereas the said C. D. was the first and eldest son of the said E. F. on the body of the said L. M. begotten, and he attained his age of twenty-one years on the   day of   ; and whereas the said A. B. died on the   day of   ; and whereas the said C. D. is desirous of barring and defeating the said estate tail, and all other estates tail of him the said C. D. of or in the hereditaments hereinafter mentioned and granted, and all remainders, reversions, estates, rights, interests and powers, to take effect after the determination or in defeazance of such estate tail or estates tail, and of limiting and assuring the same hereditaments to the uses, upon the trusts and subject to the power of appointment hereinafter limited and contained, subject nevertheless and without prejudice to the estates by the said indenture of the   day of   limited, which precede the estate tail thereby limited to the first son of the said E. F. on the body of the said L. M. to be begotten, and to the powers and privileges to the same preceding estates annexed, or belonging or exercisable during the continuance thereof, so far as the same estates, powers and privileges are now subsisting or capable of taking effect; and whereas the said E. F., as protector of the said settlement, hath agreed to become a party to these presents for the purpose of giving his consent to the disposition intended to be hereby made by the said C. D.: Now this indenture witnesseth, that for effectuating the said desire of the said C. D., and in consideration of the premises, he the said C. D., with the consent of the said E. F., testified by his being a party to and executing these presents, doth by these presents grant, dispose of and confirm unto the said G. H. and his heirs, all [*parcels*], and also all other the hereditaments (if any) which are now subject at law or in equity to the subsisting uses of the said indenture of the   day of   , To hold the said hereditaments unto the said G. H. and his heirs, subject nevertheless to the estates by the said indenture of the   day of   limited, which precede the estate tail by the same indenture limited to the said C. D., and to the powers and privileges to the same precedent estates annexed during the continuance thereof, so far as the same are now subsisting or capable of taking effect, but freed and discharged from the said estate tail, and all other estates tail of the said C. D., and all remainders, reversions, estates, rights, titles, interests and powers, to take effect after the determination of such estate or estates tail, to such uses [*here, if such be the intention, insert a power of appointment or the usual uses to bar dower, or any other uses that the parties may wish to have inserted*].

In witness, &c.

DISTRINGAS.

82.

Affidavit to obtain Distringas on Stock.

A. B. [*the name of the party or parties in whose behalf the writ is issued*],

against

The Governor and Company of the Bank of England.

I, A. B., of   , in the county of   , do solemnly swear, that, according to the best of my knowledge, information and belief, I am [*or, if the affidavit is made by the solicitor, A. B., of   is*] beneficially interested in the stock hereinafter particularly described, that is to say, the sum of £   3*l.* per Cent. Consolidated Bank Annuities, now standing in the Books of the Governor and Company of the Bank of England in the name of C. D., of   , in the county of   , gentleman.

Sworn, &c.

83.

Notice to the Bank of England.

IN CHANCERY.

  A. B.
   against
  The Governor and Company of the Bank of
   England.

TAKE NOTICE, that the writ of distringas served herewith is for the purpose of restraining, and you are hereby required not to permit, the transfer of the stock or sum hereinafter particularly mentioned and described, that is to say, £   3*l.* per Cent. Consolidated Bank Annuities, standing in the name of C. D., of   , in the county of   , gentleman, in your books at the Bank of England. Dated this   day of   , 18 .

Yours, &c.
E. F.,
of 11, Chancery Lane, in the county of
Middlesex, solicitor for the above-
named A. B.

To the Governor and Company
 of the Bank of England, and
 Messrs. Freshfield, their solicitors.

 Additional remedy given by sect. 4 of 5 Vict. c. 5, to restrain the Bank of England, or any other company incorporated or not, from permitting transfer of stock or shares in any public company, or from paying dividends due thereon.

 Application for such restraining order to be made to the

Court of Chancery by any person interested by motion or petition in a summary way without bill filed, founded on affidavit verifying the special grounds for such application.

Sect. 5 is confined to distringas on stock, &c. in the Bank of England. As to practice under 4th sect., see *In re Marquis of Hertford*, 1 Hare, 584, 586; 1 Phil. 203; and see 15 & 16 Vict. c. 86, s. 59.

ENFRANCHISEMENTS.

[*See " Copyholds," page* 241.]

GRANT.

84.

In Fee of a Plot of Land subject to a Yearly Rent-Charge.

THIS INDENTURE, made the   day of   , 18 , between A. B., of &c. [*grantor*] of the first part, C. D., of &c. [*grantee*] of the second part, E. F., of &c. [*grantee of a piece of land adjoining by the same grantor*] of the third part, and G. H., of &c. [*trustee to bar dower*] of the fourth part, Witnesseth, that, in consideration of the rent hereinafter limited, and of the covenants and agreements hereinafter contained on the part of the said C. D., his heirs, executors, administrators and assigns, to be paid, observed and performed, the said A. B. doth hereby grant unto the said C. D. and his heirs, all [*parcels*], and which said plot of land contains in the whole   superficial square yards of land or thereabouts, be the same more or less, and is, with its boundaries, dimensions and other particulars, more fully delineated in the plan drawn in the margin of these presents, and therein coloured "red," and also all and singular the dwelling-house and other buildings already erected by the said C. D. on the said plot of land, or any part thereof, with the appurtenances to the said plot of land belonging or appertaining, (save and except out of these presents all mines, minerals and materials lying within or under the said plot of land, with liberty to get and dispose of the same, as well as the mines lying under any other lands, leaving sufficient pillars to support the surface of the same plot and any erections now erected or hereafter to be erected thereon,) To hold the premises hereby granted unto the said C. D. and his heirs, to the several uses and upon the trusts hereinafter limited and declared concerning the same (that is to say), to the use, intent and purpose that the said A. B., his heirs and assigns, may out of the said premises for ever hereafter receive and take one clear rent of £   sterling, to be issuing and payable thereout by two equal half-yearly payments, on the   day of   and the   day of   in every year, free from all deductions whatsoever, the first half-yearly payment whereof will become due on the   day of   next: And to the further use, intent and purpose, that if the said yearly rent-charge or any part thereof shall be in arrear and unpaid for the space of twenty days after the same shall become due, then it shall be lawful for the said A. B., his heirs and assigns, to enter into and upon the said premises, and to distrain for the said rent in arrear, and the distress or distresses so taken to sell and dispose of and to demean therein according to law as landlords are authorized to do in respect of distresses for arrears of rent upon leases for years, so that the said A. B., his heirs or assigns, may be paid and satisfied the said yearly rent, or so much thereof as shall then remain due and unpaid, and all costs and expenses occasioned by the nonpayment thereof: And to the further use, intent and purpose, that in case the said yearly rent-charge or any part thereof shall be in arrear and unpaid for the space of forty days next after the same shall become due, then (although no legal demand shall have been made thereof) it shall be lawful for the said A. B., his heirs and assigns, from time to time into and upon the said premises to enter, and receive and take the rents thereof for his and their own use, until not only all arrears of the said yearly rent but also all such rent as shall accrue during such possession, and all expenses incurred on account of such entry or entries and receipt of rents shall be fully paid, and such possession when taken shall be without impeachment of waste: [And to this further use and intent, that if it shall happen that the said yearly rent or any part thereof shall be behind or unpaid for the space of two years next after any of the said days or times of payment on which the same ought to be paid as aforesaid, and no sufficient distress or distresses can or may be found in or upon the said premises, it may be lawful for the said A. B., his heirs or assigns, into and upon the said premises, or any part thereof in the name of the whole, to re-enter and the same to have again, re-possess and enjoy, and receive and take the rents and profits for his and their own benefit as in his or their first and former estate;] and as to the said premises, subject to and charged with the said yearly rent and the remedies hereby provided for recovery thereof, and to the several limitations hereinbefore contained, [to the use of the said C. D. and his assigns for his life, and immediately after the determination of that estate in his lifetime, to the use of the said G. H., his executors and administrators, during the life of the said C. D. in trust for him and his assigns, and after the determination of the estate lastly hereinbefore limited,] to the use of the said C. D., his heirs and assigns: [And the said C. D. doth hereby declare that neither his present nor any future wife shall be entitled to dower out of or upon the same hereditaments and premises or any part thereof;] and the said C. D. for himself, his heirs, executors and administrators, doth hereby covenant with the said A. B., his heirs and assigns, that he the said C. D., his heirs and assigns, will yearly for ever hereafter pay unto the said A. B., his heirs and assigns, the said yearly rent of £   , by equal half-yearly payments, upon the days and in manner aforesaid, without any deductions whatsoever (the property tax in respect of the said yearly rent only excepted), and will within one year from the date hereof erect and build upon the land hereby granted one or more substantial dwelling-houses or other erections and buildings of brick or stone, or both, to be set with good lime and sand mortar, and covered with slates or tiles, of the value, to be let at £   a year at least, and will at all times hereafter keep the same buildings in good substantial repair and condition, and in case of accident or decay will from time to time rebuild the same, so that there shall always be buildings upon the said premises of the said yearly value: and the said E. F. for himself, his heirs, executors and administrators, conformably with the contract for the said plot of land, and in consideration of a similar privilege contained in the grant to him, doth hereby covenant with the said C. D., his heirs and assigns, that it shall be lawful for the said C. D., his heirs or assigns, to lay and tie the bricks, stones and timber of any building or buildings which he or they may erect in or upon the gable end or gable ends of any building or buildings which shall be erected by the said E. F., his heirs or assigns, abutting upon the extreme southwesterly side of the land hereby granted, on paying to him one half part of the expense of such gable end or gable ends which shall be so abutted upon, laid or tied, and also one half part of the future repairs thereof; and the said A. B. doth hereby for himself, his heirs, executors and administrators, covenant with the said C. D., his heirs and assigns, that, notwithstanding any act or thing by him to the contrary, he the said A. B. now hath in himself full power and authority to grant the said premises to the uses and in manner aforesaid, free from incumbrances; and that the said A. B., and every person claiming through or in trust for him, will at all times hereafter, at the costs of the said C. D., his heirs or assigns, do and execute all such acts and assurances for more effectually assuring the said premises to the uses aforesaid, or otherwise according to the direction of the said C. D., his heirs or assigns (subject, nevertheless, as herein mentioned), as by him or them shall be reasonably required; and, lastly, that he the said A. B., his heirs and assigns, will at all times hereafter (unless prevented by inevitable accident or unavoidable cause), at the request and costs of the said C. D., his heirs and assigns, produce all deeds and documents whatsoever in the possession or control of the said A. B., his heirs or assigns, for the manifestation or defence of the title of the said C. D., his heirs or assigns, to the premises hereby granted, and, at the like request and costs, furnish to him or them copies or abstracts of or extracts from the said deeds and documents, and permit the same to be examined with the originals, and in the meantime preserve the same deeds and documents whole and uncancelled.

In witness, &c.

' 85.

Of a Yearly Rent-Charge.

THIS INDENTURE, made the   day of   , 18 , between A. B., of &c., of the one part, and C. D., of &c., of the other part, Witnesseth, that in consideration of £   sterling to the said A. B. paid by the said C. D. on the execution hereof, the receipt whereof the said A. B. doth hereby acknowledge and discharge the said C. D., his heirs, executors, administrators and assigns therefrom, he the said A. B. doth hereby grant unto the said C. D., his heirs and assigns, one clear annuity or yearly rent-charge of £   sterling, to be issuing from and out of and to be charged and chargeable upon all [*parcels*], To have, receive and take the said annuity or yearly rent-charge of £   unto the said C. D., his heirs and assigns: And it is hereby declared, that the said annuity or yearly rent-charge shall be paid and payable half-yearly in equal portions on the   day of   and the   day of   in every year, and the first payment thereof shall begin and be made on the   day of   next: Provided always, and it is hereby declared and agreed, and the said A. B. doth hereby grant, that if the said annuity or yearly rent-charge shall be in arrear and unpaid for the space of thirty days next after either of the said days of payment (the same being first lawfully demanded), then and so often as the case may happen it shall be lawful for the said C. D., his heirs, executors, administrators and assigns, into and upon the hereditaments hereby charged therewith, or into any part thereof in the name of the whole, to enter and distrain for the same annuity or yearly rent-charge and all arrears thereof, and the distress and distresses then and there found to detain, sell and dispose of in the same manner in all respects as distresses for rents reserved upon leases for years, to the intent that the said C. D., his heirs, executors, administrators and assigns, may thereby or otherwise be fully satisfied and paid the said annuity or yearly rent-charge, and all the arrears thereof, and all costs and expenses attending the nonpayment of the same; and the said A. B. doth hereby for himself, his heirs, executors and administrators, covenant with the said C. D., his heirs and assigns, that, notwithstanding any act or deed made, done or permitted by the said A. B. to the contrary, he the said A. B. has good right and full power to grant the said annuity or yearly rent-charge in manner aforesaid, free from incumbrances; and moreover, that the said A. B., and every person having or claiming through or in trust for him any estate or interest in, to or out of the said hereditaments, will at all times hereafter, at the request and costs of the said C. D., his heirs or assigns, execute and perfect all such further assurances for more effectually granting and assuring to the said C. D., his heirs and assigns, or as he or they shall direct, the said annuity or yearly rent-charge intended to be hereby granted, as by him or them shall be reasonably required. [*Here insert a covenant by A. B. for production of title deeds.*]

In witness, &c.

86.

Of a Right of Road.

TOGETHER with full and free liberty and privilege for the said E. F., his heirs and assigns, and his and their agents and tenants, and the owners and occupiers for the time being of the plot of land hereby granted, and the servants, workpeople and others from time to time employed in the service of him and them respectively, from time to time and at all times for ever hereafter, at his and their respective wills and pleasures, and for all purposes, to go, return, pass and repass, with and without horses, carts, waggons and other carriages, laden or unladen, and also to drive cattle and other beasts in, through, along and over a certain road or way of four yards wide at the least, to be forthwith laid out, levelled and found by the said A. B., pursuant to his covenant in that behalf hereinafter contained, across the land of the said A. B., in the course and direction shown and delineated in the said plan, being thereon coloured brown, or in some other equally convenient course and direction, and communicating between the land hereby granted and a certain public road or way leading from   to   .

87.
Special Grant of Right of Road to Railway.

TOGETHER with full and free liberty for the said E. F., his heirs and assigns, and his and their agents and tenants, and the owners and occupiers for the time being of the land hereby granted, and the servants, work-people and others from time to time employed in the service of him and them respectively, from time to time and at all times for ever hereafter, at his and their respective will and pleasure, and for all purposes, to go, return, pass and repass, with or without engines, waggons and other carriages, laden or unladen, and propelled by steam or horse power or otherwise, on, along and over the railway hereinafter covenanted by the said A. B., to be formed by him as a branch railway from the land hereby appointed and released at the point marked A. on the said plan, through and over the land of him the said A. B. to a branch of the   Railway, and so and in such manner that he the said E. F., his heirs and assigns, and his and their tenants and occupiers may at all times after the construction of the said railway have a direct means of transit by such railway for his and their goods, merchandize and other commodities to and from and between the said land hereby granted, and the said   Railway, without and free from the payment of any toll, tonnage or other charge whatsoever, other than such as may be imposed by the said   Railway Company in respect of so much, if any, of the said intended branch railway as may be found by or belong to such company.

88.

Covenants and Proviso relating to the said Grants of Rights of Way.

AND the said A. B. for himself, his heirs, executors, administrators and assigns, doth hereby covenant with the said E. F. and his heirs that the said A. B., his heirs, executors, administrators or assigns, will at his and their own costs forthwith lay out, level and form, and afterwards at all times maintain and keep in repair in a good, substantial and workmanlike manner, a road or way, of four yards wide at the least for the whole length thereof, over and across the land of him the said A. B., in the course and direction shown and delineated in the said plan hereupon indorsed, being thereon coloured brown, or in some other equally convenient course and direction, so as to form a communication for horses, cattle, waggons and other carriages, between the said land hereby granted, and the public road or way leading from   to   , so that the same may at all times afterwards be used and enjoyed by the said E. F., his heirs and assigns, and his and their tenants, occupiers and servants, pursuant to and in accordance with the liberty and privilege in that behalf hereinbefore granted: And also that he the said A. B., his heirs, executors, administrators or assigns, will, when and so soon as the   Railway Company, or any other company, person or persons, shall make and form a branch railway from the main line of the said   Railway to the land of him the said A. B., on the   side of and adjoining to the land hereby granted, lay down and construct in a good, substantial and workmanlike manner a railway or tramroad from the said land hereby granted, at the point marked A. on the said plan, on and over his said adjoining land in a direction towards and to communicate with the aforesaid branch of the said   Railway, and will afterwards and from time to time for ever hereafter maintain and keep the same in good working repair, order and condition, and so and in such manner that the same may at all times be used and enjoyed by the said E. F., his heirs and assigns, and his and their tenants and occupiers and servants, pursuant to and in accordance with the liberty and privilege in that behalf hereinbefore granted: Provided nevertheless, and it is hereby declared and agreed by and between the said A. B. and E. F., that the costs and charges of making and repairing the railway hereinbefore covenanted to be made and repaired by the said A. B. shall be borne and paid by the said A. B. and E. F. and their respective heirs and assigns, in the proportions following, that is to say, two third parts thereof by the said A. B., his heirs and assigns, and one third part thereof by the said E. F., his heirs and assigns, save and except nevertheless as regards such repairs as may from time to time be rendered necessary through any breakage or other damage which may have been made or occasioned by or through the negligence or carelessness of either of the said parties, which shall be made by and at the sole costs of the party occasioning the same.

89.

Instructions to be sent to a Non-professional Person with a Deed for Signature.

Instructions for Execution of the accompanying Deed.

SIGN the deed at the foot, in front, opposite the seal [and also under the receipt indorsed at the back], in the place where your name is written in pencil; place a finger on the seal and say, "I deliver this as my act and deed." A witness should see you sign the deed [and receipt] and should write his or her name, place of abode and profession or calling, under the attestation at the back where "Witness's name,

&c.," is written in pencil, and should write his or her name only under the receipt where " Witness's name only" is written in pencil.

LEASES.

90.

Of Public House and Premises.

THIS INDENTURE, made the   day of   , 18 , between A. B., of &c., of the one part, and C. D., of &c., of the other part, Witnesseth, that, in consideration of the rent hereinafter reserved and of the covenants and agreements hereinafter contained, and on the part of the said C. D., his executors, administrators and assigns, to be paid, observed and performed, he the said A. B. doth demise unto the said C. D., his executors, administrators and assigns, all that messuage, tenement or public-house, called or known by the sign of the situate in   Street, in the parish of   in the said county of Middlesex, as the same is now in the occupation of the said C. D., together with all easements, vaults, cellars, yards and appurtenances whatsoever to the said premises belonging or appertaining, To hold the said premises, with the appurtenances, unto the said C. D., his executors, administrators and assigns, from the   day of   next, for twenty-one years thence next ensuing, yielding and paying during the continuance of the said term unto the said A. B., his heirs and assigns, the yearly rent of £   sterling, by four equal quarterly payments on the 29th day of September, the 25th day of December, the 25th day of March, and the 24th day of June in every year, clear of the land tax, sewers rate, and all manner of parliamentary and parochial taxes, rates or assessments whatsoever, whether now or at any time hereafter imposed or payable in respect of the said premises, and whether any such future taxes, rates or assessments shall be in the nature of those now in being or not; the first quarterly payment of the said rent to be made on the   day of next ensuing: And the said C. D. doth hereby for himself, his heirs, executors, administrators and assigns, covenant with the said A. B., his heirs and assigns, as follows, that he the said C. D., his executors, administrators and assigns, will during the continuance of the said term pay unto the said A. B., his heirs or assigns, the said rent of £   sterling in manner hereinbefore appointed for payment thereof; and also will pay the land tax, sewers rate, and all taxes, rates and assessments, parliamentary or parochial, whether now or at any time hereafter payable in respect of the said premises, and whether such future taxes, rates or assessments shall be in the nature of those now in being or not; and also will, at all times during the said term, sufficiently repair and maintain, and keep in repair with good materials, the premises hereby demised, together with the glass and other windows, window shutters, doors, locks, fastenings, bells, partitions, ceilings, chimney-pieces, pavements, pitchings, privies, drains, sinks, cesspools, cisterns, pumps, wells, pipes, water-closets and water-courses, to the said premises belonging, and all such buildings, improvements and additions whatsoever as at any time during the said term shall be erected or made by the said C. D., his executors, administrators or assigns, upon the said premises; and will, once in every three years during the said term, paint in good oil colours all the doors, rails, window frames and other the outside wood and iron work of the said premises, and once in every seven years during the said term (one of such times to be during the last three years of the said term) in like manner paint the inside wood, iron and other works now or usually painted, with two coats of proper oil colours, and also wash, stop, whiten and colour such part of the same premises as shall respectively be coloured and whitewashed; and the said premises, being so well and sufficiently repaired, maintained, cleansed and scoured, at the end or other sooner determination of the said term, will peaceably yield up unto the said A. B., his heirs and assigns: And also, that it shall be lawful for the said A. B., his heirs or assigns, and his or their surveyor, either alone or with workmen or others, twice in every year during the said term, at seasonable times in the day time, to enter into and upon the said premises, for the purpose of viewing the condition thereof; and in case any want of reparation of the said premises shall be found, he the said C. D., his executors, administrators or assigns, will, upon having three calendar months' notice thereof in writing given to him or them by the said A. B., his heirs or assigns, cause the said premises to be sufficiently repaired in all things within the term aforesaid: And also, that he the said C. D., his executors, administrators or assigns, will not, during the continuance of the said term, use, exercise or carry on, or permit or suffer to be used, exercised or carried on, in or upon the said premises, any noxious, noisome or offensive trade or business, without the consent in writing of the said A. B., his heirs or assigns, first obtained: And also, that he the said C. D., his executors, administrators and assigns, will not at any time during the continuance of the said term, without the consent in writing of the said A. B., his heirs or assigns, first obtained, convert the premises hereby demised, or any part thereof, into a shop, warehouse, shed or place of sale for goods or merchandize, or into a private dwelling-house, or open or use or suffer the same respectively to be opened or used for any other purpose than as an hotel or inn, public-house or tavern: And also, that the said C. D., his executors, administrators and assigns, or such other person or persons as shall for the time being inhabit, keep, occupy or conduct the business of the said messuage, tenement or public-house, will at all times during the continuance of the said term keep and conduct the same in a regular and proper manner in every respect, and will immediately apply for and use his and their best endeavours to obtain a certificate, licence or permission of her Majesty's justices of the peace for the vending of wines, spirituous liquors and beer on the said premises, and shall not knowingly or willingly do any act whereby the same may become legally or justly abrogated, forfeited or refused: And also will at all times during the said term manage or conduct the business of the said public-house, hotel or inn, under the name of and constantly keep up the effigy or sign of the "   "; and will at the end or other sooner determination of the said term, upon demand by the said A. B., his heirs or assigns, or his or their incoming tenant, deliver up the said several certificates, licences or permissions of her said Majesty's justices of the peace, granted during the then current year, for the vending of any wines, spirits, liquors, beer, ale or tobacco upon the said demised premises, and also all and every the excise licences for the unexpired term they may have then to run: And also, that the said C. D , his executors, administrators and assigns, will forthwith insure the said premises to the full value thereof in some respectable insurance office in London or Westminster in the joint names of the said A. B., his heirs or assigns, and the said C. D., his executors, administrators or assigns, and keep the same so insured during the said term, and will, upon the request of the said A. B., his heirs or assigns, or his or their agent, show the receipt for the last premium paid for such insurance for every current year, and as often as the said premises shall be burnt down or damaged by fire, all the money which shall be received by the said C. D., his executors, administrators or assigns, for or in respect of such insurance, shall be expended by him or them in building or repairing the said premises or such parts thereof as shall be burnt down or damaged by fire as aforesaid: Provided always, and it is hereby agreed, that if the rent hereby reserved or any part thereof shall be unpaid for fifteen days after any of the days on which the same ought to have been paid, or in case of the breach or nonperformance of any of the covenants or agreements herein contained on the part of the said C. D., his executors, administrators or assigns, then and in either of such cases it shall be lawful for the said A. B., his heirs or assigns, at any time thereafter into and upon the said premises, or any part thereof in the name of the whole, to re-enter, and the same to have again, repossess and enjoy, as in his or their former estate: And the said A. B. doth hereby for himself, his heirs, executors, administrators and assigns, covenant with the said C. D., his executors, administrators and assigns, that he the said C. D., his executors, administrators and assigns, paying the rent hereby reserved

276   PRECEDENTS.

at and upon the days and times, and in the manner hereinbefore appointed for payment thereof, and performing and observing the covenants and agreements hereinbefore on his and their part contained, shall quietly enjoy the premises hereby demised, with their appurtenances, during the term hereby granted without any interruption whatsoever by the said A. B. or his heirs, or any other person or persons lawfully claiming by, from or under him or them.

In witness, &c.

91.

Of Land for Building Purposes.

THIS INDENTURE, made the   day of   , 18 , between A. B. of the one part, and C. D. of the other part: Witnesseth, that, in consideration of the rent, covenants and conditions hereinafter reserved and contained, he the said A. B. doth by these presents demise and lease unto the said C. D., his executors, administrators and assigns, all &c., situate   , in the said county; and which said plot or parcel of land so demised to the said A. B. as aforesaid forms part of a piece or parcel of land called   , and contains in the whole by admeasurement   square yards or thereabouts; and is more particularly delineated or described in the plan or ground plot thereof, drawn in the margin hereof, together with the appurtenances to the same belonging, [save and except out of this present demise all mines, veins, beds and seams of coal and cannel, and all other minerals whatsoever, now being thereunder, with liberty for the said A. B., his heirs and assigns, and his and their tenants, agents, servants, workmen and others, with his and their permission and authority, to win, work, get and carry away the same, when and as he and they shall think proper; and also to erect engines and machinery, and make roads, and do all such acts and exercise all such powers and privileges as shall be necessary for the more profitable winning, working, getting and carrying away of the said mines and minerals, when and as he and they shall think fit:] To hold the premises hereby demised with their appurtenances unto the said A. B., his executors, administrators and assigns, from the making of these presents, for and during and unto the full end and term of ninety-nine years thence next ensuing, and fully to be complete and ended; yielding and paying, therefore, yearly and every year during the said term hereby granted, unto the said A. B., his heirs and assigns, the rent or sum of £   sterling, by equal quarterly payments, on the   day of   , the   day of   , the   day of   , and the   day of   in every year, free from all taxes, charges, impositions and assessments whatsoever, now or hereafter to be imposed upon or in respect of the said demised premises or any part thereof by authority of parliament or otherwise however; the first quarterly payment of the said yearly rent of £   , to be made on the   day of   , now next ensuing: And the said C. D. for himself, his heirs, executors, administrators and assigns, doth hereby covenant with the said A. B., his heirs and assigns, in manner following; that is to say, that he the said A. B., his executors, administrators or assigns will pay unto the said A. B., his heirs and assigns the yearly rent of £   , clear of all taxes and deductions as aforesaid, on the days and times hereinbefore mentioned: And also, that the said C. D., his executors, administrators and assigns, will, during the term hereby granted, pay and discharge all rates, taxes, lays, duties, assessments, outgoings, and all other taxes, charges and impositions whatsoever, which are or shall be assessed or charged on, or in anywise imposed upon, or in respect of the same premises, hereby intended to be demised, or any part thereof, or upon the lessor for the time being in respect thereof, or upon the lessee or lessees, tenants or occupiers of the same premises, by authority of parliament, or otherwise howsoever: And also, that he the said C. D., his executors, administrators and assigns, will, at his and their proper costs and charges, within the space of two years, to be computed from the day of the date hereof, in a good substantial and workmanlike manner, erect, build and completely finish, fit for habitation and use, upon the land hereby demised, one or more messuage or tenement, messuages or tenements, to be built with the best sound material of all sorts, and will roof and cover in such messuages or tenements with good blue slate; and also, will fence off the land hereby demised, on the   sides thereof respectively, by a good brick wall, six feet in height at the least, from other parts of the land adjoining, it being expressly understood and agreed by and between the parties hereto, that in such messuage or tenement, messuages or tenements, so to be erected and built as aforesaid, there shall not be any window, door or other communication from the   sides of such building or buildings respectively, with the lands or buildings immediately adjoining or contiguous thereto, so that the value of such buildings, or the lands, as now or hereafter to be laid out, on the   side thereof, may not be in any way injured or depreciated for building purposes: And such messuage or tenement, messuages or tenements, when so erected and built as aforesaid, shall be worth, to let to a tenant or tenants, by the year, not less than double the amount of the yearly rent hereby reserved; and also, that he the said A. B., his executors, administrators and assigns, will, as occasion shall require, during the said term, well and sufficiently repair, maintain, pave, empty, cleanse, amend, and keep the said premises, with the appurtenances, in such good and substantial repair as is necessary for the occupation of a tenant or tenants at rack rents; and the said premises, being in all things repaired, maintained, paved, emptied, cleansed, amended and kept, as aforesaid, at the end or other sooner determination of the said term, will quietly yield up unto the said A. B., his heirs or assigns, together with all chimney-pieces, windows, doors, fastenings, water-closets, cisterns, partitions, fixed presses, shelves, pipes, pumps, pales, rails, locks and keys, and all other things, which, at any time during the last seven years of the said term, shall be fastened to the said demised premises and come within the denomination of fixtures: And also, that it shall be lawful for the said A. B., his heirs or assigns, and any persons deputed by him or them, at any reasonable hours, in the day-

time, during such last seven years, to enter upon all and every the said demised premises, and take a schedule or schedules of the same fixtures and things respectively: And also, that the said C. D., his executors, administrators and assigns, will, in every third year of the said term, paint all the outside woodwork and iron work belonging to the said premises, with two coats of proper oil colours, in a workmanlike manner, and shall in every seventh year of the said term paint and paper in like manner all the internal parts of such messuage and tenement, messuages and tenements as shall have been painted and papered: And also, that the said C. D., his executors, administrators and assigns, will, on demand, pay and allow to the said A. B., his heirs and assigns, one-half the expense of making and forming an intended new street of ten yards wide, and now forming part of   , other land belonging to the said A. B.; and also of making a covered drain or drains, from the front of the said messuage or tenement, messuages or tenements and buildings, and leading from the common sewer: And shall bear the like proportion of laying down and paving the said street, so far as the same shall run co-extensively with the premises hereby demised, such street, drain and pavement to be made to the satisfaction of the surveyor for the time being of the said A. B., his heirs or assigns, and also will at his or their own proper costs and charges, and to the satisfaction of the said A. B., his heirs or assigns, pave with good flagging stones, the footways to be made on the side of the said intended new street as aforesaid, and shall also at his and their own expense, and to the satisfaction of the said A. B., his heirs or assigns, pave with good flagging stones, before the fronts of the said messuages or tenements, and lay down edging-stones to the aforesaid foot-paths, respectively, so far as such foot-paths run co-extensively with the hereby demised premises, and also will, from time to time, and at all times during the said term, repair and keep in repair the whole of the said foot-paths, as well in the front of the said messuage or tenement, messuages or tenements, on the
part thereof, so far as the same respectively run co-extensively with the said premises; and also will bear, pay and discharge

one moiety, half part, or share of the charges and expenses of making, supporting, repairing and amending all party walls and gutters, which during the said term shall belong to the said premises, or which shall be used in common by the said C. D. or his assigns, and the takers or occupiers of the adjoining or contiguous premises respectively: And, moreover, that it shall be lawful for the said A. B., his heirs and assigns, and for any person and persons to be deputed by him or them, with or without workmen in his or their company, twice or oftener in every year, during the term hereby granted at seasonable and convenient times in the day time, to enter and come into and upon the said premises or any part thereof, to view and examine the state and condition of the repairs thereof, and of all defects and wants of reparation and amendment, and upon every such view to give or leave notice or warning in writing at the said demised premises; and that the said C. D., his executors, administrators and assigns, will, within three calendar months next after such notice and warning, well and sufficiently repair and amend the same, according to such notice and warning so given or left as aforesaid : And further, that the said C. D., his executors, administrators and assigns, shall not nor will exercise, or carry on, or permit or suffer to be exercised or carried on by any person whomsoever, upon any part of the premises hereby demised, the trade of a boiler of horse flesh, slaughterman, soap maker or boiler, melter of tallow, distiller, brewer, victualler, beer shop or alehouse keeper, blacksmith, boiler maker, or any other noisome, dangerous or offensive trade or business whatsoever, without the express consent in writing, under the hand of the said A. B., his heirs or assigns, first had and obtained for that purpose, such consent, if the same have reference to the trades of a victualler or beer shop or alehouse keeper, to be applied for yearly and every year, and to be granted at the discretion of the said A. B., his heirs or assigns ; nor shall the said C. D., his executors, administrators or assigns do, or cause or wittingly or willingly suffer to be done, any act or thing on the said demised premises, or any part thereof, which may grow to the annoyance, damage or disturbance of the said A. B., his heirs or assigns, or his or their tenant or tenants; and, moreover, that he the said C. D , his executors, administrators and assigns will insure the buildings to be erected on the ground hereby demised, in the joint names of him or them and the said A. B., his heirs or assigns to the full value thereof, in such fire insurance office as the said A. B., his heirs or assigns shall direct, and keep the same so insured during the said term; and upon the request of the said A. B., his heirs or assigns, or his or their solicitor, steward, or agent, produce and show the receipt for the premium for such insurance for the then current year; and also will during the said term, as often as the buildings to be erected on the ground hereby demised or any part thereof shall be burnt down or destroyed by fire, forthwith reinstate the same under the direction and to the satisfaction of the surveyor for the time being of the said A. B., his heirs or assigns, and will pay the said rent hereby reserved in the same manner as if no such accident by fire had happened; and, the same premises being so rebuilt as aforesaid, the said A. B., his heirs or assigns will allow the said C. D., his executors, administrators and assigns to retain and keep to his and their own use any sum or sums of money to be received by him or them by virtue or in consequence of any such policy or policies of insurance so to be effected as aforesaid: And the said C. D. for himself, his heirs, executors, administrators and assigns, doth hereby covenant with the said A. B., his heirs and assigns, that in case the said C. D., his executors, administrators or assigns, shall at any time or times hereafter sell, assign or underlet the piece or parcel of land or ground hereby demised, or any part thereof, and the buildings and erections thereon, or part with this present indenture of lease, that then and in any or either of the said cases the said C. D., his executors, administrators and assigns, shall within twenty-one days after any agreement of sale, assignment or underlease as aforesaid shall be made, deliver a true copy of such agreement of sale, assignment or underlease to the said A. B., his heirs or assigns; and that the said C. D., his executors, administrators or assigns, shall not during the last seven years of the said term, sell, assign, demise or make over or part with the said premises or any part thereof, for all or any part of the residue of the said term, without the consent in writing of the said A. B., his heirs or assigns: Provided always, that if it shall happen that the said yearly rent or sum of £   shall be unpaid in the whole or in part by the space of twenty-one days next after the said days of payment on which the same ought to be paid as aforesaid, the same being first lawfully demanded upon or at any time after the expiration of the said twenty-one days, and not paid when demanded, or if default shall be made in the observance or performance of all or any of the covenants, clauses or agreements herein contained on the part of C. D., his executors, administrators or assigns to be performed, then and thenceforth, and in any of the said cases, it shall be lawful for the said A. B., his heirs or assigns, into and upon the said demised premises or any part thereof, in the name of the whole, to re-enter as in his or their first and former estate.

In witness, &c.

92.

Of a House.

THIS INDENTURE, made the   day of   , 18 , between A. B., of &c., of the one part, and C. D., of &c., of the other part, Witnesseth, that, in consideration of the rent hereby reserved, and the covenants hereinafter contained, and on the part of the lessee, his executors, administrators and assigns to be paid and performed, he the said A. B. doth demise unto the said C. D., all &c., To hold unto the said C. D., his executors, administrators and assigns, for   years from   18 , yielding and paying, therefore, yearly unto the said A. B., his heirs and assigns, the rent of £   by quarterly payments on the usual quarterly days, the first payment to be made on the   day of   next; and the said C. D. doth hereby for himself, his heirs, executors, administrators and assigns, covenant with the said A. B., his heirs and assigns, in manner following (that is to say), that he the said C. D., his executors, administrators and assigns, will during the said term pay unto the said A. B., his heirs and assigns, the rent hereby reserved in manner hereinbefore mentioned, without any deduction; and also will pay all taxes, rates, duties and assessment whatsoever, whether parochial, parliamentary or otherwise, now charged or hereafter to be charged on the said premises or the lessor on account thereof (except only the property tax); and also will during the said term well and sufficiently repair, maintain, pave, empty, cleanse, amend and keep the demised premises and every part thereof, with the appurtenances, in good and substantial repair and condition; and also will in every fourth year of the said term paint all the outside wood work and iron work belonging to the said premises with two coats of proper oil colours in a workmanlike manner; and also will in every seventh year paint the inside wood, iron and other work now or usually painted with two coats of proper oil colours in a workmanlike manner; and also repaper with paper of a quality as at present such parts of the premises as are now papered; and also wash, stop, whiten or colour such parts of the premises as are now plastered; and also will forthwith insure the said premises in the sum of £ in some respectable insurance office in the joint names of the said A. B., his heirs or assigns, and the said C. D., his executors, administrators and assigns, and keep the same so insured during the said term, and will upon the request of the said A. B., his heirs or assigns, or his or their agent, show the receipt for the last premium paid for such insurance for every current year, and as often as the said premises shall be burnt down or damaged by fire all and every the sums or sum of money which shall be recovered or received by the said C. D., his executors, administrators or assigns, for or in respect of such insurance shall be laid out and expended by him or them in building or repairing the demised premises, or such parts thereof as shall be burnt down or damaged by fire; and that it shall be lawful for the said A. B., his heirs or assigns, and his or their agents at all seasonable times during the said term to enter the demised premises to take a schedule of the fixtures and things made and erected thereupon, and to examine the condition of the said premises, and that all wants of reparation which upon such views shall be found, and for the amendment of which notice in writing shall be left at the premises, the said C. D., his executors, administrators and assigns will within three calendar months next after every such notice well and sufficiently repair and make good accordingly; and also will not convert, use or occupy the said premises or any part thereof into or as a shop, warehouse or other place for carrying on any trade or business whatsoever, or suffer the said premises to be used for any such purpose or otherwise than as a private dwelling-house, nor at any time during the said term assign, transfer or underlet the demised premises or any part thereof to any person or persons whomsoever without the consent in writing of the said A. B , his heirs or assigns first obtained; and also will at the expiration or other sooner determination of the said term peaceably yield up the demised premises with the appurtenances unto the said A. B., his heirs or assigns, together with all buildings, erections and fixtures now or hereafter to be built or erected thereon, in good and substantial repair and condition in all respects: provided always, and it is expressly agreed, that if the rent hereby reserved or any part thereof shall be unpaid for twenty-one days after any of the days on which the same ought to have been paid (although no formal demand shall have been made thereof), or in case of the breach or nonperformance of any of the covenants herein contained on the part of the said C. D., his executors, administrators and assigns, then and in either of such cases it shall be lawful for the said A. B., his heirs or assigns, at any time thereafter unto and upon the demised premises or any part thereof in the name of the whole to re-enter, and the same to have again as in his or their former estate: And the said A. B. doth hereby for himself, his heirs, executors, administrators and assigns, covenant with the said C. D., his executors, administrators and assigns, that he and they, paying the rent hereby reserved and performing the covenants hereinbefore on his and their parts contained, may peaceably enjoy the demised premises for the term hereby granted without any interruption or disturbance from the said A. B., his heirs or assigns, or any person or persons lawfully claiming by, from or under him, them or any of them.

In witness, &c.

93.

Covenant for Production of Original Lease contained in an Underlease.

AND further, that the said A. B., his executors, administrators and assigns, will during the term hereby granted (if not prevented by fire or other inevitable accident), at the request and costs of the said C. D., his executors, administrators or assigns, produce unto him or them, or as he or they may direct, in England, and not elsewhere, the hereinbefore-recited [*or* mentioned] indenture of lease of the   day of   , 18 ; and will at the like request and costs furnish to the said C. D., his executors, administrators or assigns, copies or extracts (attested, if required) of or from the same indenture of lease or any part thereof.

94.

Arbitration Clause in Lease.

AND in case of any dispute or difference in opinion between the said parties hereto with respect to the state, condition and value of the said several articles, matters and things enumerated in the said schedule at the expiration or other sooner determination of the said term, the same shall be referred to the arbitration and final determination of two indifferent persons, one to be chosen by the said [*lessor*], his heirs or assigns, and the other by the said [*lessee*], his executors, administrators or assigns, or if the two persons chosen shall disagree, then by an umpire to be chosen by such two persons before entering on their valuation; and if either of them the said [*lessor*], his heirs or assigns, and [*lessee*], his executors, administrators or assigns, shall neglect or refuse, after the expiration of fourteen days' notice in writing by the other party to appoint a person, in pursuance of the provision aforesaid, or the person appointed by one of them shall neglect or refuse, after such notice as aforesaid, to act, then and in either of such cases the person appointed by the other of them shall alone make such valuation or decision as aforesaid, and such valuation or decision shall in all cases be binding and conclusive.

95.

Clause in Lease suspending Rent during Fire.

AND it is hereby declared and agreed, that in case the premises hereby demised, or any part thereof, shall at any time during the term hereby granted be burnt down or damaged by fire so as to render the same unfit for habitation, then and so often as the same shall happen the rent hereby reserved, or a proportionate part thereof, according to the nature and extent of the injury sustained, and all remedies for recovering the same, shall be suspended and abated until the said premises shall have been rebuilt and made fit for habitation.

96.

Exception out of Lease of Water from Well.

EXCEPT and reserved out of this demise unto the said lessors, their heirs and assigns, and the occupier and occupiers of any other buildings, lands and premises late of or the site whereof was late of or belonging to the said G. C. deceased, the full and free liberty of ingress, egress and regress, in, to, from and out of the said pieces or parcels of ground coloured blue in the said plan, to take in common with the said J. P., his executors, administrators and assigns, and his and their under-tenants of the premises hereby demised, the water from the well therein sunk, and to sink any other well or wells, and make any tank or reservoir in or upon the said pieces of ground coloured blue, and to take and lay down any pipes or aqueducts in and through any part or parts of the said plots of ground hereby demised, not being the site of any building, for conveying the water therefrom in order to supply with water any other messuages or tenements of the said lessors, their heirs or assigns; and also, except and always reserved out of this demise unto the said lessors, their heirs and assigns, and the occupier and occupiers of adjoining and neighbouring buildings, lands and premises late of or the site whereof was late of or belonging to the said G. C. deceased, the free passage of water and soil in, by and through the channels and drains belonging or to be made upon or through the said hereby demised premises, or any part thereof, To have and to hold, &c.

97.

Licence by Lessor to Lessee to permit Sale by Auction on Premises.

WHEREAS, by indenture of lease bearing date the   day of   , 18 , made between the undersigned S. B. of the one part, and J. H. of the other part, the said S. B. demised the premises therein mentioned, situate in the parish of B., in the county of M., for the term and at the yearly rent therein mentioned; and in which said indenture the said J. H. covenanted that he would not permit or suffer any auction or sale of household goods, furniture or other things to be made in or upon the said premises, without the licence or consent in writing of the said S. B., his executors, administrators or assigns, first had and obtained: Now the said S. B. doth hereby give full liberty and licence unto the said J. H. to make sale by auction of the said lease and also of his present household goods, furniture and effects in and upon the said premises; nevertheless, the licence so hereby given by the said S. B. to the said J. H. as aforesaid is, and he doth hereby accept the same, upon this express condition, that such licence shall not extend nor be deemed or construed to extend to permit the said J. H. to make any further sale by auction of household goods, furniture or other things in or upon the said demised premises without the like licence and consent of the said S. B., his executors, administrators and assigns, first had and obtained for that purpose. Dated this   day of   , 18   .   S. B.

98.

Notice to Quit.

To Mr. J. P., or whom else it may concern. I hereby give you notice, that I require you to quit and deliver up to me on or before the   day of   now next ensuing the peaceable and quiet possession of all that messuage or tenement, with the shed and outbuildings and front garden, containing 1A. 2R. 3P., and all that piece or parcel of arable land containing 1A. 2R. 3P., situate in the parish of E., in the county of M., which you now hold of me as tenant, or otherwise that you deliver up the said messuage or tenement, lands and premises to me at the end of the year of your tenancy which shall expire next after the end of one half year from the date hereof. Dated this   day of   18 .

Yours, &c., A. B.

By C. D., his agent.

99.

Clause, restrictive as to Assignment, but not to be unreasonably withheld.

AND further, that he the said A. B., his executors, administrators or assigns, shall not nor will, at any time during the said term, assign these presents or underlet the premises hereby demised, or any part thereof, to any person or persons whomsoever, without the consent of the said E. D., his heirs or assigns, in writing for that purpose first obtained: [provided nevertheless, and it is hereby declared, that the covenant last hereinbefore contained is and is meant for the sole end and intent that the said premises shall not be so assigned or let unto or become the property of any indigent or improper person or persons, and not to restrain or prevent the said A. B., his executors or administrators, from assigning, letting or parting with or disposing of the said premises, or any part thereof, to any responsible and substantial person or persons who may be desirous of taking the same; and that the said E. D., his heirs or assigns, shall not nor will substantially and without good and sufficient reason and cause assigned refuse such consent as aforesaid, nor demand or require any premium or gratuity for giving or granting the same] or [but it is hereby declared that such consent shall not be unreasonably or capriciously withheld].

100.

Proviso to determine Lease at the option of either Party at the end of the first Seven or Fourteen Years.

PROVIDED always, and it is hereby agreed, that if the said G. F.; his executors, administrators or assigns, or the said G. T. K, his executors, administrators or assigns, shall be desirous to determine this present demise at the end of the first seven or fourteen years of the said term of twenty-one years, and of such his or their respective desire shall give six calendar months' notice in writing to the other or others of them respectively before the expiration of the said first seven or fourteen years, then and in that case this lease and every clause and thing herein contained, and the term hereby granted, shall at the expiration of the said seven or fourteen years thenceforward cease, and be void and determine, in like manner as if the whole of the said term of twenty-one years had run out and expired, or the said demise or lease had been made or granted for seven or fourteen years only.

101.

Proviso in Lease requiring Lessee to give up any Part of demised Premises on receiving Notice from Lessor.

PROVIDED always, and it is hereby declared and agreed, by and between the said parties hereto, that in case the said [*lessor*], his heirs or assigns, shall at any time, or from time to time, during the continuance of the term hereby granted, be desirous of having any part of the said piece or parcel of land and premises hereby demised delivered up to him or them, and of such his or their desire shall give three calendar months' notice in writing to the said [*lessee*], his executors, administrators or assigns, at his or their last or usual place of abode, or upon the said demised premises, such notice to expire at any period, then at the expiration of such notice the said [*lessee*], his executors, administrators or assigns, doth hereby covenant and agree peaceably and quietly to yield and surrender up, and that the said [*lessor*], his heirs or assigns, shall and may take peaceable and quiet possession of, such part or parts of the said piece or parcel of land and premises hereby demised as shall be mentioned and included in such notice as aforesaid, he the said [*lessor*], his heirs or assigns, paying to the said [*lessee*], his executors, administrators or assigns, a reasonable and fair compensation in respect of the monies which may have been laid out by the said [*lessee*], his executors, administrators or assigns, in improving the condition of so much of the said piece or parcel of land as shall be so given up to the said [*lessor*], his heirs or assigns, as hereinbefore mentioned, and then and from thenceforth the rent reserved by this indenture shall be reduced at the rate of

for each and every acre, and so in proportion for a less quantity than an acre, of the said land that may be given up to the said *lessor*], his heirs or assigns, as aforesaid, and the remainder of the said land shall be held by the said [*lessee*], his executors, administrators or assigns, at such reduced rent; and the said [*lessor*], his heirs or assigns, shall have the same powers and remedies in all respects as if this lease had been originally granted at such reduced rent; and all and every the covenants, clauses, provisoes, stipulations and agreements herein contained shall be as valid and effectual of and for so much of the land hereby demised as shall not be included in any such notice; and this indenture shall be read and construed in all respects with reference thereto as if such reduced rent had been the original rent reserved therein, and the land originally demised had been the land not included in such notice as aforesaid, and the covenants, clauses, provisoes, stipulations and agreements herein contained had only related to such last-mentioned land.

[N.B.—The above is a condition, and not only a covenant.

Under the above clause the lessor, if he thought fit, could re-enter upon the whole of the demised premises, upon giving three months' notice. *Doe* d. *Gardner* v. *Kennard*, 12 Jurist, 821.]

102.

Proviso to be inserted in Mining Lease providing for Reduction of Rent if Faults met with.

PROVIDED nevertheless, that in measuring and ascertaining the quantity or several quantities of coals gotten by virtue of this demise, an adequate deduction and allowance from such measurement shall from time to time be made to the lessees for or in respect of any fault or faults which in the working the said mines or any of them shall be met with and discovered therein, and if the extent of the quantity to be deducted by reason of such fault or faults cannot be agreed upon by the said [*lessor*] and [*lessee*], then the same shall be decided by arbitration pursuant to the clause in that behalf hereinafter contained.

103.

Proviso in Lease authorizing Lessor to dispose of Part of demised Land on allowing abatement or expending Money received.

PROVIDED always, and it is hereby declared and agreed, that it shall at all times, during the continuance of the said term, be lawful for the said [*lessor*], his heirs or assigns, from time to time to sell to or exchange with any person or persons whomsoever any part of the land hereby demised, or to sell or give up to the commissioners of the town of   for the time being any part of the said land for the widening and improvement of the roads adjoining the same, and for that purpose by any writing under his, her or their hands or hand, to revoke and determine this demise in respect of so much of the said premises as shall be so exchanged, sold or given up, but in every such case the person or persons so exchanging, selling or giving up shall make compensation to the said [*lessees*], their executors, administrators or assigns, either by an abatement from the rent hereby reserved, or by expending, with all reasonable speed, upon the premises hereby demised such sum or sums of money as shall have been received from the said commissioners of the town of   at the option of such person or persons so exchanging, selling or giving up as aforesaid; such expenditure or abatement to be settled in case the parties shall differ by three indifferent persons or the major part of them, one to be chosen by each of the contending parties, and the third by the two so chosen; but if the sum so received from the said commissioners of the town of   shall be expended upon the said premises as aforesaid, the whole of the rent hereby reserved, or if an abatement of the rent shall be elected the residue of such rent, shall be paid and payable, and recoverable by distress or otherwise, in all respects as if no such exchange, sale or gift had taken place.

104.
Notice to Lessee to abate Nuisance.

To Mr. N. O., or whomsoever else it may concern: Whereas by indenture of lease, dated the   day of   18 , and made between A. B., C. D. and E. F. of the first part, G. H. of the second part, and you, the said N. O. of the third part, a piece of ground with the messuage and buildings thereon erected, situate in the parish of   , in the county of   , was demised to you for the term of forty years, at the yearly rent of 60l., and subject to the covenants on your part to be observed and performed, and in the said lease is contained a covenant in the words or to the effect following (that is to say), that you would not erect on the said piece of ground thereby demised any new or additional erection or building, nor use, or exercise, or permit, or suffer to be used or exercised in or upon the said messuage and premises thereby demised, any trade or business whatsoever, without the consent in writing of the said lessors, their heirs or assigns: Now we hereby give you notice, and require you within the space of fourteen days from the date hereof, to take down the cart-shed and stable you have lately erected on the said demised premises, contrary to the covenant contained in the said lease, and we also require you immediately to discontinue the trade or business of a   now carried on by you or on your account, or with your consent, or by your sufferance, contrary to the covenant in the said lease; and we further give you notice, that the lessors will enter upon the demised premises as of their former estate, and make void the above-mentioned lease, if you disregard the requisition aforesaid, and do not observe and perform the covenants on your part in the said indenture of lease contained.

Dated this   day of   , 18 .

M. and N.,
Solicitors for the above-named lessors.

105.

Surrender of Lease by Indorsement.

THIS INDENTURE, made the   day of   18 , between [the within-named] C. D. [*lessee*], of the one part, and [the within-named] A. B. [*lessor*] of the other part: [Whereas by virtue of divers assignments and acts in the law, and ultimately by an indenture, dated the   day of   18 , made between E. F. of the one part, and the said C. D. of the other part, the messuage or tenement, and all other the premises demised by the within indenture were assigned to and are now vested in the said C. D. for all the residue of the term granted by the within indenture]; [and whereas by divers mesne conveyances and acts in the law, and ultimately by an indenture, dated the   day of   18 , made between G. H. of the one part, and the said A. B. of the other part, the reversion and inheritance of and in the premises demised by the within indenture immediately expectant on the term thereby granted became vested in the said A. B., his heirs and assigns]; and whereas the said C. D. hath contracted with the said A. B. to surrender to him the said premises in manner hereinafter mentioned: Now this indenture witnesseth, that, in consideration of the premises, he the said C. D. doth by these presents surrender and yield up unto the said A. B. the messuage or tenement and all other the premises demised by the within indenture or intended so to be, with their rights, members and appurtenances, to the intent that the residue of the term of   years granted by the within indenture may forthwith, or as soon as circumstances will permit, be extinguished in the reversion and inheritance of and in the said premises; and the said C. D. doth hereby for himself, his heirs, executors, and administrators, covenant with the said A. B., his heirs and assigns, that he the said C. D. hath not at any time heretofore done or knowingly permitted or suffered any act, deed or thing whereby or by means whereof the said premises are or may be charged, incumbered or prejudicially affected, or whereby the said C. D. can be in any manner hindered or prevented from surrendering the same in manner aforesaid. In witness, &c.

106.

Waiver by Lessor of past Breaches of Covenant by a Lessee.

IN consideration of £ paid to me the undersigned by the present owner (under the lease hereinafter referred to) of the leasehold messuage or tenement and premises at   comprised in an indenture of lease, dated the   day of 18 , and made between, &c., I the said   [*the person entitled to the reversion in the said premises expectant on the term granted by the said lease*] agree to waive and do hereby waive any past breach or breaches in the observance or performance of the covenants and agreements in the said lease contained, and which on the part of the lessee or assignee of the premises thereby demised ought to have been observed and performed. Dated this   day of   18 .

107.

Licence by Lessor to assign Lease.

WHEREAS by indenture of lease, dated the   day of   , 18 , made between the undersigned L. B. of the one part, and S. T. of the other part, the said L. B. did demise certain premises situate in the parish of   , in the county of   , for the term and at the yearly rent therein mentioned, and in which said indenture the said S. T. covenanted that he would not assign, demise, underlet or otherwise part with the possession of the said demised premises or any part thereof without the license or consent in writing of the said L. B., his executors, administrators or assigns first had and obtained; now the said L. B. doth hereby give full liberty and license unto the said S. T. to assign the said lease and all his estate and interest therein, unto Y. Z., of   .

[The act 22 & 23 Vict. cap. 35, sect. 1, enacts, that such a licence as the above shall only extend to the particular assignment mentioned in the licence.]

MEMORIALS.

108.

Of a Lease for Registration.

B. } A MEMORIAL to be registered of .
to } An indenture of lease, bearing date the day
D. } of , 18 , made between A. B., of &c., of the one part, and C. D., of &c., of the other part: Whereby all [*insert parcels from the lease verbatim*], with their rights, members and appurtenances, were demised by the said A. B. to the said C. D. for years, and which said indenture, as to the execution thereof by the said A. B. is witnessed by E. F., of &c., and the same is required to be registered by the said A. B.

As witness his hand and seal. (L.S.)
Signed and sealed in the presence of
[*Two witnesses.*]

109.

Of Conveyance.

A. } A MEMORIAL to be registered of .
to } An indenture, bearing date the day of ,
B. } 18 , made between [*parties verbatim as in deed*]: Whereby the said did grant unto the said all [*parcels verbatim*], with their rights, easements and appurtenances, To hold the same unto and to the use of the said , his heirs and assigns, which said indenture, as to the execution thereof by the said is witnessed by of , and as to the execution thereof by the said is witnessed by of , and the same is hereby required to be registered by the said .

As witness his hand and seal. (L.S.)
Signed and sealed in the presence of
[*Two witnesses.*]

[N.B.—If the conveyance is to the ordinary uses to bar dower, then, instead of the above limitation, it will be as follows: " To uses for the benefit of the said   his heirs and assigns, being the ordinary uses to bar dower."]

110.

Of an Assignment.

A. ⎫ A MEMORIAL to be registered of
to ⎬ An indenture, bearing date the   day of   ,
B. ⎭ 18 , made between [*parties verbatim as in deed*]: After reciting an indenture of lease whereby [*parcels from the lease as set out in the recital of that document in the assignment*] were demised to   , it was by the indenture now intended to be registered witnessed, that the said   did assign unto the said   all [*parcels verbatim from the body of the assignment*] with their rights, easements and appurtenances, To hold unto the said   , his executors, administrators and assigns, for the remainder of a term of   years created by the said indenture of lease, subject to the payment of the rent reserved by and to the performance of the conditions contained in the same indenture, which said indenture as to the execution thereof by the said   is witnessed by   of   , and as to the execution thereof by the said   is witnessed by   of   , and the same is hereby required to be registered by the said   .

As witness his hand and seal.   (L.S.)

Signed and sealed in the presence of   .

[*Two witnesses.*]

111.

Of a Mortgage.

A. ⎫ A MEMORIAL to be registered of
to ⎬ An indenture, bearing date the   day of   ,
B. ⎭ 18 , made between [*same as No.* 109 *or No.* 110, *as the case may be, except that at the end of the habendum the*

following words should be inserted, " subject to a proviso for re-conveyance of the said hereditaments on payment by the said   , his heirs, executors or administrators, unto the said   , his executors, administrators or assigns, of the sum of £   with interest, after the rate, on the day, and in the manner therein mentioned,"] [the conclusion will be as before].

[N.B.—If the deed and memorial are executed in the country, no affidavit is now required, but it is sufficient that the following be indorsed on the memorial, and one of the witnesses will attend before the commissioner and make the oath.]

112.

Memorandum to be indorsed on the Memorial where Deed and Memorial executed in the Country.

I HEREBY certify that the within-named A. B. made oath of the signing and sealing of this memorial, and of the due execution of the deed to which it refers, before me.

A commissioner to administer oaths
in Chancery in England.

113.

Of an endorsed Deed.

A MEMORIAL to be registered of   .

An indenture, dated the   day of   , 18   [*indorsed on an indenture, dated the   day of   , 18   , made between A. B., of &c., of the one part, and C. D., of &c.,* of the other part: A memorial whereof was registered on the   day of   , 18   , B., No.   ]. The indenture, of which this is a memorial, is made between the therein within-named C. D. of the one part, and E. F., of &c., of the other part: Whereby, for the considerations therein mentioned, the said C. D. did assign unto the said E. F. [*all and singular the messuages or tenements and other hereditaments comprised in and demised by the therein within-named written indenture with the appurtenances*] : And which premises are in the therein within-written indenture described to be situate in the parish of , in the county of Middlesex. To hold, &c.

[Conclude as before.]

Mortgages.
114.
Of Freeholds to a Building Society.

THIS INDENTURE, made the day of , 18 , between A. B., of &c. (a member of a certain society called " The Society," established pursuant to the statute in that behalf made and provided) of the one part, and C. D., E. F. and G. H. (trustees of the said society, and who are hereinafter called "trustees"), of the other part: Witnesseth, that, in consideration of £ sterling, to which sum the said A. B. as a member of the said society is entitled under the rules thereof, by the said trustees paid to the said A. B. on the execution hereof, the receipt whereof he doth hereby acknowledge, he the said A. B. doth grant unto the said trustees and their heirs, all [*parcels*], together with all buildings now or at any time hereafter to be erected on the same, with the appurtenances to the same belonging, To hold the same unto the said trustees and their heirs, to the use of the said trustees, their heirs and assigns, upon trust so long as the said A. B., his heirs or assigns, shall duly make the several subscriptions and payments, and observe and perform the regulations prescribed by the rules of the said society, and which on the part of him the said A. B., his heirs, executors and administrators, ought to be paid, observed and performed (including the repayment to the said society of the monthly sum of £ , the amount by the rules of the said society payable in respect of the said advance of £ , on every monthly meeting of the said society, commencing on and from the day of until the day of 18 , both inclusive), and shall also observe and perform the covenants hereinafter contained on his and their part, to permit the said A. B., his heirs and assigns, to hold the said premises and receive the rents and profits thereof for his and their own benefit; but in case neglect or default shall be made by him or them for three general monthly meetings of the said society in making any of the said subscriptions and payments, or in the observance or performance of any of the regulations of the said society, then upon trust at any time thereafter for the said trustees or the survivors or survivor of them, or the executors or administrators of such survivor, their or his assigns (all and every of whom are comprehended within the terms hereinafter used of "trustees and trustee" or "trustees or trustee,") when and as they or he in their or his discretion shall think fit, to enter into possession, and either by themselves or himself, or by a person or persons to be appointed by them or him, to collect the rents and profits of the said premises, and to make any demise or lease of the said premises, or any part thereof, from year to year, or for any shorter period, or for any term of years, at such rent, and upon such terms (including the receipt of any fine or premium), as they or he shall think proper: and also either before or after such demise, at their or his discretion, and without the concurrence or consent of the said A. B., his heirs, executors, administrators or assigns, to sell and absolutely dispose of all or any part of the said premises as they or he shall think proper, either by public auction or private contract, or partly by either, and subject or not to any special conditions, with liberty to buy in the said premises or any part thereof, or rescind or vary any contract for sale and to resell the same in manner aforesaid, without being answerable for any loss, but so, nevertheless, that the premises be sold for the most money that can be obtained, and to assure the same unto the purchaser or purchasers thereof, his or their heirs or assigns, or as he or they shall direct; and it is hereby declared, that the said trustees or trustee shall, out of the rents and fines, or premiums and purchase-money, of the said premises, in the first place retain and pay all costs, charges and expenses which may be incurred on account of such collection of rents and profits, or of any sale of the said premises or otherwise in relation to the trusts aforesaid, and in the next place shall retain unto themselves and himself, on account of the said society, all such principal money, subscriptions and other payments as shall then be due and payable by the said A. B., his heirs, executors, administrators or assigns, and as thereafter may become payable by him or them under or by virtue of the said rules and these presents in respect of the said advance of £ , and to pay the surplus (if any) unto the said A. B., his executors, administrators or assigns, as personal estate; and it is hereby also declared, that every receipt in writing of the said trustees or trustee for any money payable to them or him by virtue of these presents shall be a sufficient discharge for the same, and that every person to whom any such receipt shall be given shall not be bound to inquire into the necessity or expediency of any such demise or sale as aforesaid, or whether any such default has been made as aforesaid, nor be affected with notice or by the fact that no such default has been made, nor by any irregularity in any such demise or sale, or that the same was not necessary or expedient: And the said A. B. doth hereby for himself, his heirs, executors, administrators and assigns, covenant with the said trustees and trustee that he the said A. B , his executors, administrators and assigns, will at all times hereafter make the several subscriptions and payments (including those hereinbefore mentioned), and observe and perform the rules and regulations for the time being of the said society in respect of the said advance of £ ; and also that the said A. B. now hath in himself good right by these presents to grant the said hereditaments in manner aforesaid, free from incumbrances; and moreover, that the said A. B. and his heirs, and all other persons lawfully claiming any estate or interest in the said hereditaments, shall, upon every reasonable request of the said trustees and trustee, their heirs or assigns, but at the costs of the said A. B., his executors, administrators or assigns, until such sale shall be made as aforesaid, and afterwards at the costs of the person or persons requiring the same, execute and perfect all such acts, deeds and assurances for more perfectly or satisfactorily assuring the said hereditaments unto the said trustees and trustee, their heirs and assigns, as they or he shall reasonably require; [and for enabling the said trustees and trustee to pursue the remedy by distress in or upon the said premises hereby granted, the said A. B. doth hereby for himself, his heirs, executors, administrators and assigns, authorize the said trustees and trustee from time to time to distrain in and upon the said premises, and the goods and chattels there, for the amount of all such subscriptions and payments as may for the time being be in arrear, and to deal with every such distress as landlords are or may be authorized by law to deal with distresses for arrears of rent, and that without prejudice to any power, trust, covenant or thing hereinbefore contained.]

In witness, &c.

[N.B.—The clause within brackets is only to be used where the mortgagor is in possession, *vide* note, page 306.]

115.

Of Leaseholds to a Building Society.

THIS INDENTURE, made the   day of   , 18 , between A. B., of &c , of the one part, and   (trustees for the time being of a certain society called the   Benefit Building Society, the rules whereof have been duly certified and enrolled agreeable to law) of the other part: Whereas [*recite lease*]; and whereas the sums to be contributed by subscription in respect of each share in the funds of the said society amount to the sum of £   and the said A. B. is entitled to receive out of the funds thereof the sum of £   in respect of   shares in the said society at the times and in the manner hereinafter mentioned, namely, the sum of £   part thereof at the execution hereof, and the residue of the said sum of £   at such time or times and in such manner as the committee for the time being of the said society shall think fit, and for securing all payments as they shall respectively become due in respect of or in anywise relating to the same shares, he has agreed to execute these presents: Now this indenture witnesseth, that, in consideration of £   sterling to the said A. B. paid by the said   (as such trustees as aforesaid), the receipt of which said sum of £

the said A. B. hereby acknowledges and therefrom releases the said society, and also in consideration of the further sum of £   to be advanced as hereinbefore mentioned, he the said A. B. doth by these presents assign unto the said   their executors, administrators, successors and assigns, all those the said   plots of land or ground hereinbefore described and demised by the said recited underlease, and all the messuages, dwelling-houses, erections and buildings whatsoever erected, built or made upon the said plots of land, or any part thereof, To hold the said premises unto the said   their executors, administrators, successors and assigns, henceforth during the residue of the said term of   : provided always, that if the said A. B., his executors, administrators or assigns, shall duly pay the monies or monthly subscriptions, interest, fines and other payments to be made in respect of the said shares in the said society, and observe and perform all and every the rules and regulations of the said society in respect of the said shares, and shall also pay the rent and perform the covenants reserved and contained in the said underlease, then after all such monies shall have been paid and satisfied, pursuant to the subsisting rules and regulations of the said society, these presents shall become void; but if default shall be made in performance of the said proviso, the said   or the trustees or trustee for the time being of the said society, or their assigns, may at any time after such default, without the concurrence of the said A. B., his executors, administrators or assigns, sell the premises hereby assigned, or any part thereof, either together or in parcels, by public auction or private contract, and under such stipulations, conditions and restrictions as to the title or otherwise as to them shall seem fit, with liberty to buy in and resell the same, with like powers as aforesaid, and out of the money arising from such sales and the rents and profits in the meantime first to retain all the costs and expenses occasioned by the nonpayment of the said principal, interest and other monies, or incurred in the execution of any of the powers of these presents, and in preserving the said premises from forfeiture by paying the rent or performing the covenants in the aforesaid underlease contained, and of obtaining possession or enforcing the performance of any contract for sale of the said premises, and in the next place to retain all such principal money, subscriptions, interest, fines or other payments as shall have been advanced to or shall be due from the said A. B., his executors, administrators and assigns, in respect of the said shares, it being agreed by the said parties hereto that, in case such sale shall take place, all the monies which shall at any time afterwards become due from him or them in respect of the said shares, according to the rules of the said society, shall be considered as then immediately due, and the same, or so much thereof as may be lawfully demanded, shall be deducted out of the monies received under the aforesaid powers, and to pay the residue of the said money unto the said A. B., his executors, administrators or assigns: And it is hereby declared, that every receipt of the trustees for the time being of the said society, or their assigns, for any money payable by virtue of these presents, shall be a sufficient discharge, and that the persons paying the same shall not be obliged to see to the application thereof, nor to inquire into the propriety or legality of such sale or sales, nor whether any such default or deficiency in payment shall have happened, nor be affected by notice thereof, or of the illegality of such sale: And the said A. B. for himself, his heirs, executors and administrators, doth hereby covenant with the said   their executors, administrators, successors and assigns, that he the said A. B., his executors, administrators or assigns, will duly and punctually pay the monies or monthly subscriptions, interest, fines and other payments to be made in respect of the above-mentioned shares in the said society, in accordance with the rules and regulations of the said society; and also that until such sale or sales as aforesaid shall be made will also duly pay the yearly ground rent of £   and perform the covenants and agreements in the hereinbefore-recited underlease reserved and contained, and from the same and also from the rent, covenants and conditions contained in the aforesaid original lease, and all liability in respect thereof, will indemnify the said trustees or the trustees for the time being of the said society and their assigns; and also that the said A. B. now hath power to assign the said premises unto the said   their executors, administrators, successors and assigns, for the term and in manner aforesaid free from incumbrances : and that he the said A. B. and every person lawfully claiming any estate or interest in the premises (except the persons claiming the said reserved rent) will, upon every reasonable request of the said   or the trustees or trustee for the time being of the said society, or their assigns, but at the costs of the said A. B., his executors, administrators and assigns (except further assurances after such sale or sales as aforesaid, which shall be at the costs of the party requiring the same) execute or procure to be executed every such further acts and assurances in the law whatsoever for the more effectually assigning the said premises, with the appurtenances, unto or according to the direction of the said   or the trustees or trustee for the time being of the said society, or their assigns, as by them or any of them shall be reasonably required : and that he the said A. B., his executors, administrators and assigns, will also duly observe the rules and regulations of the said society with regard to the insurance of the aforesaid premises from loss or damage by fire; and that all monies, interest and fines which shall become due to the said society from the said A. B., his executors, administrators or assigns, in respect of any insurance or insurances to be effected conformably with the rules and regulations for the time being of the said society, shall be a charge upon the aforesaid premises ; and all monies to be received under or by virtue of such insurance or insurances shall be applied in manner directed by the rules and regulations for the time being of the said society : [And it is hereby declared and agreed, that the said A. B. shall hold the said premises as tenant at will to the said trustees or trustee at the clear yearly rent of £   payable quarterly, for which rent it shall be lawful for the said trustees or trustee to distrain on the said premises, or any part thereof, as landlords may for rent reserved on leases for years ; but it is hereby also agreed that it shall be lawful for the said trustees or trustee at any time to determine such tenancy, by leaving notice in writing for such purpose on the said premises, or any part thereof.]

In witness, &c.

[N.B.—Notwithstanding the mortgagor may quit the premises, and a new tenant take possession, the mortgagee may distrain for the rent under the above clause. *Pinhorn v. Souster*, 21 L. T. 92.]

116.

Another Form of Power of Distress by Mortgagor.

AND the said [*mortgagor*] doth hereby grant unto the said [*mortgagee*], his executors, administrators and assigns, that when and so often from time to time as any interest for money due on the security of these presents shall be in arrear for   days, it shall be lawful for the said [*mortgagee*], his executors, administrators or assigns, into the hereditaments hereby granted to enter and distrain for the same interest, and the distress and distresses then and there found to dispose of, in the same manner in all respects as landlords are authorized to do with respect to distresses for arrears of rent reserved upon leases for years, to the intent that the said [*mortgagee*], his executors, administrators and assigns, shall by the same distress or distresses be from time to time paid and satisfied all arrears of the said interest, and all costs and charges occasioned by the nonpayment thereof.

117.

Another Form of Power in Mortgage Deed for Mortgagee to distrain for Interest in Arrear, when Property in possession of Mortgagor.

AND in case the said interest hereby reserved or any part of the same shall be in arrear for the space of   days next, after any of the days hereinbefore appointed for payment thereof, it shall be lawful for the said [*mortgagee*], his heirs, executors, administrators or assigns into and upon the said hereditaments and premises to enter, and then and there to distrain for such interest so in arrear as aforesaid, and impound or dispose of the distress or distresses so taken, or otherwise to act therein according to due course of law as in cases of distress for nonpayment of rent reserved upon common demise or lease.

118.

Mortgage of Leaseholds for a Sum certain and further Advances.

THIS INDENTURE, made the   day of   , 18 , between A. B., of &c., of the one part, and C. D., of &c., of the other part: Whereas by an indenture, dated the   day of   , 18 , and made between [*lessor*] of the one part, and [*lessee*] of the other part, for the considerations therein mentioned, all [*copy parcels from lease verbatim*], with the appurtenances, were demised unto the said [*lessee*], his executors, administrators and assigns, from the   day of   then last, for   years, at the yearly rent of £   , and subject to the covenants and agreements therein contained; and whereas by divers mesne assignments, and ultimately by an indenture, dated the   day of   , 18 , and made between   of the one part, and the said A. B. of the other part, the said piece or parcel of ground, with the two several messuages or tenements thereon erected, and then known as Nos.
and   in   Street aforesaid, became vested in the said A. B., his executors, administrators and assigns, for all the residue of the term therein, subject to the payment of the rent reserved by and to the performance of the covenants and agreements contained in the said indenture of lease; and whereas the said A. B. being justly and truly indebted to the said C. D. in the sum of £   was required by the said A. B. to forthwith pay the said sum, but being unable to do so, he hath requested the said C. D. to forbear pressing for the immediate payment of such sum, and also to lend him the further sum of £   , which the said C. D. hath agreed to do, and in consideration of such forbearance and of the said

further advance, he the said A. B. hath agreed to execute these presents, being a security to the said C. D. for the repayment of the said two sums of £   and £   (making together the sum of £   ), and also for such further sum or sums of money as may from time to time be due and owing from the said A. B. to the said C. D. in the trading account between them or otherwise, with interest on all the said sums after the rate of £5 per cent. per annum: Now this indenture witnesseth, that, in consideration of the said sum of £   so due and owing as aforesaid, and of the said C. D. having at the request of the said A. B. forborne to press for the immediate repayment of the same, and also in consideration of the sum of £   sterling on the execution hereof paid by the said C. D. to the said A. B., the receipt of which said sum of £   and that the said sum of £
is now justly due and owing from him to the said C. D., he the said A. B. doth hereby acknowledge and doth discharge the said C. D., his heirs, executors and administrators therefrom, and also in order to secure to the said C. D. the repayment of such further sum or sums of money and interest as aforesaid, he the said A. B. doth by these presents assign unto the said C. D., his executors, administrators and assigns, all that the piece or parcel of ground comprised in and demised by the hereinbefore-recited indenture of lease, together with the two several messuages or tenements thereon erected and built, and which are now known and distinguished by the Nos.   and   in   Street aforesaid, and now or late in the occupation of   and   , and all other the messuages or tenements and buildings erected or standing on the said piece or parcel of ground, with the rights, easements and appurtenances thereto belonging or enjoyed therewith, To hold the said premises unto the said C. D., his executors, administrators and assigns, henceforth for all the remainder of the said term of   years granted by the hereinbefore-recited indenture: provided always, that if the said A. B., his executors, administrators or assigns, shall on or before the   day of   next, pay unto the said C. D., his executors, administrators or assigns, the sum of £   sterling, together with

interest for the same in the meantime, after the rate of £5 per cent. per annum, and shall on demand pay to the said C. D., his executors, administrators or assigns, all such further sum or sums of money as may at any time hereafter be due on the trading account between him and the said A. B. or otherwise, without any deduction, then the said C. D., his executors, administrators or assigns, will, at the request and costs of the said A. B., his executors, administrators or assigns, reassign the said premises unto the said A. B., his executors, administrators or assigns, or as he or they may direct; provided also, that if default shall be made in the performance of the proviso lastly hereinbefore contained in any of its terms, then it shall be lawful for the said C. D., his executors, administrators or assigns, at any time thereafter, without any further consent on the part of the said A. B., his executors, administrators or assigns, to sell the premises hereby assigned, or any part thereof, either together or in parcels, and either by public auction or private contract, and subject to such conditions of sale and generally in every respect as the said C. D., his executors, administrators or assigns shall deem fit, with power to buy in the same at any auction, or rescind any contract for sale of the same, and to resell the same from time to time in manner aforesaid, without being responsible for any loss occasioned thereby, and upon any such sale to assign the premises sold unto the purchaser or purchasers, his or their executors, administrators and assigns, or as he or they may require; and it is hereby declared that the said C. D., his executors, administrators and assigns, shall stand possessed of the monies to arise from any such sale, upon trust in the first place to pay the costs, charges and expenses of and incidental to such sale and the carrying the contract thereof into complete execution, and in the next place upon trust to repay himself and themselves such sum or sums of money as may then be due or owing to him or them under or by virtue of this security, and to pay the surplus (if any) of the monies arising from such sale unto the said A. B., his executors, administrators or assigns: And it is hereby declared, that every receipt which shall be given by the said C. D., his executors, administrators or assigns, for any purchase or other monies to be derived from any such sale or sales, or otherwise under these presents, shall be an effectual discharge to the person or persons to whom such receipt or receipts shall be given for the money therein acknowledged to be received; and that the person or persons taking such receipt shall not be answerable or accountable for the misapplication or non-application of the money therein mentioned to be received, nor for any irregularity or impropriety whatsoever in any such sale or sales, nor be bound to inquire whether any default has been made in payment of the said principal money and interest, or any part thereof: And the said A. B. doth hereby for himself, his heirs, executors and administrators, covenant with the said C. D., his executors, administrators and assigns, as follows, namely, that he the said A. B., his executors or administrators, will on or before the   day of   next, pay unto the said C. D., his executors, administrators or assigns, the sum of £   sterling, together with interest for the same in the meantime after the rate of £5 per cent. per annum, without any deduction, and will on demand pay to the said C. D., his executors, administrators or assigns, all such further sum or sums of money as may at any time hereafter be due on the trading account between him and the said A. B., or otherwise, without any deduction; and also that at the time of the execution hereof the said indenture of lease is a good, valid and subsisting lease, and not forfeited or surrendered; and that all and every the covenants therein contained, and on the part of the lessee, his executors, administrators or assigns, to be observed or performed, have been observed and performed up to the date of these presents; and also, that he the said A. B. now hath in himself good right to assign the said premises unto the said C. D., his executors, administrators and assigns in manner aforesaid, free from incumbrances; and also, that the said A. B., his executors or administrators, and all other persons having or claiming any estate, or interest in, or out of the said premises, will at all times hereafter, at the request of the said C. D., his executors, administrators or assigns, but at the costs of the said A. B., his executors, administrators or assigns, execute every such further assurance for further assuring the said premises unto the said C. D., his executors, administrators and assigns, as he or they shall require; and also will at all times hereafter, so long as any money shall remain due on this security, perform and observe all the covenants and agreements (and particularly the covenant for insurance against loss or damage by fire) contained in the hereinbefore-recited lease, and on the part of the lessee, his executors, administrators or assigns, to be observed or performed, and keep the said C. D., his executors, administrators and assigns, indemnified from and against any breach of the same; and also will, at the request of the said C. D., his executors, administrators or assigns, produce to him or them from time to time the receipt for the premiums and duty payable on such insurance for the current year.

In witness, &c.

119.

Mortgage of Leaseholds for a Sum certain.

THIS INDENTURE, made the   day of   , 18 , between A. B., of &c., of the one part, and C. D., of &c., of the other part: Whereas by an indenture, dated the   day of   , 18 , and made between [*lessor*] of the one part, and [*lessee*] of the other part, for the considerations therein mentioned, all [*copy parcels from lease verbatim*], with the appurtenances thereunto belonging, were demised unto the said [*lessee*], his executors, administrators and assigns, from the   day of   then last, for the term of   years, at the yearly rent of £   , and subject to the covenants and agreements therein contained; and whereas by divers mesne assignments, and ultimately by an indenture, bearing date the   day of   , 18 , and made between   of the one part, and the said A. B. of the other part, the said piece or parcel of ground, with the two several messuages or tenements thereon erected, and then known as Nos.   and   in   Street aforesaid, became vested in the said A. B., his

executors, administrators and assigns, for all the residue of
the term therein, subject to the payment of the rent reserved
by and to the performance of the covenants and agreements
contained in the said indenture of lease; and whereas the
said C. D. hath agreed to advance the said A. B. £   on
having the same with interest secured in manner hereinafter
appearing: Now this indenture witnesseth, that, in consideration of £   sterling on the execution hereof paid by the
said C. D. to the said A. B., the receipt of which said sum
of £   the said A. B. doth hereby acknowledge and doth
discharge the said C. D., his heirs, executors and administrators therefrom, he the said A. B. doth by these presents
assign unto the said C. D., his executors, administrators and
assigns, all that the piece or parcel of ground comprised in
and demised by the hereinbefore-recited indenture of lease,
together with the two several messuages or tenements thereon
erected and built, and which are now known and distinguished
by the Nos.   and   in   Street aforesaid, and now
or late in the occupation of   and   , and all other the
messuages or tenements and buildings erected or standing on
the said piece or parcel of ground in and demised by the
hereinbefore-recited indenture of lease, with the easements
and appurtenances thereto belonging or enjoyed therewith,
To hold the said premises with their appurtenances, unto the
said C. D., his executors, administrators and assigns, henceforth for all the remainder of the said term of   years
granted by the hereinbefore-recited indenture of lease: provided always, that if the said A. B., his executors, administrators or assigns, shall on or before the   day of
next pay unto the said C. D., his executors, administrators or
assigns, the sum of £   sterling, together with interest for
the same in the meantime, after the rate of £5 per cent. per
annum, without any deduction, then the said C. D., his executors, administrators or assigns, will thereupon, at the
request and costs of the said A. B., his executors, administrators or assigns, reassign the said premises unto the said
A. B., his executors, administrators or assigns, or as he or
they may direct; provided also, that if default shall be made

in such payment, it shall be lawful for the said C. D., his executors, administrators or assigns, at any time thereafter, without any further consent on the part of the said A. B., his executors, administrators or assigns, to sell the premises hereby assigned, or any part thereof, either together or in parcels, and either by public auction or private contract, and subject to such conditions of sale and generally in every respect as the said C. D., his executors, administrators or assigns shall deem fit, with power to buy in the same at any auction, or rescind any contract for sale of the same, and to resell the same from time to time in manner aforesaid, without being responsible for any loss occasioned thereby, and upon any such sale to assign the premises sold unto the purchaser or purchasers, his or their executors, administrators and assigns, or as he or they may require: and it is hereby declared that the said C. D., his executors, administrators and assigns, shall stand possessed of the monies to arise from any such sale, upon trust, in the first place to pay the costs, charges and expenses of and incidental to such sale and the carrying the contract thereof into complete execution, and in the next place upon trust to repay himself and themselves all and every such sum or sums of money as may then be due or owing to him or them under or by virtue of this security, and to pay the surplus (if any) of the monies arising from such sale unto the said A. B., his executors, administrators or assigns: And it is hereby declared, that every receipt which shall be given by the said C. D., his executors, administrators or assigns, for any purchase or other monies to be derived from any such sale or sales, or otherwise under these presents, shall be an effectual discharge to the person or persons to whom such receipt or receipts shall be given for the money therein acknowledged to be received; and that the person or persons taking such receipt shall not be answerable or accountable for the misapplication or non-application of the money therein mentioned to be received: And the said A. B. doth hereby for himself, his heirs, executors and administrators, covenant with the said C. D., his executors, administrators and assigns, as follows, namely, that he the said A. B., his executors or administrators, will on or before the   day of   next pay unto the said C. D., his executors, administrators or assigns, the sum of £   sterling, together with interest for the same in the meantime after the rate of £5 per cent. per annum, without any deduction; and also, that at the time of the execution hereof the said indenture of lease is a good, valid and subsisting lease, and not forfeited or surrendered; and that all and every the covenants therein contained, and on the part of the lessee, his executors, administrators or assigns to be observed or performed, have been observed and performed up to the date hereof; and also, that he the said A. B. now hath in himself good right to assign the said premises unto the said C. D., his executors, administrators and assigns, in manner aforesaid free from all incumbrances; and also, that the said A. B., his executors or administrators, and all other persons having or claiming any estate, or interest in, or out of the said premises, will at all times hereafter at the request of the said C. D., his executors, administrators or assigns, but at the costs of the said A. B., his executors, administrators or assigns, execute every such further assurance for better assuring the said premises unto the said C. D., his executors, administrators and assigns, as he or they shall require; and also will from time to time and at all times hereafter, so long as any money shall remain due on the security of these presents, perform and observe the covenants (and particularly the covenant for insurance against loss or damage by fire) contained in the hereinbefore-recited indenture of lease, and on the part of the lessee, his executors, administrators or assigns, to be observed or performed, and keep the said C. D., his executors, administrators and assigns indemnified from and against any breach of the same; and also will at the request of the said C. D., his executors, administrators or assigns, produce to him or them from time to time the receipt for the premiums and duty payable on such insurance for the current year.

In witness, &c.

120.

Of a Pecuniary Legacy.

THIS INDENTURE, made &c., between A. B., of &c., of the one part, and C. D., of &c., of the other part: Whereas E. F., late of &c., deceased, by his will dated the   day of   , 18 , and proved in the   Registry of the Court of Probate on the   day of   , 18 , bequeathed unto G. H. and I. K., the sum of £2,000 sterling, upon trust to invest the same in the government stocks or funds, and to pay the income thereof unto L. F., spinster, the said testator's sister, during her natural life, and at her decease to pay and transfer the said sum of £2,000 sterling, and the stocks, funds and securities, upon which the same should be invested unto the said A. B., his executors, administrators and assigns, for his and their absolute use and benefit; and whereas the said L. F. is still living; and whereas the said C. D. has agreed to lend the said A. B. the sum of £700 at interest on the security of his said legacy: Now this indenture witnesseth, that, in consideration of £700 sterling paid by the said C. D. to the said A. B. on the execution hereof, the receipt whereof the said A. B. doth acknowledge, and therefrom doth release the said C. D., his heirs, executors, administrators and assigns, he the said A. B. doth assign unto the said C. D., his executors, administrators and assigns, all that the legacy or sum of £2,000 so bequeathed to him the said A. B. in and by the hereinbefore-recited will of the said E. F. as aforesaid, and all sum and sums of money to become due and payable in respect of the same legacy, and all stocks, funds and securities in or upon which the said legacy, sum and sums of money or any of them shall for the time being be invested, To have and receive the said legacy, sum and sums of money and other the premises hereby assigned unto the said C. D., his executors, administrators and assigns, for his and their own use absolutely, subject nevertheless to the life interest of the said L. F. in the said legacy or sum of £2,000, and the interest, dividends and annual income thereof, and subject also to the proviso next hereinafter contained: Provided always, that if

the said A. B., his executors, administrators or assigns,
shall on the   day of   next pay to the said C D.,
his executors, administrators or assigns, the sum of £700
sterling, with interest for the same at the rate of £5 per cent.
per annum, without deduction, then these presents shall be
void; but in case default shall be made in payment of
the said principal sum and interest or any part thereof on
the said   day of   next, it shall be lawful for the
said C. D., his executors, administrators or assigns, without
any further consent of the said A. B., his executors or administrators, to sell the said legacy or sum of £2,000 and premises hereby assigned by public auction or private contract,
and subject to such conditions as he or they shall think
proper, with liberty to buy in the same at any auction or auctions, if it shall be deemed expedient to do so, and vary the
terms of and rescind any contract for sale which may have
been entered into, and to assign and assure the same when
sold unto the purchaser or purchasers thereof, or as he or
they shall direct: And it is hereby declared, that the said
C. D., his executors, administrators or assigns, shall hold the
monies to arise from any such sale, upon trust, first to retain
and pay all the costs and charges attending such sale and
otherwise incidental thereto, and to the trusts of these
presents, and next to retain and pay to himself and themselves the said C. D., his executors, administrators or assigns,
the principal monies and interest intended to be hereby
secured, which shall be then due and owing to him and them,
and to pay the surplus (if any) unto the said A. B., his executors, administrators or assigns: And it is hereby declared,
that the receipt or receipts of the said C. D., his executors,
administrators or assigns, for any sum or sums of money to
be received by him or them under or by virtue of these presents shall effectually discharge the person or persons paying
the same from all responsibility in respect of the application
thereof; and the said A. B., for himself, his heirs, executors
and administrators, doth hereby covenant with the said C. D.,
his executors, administrators and assigns, that he the said
A. B., his heirs, executors, administrators or assigns, will pay

unto the said C. D., his executors, administrators or assigns, the sum of £700 sterling, with interest thereon at the rate of £5 per cent. per annum, on the   day of   next, and also that the legacy or sum of £2,000 hereby assigned is now (subject as aforesaid) absolutely owing to the said A. B., according to the tenor and effect of the above-recited will, and that no part thereof hath been received, released, assigned or incumbered by the said A. B., and that he now hath absolute right to assign the same legacy, subject and in manner aforesaid, and will not at any time during the continuance of this security, receive or release the said legacy, or the stocks, funds or securities in or upon which the same or any part thereof may for the time being be invested, nor do or suffer any thing whereby the said legacy, stocks, funds, securities and premises hereby assigned can or may be forfeited or incumbered, or whereby the said C. D., his executors, administrators or assigns, may be hindered or prevented from recovering the principal money and interest hereby secured or any part thereof respectively; and moreover, that he the said A. B., his executors and administrators, will at all times hereafter, on the request of the said C. D., his executors, administrators or assigns (at the cost until sale or foreclosure of the said A. B., his executors or administrators, and afterwards of the person requiring the same) execute and do every such further deed and thing for more effectually assigning the said legacy and premises hereinbefore assigned (subject as aforesaid) unto the said C. D., his executors, administrators and assigns, or for enabling or empowering him or them to recover and receive the monies hereby assigned, as by him or them shall be reasonably required.

In witness, &c.

[N.B.—In this case it is necessary that the following notice be sent to the trustees] :—

Notice to Trustees.

To Messrs. G. H. and I. K.,
    Gentlemen,
          I hereby give you notice, that by an indenture made the   day of   , 18 , between A. B., of &c., of the

one part, and C. D., of &c., of the other part, the said A. B. assigned unto the said C. D., his executors, administrators and assigns, the legacy or sum of £2,000, and the stocks, funds and securities upon which the same may be invested, and to which under the will of E. F., late of &c., deceased, the said A. B. is absolutely entitled, subject to the life interest in the dividends, interest and annual income thereof of the said testator's sister L. F. for her life, and which said sum of £2,000 is now invested in the names of you the said G. H. and I. K., as the trustees and executors of the said will of the said E. F. in the Three per Cent. Consolidated Annuities, by way of mortgage for securing to the said C. D., his executors, administrators and assigns, the repayment of the sum of £700 money lent to the said A. B., with interest thereon in the meantime at the rate of £5 per cent. per annum.

Dated this   day of   , 18 .

Yours, &c.,

Y. Z.,

Solicitor for the said C. D.

121.

Of Freehold Houses to One Mortgagee.

THIS INDENTURE, made the   day of   , 18 , between A. B., of &c., of the one part, and C. D., of &c., of the other part : Whereas the said A. B. is seised to him and his heirs, or otherwise well and sufficiently entitled to the hereditaments hereinafter described and granted for an estate in fee simple in possession, free from incumbrances; and whereas the said C. D. hath agreed to advance the said A. B. the sum of £   on having the repayment of the same with interest thereon in the meantime, after the rate of £5 per cent. per annum, secured in manner hereinafter mentioned : Now this indenture witnesseth, that, in consideration of £   sterling to the said A. B. paid by the said C. D. upon the execution hereof, the receipt whereof the said A. B. doth hereby acknowledge and therefrom doth discharge the said C. D., his heirs, executors, administrators and assigns,

he the said A. B. doth by these presents grant unto the said
C. D. and his heirs, all those messuages or tenements situate
and being Nos. 2 and 4,   Street, in the city of London,
now in the occupation of   and   , together with all
ways, lights, easements and appurtenances thereunto belonging or appertaining, To hold the said premises unto and to
the use of the said C. D. his heirs and assigns: provided
always, that if the said A. B., his heirs, executors, administrators or assigns, shall pay unto the said C. D., his executors, administrators or assigns, the sum of £   sterling, together with interest for the same in the meantime after the
rate of £5 per cent. per annum, on the   day of
next, without deduction, then the said C. D., his heirs or
assigns, will, upon the request and at the costs of the said
A. B., his heirs, executors, administrators or assigns, reconvey
the hereditaments hereby granted to the use of the said A. B.,
his heirs and assigns, or as he or they shall direct; but if
default shall be made in payment of the said sum of £   ,
or the interest thereon, or any part thereof respectively, on
the said   day of   next, it shall be lawful for the
said C. D., his executors, administrators or assigns, without
any further consent on the part of the said A. B., his heirs
or assigns, to sell the hereditaments hereby granted, together
or in parcels, and either by public auction or private contract,
with power upon any such sale to make any stipulations as
to title or evidence of title, or otherwise, which the said C. D.,
his executors, administrators or assigns shall deem proper,
and also with full power to buy in or rescind any contract for
sale of the said premises, and to resell the same without
being responsible for any loss occasioned thereby, and for the
purposes aforesaid, or any of them, to make and execute all
such agreements and assurances as he or they shall think fit:
[provided always, that the said C. D., his executors, administrators or assigns, shall not execute the said power of sale,
unless or until he or they shall have given a notice in writing
to the said A. B., his heirs, executors, administrators or
assigns, or sent the same through the General Post Office,
addressed to his or their last known place of abode, requir-

ing him or them to pay off the monies for the time being owing on the security of these presents, or left a notice in writing to that effect at or upon some part of the said premises, and default shall have been made in payment of such monies, or some part thereof, for six calendar months from the time of giving or sending or leaving such notice, as the case may be; but no purchaser at any such sale shall be obliged or concerned to inquire whether such notice has been given or sent, or whether default has been made in payment of the said principal money and interest, or any part thereof:] And it is hereby declared, that upon any such sale as aforesaid the receipts of the said C. D., his executors, administrators or assigns, for the purchase-money of the premises sold, shall be effectual discharges for the money expressed to be received, and that no purchaser shall be concerned to see to the application of his purchase-money, or be answerable for any loss, misapplication or nonapplication thereof: And it is hereby further agreed and declared, that the said C. D., his executors, administrators or assigns, shall hold the monies to arise from any such sale upon trust, in the first place thereout to reimburse himself or themselves, or pay and discharge all the costs and expenses attending or incurred in or about such sale, or otherwise in respect of the premises, and in the next place to apply such monies in or towards satisfaction of all and singular the monies for the time being owing on the security of these presents, and to pay the surplus (if any) of the said monies unto the said A. B., his heirs, executors, administrators or assigns: And the said A. B. doth hereby for himself, his heirs, executors and administrators, covenant with the said C. D., his heirs, executors and administrators respectively, that he the said A. B., his heirs, executors or administrators, will pay unto the said C. D., his executors, administrators or assigns, the sum of £   sterling, together with interest for the same in the meantime after the rate of £5 per cent. per annum, on the   day of   next, without deduction; and also that he the said A. B. now hath full power to grant the hereditaments hereinbefore expressed to be granted to the use of the said C. D., his heirs and assigns, free from incumbrances; and moreover, that the said A. B. and his heirs, and every other person having or claiming any estate or interest, in or to the said hereditaments will at all times, upon the request of the said C. D., his heirs, executors, administrators or assigns, but at the costs of the said A. B., his heirs, executors or administrators, execute every such assurance for more perfectly assuring the said hereditaments to the use of the said C. D., his heirs and assigns, in manner aforesaid, as by the said C. D., his heirs, executors, administrators or assigns, shall be reasonably required; and also, that he the said A. B., his heirs, executors, administrators or assigns will, so long as any money shall remain on this security, keep all the said messuages and buildings insured in some respectable fire insurance office in London or Westminster against loss or damage by fire in the sum of £   at the least, and pay all premiums and sums of money necessary for such purpose on the first day on which the same respectively ought to be paid, and will on demand deliver to the said C. D., his executors, administrators or assigns, the policy or policies of such insurance, and the receipt for every such payment; and that if default shall be made in keeping the said premises so insured, it shall be lawful for the said C. D., his executors, administrators or assigns, to insure and keep insured the said premises in any sum not exceeding the sum of £   ; and that the said A. B., his executors, administrators or assigns, will repay to the said C. D., his executors, administrators or assigns, every sum of money expended for that purpose by him or them, with interest thereon at the rate aforesaid, from the time of the same respectively having been so expended, and that until such repayment the same shall be a charge upon the hereditaments hereby granted.

In witness, &c.

122.

Of Freehold Houses to Two Mortgagees.

THIS INDENTURE, made the   day of   , 18 , between A. B., of &c., of the one part, and C. D., of &c. and E. F., of &c., of the other part: Whereas the said A. B. is seised to him and his heirs, or otherwise well and sufficiently entitled to the hereditaments hereinafter described for an estate in fee simple in possession, free from incumbrances; and whereas the said A. B. hath requested the said C. D. and E. F. to lend him the sum of £   which they have agreed to do out of money belonging to them on a joint account, on having the repayment of the same with interest thereon in the meantime, after the rate of £5 per cent. per annum, secured in manner hereinafter mentioned: Now this indenture witnesseth, that, in consideration of £   sterling to the said A. B. paid by the said C. D. and E. F. upon the execution hereof, the receipt whereof the said A. B. doth hereby acknowledge and therefrom doth discharge the said C. D. and E. F., their heirs, executors, administrators and assigns, he the said A. B. doth by these presents grant unto the said C. D. and E. F. and their heirs, all those messuages or tenements situate and being Nos. 2 and 4,   Street, in the city of London, now in the occupation of   and   , together with all the easements and appurtenances thereunto belonging or appertaining or used, occupied or enjoyed therewith, To hold the said premises unto and to the use of the said C. D. and E. F., their heirs and assigns: provided always, that if the said A. B., his heirs, executors, administrators or assigns, shall pay unto the said C. D. and E. F., or the survivor of them, his executors or administrators, or their or his assigns, the sum of £   sterling, together with interest for the same in the meantime after the rate of £5 per cent. per annum on the   day of   next, without deduction, then the said C. D. and E. F., or the survivor of them, or his heirs, or their or his assigns, will upon the request and at the costs of the said A. B., his heirs, executors, administrators or assigns, reconvey the said premises to the use of the said A. B., his heirs and assigns, or as he or they shall direct; but if default shall be made in payment of the said sum of £   , or the interest thereon, or any part thereof respectively, on the said   day of   next, it shall be lawful for the said C. D. and E. F., or the survivor of them, his executors or administrators, or their or his assigns, without any further consent on the part of the said A. B., his heirs or assigns, to sell the said premises, together or in parcels, and either by public auction or private contract, with power upon any such sale to make any stipulations as to title or evidence of title, or otherwise, which the said C. D. and E. F., or the survivor of them, his executors or administrators, or their or his assigns, shall deem proper, and also with full power to buy in or rescind any contract for sale of the said premises, or any part thereof, and to resell the same without being responsible for any loss occasioned thereby, and for the purposes aforesaid, or any of them, to make and execute all such agreements and assurances as they or he shall think fit; [provided always, that the said C. D. and E. F., or the survivor of them, his executors or administrators, or their or his assigns, shall not execute the said power of sale, unless or until they or he shall have given a notice in writing to the said A. B., his heirs, executors, administrators or assigns, or sent the same through the General Post Office addressed to his or their last known place of abode, requiring him or them to pay off the monies for the time being owing on the security of these presents, or left a notice in writing to that effect at or upon some part of the said premises, and default shall have been made in payment of such monies, or some part thereof, for six calendar months from the time of giving or sending or leaving such notice, as the case may be; but no purchaser at any such sale shall be obliged or concerned to inquire whether such notice has been given or sent, or whether default has been made in payment of the said principal money and interest, or any part thereof;] and it is hereby declared, that upon any such sale as aforesaid the receipts of the said C. D. and E. F., or the survivor of them, his executors or administrators, or their or his assigns, for the purchase-money of the premises sold, shall be effectual discharges for the money expressed to be received, and that no purchaser shall be concerned to see to the application of his purchase-money, or be answerable for any loss, misapplication or nonapplication thereof: And it is hereby further agreed and declared, that the said C. D. and E. F., and the survivor of them, his executors or administrators, or their or his assigns, shall hold the monies to arise from any such sale upon trust in the first place thereout to reimburse themselves or himself, or pay and discharge all the costs and expenses attending or incurred in or about such sale, or otherwise in respect of the premises, and in the next place to apply such monies in or towards satisfaction of all and singular the monies for the time being due or owing on the security of these presents; and to pay the surplus (if any) of the said monies unto the said A. B., his heirs, executors, administrators or assigns; and the said A. B. doth hereby for himself, his heirs, executors and administrators, covenant with the said C. D. and E. F., their heirs, executors, administrators and assigns, respectively as follows, that the said A. B., his heirs, executors or administrators, will pay unto the said C. D. and E. F., or the survivor of them, his executors or administrators, or their or his assigns, the sum of £   sterling, together with interest for the same in the meantime after the rate of £5 per cent. per annum, on the   day of   next, without deduction; and also, that the said A. B. now hath full power to grant the said premises to the use of the said C. D. and E. F., their heirs and assigns, in manner aforesaid, free from incumbrances; and that the said A. B. and his heirs, and all persons having or claiming any estate or interest, in or to the said premises, will at all times, upon the request of the said C. D. and E. F., or the survivor of them, his heirs, executors or administrators, or their or his assigns, but at the costs of the said A. B., his heirs, executors or administrators, execute every such assurance for more perfectly assuring the said premises to the use of the said C. D. and E. F., their heirs and assigns, in manner aforesaid, as by the said C. D. and E. F., or the survivor of them, his heirs, executors or administrators, or their or his assigns, shall be reasonably required; and also, that the said A. B., his heirs, executors, administrators or assigns will,' so long as any money shall remain on this security, keep all the said messuages and buildings insured in some respectable fire insurance office in London or Westminster against loss or damage by fire in the sum of £   at the least, and pay all premiums and sums of money necessary for such purpose on the first day on which the same respectively ought to be paid, and will on demand deliver to the said C. D. and E. F., or the survivor of them, his executors or administrators, or their or his assigns, the policy or policies of such insurance, and the receipt for every such payment; and that if default shall be made in keeping the said premises so insured, it shall be lawful for the said C. D. and E. F., or the survivor of them, his executors or administrators, or their or his assigns, to insure and keep insured the said premises in any sum not exceeding the sum of £   ; and that the said A. B., his executors, administrators or assigns, will repay to the said C. D. and E. F., or the survivor of them, his executors or administrators, or their or his assigns, every sum of money expended for that purpose by them or him, with interest thereon at the rate aforesaid, from the time of the same respectively having been so expended, and that until such repayment the same shall be a charge upon the hereditaments hereby granted: provided always, and it is hereby declared, that the said sum of £ advanced by the said C. D. and E. F. as aforesaid was money belonging to them on a joint account in equity as well as at law, and that they shall remain jointly entitled in equity as well as at law to the said sum of £   and interest, and accordingly that the receipt of the survivor of them, or of the executors or administrators of such survivor, shall be an effectual discharge for the said sum of £   and interest.

In witness, &c.

123.

Further Charge.

THIS INDENTURE, made the   day of   , 18 , between
A. B., of &c., of the one part, and C. D., of &c., of the other
part: Whereas by an indenture bearing date the   day
of   , 18 , and made between the said A. B. of the one
part, and the said C. D. of the other part, in consideration of
£   advanced to the said A. B. by the said C. D., he the
said A. B. assigned unto the said C. D., his executors, administrators and assigns, a certain sum of £   3*l*. per Cent.
Reduced Bank Annuities, standing in the name of E. F. in
the books of the governor and company of the Bank of
England, and representing a sum of £   sterling, together
with the benefit of all investments thereof: and also all those
leasehold messuages or dwelling-houses and premises situate
and being Nos.   ,   ,   Street, To hold the said
sum of £   unto the said C. D., his executors, administrators and assigns absolutely, and to hold the said leasehold
premises unto the said C. D., his executors, administrators and
assigns, for all the residue of the respective terms therein;
and in the indenture now being recited is contained a proviso
for reassignment of the said money and premises on payment
by the said A. B., his executors, administrators or assigns,
unto the said C. D., his executors, administrators or assigns,
of the sum of £   with interest thereon in the meantime
after the rate, on the day and in manner therein mentioned;
and whereas the said principal sum of £   remains due to the
said C. D. upon the security of the said indenture, together
with the current half-year's interest thereon; and whereas the
said C. D. hath agreed to lend the said A. B. the further sum
of £   on having the repayment thereof, with interest, secured
in manner hereinafter appearing: Now this indenture witnesseth, that, in consideration of £   sterling paid by the
said C. D. to the said A. B. on the execution hereof (the
receipt whereof the said A. B. doth hereby acknowledge, and
therefrom doth discharge the said C. D., his heirs, executors

and administrators, by these presents), he the said A. B. doth hereby for himself, his heirs, executors and administrators, covenant with the said C. D., his executors and administrators, that he the said A. B., his heirs, executors or administrators, will pay unto the said C. D., his executors, administrators or assigns, the sum of £ , with interest for the same after the rate of £5 per centum per annum on the day of next, without any deduction whatsoever; and in case the said sum of £ shall not be paid on the said day of next, shall and will thenceforth during the continuance of this security pay unto the said C. D., his executors, administrators or assigns, interest after the rate aforesaid for the said sum of £ or for so much thereof as shall for the time being remain unpaid, by equal half-yearly payments, on the day of and the day of in every year: And it is hereby agreed and declared, and the said A. B. doth hereby for himself, his heirs, executors and administrators, covenant with the said C. D., his executors, administrators and assigns, that the hereinbefore-mentioned sum of £ 3l. per Cent. Reduced Bank Annuities, and also the said sum of £ sterling so represented by the said sum of £ stock as aforesaid, and also the messuages and other premises by the hereinbefore-recited indenture assigned with their appurtenances, shall respectively be and remain a security for and stand charged and chargeable with the payment to the said C. D., his executors, administrators and assigns, as well of the said sum of £ and interest for the same according to the covenant hereinbefore contained, as of the before-mentioned sum of £ and all interest due and to grow due for the same; and that the said stock, money, securities, messuages and premises respectively shall not in anywise be redeemed or redeemable but upon payment by the said A. B., his heirs, executors, administrators or assigns, unto the said C. D., his executors, administrators or assigns, as well of the said sum of £ and interest for the same as aforesaid, as of the said sum of £ and the interest due and to grow due for the same: And it is hereby agreed and declared, that the power of sale in the hereinbefore-recited indenture contained for better securing the payment of the said sum of £   and interest, and all trusts and provisions in relation thereto, shall extend and be applicable, so as to be a further security for the said sum of £   and interest, in the same manner as if the said sum of £   had formed part of the principal money secured by the hereinbefore-mentioned indenture.

In witness, &c.

124.

Further Charge, by Indorsement on Mortgage Deed.

THIS INDENTURE, made the   day of   , 18 , between the within-named A. B. of the one part, and the within-named C. D. of the other part: Whereas the within-mentioned sum of £   remains due to the said C. D., but all interest for the same has been paid up to the   day of   last; and whereas the said C. D. has at the request of the said A. B. agreed to advance him the further sum of £   on having the repayment thereof, with interest after the rate of £   per cent. per annum, secured in manner hereinafter appearing: Now this indenture witnesseth, that, in consideration of £   sterling paid by the said C. D. to the said A. B. on the execution hereof (the receipt whereof the said A. B. doth hereby acknowledge and discharge the said C. D., his heirs, executors, administrators and assigns therefrom), he the said A. B. doth hereby for himself, his heirs, executors and administrators, covenant with the said C. D., his executors and administrators, that he the said A. B., his executors, administrators or assigns, will pay unto the said C. D., his executors, administrators or assigns, the sum of £   with interest thereon at the rate of £   per cent. per annum on the   day of   next, without deduction: And it is hereby agreed and declared, and the said A. B. doth hereby for himself, his heirs, executors and administrators, covenant with the said C. D., his executors, administrators and assigns, that the hereditaments granted by the within indenture, with their appurtenances, shall be and remain a security for and stand charged with the payment to the said C. D., his executors, administrators and assigns, as well of the said sum of £   and interest for the same according to the covenant of the said A. B. hereinbefore contained, as of the within-mentioned sum of £   and all interest due and to grow due for the same, and that the said messuages and hereditaments shall not be redeemed or redeemable but upon payment by the said A. B., his heirs, executors, administrators or assigns, unto the said C. D., his executors, administrators or assigns, as well of the said sum of £   and interest for the same, as of the said sum of £   and the interest due and to grow due for the same: And it is hereby further agreed and declared, that the power of sale in the within indenture contained for better securing the payment of the said sum of £   and interest, and all trusts and provisions in relation thereto, shall extend and be applicable so as to be a further security for the said sum of £   and interest, in the same manner as if the said sum of £   had formed part of the principal money secured by the within indenture.

In witness, &c.

125.

Reconveyance of Freehold Hereditaments.

THIS INDENTURE, made the   day of   , 18 , between [*mortgagee*] of the one part, and [*mortgagor*] of the other part: Whereas by an indenture dated the   day of   , and made between the said [*mortgagor*] of the one part, and the said [*mortgagee*] of the other part, in consideration of £   sterling paid to the said [*mortgagor*] by the said [*mortgagee*], he the said [*mortgagor*] did grant unto the said [*mortgagee*], his heirs and assigns, all [*parcels*], To hold the same unto the said [*mortgagee*], his heirs and assigns, to the use of the said [*mortgagee*], his heirs and assigns, subject nevertheless to a proviso contained in the indenture now being recited for reconveyance of the said premises on payment by the said [*mortgagor*], his heirs, executors, administrators or assigns, unto the said [*mortgagee*], his executors, administrators or assigns, of   , together with interest for the same in the meantime after the rate, on the days and in the manner therein appointed for payment thereof; and whereas the said principal sum of £   still remains owing to the said [*mortgagee*] upon the security of the hereinbefore-recited indenture, but all interest for the same has been paid up to the date hereof, as the said [*mortgagee*] doth hereby acknowledge; and whereas the said [*mortgagor*] is desirous of paying off the said principal sum of £   , and that the messuages and other hereditaments, with the appurtenances, by the said indenture granted, shall be reconveyed unto and to the use of him the said [*mortgagor*], his heirs and assigns, in manner hereinafter mentioned: Now this indenture witnesseth, that for effectuating the said desire, and in consideration of £   to the said [*mortgagee*] on the execution hereof paid by the said [*mortgagor*] (the receipt of which said sum of £   he the said [*mortgagee*] doth hereby acknowledge, and of and from the same and every part thereof doth discharge the said [*mortgagor*], his heirs, executors, administrators and assigns, by these presents), he the said [*mortgagee*] doth by these presents grant and release unto the said [*mortgagor*] and his heirs, all and singular the said messuage or dwelling-house and shop, known as   , with the several warehouses, outbuildings, ground and hereditaments thereto belonging and occupied therewith, comprised in and granted by the hereinbefore-recited indenture or intended so to be, and all other the messuages, hereditaments and premises comprised in or conveyed by the said indenture or intended so to be, with their and every of their rights, easements and appurtenances, To hold the premises hereby granted unto the said [*mortgagor*], his heirs and assigns, to the use of the said [*mortgagor*], his heirs and assigns, discharged from all principal monies and interest intended to be secured by the hereinbefore-recited indenture, and from all actions, suits, claims and demands whatsoever, for, upon account or in respect of the said principal monies or interest or any part thereof respectively, or for, upon account or in respect of the hereinbefore-recited indenture: And the said [*mortgagee*] doth hereby for himself, his heirs, executors and administrators, covenant with the said [*mortgagor*], his heirs and assigns, that the said [*mortgagee*] hath not at any time heretofore made or executed, or knowingly or willingly permitted or suffered or been party or privy to any act or thing, whereby the said hereditaments can or may be charged, incumbered or prejudicially affected.

In witness, &c.

[N.B.—This may be easily altered so as to be a reconveyance by indorsement, by describing the parties as the within-named A. B. and C. D., and omitting the recital of the mortgage and substituting the "within-named" for the word "said" in mentioning either the money or the premises.

Precedent No. 124 will give some assistance in making the necessary alterations.]

126.

Re-assignment of Leasehold Premises.

THIS INDENTURE, made the   day of   , 18 , between [*mortgagee*] of the one part, and [*mortgagor*] of the other part: Whereas by an indenture dated the   day of   , 18 , made between the said [*mortgagor*] of the one part, and the said [*mortgagee*] of the other part, in consideration of £   sterling paid to the said [*mortgagor*] by the said [*mortgagee*], the said [*mortgagor*] assigned unto the said [*mortgagee*] all [*parcels*], To hold the same unto the said [*mortgagee*], his executors, administrators and assigns, subject nevertheless to a proviso therein contained for re-assignment of the said premises on payment by the said [*mortgagor*], his executors, administrators or assigns, unto the said [*mortgagee*], his executors, administrators or assigns, of £   , together with interest for the same in the meantime after the rate, on the days and in manner therein appointed for payment thereof; and whereas the said principal sum of £   still remains owing to the said [*mortgagee*] upon the security of the hereinbefore-recited indenture, but all interest for the same has been paid up to the date hereof as the said [*mortgagee*] doth hereby acknowledge; and whereas the said [*mortgagor*] is desirous of paying off the said principal sum of £   , and that the premises by the said indenture assigned shall be re-assigned to the said [*mortgagor*], his executors, administrators and assigns: Now this indenture witnesseth, that, in consideration of £   to the said [*mortgagee*] on the execution hereof paid by the said [*mortgagor*] (the receipt whereof the said [*mortgagee*] doth hereby acknowledge, and from the same doth discharge the said [*mortgagor*], his heirs, executors, administrators and assigns, by these presents), he the said [*mortgagee*] doth hereby assign unto the said [*mortgagor*] all and singular the said messuage or dwelling-house and shop, known as   , with the several warehouses, outbuildings, ground and hereditaments thereto belonging and occupied therewith, comprised in and assigned by the hereinbefore-recited indenture, and all other the premises assigned by the said indenture, with their easements and appurtenances, To hold the said premises unto the said [*mortgagor*], his executors, administrators and assigns, discharged from all principal monies and interest intended to be secured by the hereinbefore-recited indenture, and from all actions and suits, upon account or in respect of the said principal monies and interest or any part thereof respectively: And the said [*mortgagee*] doth hereby for himself, his heirs, executors and administrators, covenant with the said [*mortgagor*], his executors, administrators and assigns, that the said [*mortgagee*] hath not at any time heretofore made, or executed, or knowingly or willingly permitted or suffered or been party or privy to any act, deed, matter or thing, whereby or by means whereof the premises hereinbefore assigned can or may be charged, incumbered or prejudicially affected.

In witness, &c.

127.

Concise Form of Transfer of Mortgage, on an intended Marriage, to the Trustees of the Settlement.

THIS INDENTURE, made the   day of   , 18 , between E. H. H., of &c., of the one part, and A. B., of &c., and

C. D., of &c., of the other part : Whereas by an indenture dated the   day of   , 18 , made between, &c., in consideration of, &c., all those, &c. [*setting out parcels at length*], were conveyed by, &c., unto the said E. H. H., his heirs and assigns, subject, &c. ; and whereas the said principal sum of £   is still due and owing, and the said E. H. H. is desirous that the said sum and the hereinbefore-recited security for the same should be vested in the said A. B. and C. D. upon the trusts and in the manner hereinafter mentioned : Now this indenture witnesseth, that, in consideration of the premises, he the said E. H. H. by these presents doth assign unto the said A. B. and C. D., their executors, administrators and assigns, all that the said sum of £   secured by the said recited indentures, and all interest due or to grow due for the same, and the covenant whereby the same sum and interest, or any part thereof, is partly secured, and all benefit and advantage thereof, and all the title, interest, property, claim and demand whatsoever, both at law and in equity, of the said E. H. H. in, to, out of or upon the said sum of £   and the interest thereof, and the security for the same, and all powers and remedies, both at law and in equity, of him the said E. H. H., for recovering and compelling payment of the same, with full power and authority to use the name or names of the said E. H. H., his executors or administrators, for that purpose, To have, hold, receive and take the said principal money, interest and premises hereby assigned unto the said A. B. and C. D., their executors, administrators and assigns : And this indenture also witnesseth, that, for the considerations aforesaid, he the said E. H. H. doth by these presents grant unto the said A. B. and C. D., and their heirs, all that the messuage, &c., comprised in and assured by the said recited indentures, together with the appurtenances whatsoever to the same belonging or in anywise appertaining, To hold the said hereditaments hereby granted unto the said A. B. and C. D. and their heirs, to the use of the said A. B. and C. D., their heirs and assigns, subject nevertheless to such right or equity of redemption as is now subsisting under the said recited indentures, on payment to the said

A. B. and C. D., their executors, administrators or assigns, of the said sum of £   and the interest thereof. [*Covenant by E. H. H. against Incumbrances.*] Declaration that the receipt or receipts of the said A. B. and C. D. and the survivor of them, his executors or administrators, or their or his assigns, for the said sum of £   and the interest thereof or any part thereof respectively, or for any other money payable to them or him under or by virtue of the said indenture of release or these presents, shall be a good and sufficient discharge for the same, and that the acts, deeds and assurances of the said A. B. and C. D., and the survivor of them, and the heirs, executors and administrators respectively of such survivor, their or his assigns, in relation to the said messuage, &c., or any of them, shall be valid and conclusive, although the said E. H. H., his heirs, executors, administrators or assigns, shall not join therein or assent thereto.

In witness, &c.

128.

Transfer of Mortgage, with Concurrence of Mortgagor.

THIS INDENTURE, made the   day of   , 18 , between A. B., of &c., of the first part, C. D., of &c., of the second part, and E. F., of &c., of the third part: Whereas by an indenture dated the   day of   , 18 , made between the said A. B. of the one part, the said C. D. of the other part, in consideration of £   to the said A. B. paid by the said C. D., all [*parcels*], with the appurtenances, were conveyed unto and to the use of the said C. D., his heirs and assigns, subject to a proviso for reconveyance of the said hereditaments on payment by the said A. B., his heirs, executors, administrators or assigns, to the said C. D., his executors, administrators or assigns, of £ , with interest thereon at the rate of £   per cent. per annum, on a day therein mentioned and since past; and whereas there is now due to the said C. D. under the said mortgage security the sum of

£   , all interest having been paid up to the date hereof; and whereas the said E. F. hath on the request of the said A. B. agreed to lend him the sum of £   to pay off the said mortgage, upon having the repayment thereof with interest secured to him in manner hereinafter expressed: Now this indenture witnesseth, that, in consideration of £   sterling to the said C. D. paid by the said E. F. on the execution hereof, at the request and by the direction of the said A. B. (the receipt whereof and that the same is in discharge of all monies owing on the said recited security the said C. D. doth hereby acknowledge and doth discharge the said E. F., his heirs, executors, administrators and assigns, and also the said A. B., his heirs, executors and administrators therefrom), he the said C. D., at the request and by the direction of the said A. B., doth hereby grant, and the said A. B. doth hereby grant and confirm, unto the said E. F. and his heirs all the said   and hereditaments hereinbefore described and comprised in and conveyed by the hereinbefore-recited indenture, with their rights, members and appurtenances, To hold the said hereditaments and premises hereby granted unto and to the use of the said E. F., his heirs and assigns, discharged from the proviso contained in the said indenture of mortgage for redemption of the said premises, but subject to the proviso next hereinafter contained: provided always, that if the said A. B., his heirs, executors, administrators or assigns, shall pay to the said E. F., his executors, administrators or assigns, the sum of £   , with interest thereon at the rate of £   per cent. per annum, on the   day of   next, without deduction, then the said E. F., his heirs or assigns, will, on the request and at the costs of the said A. B., his heirs, executors, administrators or assigns, reconvey the said hereditaments to the use of him or them, or as he or they may direct; but if default shall be made in payment of the said sum of £   , or the interest thereon, or any part thereof, on the day hereinbefore appointed for payment thereof, it shall be lawful for the said E. F., his executors, administrators and assigns, without any further concurrence or consent of the said A. B., his heirs or assigns, to [enter upon the hereditaments hereby assured, and take the rents and profits thereof, and, whether in or out of possession of the same, to make any lease or leases thereof, or of any part thereof, as he or they shall think fit, and also at his or their sole discretion to] sell and absolutely dispose of the said hereditaments, or any part thereof, by public sale or private contract, in such manner, at such times and subject to such conditions as to him or them shall seem meet (with power to buy in the same at any auction, and to rescind any contract without being responsible for any deficiency on any subsequent sale), and to assure the said hereditaments when sold to the purchaser or purchasers thereof, his or their heirs and assigns, or as he or they shall direct; and it is hereby declared, that the said E. F., his executors, administrators and assigns, shall stand possessed of the rents and profits of the said hereditaments until sale, and after sale then of the proceeds arising therefrom, upon trust first to deduct thereout all expenses incurred by him or them in respect of the said sale or in making a title to the said hereditaments, or in the execution of the powers and trusts hereby reposed in him and them; secondly, to retain the said sum of £   and interest and all monies due to him or them under or by virtue of these presents, and then to pay the surplus (if any) unto the said A. B., his heirs, executors, administrators and assigns; and it is hereby declared, that the receipts of the said E. F., his executors, administrators or assigns, shall be sufficient discharges to purchasers and others taking the same, and shall absolve them from the responsibility of seeing to the application, or being accountable for the misapplication or nonapplication of the money therein expressed to be received; and the said C. D. doth hereby for himself, his heirs, executors and administrators, covenant with the said E. F., his heirs and assigns, that he the said C. D. hath not made, done, executed or knowingly permitted any act, deed, matter or thing by means whereof the hereditaments hereby granted, or any part thereof, are, is or can be in anywise charged, incumbered or prejudicially affected in title, estate or otherwise howsoever; and the said A. B. doth hereby for himself, his heirs, executors and administrators, covenant with the said C. D., his heirs, executors, administrators and assigns respectively, as follows, namely, that he the said A. B., his heirs, executors or administrators, will pay to the said C. D., his executors, administrators or assigns, the sum of £   with interest thereon after the rate of £   per cent. per annum, on the   day of   next, without deduction; and also that they the said A. B. and C. D. now have in themselves, or one of them now hath in himself, full power to grant the said hereditaments in manner aforesaid, free from all charges and incumbrances whatsoever; and moreover, that they the said A. B. and C. D., and each of them, and their respective heirs, and all other persons claiming any estate or interest in the said hereditaments, shall at the expense of the said A. B., his heirs, executors or administrators, make and execute all such further assurances for more perfectly assuring the said hereditaments unto the said E. F., his heirs and assigns, subject to the proviso herein contained for redemption of the said premises, as he or they may reasonably require: [And further, that the said A. B., his heirs, executors, administrators and assigns, will, so long as any money is owing on the security of these presents, insure from damage by fire the erections and buildings for the time being standing on the said premises, in the full value thereof, in the name of the said E. F., his executors, administrators or assigns, in some reputable insurance office, and produce to him or them on demand the policy of and vouchers for such insurance, and on neglect or refusal to produce such policy or vouchers it shall be lawful for the said E. F., his executors, administrators or assigns, to effect such insurance, and the monies expended by him or them in and about the same shall be a charge on the hereditaments hereby granted, and bear interest after the rate aforesaid, and if any damage by fire shall happen to the said premises, the money recoverable under such insurance shall be received by the said E. F., his executors, administrators or assigns, and be applied at his or their option, either in reinstating the buildings, or in payment of the money then due on this security]; [and the said

E. F. doth hereby for himself, his heirs, executors and administrators (but so only as to bind himself and themselves during such time as he or they may be the mortgagee or mortgagees of the said hereditaments, and by no means after any transfer of this security), covenant with the said A. B., his heirs, executors, administrators and assigns respectively, that no sale of the said hereditaments, or any part thereof, shall take place until one calendar month's previous notice in writing of such intended sale shall have been given by the said E. F., his heirs, executors, administrators or assigns, or some or one of them, to the said A. B., his heirs or assigns, or left for him or them at or sent through the Post Office addressed to his or their last or most usual place of abode in England, or at the said premises; but this covenant shall not oblige any purchaser to inquire whether such notice shall have been given, nor shall the non-delivery of such notice affect the title of any purchaser.]

In witness, &c.

129.

Transfer of Mortgage, with further Advance.

THIS INDENTURE, made the   day of   , 18 , between A. B., of &c., of the first part, C. D., of &c., of the second part, and E. F., of &c., of the third part: Whereas by an indenture, dated the   day of   , 18 , made between the said A. B. of the one part, and the said C. D. of the other part, in consideration of £   to the said A. B. paid by the said C. D., all [*parcels*] with the appurtenances were conveyed unto and to the use of the said C. D., his heirs and assigns, subject to a proviso for reconveyance of the said hereditaments on payment by the said A. B., his heirs, executors, administrators or assigns, to the said C. D., his executors, administrators or assigns, of £   , with interest thereon at the rate of £   per cent. per annum, on a day therein mentioned and since past; and whereas there is now owing to the said C. D., under the said mortgage security, the sum of £   , all interest having been paid up to the date of these presents; and whereas the said E. F. hath agreed to lend the said A. B. the sum of £   to pay off the said mortgage, and also the further sum of £   , upon having the repayment thereof with interest secured in manner hereinafter expressed: Now this indenture witnesseth, that, in consideration of £   sterling to the said C. D. paid by the said E. F. on the execution hereof (at the request of the said A. B.), the receipt whereof, and that the same is in full satisfaction and discharge of all monies owing on the said recited security, the said C. D. doth hereby acknowledge, and from the same doth discharge the said E. F., his heirs, executors, administrators and assigns, and also the said A. B., his heirs, executors and administrators, and also in consideration of £   sterling to the said A. B. at the same time paid by the said E. F., the receipt of which several sums of £ and £   (making together the sum of £   ) the said A. B. doth hereby acknowledge, and doth discharge the said E. F., his heirs, executors, administrators and assigns, therefrom, he the said C. D., at the request of the said A. B., doth grant, and the said A. B. doth grant and confirm, unto the said E. F. and his heirs, all the said   and hereditaments hereinbefore described and comprised in and conveyed by the hereinbefore-recited indenture, with their appurtenances, To hold the said premises hereby granted unto and to the use of the said E. F., his heirs and assigns, discharged from the proviso contained in the said indenture of mortgage for redemption of the said premises, but subject to the proviso next hereinafter contained. [*Here insert the proviso for redemption and other provisions, as in the last Precedent, the amount of mortgage money being the aggregate of the amount paid to the prior mortgagee and the further advance.*]

In witness, &c.

130.

Release of Equity of Redemption, by Indorsement.

THIS INDENTURE, made the   day of   , 18 , between the within-named A. B. of the one part, and the within-named C. D. of the other part: Whereas the principal sum of £   secured by the within indenture was not paid at the time within mentioned, and is still owing to the said C. D., but all interest thereon hath been paid up to the date hereof; and whereas the said A. B. hath contracted with the said C. D. for the absolute sale to him of the equity of redemption of and in the within-mentioned hereditaments for the sum of £   : Now this indenture witnesseth, that, in consideration of the release by the said C. D. hereinafter contained, and of £   sterling paid by him to the said A. B. on the execution hereof, the receipt whereof the said A. B. doth hereby acknowlege, and from the same discharge the said C. D., his heirs, executors, administrators and assigns, he the said A. B. doth grant and release unto the said C. D. and his heirs, all the within-mentioned hereditaments and premises, with the appurtenances, To hold the said hereditaments, with the appurtenances (freed and discharged from the proviso for redemption contained in the within indenture, and all claims and demands in respect of the same), unto and to the use of the said C. D., his heirs and assigns; and the said A. B. doth hereby for himself, his heirs, executors and administrators, covenant with the said C. D., his heirs and assigns, that (notwithstanding any act, deed or thing done or permitted by the said A. B. to the contrary) he now hath in himself full power to assure the said hereditaments to the use of the said C. D., his heirs and assigns, free from incumbrances; and moreover, that he the said A. B., and every person having or claiming any estate or interest in or out of the said hereditaments through, under or in trust for him, shall at all times hereafter, at the request and costs of the said C. D., his heirs or assigns, execute and perfect all such further assurances for more effectually assuring the said hereditaments, with the appurtenances, unto the said C. D., his heirs or assigns, discharged from the said mortgage and all claims and demands in respect of the same, as by him or them shall be reasonably required; and the said C. D. doth hereby, in consideration of the grant and release hereinbefore contained, release and discharge the said A. B., his heirs, executors, administrators and assigns, of and from the payment of the within-mentioned principal sum of £   and interest, and all claims and demands in respect of the same.

, In witness, &c.

[N.B.—If the mortgagee was married before the 1st January, 1834, and his wife be living, a dower trustee should be added, and the usual provisions to bar dower inserted.]

131.

Proviso that Mortgagor, being a Solicitor, shall have his Costs.

PROVIDED LASTLY, and it is hereby agreed and declared, that the said G. H. shall be entitled to charge and shall be paid for all business done by him as an attorney or solicitor in relation to these presents or the trusts thereof, in the same manner and to the same extent as he might do if he were acting as solicitor for a mortgagee and had not himself advanced the said sum of £   , any rule of equity to the contrary notwithstanding.

132.

Proviso in Mortgage for Money to remain for a Term certain.

PROVIDED ALWAYS, and it is hereby declared and agreed, that in case the said [*mortgagor*] shall duly and punctually pay all premiums and other monies necessary for keeping on foot the said policy of assurance when and as the same shall become due and payable, and shall also duly pay the interest on the said sum of £   on the days and in the manner hereinbefore mentioned, or within thirty days after the expiration of any or either of such days, the said [*mortgagee*], his executors, administrators or assigns, will not call in or compel payment of the said sum of £   , or proceed to the exercise of the power of sale hereinbefore contained, until the   day of   , 18 : Provided also, that for the considerations aforesaid the said [*mortgagor*] shall not nor will require the said [*mortgagee*], his executors, administrators or assigns, to receive payment of the said sum of £   until the said   day of   , 18 .

133.

Form of Receipt to be indorsed on Mortgage when Mortgage Money paid and no Reconveyance then taken.

MEMORANDUM. I acknowledge that the within-named A. B. hath paid to me all principal and interest monies intended to be secured by the within indenture, and I undertake, when requested, at the costs in all things of the said A. B., to execute such reconveyance of the within-mentioned hereditaments and premises as he may direct.

C. D.

134.

Notice of Sale by Mortgagee.

To Mr.   and whom else it may concern:

I hereby request payment of the sum of £   , with interest thereon, from the   day of   last, owing to me by virtue of the indenture of mortgage executed by you, bearing date the   day of   , 18 ; and I hereby give you notice, that unless the same be paid within   calendar months from the delivery hereof, I shall proceed to a sale of the   and hereditaments in the said indenture comprised, in execution of the power thereby vested in me. Dated this   day of   , 18 .

135.

Form of Letter or Undertaking to be given by Solicitor of intending Mortgagor [or by the Mortgagor] to intending Mortgagee's Solicitor before the Title is investigated.

A. to B.

SIR,—In the event of the proposed mortgage from my client Mr. A. [*or* " from me the undersigned J. A."] to your client Mr. B. of premises at   for £   and interest not being carried out and completed either from the security being insufficient in value or the title to the property being unsatisfactory in the opinion of Mr. B.'s counsel, or from any cause other than the neglect or default of Mr. B. to advance the said sum of £   on mortgage of the said premises, I undertake that Mr. A. shall [*or* " I undertake to"] pay all expenses for valuing the said premises, and also all reasonable and proper charges and payments for investigating the title and otherwise incidental to the matter.

To G. H.   Yours, &c.

136.

Release by Mortgagee in Fee of Part of the Hereditaments subject to his Mortgage.

THIS INDENTURE, made the   day of   , 18   , between A. B., of &c., of the one part, and C. D., of &c., of the other part: Whereas by an indenture dated the   day of   , 18   , and made between K. L. (the father of the said C. D.) of the one part, and the said A. B. of the other part, the said K. L. granted and conveyed unto the said A. B., his heirs and assigns, (among other hereditaments) the hereditaments hereinafter described, subject to a proviso for redemption on payment by the said K. L., his executors, administrators or assigns, to the said A. B., his executors, administrators or assigns, of 3,000*l*., and such other principal sums, not exceeding therewith the total sum of 5,000*l*., as might become due, and interest thereon at the rate and times and in manner therein mentioned; and whereas the said K. L., by his will dated the   day of   , 18   , devised the hereditaments comprised in and then subject to the before-recited mortgage unto his son the said C. D., his heirs and assigns, for his and their own use and benefit; and whereas the said K. L. died on the   day of   , 18   , and his said will was proved in the principal registry of the Court of Probate; and whereas the sum of 3,000*l.*, together with some interest thereon, is still owing to the said A. B. by virtue of the said mortgage; and whereas the said A. B. hath agreed to release from his said mortgage the hereditaments hereinafter described: Now this indenture witnesseth, that, in consideration of the premises, he the said A. B. doth hereby grant unto the said C. D. and his heirs all [*setting out the portion of the mortgaged premises to be released*], and the same are now in the occupation of   as tenant thereof, with their rights, easements and appurtenances, To hold the said premises, discharged from the said mortgage and all monies thereby secured, unto and to the use of the said C. D., his heirs and assigns; and the said A. B. doth hereby for himself, his heirs, executors and administrators, covenant with the said C. D., his heirs and assigns, that he the said A. B. hath not at any time heretofore done or executed or knowingly permitted any deed or thing whereby the said hereditaments hereby granted are or may be charged, affected or incumbered.

In witness, &c.

Notices.

137.

To Quit, from Landlord to Tenant.

To Mr. J. P., or whom else it may concern:

I hereby give you notice, that I require you to quit and deliver up to me on or before the   day of   now next ensuing the peaceable and quiet possession of all that messuage or tenement, outbuildings, garden and arable land, situate in the parish of E., in the county of M., which you now hold of me as tenant, or otherwise that you deliver up the said premises to me at the end of the year of your tenancy which shall expire next after the end of one half year from the date hereof. Dated this   day of   , 18 .

      Yours, &c., A. B.
      By C. D., his agent.

138.
To Quit, from Tenant to Landlord.

To Mr. J. P., or whom else it may concern:

I hereby give you notice, that it is my intention to quit and deliver up to you on the   day of   next possession of all that messuage or tenement, outbuildings, garden and arable land, situate in the parish of E., in the county of M., which I now hold of you as tenant. Dated this   day of   , 18 .

      Yours, &c.
      A. B.

139.
To Quit and for Double Rent.

To Mr. A. B., or whomsoever else it may concern:

I do hereby give you notice to quit and deliver up to me, or to the landlord for the time being, possession of the several pieces or parcels of land, hereditaments and premises, situate in the parish of   in the county of   , which you now hold as tenant from year to year, and which are more particularly described in the schedule hereunder written, on the   day of   now next ensuing, or at the end of the year of your tenancy which shall expire next after the end of one half year from the date hereof, and on failure thereof I shall require you to pay thenceforth double the former rent, or double the yearly value of the said several pieces or parcels of land, hereditaments and premises, according to the form of the statute in that case made and provided. Dated this day of , 18 .

Yours, &c.,
J. O.,
Solicitor and agent for the landlord or landlords of the said premises.

[Schedule.]

140.

To a Railway Company from a Claimant requiring Compensation as Occupier, in respect of Property injuriously affected, under the 68th Section of " The Lands Clauses Consolidation Act, 1864."

To the   Railway Company:

I the undersigned A. B., of &c., do hereby give you notice, that I am the occupier of a dwelling-house and shop situate in   Street in the parish of   and county of   , and that I hold the said dwelling-house and shop as tenant from year to year, and that the said dwelling-house and shop are used by me for carrying on therein my business as a   , and that you have during and in consequence of the construction of the railway called the   Railway and other the works authorized by " The   Railway Act, 18 ," injuriously affected my said dwelling-house and shop, and occasioned loss and damage to me in my business by the blocking up of [*state the grievance*], and thereby preventing the passing of customers to my said dwelling-house and shop and causing a diminution in my business; and I give you notice, that I claim the sum of £   as the compensation to be paid to me for the injury done to my said dwelling-house and shop, and the loss and damage which I have sustained as aforesaid, by the making of the said railway and the construction of the works thereof, and that in case you the said company shall dispute my said claim for compensation it is my desire to have the amount of such compensation settled by a jury in the manner mentioned in and according to " The Lands Clauses Consolidation Act, 1845." Dated this day of , 18 .

A B.

[The above is a claim for compensation by a tenant from year to year for injury done to his business by the blocking up of a street during the construction of the railway. If the tenant has a lease state it; for instance, " in my occupation and held by me under a lease for years at a rent of £ per annum, of which term years are unexpired."

It is quite clear that such a claim comes within the 68th section; *Chamberlain* v. *West End Railway Company* (11 Weekly Rep. 472); *Senior* v. *Metropolitan Railway Company* (11 Weekly Rep. 836); *Cameron* v. *Charing Cross Railway Company* (12 Weekly Rep. 803).

In such a case as the above the tenant is not obliged to go before two justices, although he is merely tenant from year to year, but he would be so obliged if the property was *taken* by the company. *Somers* v. *Metropolitan Railway Company* (10 Weekly Rep. 717).]

141.

To a Railway Company from a Claimant requiring Compensation as Owner of Property, taken by the Railway, under the 68th *Section of* " *The Lands Clauses Consolidation Act,* 1864."

To the Railway Company:

Whereas by a notice in writing numbered , bearing date the day of , 18 , under the hand of your secretary, you the said company gave notice to A. B., that you required to purchase and take under the powers and for the purposes of " The Railway Act, 1861," so much and such part or parts of the land or ground and hereditaments of which the particulars (as described or referred to in the map or plan and book of reference mentioned in the said act to have been deposited with the respective clerks of the peace for the city of London and county of Middlesex) were contained in the Schedule to the said notice, and as was or were delineated in the plan attached thereto and therein distinguished by a red colour, together with all buildings thereon, and that you the said company were willing to treat with the said A. B. for the purchase of the land and hereditaments so required as aforesaid, with the appurtenances, and as to the compensation to be made to the said A. B., for the damage that might be sustained by him by means of the execution of the works authorized by the said act; and whereas the lands, hereditaments and premises comprised in or affected by the said notice consist of two messuages, yards, gardens, stables and premises situate and being Nos.   ,   Street, in the parish of   in the county of Middlesex, and the same are numbered   in the map or plan and book of reference referred to in the said notice; and whereas by a notice in writing to you the said company under the hand of the said A. B., dated on or about the   day of   , 18 , he the said A. B. required the sum of £   for the land, hereditaments and premises mentioned in the said notice so given by the said company; and whereas the interest of the said A. B. in the said land, hereditaments and premises consists of a lease granted to him for the term of   years from   , 18 , subject to the payment of a yearly rent of £   per annum, and the said A. B. is the sole owner of such lease; and whereas the said premises are in the occupation of C. and D. respectively, as tenants from year to year; and whereas the price required by the said A. B. for the purchase of or compensation money for the said land, hereditaments and premises is the sum of £   ; and whereas no award has been made or agreement entered into respecting the said purchase or compensation: Now therefore, I, the said A. B., do hereby give you notice, that I desire to have the question of compensation to be paid to me for and in respect of my interest in the said lands, hereditaments and premises settled by a jury pursuant to the provisions of "The Lands Clauses Consolidation Act, 1845," and I do require you the said company within twenty-one days from the receipt of this notice to issue your warrant to the sheriff to summon a jury for settling the amount of the said compensation according to the provisions of "The Lands Clauses Consolidation Act, 1845." Dated this   day of   , 18 .   A. B.

[If the property be freehold then alter the notice accordingly; if in the owner's occupation, say so; if in the occupation of tenants, say so; and state how they hold.

This notice cannot be given until the property has been taken by the company. If, therefore, the company give a notice to treat for two houses, and only take one, the above notice must be confined to that one, otherwise it will be bad. And, with respect to the other, the proper course is for the owner to apply for a mandamus compelling the company to issue their warrant to summon a jury.]

142.

By Mortgagee to Tenant to pay Rent to him.

I HEREBY give you notice, that by an indenture dated, &c., made between, &c., the house and premises at   now in your occupation was mortgaged to me for securing £
and interest, and the said house and premises are now vested in me by virtue of the said indenture : And I require you to pay to me or to my authorized agent all rent now due and hereafter to become due in respect of the same premises. Dated, &c.

To Mr.   .   A. B.

143.

By Second Mortgagee to First.

I HEREBY give you notice, that by indenture dated, &c., made between A. B. of the one part, and me the undersigned C. D. of the other part, the hereditaments now in mortgage to you situate in , were assured to me by the said A. B. for securing the sum of £ and interest. Dated, &c.

C. D.

To Mr. [*first mortgagee*].

PARTITION DEED BY TENANTS IN COMMON.

144.

THIS INDENTURE, made the day of , 18 , between A. B., of &c., of the first part, C. D., of &c., of the second part, and E. F. (releasee to uses) of &c., of the third part: Whereas G. H., late of &c., deceased, by his will, dated &c., devised the hereditaments hereinafter mentioned unto the said A. B. and C. D., their heirs and assigns, as tenants in common; and whereas the said A. B. and C. D. are desirous to make a partition of the hereditaments so devised to and now held by them as aforesaid, and they have agreed that the messuage and hereditaments in shall be taken and enjoyed by the said A. B. in severalty in lieu of his undivided share of the entirety of the said hereditaments, and that the land and hereditaments in shall be taken and enjoyed by the said C. D. in severalty, in lieu of his undivided share of the entirety of the said hereditaments; and whereas the said A. B. and C. D. are desirous that the hereditaments so to be allotted to them respectively should be conveyed and assured in manner hereinafter appearing: Now this indenture witnesseth, that, in pursuance of the said agreement, and in consideration of the premises, they the said A. B. and C. D. do and each of them doth grant unto the said E. F., and his heirs first all [premises to be taken by A.] now in the tenure or occupation of ; secondly, all [premises to be taken by B.] now in the several tenures or occupations of , together with the appurtenances to the said premises respectively belonging or appertaining, To hold the said premises hereby granted unto the said E. F. and his heirs, to the uses following, namely, as to the premises first hereinbefore described, to the use of the said A. B., his heirs and assigns, and as to the premises secondly hereinbefore described, to the use of the said C. D., his heirs and assigns, and the said A. B., so far as respects one undivided moiety of the said premises, and the said C. D., so far as respects the other undivided moiety of the said premises, do hereby severally covenant with the said E. F. and his heirs, that, notwithstanding any act, deed or thing made, done or permitted by the said A. B. and C. D. respectively or the said G. H. deceased to the contrary, the said A. B. and C. D. respectively have good right to grant the said hereditaments with their appurtenances, unto the said E. F. and his heirs, to the uses and in manner aforesaid free from incumbrances : And further, that the said A. B. and C. D. respectively, and their respective heirs and every person rightfully claiming under them respectively, or under the said G. H. deceased, will at all times hereafter, at the request and costs of the said E. F., his heirs or assigns, execute every such deed for more effectually assuring the hereditaments hereby granted unto the said E. F. and his heirs, to the uses and in manner aforesaid, as the said E. F., his heirs or assigns, may reasonably require.

In witness, &c.

PARTNERSHIP.

145.

Deed of Copartnership between two Traders, with usual Clauses.

THIS INDENTURE, made the   day of   , 18 , between A. B., of &c., of the one part, and C. D., of &c., of the other part: Whereas the said A. B. hath for some time past carried on the trade or business of   , at No.   ,   street, in the county of   ; and whereas the said A. B. has agreed to admit the said C. D. into partnership in the said trade or business, as and from the   day of   last, for the term and upon the conditions and stipulations hereinafter expressed and declared; and whereas upon the treaty for the said partnership it was agreed, that the value of the stock in trade, plant and materials used in carrying on the said trade or business should be taken at the sum of £   , and that the said C. D. should pay to the said A. B. the sum of £   , as and for the purchase of one   part or share of and in the said trade or business, and the stock in trade, plant and materials used in carrying on the same; and whereas the said C. D. has immediately before the execution hereof paid to the said A. B. the sum of £   , as he doth hereby acknowledge and declare: Now this indenture witnesseth, that, for the considerations aforesaid, and also in consideration of the mutual trust and confidence which the said A. B. and C. D. have and repose in each other, each of them the said A. B. and C. D., as far as the covenants and agreements hereinafter contained are to be observed or performed by him, his heirs, executors or administrators, doth for himself, his heirs, executors and administrators, covenant with the other of them, his executors and administrators, by these presents, in manner following; that is to say,

1. That they the said A. B. and C. D. shall and will become, be and remain copartners in the trade or business of   , for the term of   years, commencing from the   day of   last, if the said partners shall so long live.

2. That the firm and style of the said copartnership shall be   .

3. That the business of the said copartnership shall be carried on at   , or at such other place or places as the said copartners shall hereafter determine.

4. That both of them, the said A. B. and C. D., shall and will at all times during the continuance of the said copartnership diligently and faithfully employ themselves in and about the business of the said copartnership, and carry on, manage and conduct the same for the greatest benefit and advantage of the said copartnership.

5. That each of them the said copartners shall and will be just and faithful to the other of them and to the said copartnership in all buyings, sellings, accounts, reckonings, receipts, payments, dealings and transactions in or about the business of the said copartnership, and shall and will give, make and render to the other of them a faithful and just account thereof

when and so often as the same shall be reasonably required, and shall and will at all times during the continuance of the said copartnership, upon any reasonable request of the other of them, inform the other of them of all such letters, accounts, writings and other things as shall or may come into his hands or knowledge in anywise touching or concerning the business of the said copartnership.

6. That neither of them the said partners shall either by himself, or with any other person or persons whomsoever, either directly or indirectly engage in any trade, manufacture or business, except upon the account and for the benefit and advantage of the said copartnership, nor take any apprentice or hire or dismiss any clerk, traveller, workman or servant in the business of the said copartnership without the consent of the other of them, nor take or go any journey or journeys, voyage or voyages for or on account of the business of the said copartnership or otherwise without such consent, and that if either of them shall, at any time or times during the continuance of the said copartnership, take or go any such journey or journeys, voyage or voyages without such consent as aforesaid, he shall for such time as he shall be upon any such journey or journeys, voyage or voyages, forfeit a proportional part of his share in the gains and profits of the said copartnership, or the sum of £   , at the option of the other partner.

7. That the capital of the copartnership shall consist of the stock in trade, plant and materials now in, upon or belonging to the premises, where the said trade or business is carried on, and also the lease of the said premises, and that the said A. B. shall be credited in the books of the said copartnership with the sum of £   and the said C. D. with the sum of £   as their proportionate share of the capital of the said copartnership at the execution hereof, and that all future capital required for carrying on the said business shall be advanced and brought into the said business by the said A. B. and C. D. in the following proportions, namely,   by the said A. B., and   by the said C. D.; and that they shall

be considered as creditors of the said copartnership in respect of such future capital, and shall be allowed interest for the same after the rate of £5 per centum per annum; and that the said capital or joint stock, and the gains and profits arising from the same, including the premiums to be paid for any apprentice to be taken by either of the said copartners, shall, subject as hereinafter mentioned, be used and employed in the business of the said copartnership.

8. That the said C. D. shall be at liberty, if he shall think proper, to use and occupy the dwelling-house at No. , street aforesaid, in the same manner as he has for some time past used and occupied the same, for the residence of himself and his family, without paying any rent and taxes for the same; that the rent of the houses and premises where the business of the said copartnership, or any of them, shall be carried on, and all repairs, additions and alterations of, to, in or about the same, and all taxes, rates, assessments, payments for insurance against loss by fire and other outgoings whatsoever for or in respect of the same, and the salaries, wages or maintenance of all clerks, travellers, workmen, servants or apprentices who shall be employed in or about the business of the said copartnership, or any of them, and all charges and expenses which shall be incurred in or about the business of the said copartnership, or in anywise relating thereto, and all duties, debts and monies which shall become payable for or upon account of the said business, and all losses and damages which shall happen in or about the same, shall be paid, defrayed and borne by and out of the joint-stock of the said copartnership, and the gains and profits arising from the same; or in case the same shall become deficient, then by the said copartners out of their respective separate estates, in the proportions to which they are entitled to the profits of the said copartnership.

9. That neither of them the said partners shall, without the consent in writing of the other of them, employ any of the monies, goods or effects belonging to the said copartnership, or engage the credit thereof, in any matter or thing, except upon the account or for the use or benefit of the said co-

partnership; and in all cases where there shall be occasion to give any bond, note, bill or other security, or sign any cheque, for the payment of any sum or sums of money on account of the said copartnership, the same shall be respectively signed and executed by both of them the said partners.

10. That neither of them the said copartners shall at any time during the continuance of the said copartnership lend any of the monies or deliver upon credit any of the goods belonging to the said copartnership to any person or persons whom the other of them shall previously by notice in writing have forbidden him to trust; and in case either of them the said copartners shall after such notice as aforesaid lend any money or deliver upon credit any goods of or belonging to the said copartnership, then and in such case the party so lending or delivering upon credit such money or goods shall pay to the said copartnership so much ready money as the full amount or value of the money or goods which he shall so lend or deliver upon credit as aforesaid.

11. That neither of them the said copartners shall, without the consent of the other of them in writing first had and obtained, enter into any bond or become bail, surety or security with or for any person or persons whomsoever, or subscribe any policy of insurance, nor do or willingly suffer to be done any act, matter or thing whatsoever whereby or by means whereof the stock in trade, capital or property of the said copartnership may be seized, attached, extended or taken in execution.

12. That each of them the said copartners shall duly and punctually pay and discharge the debts now due and owing, or hereafter during the continuance of the said copartnership to become due and owing from him, to any person or persons whomsoever; and shall at all times hereafter, during the continuance of the said copartnership, save, defend and keep harmless and indemnified the other of them, and his heirs, executors and administrators, and the stock in trade, capital and property of the said copartnership, and the increase thereof, of and from his private and separate debts and engagements, whether already contracted or entered

into or hereafter during the continuance of the said copartnership to be contracted or entered into, and of and from all actions, suits, costs, damages and expenses on account thereof.

13. That the said copartners respectively shall keep or cause to be kept proper books of account in writing of all monies received and paid, all contracts entered into and all business transacted on account of the said copartnership, and all other matters of which accounts ought to be kept according to the usual and regular course of the said trade or business, and which accounts, together with all deeds, securities for money and papers belonging to the said copartnership, shall be kept at the principal place where the said trade or business shall be carried on, and not elsewhere; and shall at all reasonable times be open to the inspection of both the said partners.

14 That as soon as conveniently may be after the day of   in every year, during the said partnership, the said partners shall make a full and correct account in writing of all such goods, wares, articles and things as shall have been bought and sold in the business of the said copartnership (in the first of such general accounts from the day of the commencement of the said copartnership, and in each of such subsequent general accounts from the day of the last preceding account), and of all monies, stock in trade, effects, debts and things belonging or due or owing to or by the said copartnership, and of all the liabilities thereof, and of all such matters and things as are usually comprehended in general accounts of the like nature taken by persons engaged in the business of   , and cause such account to be written in two books, to be respectively signed by the said copartners within one calendar month after the time appointed for taking thereof respectively; and that after such signature each of them the said copartners shall take one of the said books into his custody, and shall be bound and concluded by every such account respectively, save and except that if any manifest error shall be found in any such account within twelve calendar months after the same shall have been so signed by both of them the said copartners, and shall be signified by

either of them the said copartners to the other of them, then and in such case such error shall be rectified; and that on the making up of every such yearly account all interest which shall become due to the said A. B. or C. D. for future capital, or such other sum or sums of money as they shall respectively advance and bring into the said copartnership, shall in the first place be deducted, and the residue of the clear profits of the said business which shall have accrued or been gained in the preceding year shall be divided among the said partners in the proportions following, namely,   parts thereof to the said A. B. and the remaining   part thereof to the said C. D.: [provided always, and it is hereby declared, that all sums of money received by the said A. B. for or on account of certain letters-patent for making or manufacturing
shall belong exclusively to the said A. B., and shall not be brought into the said copartnership.]

15. That the said A. B. shall be at liberty from time to time to draw out of the said business any sum or sums not exceeding the sum of £   per week for his own use, and the said C. D. shall be at liberty to draw out of the said business any sum or sums not exceeding the sum of £
per week for his own use, but in case at the end of the year it shall appear, upon making the general annual account hereinbefore directed to be made, that the net gains and profits of such year shall not have amounted to the aggregate sum drawn out by the said partners as hereinbefore mentioned, then and in such case, immediately after such general annual account shall have been made and settled, the said A. B. and C. D. shall repay to the said copartnership the difference (if any) between the amount of the sums which he shall actually have received in respect of such weekly payment, and the sum which he shall have been entitled to receive as his share of the net gains and profits of the said business.

16. That within the space of six calendar months after the expiration or determination of the said copartnership a full and general account in writing shall be made and taken by the said partners of all monies, stock in trade, debts, effects and things belonging to the said copartnership, and of all

monies and debts due or owing by the said copartnership, and of all the liabilities of the said copartnership, and a just valuation and appraisement shall be made of all the particulars included in such account which require and are capable of valuation or appraisement, and immediately after such last-mentioned account shall have been so taken and settled the said partners shall forthwith make due provision for the payment of all monies and debts then due or owing by the said copartnership, and for meeting all the liabilities thereof, and subject thereto all the monies, stock in trade, debts, effects and things then belonging to the said copartnership shall be divided between the said partners in the proportions aforesaid, and such instruments in writing shall be executed by them for facilitating the getting in of the outstanding debts and effects of the said copartnership, and for indemnifying each other touching the premises, and for vesting the sole right and property in the respective shares of and in the stock in trade, property and effects, in the parties to whom the same respectively shall upon such division belong, and for releasing to each other all claims on account of the said partnership as are usual in cases of the like nature.

17. [Provided always, and it is hereby agreed, that it shall be lawful for the said C. D. at the end of the said copartnership, on giving to the said A. B. six calendar months' previous notice of his desire so to do, to renew the said copartnership for a similar term of years, and to elect to take an equal interest with the said A. B. in the said copartnership; and on payment by the said C. D. to the said A. B. of such a sum of money as will make the difference between the value of one-third of the stock in trade, plant, materials and capital of the said copartnership, and one-half part thereof, the said A. B. and C. D. shall be interested in the said copartnership, and the capital, stock in trade and effects thereof, and the profits arising therefrom, in equal shares, and shall enter into such further articles of copartnership as may be necessary for carrying into effect this provision.]

18. [That it shall be lawful for the said A. B., at any time or times during the continuance of the said copartnership, to

assign and transfer, subject as hereinbefore mentioned, the whole or any part of his share in the said trades or businesses, or any of them, and the capital, stock in trade, plant, materials and profits thereof, to any person or persons whomsoever, who shall thereby become and be admitted a partner or partners of the said trades or businesses, or any of them, unless, and subject to the proviso after mentioned, the said C. D. shall make some substantial objection in writing to the person or persons proposed by the said A. B. to be brought into the said copartnership within one calendar month after he shall have received such notice in writing from the said A. B. of his intention to make any such assignment or transfer: Provided always, that in case the said C. D., within the period last mentioned, shall signify in writing to the said A. B. his desire to purchase the whole or any part of the share of the said A. B., intended to be disposed of by him, and shall pay to him the amount or value of the same, then and in such case the said C. D. shall be at liberty to purchase the same.]

19. That in case either of the said partners shall die during the continuance of the said partnership, then and in such case the share and interest of such deceased copartner in such copartnership shall be taken to be the amount which appeared as his share of the capital in the last preceding balance-sheet, and that the executors or administrators of such deceased copartner shall be entitled to receive from such surviving partner such amount, together with or less by any sum which may be due from or to the firm to or from the said deceased copartner at the time of his death, in respect of monies advanced to or from the said copartnership, to or by such deceased partner, and to or by such sum in lieu of profits from the date or time to which the last preceding balance-sheet shall have been made, up to the time of death, as would be receivable for such period after the rate at which such deceased copartner had drawn out, in respect of net profits for the year immediately preceding such last balance-sheet, after allowing for all sums then previously drawn out by such deceased copartner since such last balance-sheet in respect of his weekly allowance or other drawing out in

respect of profits, together with interest after the rate of £5 per cent. per annum on the said aggregate amount from the day of the death of such deceased copartner until payment, it being the true intent and meaning of such copartners that such sums shall be given and taken in full for the share and interest of such deceased partner in the said copartnership at the time of his death, without any account being taken or any addition or deduction being made thereto or therefrom on any account whatsoever; and that the surviving partner shall, within two months next after the death of the deceased copartner, give such surety as shall be to the satisfaction of the executors or administrators of such deceased partner for the payment and discharge of the debts and liabilities of the said copartnership due at the time of the death, and for indemnifying the estate and effects of the deceased copartner therefrom; and also for securing to such executors or administrators the payment of such aggregate amount as aforesaid by three equal yearly instalments, payable respectively at the expiration of one, two and three years after the death of the deceased partner, and with each of such instalments the sum due at the date of each such payment in respect of such interest as aforesaid on the said aggregate amount, or on so much thereof as shall for the time being remain unpaid; and that until such security shall be so given the said aggregate amount and interest shall be the primary charge on all the estate and effects belonging to the said copartnership at the time of the death of the said copartner, after payment of the debts and liabilities thereof, and that no part of the assets or monies of the said copartnership shall be received by the surviving copartner for his own benefit, or be applied or disposed of by him except for the necessary payment of the debts or liabilities of the firm; and that when the whole of the said aggregate amount and interest, and the debts and liabilities, shall have been fully paid and discharged, then, or at any time thereafter, the executor or administrator of such deceased partner shall, at the request and costs of the surviving partner, his executors or administrators, execute to him or them a sufficient release of the said security so to be given as aforesaid, and also of and from all claims and demands respecting the said copartnership.

20. [That for the purpose of giving proper effect to the last preceding clause, in the event of the death of either of the said partners taking place during the first year of the said copartnership, it is agreed that the profits of the said copartnership for such year shall be and are hereby fixed at the sum of £   , and in the event of such death taking place during the second year of the said copartnership, then the said profits shall consist of the net profits of the preceding year (as appearing by the balance-sheet of that year), and the hereinbefore-mentioned sum of £   added thereto.]

21. That if at any time during the said copartnership, or at any time after the expiration or determination thereof, any dispute, doubt or question shall arise between the said partners, or their respective heirs, executors or administrators, either on the construction of these presents, or respecting the accounts, transactions, profits or losses of the business of the said copartnership, then every such dispute, doubt or question shall be referred to the arbitration of two indifferent persons, one to be named by each party in dispute, or in case either of the parties in dispute shall, upon the request of the other of the said parties, or within the seven days following such request, refuse or neglect to join in such nomination, then both of the said arbitrators shall be named by the other of the said parties; and in case such referees cannot agree upon an award, then the said dispute, doubt or question shall stand referred to the umpirage or arbitration of such one person as the two referees shall, before they shall proceed in the reference, by any writing under their hands appoint, so that every such reference shall be made within forty days next after such dispute, doubt or question shall arise: and the award or determination which shall be made by the said two referees or by their umpire concerning the premises shall be final and conclusive on the parties respectively, and their respective heirs, executors and administrators, so as such referees shall make their award in writing under their hands, or appoint an umpire, within forty days next after the reference to them, and so as

such umpire shall make his determination in writing under his hand within twenty days after the time appointed for making the award of the said referees shall be expired; and it is hereby further agreed, that this submission to reference shall be made a rule of her Majesty's Court of Queen's Bench at Westminster, on the application of either of the parties to the reference; and also, that no suit at law or in equity shall be commenced or prosecuted against the referees or their umpire concerning any of the matters or things so to be referred to them or him as aforesaid, or concerning their or his award or determination; and that the several and respective parties to such reference shall submit to be examined by the said referees or their umpire upon oath, to be administered in such manner as the said arbitrators or umpires shall direct, for the discovery of any of the dealings or transactions of the said partnership relating to the matters so referred as aforesaid; and it is hereby further agreed, that no suit at law or in equity shall be commenced or instituted by either of the said partners, his heirs, executors or administrators, against the other of them, his heirs, executors and administrators, touching the matters in dispute before the partner, his heirs, executors and administrators, to be made defendant or defendants to such suit or suits shall have refused or neglected to refer the matter in difference to arbitration pursuant to the agreement hereinbefore contained, or unless the time limited for making such award or determination shall have elapsed or expired without any such award having been made.

22. That the said A. B. shall, when required by the said C. D., at the expense of the said copartnership estate, execute such assignments or other assurances for well and effectually vesting the premises where the said copartnership trades or businesses are carried on in the said A. B. and C. D. jointly for the remainder of the respective terms therein, subject to the payment of the rent and performance of the covenants therein contained, as the said C. D. may require.

In witness, &c.

146.

Deed of Dissolution of Partnership.

THIS INDENTURE, made the   day of   , 18 , between A. B., of &c., of the one part, and C. D., of &c., and E. F., of &c., of the other part: Whereas from the   day of   to the   day of   last, the said A. B. and C. D. carried on the business of   in copartnership, under the firm of B. & Co. at   aforesaid, pursuant to certain articles of copartnership, dated the   day of   , and made between the said A. B. of the first part, the said C. D. of the second part, and the said E. F. of the third part, by which articles the said A. B., C. D. and E. F. bound themselves, &c. [*shortly recite so much of the partnership deed as is necessary*]; and whereas the parties hereto have agreed that the said copartnership shall be dissolved from the date hereof, so far as relates to the said A. B., and that the same shall henceforth be carried on by the said C. D. and E. F.; and whereas an account hath been stated and settled between the said parties, of all the debts and effects due or owing or belonging to the said copartnership on the date hereof, and of all the present outstanding bills or notes, and other debts or engagements of the said copartnership; and whereas the respective shares of the parties hereto of and in the net gains and profits of the said copartnership up to the day of the date of these presents have been paid to or received by them respectively, and all allowances for house rents and taxes which the parties hereto respectively have become entitled to under the said articles up to the date hereof have also been paid to or received by them respectively: Now this indenture witnesseth, that, in consideration of the premises, the parties hereto do with mutual consent hereby determine and dissolve the aforesaid copartnership, so far as relates to the said A. B., from the date hereof: And this indenture also witnesseth, that, in consideration of the premises, he the said

A. B. doth hereby assign unto the said C. D. and E. F., their executors and administrators, all the part, share and proportion of him the said A. B. of and in the monies, debts, bills, notes, bonds and other securities for money, chattels and effects whatsoever belonging, due or owing to the said copartnership, To have and receive the same unto the said C. D. and E. F., their executors, administrators and assigns, absolutely; and for the more effectually receiving the said several debts, monies and premises, he the said A. B. doth by these presents appoint the said C. D. and E. F., and each of them, their and each of their executors and administrators, and their or his substitute or substitutes jointly and severally, the attornies and attorney of the said A. B., in his name, or otherwise, but for the benefit of the said C. D. and E. F., their executors and administrators, to demand and receive the said debts, monies and premises from the persons liable to pay the same, and to prosecute all lawful or equitable courses for recovering the same, and to give effectual discharges for the same, and to sign the name of the said A. B. to any bill or note, the indorsement or acceptance of which by the said A. B. shall be necessary or convenient, and to do or cause to be done every or any other matter or thing necessary or convenient in or about the premises in as full, ample and beneficial a manner to all intents and purposes as the said A. B. might have done in case the said copartnership had not been dissolved; and the said A. B. doth hereby for himself, his heirs, executors and administrators, covenant with the said C. D. and E. F., their executors, administrators and assigns, that the said A. B. hath not contracted any debt or become bound to pay any debt or sum of money which can charge or affect the effects of the said copartnership, or for the payment whereof any of the members of the said copartnership may be subject or liable to be sued, except such debts as are entered in the books of the said copartnership, nor at any time assigned, released or received any of the said debts or done any other act whereby the same may be discharged or encumbered; and that he the said A. B., his executors or administrators, will justify and ratify whatsoever the said C. D.

and E. F. or either of them, their or either of their executors, administrators or assigns, substitute or substitutes shall lawfully do or cause to be done in or about the premises, and will at all times hereafter, at the request and costs of the said C. D. and E. F., or either of them, their or either of their executors, administrators or assigns, do and execute all such further acts and deeds for the better enabling the said C. D. and E. F., their executors, administrators or assigns, to recover and receive the said monies, debts and effects belonging to the said late copartnership, for their own use, as by the said C. D. and E. F., or either of them, their or either of their executors, administrators or assigns, shall be required; and also will not revoke any of the powers or authorities hereby given to the said C. D. and E. F., or either of them, their or either of their executors or administrators, substitute or substitutes, nor release, discharge or receive any of the debts or effects of the said copartnership, nor release or become nonsuit in any action or suit which may be brought for or in respect of the same, nor do any act or thing whereby the recovery of the same premises may be impeded or delayed, nor interfere in the same premises further than the said C. D. and E. F., their executors, administrators or assigns shall require; and the said C. D. and E. F. do hereby for themselves, their heirs, executors and administrators, and each of them doth hereby for himself, his heirs, executors and administrators, covenant with the said A. B., his executors and administrators, that the said C. D. and E. F., or one of them, their or one of their heirs, executors or administrators, will, with all convenient speed, pay all bills or notes of the said copartnership, now in circulation, and all other the debts and money due and owing from or by the said late copartnership, or the said parties hereto in respect thereof, and which appear in the books or accounts of the said late copartnership, and fulfil and perform all other the engagements whatsoever of the said copartnership, or to which the said parties or any of them are, is or shall be liable on account of the same; and will indemnify the said A. B , his heirs, executors and administrators, against all damages and expenses which may be incurred or become payable by reason of the nonpayment or nonperformance of any of the said bills, notes, debts, sums of money or engagements or in anywise relating thereto, or by reason of any action, suit or other proceeding which may be brought by virtue of or under any authority hereby given, or in pursuance hereof to be given, to the said C. D. and E. F., or either of them, their or either of their executors, administrators or assigns, or their or any of their substitute or substitutes: And this indenture also witnesseth, that, in pursuance of the said agreement in this behalf, they the said C. D. and E. F. do and each of them doth hereby release the said A. B., his heirs, executors and administrators, and the said A. B. doth hereby release the said C. D. and E. F., and each of them, their and each of their heirs, executors, administrators and assigns, from all actions, suits, accounts and demands on account of the said copartnership, or any clause, covenant, matter or thing contained in the said articles, or of any act, deed or thing in anywise relating thereto.

In witness, &c.

---

146 a.

Notice of Dissolution of Partnership.

NOTICE is hereby given, that the partnership lately subsisting between us the undersigned A. B., C. D. and E. F. as   , at   , in the county of   , under the firm of   , was on the   day of   last dissolved by mutual consent, so far as regards the said A. B., who on that day retired from the concern; and that all debts due and owing to or by the late firm will be received and paid by the said C. D. and E. F.

As witness our hands this   day of   , 18   .

A. B.
C. D.
Witness, S. H. .   E. F.

Powers of Attorney.
147.
Under Tithe Commutation Act.
WE the Reverend A. B., of &c., and C. D., of &c., do hereby appoint E. F., of &c., to be our and each of our lawful attorney, to act for us and each of us, in all respects as if we and each of us were present and acting, in the execution of an Act passed in the 6th and 7th years of his late Majesty King William the 4th, intituled " An Act for the Commutation of Tithes in England and Wales." Dated this   day of   , 18 .

Witness.

A. B.
C. D.

148.
Under Inclosure Act.
WE A. B., of &c., and C. D., of &c., do hereby appoint E. F., of &c., our and each of our lawful attorney for all the purposes of an Act passed in the 8th and 9th years of her present Majesty, intituled " An Act to facilitate the Inclosure and Improvement of Commons and Lands held in common, and the division of intermixed Lands, to provide remedies for defective or incomplete Executions and for the non-execution of the powers of General and Local Inclosure Acts, and to provide for the revival of such Powers in certain Cases." . Dated this   day of   , 18 .

Witness.

A. B.
C. D.

149.
To recover a Debt.
To all to whom these presents shall come, I, A. B., of &c., send greeting: Whereas C. D., of &c., is indebted to me in the sum of £   , and for the purpose of recovering the same I am desirous of appointing an attorney: Now there-

fore know ye, that I have appointed, and by these presents doth appoint E. F., of &c., my attorney, to ask and demand of the said C. D. the sum of £   , and on nonpayment thereof, or any part thereof, to commence and prosecute any action or actions for the recovery of the same in my name, and generally to do all and every or any other acts, deeds, matters and things whatsoever in or about the premises as fully and effectually to all intents and purposes as I could do if personally present, I hereby ratifying and confirming all and whatsoever the said E. F. shall lawfully do or cause to be done in or about the premises aforesaid by virtue hereof.

In witness, &c.

150.

From a Brewer to his Manager.

To all to whom these presents shall come, A. B., of &c., brewer, sends greeting: Whereas the said A. B. some time since took C. D., of &c., as his chief clerk, for the managing, superintending and conducting the trade or business of a brewer, carried on by the said A. B. at   aforesaid, and as his receiver of the rents and profits of his messuages, lands and hereditaments in the county of   ; and whereas the said A. B. is desirous of appointing the said C. D. as his attorney for the purposes hereinafter expressed: Now therefore know ye, that the said A. B. hath appointed, and by these presents doth appoint, the said C. D. his attorney, to act in, conduct, superintend and manage the said trade or business, and every or any other business now carried on by the said A. B., and for that purpose doth by these presents authorize and empower the said C. D., in the name and on behalf of the said A. B., to ask, demand, sue for, recover and receive of and from all and every person and persons whomsoever, and also of and from all and every body or bodies politic or corporate, whom it doth, shall or may concern, all and every sum and sums of money, debts, dues, goods, wares, merchandizes, chattels, effects and things of what nature or description soever which now are or is, or which at any time or times during the subsistence of these presents shall or may be or become due, owing, payable or belonging to the said A. B., and upon receipt thereof, or of any part thereof, for and in the name of him the said A. B. or of him the said C. D. or otherwise, as the case may require, to make, sign, execute and deliver such receipts, releases or other discharges, acquittances or acknowledgments for the same respectively as he the said C. D. shall think fit or be advised, and also for him the said A. B. and in his name to settle any account or accounts, or reckoning or reckonings, whatsoever wherein the said A. B. now is or at any time or times hereafter shall or may be in anywise interested or concerned with any person or persons whomsoever, and to pay or receive the balance or balances thereof, as the case may be or require; and also for him the said A. B., and in his name or otherwise, to compound with any person or persons for or in respect of the aforesaid debts or of any sums of money or of any other debt or debts or demands whatsoever which now is or are or shall or may at any time or times hereafter become due or payable to him the said A. B., and take or receive any composition or dividend thereof or thereupon, and give receipts, releases or other discharges for the whole of the same debts, sums or demands, or to submit to arbitration all and every or any such debts or demands as the said C. D. shall think most advisable for the benefit and advantage of the said A. B., and for that purpose and in his name to enter into, make, sign, execute and deliver such bonds of arbitration, or other deeds or instruments as are usual in like cases; and also for him the said A. B. and in his name to appear, and his person to represent in all or any court or courts and before all or any magistrates or officers of or in law or equity whatsoever, as by the said C. D. shall be thought advisable or as he shall think fit, and to sue, arrest, distrain upon and imprison, and out of prison again to liberate, release, acquit and discharge all and every or any person or persons whomsoever now indebted or who shall or may at any time hereafter become indebted to the said A. B., or upon whom he now has or hereafter shall or may have any lawful claim or demand; and also for and in the name of the said A. B. or otherwise to commence any action or actions for the recovery of any debt or sum or sums of money now due or payable or to become due or payable to the said A. B. by reason or on account of the said trades or businesses, or the possession of messuages or tenements held or connected therewith, and the same action or actions to prosecute and follow or to discontinue or become nonsuit therein if the said C. D. shall see cause; and also for him the said A. B. and in his name, or in the name of the said C. D. by procuration of the said A. B., but to and for his the said A. B.'s use and benefit, to make, draw or sign any bill or bills of exchange which in the due course and conduct of the business of the said A. B. shall be necessary; and also to draw drafts or orders on the banker of the said A. B. for payment of money which in the due course of the said business shall be required; and also to indorse the said bills of exchange or any note or order requiring such indorsement, for the purpose of enabling the bankers of the said A. B. to receive the same, but not so as to make the said A. B. personally liable for the amount thereof; and also to view, search and see the state, condition and defects of the reparation of the messuages, farms, lands and hereditaments of him the said A. B., and from time to time to give proper notices and directions for repairing the same, and to oversee, set, let, manage and improve the same to the best advantage; and also to pay and allow all taxes, rates, charges, and deductions and expenses, and all other payments and outgoings whatsoever due and payable or to grow due and payable for or on account of the said lands, hereditaments and other estates and premises of the said A. B.; and also for and in the name of the said A. B. to ask, receive and recover of and from all the farmers, tenants and other occupiers whatsoever of the messuages, lands, tenements and other hereditaments of the said A. B. all rents, arrears of rent, issues, profits and sum and sums of money now due, owing and payable, or at any time hereafter to grow and become due, owing and payable, for or in respect or on account of the same premises in any manner whatsoever; and also on non-payment thereof, or of any part thereof, to enter and distrain, and the distress and distresses there found to detain and keep, or otherwise to sell and dispose of according to law; and generally to do all and every or any other acts, deeds, matters and things whatsoever in or about the premises as fully and effectually to all intents and purposes as he the said A. B. could do or might have done in his own proper person if these presents had not been made, he the said A. B. hereby ratifying and confirming and promising and agreeing at all or any time or times to allow, ratify and confirm all and whatsoever the said C. D. shall lawfully do or cause to be done in or about the premises aforesaid by virtue hereof: [provided always, that these presents, or the power hereby given, shall in nowise extend nor be deemed nor construed to extend or revoke, determine or make void any of the former or other powers or authorities contained in certain articles of agreement bearing date the   day of   , and made between the said A. B. of the one part, and the said C. D. of the other part, nor to make void or abridge the stipulations, clauses and agreements therein contained, nor to entitle the said C. D. to any further or other compensation than is therein stipulated for, but all such powers, stipulations, clauses and agreements shall remain and be of the same validity, force and effect as if these presents had not been made.]

In witness whereof the said A. B. hath hereunto set his hand and seal the   day of   , 18 .

151.

By an Executor about to leave England.

To all to whom these presents shall come, I, A. B., of &c., send greeting : Whereas B. H., late of   aforesaid, merchant, made his last will and testament, bearing date on or about the   day of   , 18 , and thereby he appointed me the said A. B. executor thereof, and the said will was proved by me in the proper ecclesiastical court on the   day of   , 18 ; and whereas I the said A. B. am now about to leave England and reside in   , and previous thereto I am desirous of appointing proper persons or a proper person as my attornies or attorney, with such powers and authorities as may be necessary to enable them or him to act for me in my absence not only in any matters in which I am personally and beneficially interested, but also in any matters connected with the said executorship: Now therefore know ye, that I the said A. B. do by these presents make, constitute and appoint C. D. and E. F., both of &c., and the survivor of them, my true and lawful attornies and attorney for me and in my name by all lawful ways and means to ask, demand, sue for, receive, recover and take possession of all and singular the messuages, lands, tenements, monies, and all other the property, estate and effects whatsoever and wheresoever now of or belonging to me, either in my own right or as an executor of the said B. H., deceased, or which shall hereafter belong to me in any manner whatsoever, and upon receiving, recovering and obtaining possession thereof, to execute and give all proper releases and discharges for the same or for the income or proceeds thereof or in respect thereof, and thereupon to manage, employ and deal with the same or any part or parts thereof respectively as I the said A. B., either in my own right or as such executor as aforesaid, could or might lawfully have done or could lawfully be required and bound to do, and in my name and as my act and deed to sign and give proper and sufficient receipts for the same respectively ; and also for me and in my name to sign, seal, and as my act and deed deliver, any deed, bond, obligation, contract or agreement, or other paper whatsoever which shall or may be deemed necessary or expedient ; and also for me and in my name, and as my act and deed, to draw upon any bank or banks, individual or individuals, for any sum or sums of money that is or may be to my credit, or which I am or may be entitled to receive, and the same to deposit in any bank or place, and again, at their or his pleasure, to draw for from time to time

as I myself might or could do; and also for me and in my
name to grant and assure any part or parts of the estates, real,
personal, mixed, leasehold or otherwise, which I am entitled
to in my own right or as executor as aforesaid, or to which I
may hereafter become entitled, either alone or jointly with
others, or howsoever I am or may be entitled to the same,
and for me, and in my name and as my act and deed, to
make, seal and deliver in due form of law all necessary contracts, leases, deeds, conveyances and assurances, in reference
thereto; and also for me and in my name to transact, manage,
negotiate and adjust all matters and things in which I may
be interested or concerned, directly or indirectly, as trustee,
guardian, executor, administrator or otherwise, and execute
in due form of law all necessary deeds, writings and instruments in regard thereto; and also for me and in my name to
commence, prosecute or defend, or suspend, abandon or determine any action or actions, suit or suits in reference to the
matters aforesaid; and also to compound, compromise, conclude and agree for the same by arbitration or otherwise, as
my said attornies or attorney shall think fit; also for me and
in my name to do all such other acts, matters and things in
relation to any property, affairs and business of every kind,
nature and description in which I am or may be interested,
either beneficially or as trustee or otherwise, as I myself
might or could do if personally present and acting therein;
and also to substitute or appoint any person or persons to
act under or in the place of the said C. D. and E. F., or the
survivor of them, in all or any of the matters aforesaid, and
every such substitution at pleasure to revoke, I the said A. B.
hereby agreeing to ratify and confirm whatsoever the said
C. D. and E. F., or the survivor of them, or their or his substitute or substitutes, shall lawfully do or cause to be done in
or about the premises by virtue of these presents; and I the
said A. B. do hereby direct that all acts which shall be had,
made or done by my said attornies, or the survivor of them,
or their or his substitute or substitutes, and all dealings and
transactions by or between my said attornies, or the survivor
of them, or their or his substitute or substitutes, and any other

person or persons before he or they shall have received notice of my death or of the revocation of the authority contained in these presents shall be as binding and valid, to all intents and purposes, as if the same had taken place previous to my death or before such revocation, any rule of law or equity to the contrary notwithstanding; and lastly, I the said A. B. do hereby direct and declare that, in the event of my decease during the existence of the authorities herein contained, these presents, so far as may be requisite or conducive to the completion or confirmation of any lawful act done or agreed to be done by virtue hereof, shall take effect as my last will and testament, and in the same event I do hereby give, devise and bequeath the said messuages, lands, tenements, monies, property, estate and effects, with the produce thereof, or my part and share of the same, or the residue thereof subsisting, unconveyed or undisposed of at the time of my decease, unto the said C. D. and E. F. and the survivor of them, his heirs, executors and administrators, upon trust, in the first place, to fulfil and carry into effect all and whatsoever I or my attornies or attorney may have previously done or engaged to do in the premises under the authorities hereinbefore contained; and upon further trust, to sell and dispose of the surplus of the said messuages, lands, tenements, monies, property, estate and effects, in such manner as they or he shall think fit, in conformity to and by way of continuation of the powers hereinbefore contained, accounting for the proceeds as part of my personal estate, but so nevertheless that the receipts of the said C. D. and E. F. and the survivor of them, his heirs, executors and administrators, shall be effectual discharges for all monies received by virtue of these presents, and shall exonerate the person or persons paying the same from all responsibility as to the application thereof.

In witness whereof I the said A. B. have hereunto set my hand and seal the   day of   , 18 .

152.

By a Person going to reside Abroad.

To all to whom these presents shall come, I, A. B., of &c., send greeting: Whereas I intend shortly to go to Australia and continue for some time in parts beyond the seas: Now know ye, that I the said A. B. have made, constituted and appointed, and by these presents do make, constitute and appoint C. D., of &c., my true and lawful attorney for me and on my behalf to ask, demand and receive, of and from all and every the person or persons to whom it doth, shall or may belong to pay the same, all and every the legacies, gifts and bequests which may at any time hereafter, during my absence, be given, bequeathed or left to me by any person or persons whomsoever, or otherwise become due or payable to me, and to make, sign, execute and deliver such receipts, releases and other discharges, acquittances and acknowledgments for the same respectively as he, the said attorney, shall think fit and be advised; and also for me, and in my name or otherwise, to receive all and every sum and sums of money whatsoever which now is or are due, arising or belonging to me, upon or by virtue of any mortgage or mortgages or other security or securities whatsoever, and on receipt thereof, for me and in my name, to make, sign and give good and sufficient receipts, releases, acquittances or other discharges for the same; and also to sign, seal and execute, make or deliver all proper and sufficient reconveyances, releases and other assurances of the lands, tenements, hereditaments and property which shall have been mortgaged for payment thereof; and also for me and in my name, or otherwise, to compound with any person or persons for or in respect of the aforesaid debts, or of any sums of money, or any other debt, debts or demands whatsoever which now is or are, or shall or may at any time or times hereafter become, due or payable to me, and take or receive any composition or dividend thereof or thereupon, and give receipts, releases and other discharges for the whole of the said debts, sums or demands; and also for me in my name, and on my behalf, to enter into any arrangements with any person or persons to whom I am or shall or may be indebted, touching or concerning the payment or liquidation of his, her or their debt or respective debts, or any part thereof respectively, and to execute and give to any such person or persons any security or securities, real or personal, or any part of my estate or effects, for the payment of his, her or their debt or respective debts, or any part or parts thereof respectively, either with or without interest, by instalments or otherwise, at such time or respective times, and under and subject to such terms, conditions, stipulations and agreements of any nature soever, as my said attorney shall think reasonable and proper; and also for me, and on my behalf, to borrow and take up at interest on any security, real or personal, any sum or sums of money my said attorney shall think proper; and for the purpose of securing any debt or debts, or sum or sums of money, now due or owing or hereafter to become due or owing from me to any person or persons, either with or without interest for the same as aforesaid, or any such sum or sums of money so to be borrowed or taken up at interest as aforesaid, or for any other purpose whatsoever which my said attorney shall think expedient or proper, for me and in my name to sign, make, indorse or accept any promissory note or notes, bill or bills of exchange, and enter into, sign, seal and execute any covenant or covenants, agreement or agreements, bond or bonds, or warrant of attorney or warrants of attorney for confessing judgment against me in any court or courts of Great Britain; and for the better doing, performing and executing all or any of the matters and things aforesaid I the said A. B. do hereby give and grant unto the said C. D. full power and authority to substitute and appoint, and in his place or stead to put, one or more attorney or attornies for me the said A. B., and as my attorney or attornies, having such appointment or appointments of attorney or attornies, from time to time to revoke or displace, and any other or others in his or their place or places to substitute or appoint, as he the said C. D. shall from time to time think fit; and generally to do and perform all other acts and things which shall be fitting, reasonable or necessary to be done in and about the said premises, as fully and effectually, to all intents and purposes whatsoever, as I the said A. B. might or could do if I were personally present, I hereby ratifying and confirming whatsoever my said attorney shall do or cause to be done in and about the premises by virtue of these presents.

In witness, &c.

RECITALS.

153.

Of Payment of Succession Duty in Conveyance.

AND whereas all duties under the act of Parliament for imposing duties on successions to real estate have been duly paid by the said A. B. as the successor [under the hereinbefore-recited indenture of the   or under the hereinbefore-recited will of the said J. K.] to the hereditaments hereinafter described and granted.

154.

Of Agreement for Sale.

WHEREAS the said A. B. is seised to him and his heirs, or otherwise well and sufficiently entitled to the fee simple and inheritance in possession, free from incumbrances, of and in the hereditaments hereinafter mentioned, and intended to be hereby granted.

[*Or*]   155.

WHEREAS the said A. B. hath contracted with the said C. D. for the sale to him of the hereditaments hereinafter described and intended to be hereby granted, and the fee simple and inheritance thereof in possession, free from incumbrances, for the sum of £   .

[*If No.* 154 *is used, then this recital should follow.*]

156.

AND whereas the said A. B. hath contracted with the said C. D. for the sale to him of the same hereditaments for the sum of £ .

157.

Of Lease.

WHEREAS by an indenture bearing date the   day of   , 18 , and made between A. B. of the one part, and C. D. of the other part: For the considerations therein mentioned the said A. B. did demise unto the said C. D. all [*parcels verbatim from lease*], with their rights, easements and appurtenances, To hold the same unto the said C. D., his executors, administrators and assigns, from the   day of   then last, for   years, subject to the payment of the yearly rent of £   and to the performance of the covenants and agreements on the part of the said C. D., his executors, administrators and assigns, thereby agreed to be performed and observed.

158.

Of Conveyance to Uses to bar Dower.

WHEREAS by an indenture dated the   day of   , 18 , made between A. B. of the first part, C. D. of the second part, and E. F. of the third part, the hereditaments hereinafter described and intended to be hereby granted were limited and assured to such uses, upon such trusts and in such manner generally as the said C. D. should by any deed or deeds appoint; and in default of and subject to any such appointment, to the use of the said C. D. and his assigns for life, with remainder to the use of the said E. F., his executors and administrators, during the life of the said C. D., in trust for him and his assigns, with remainder to the use of the said C. D., his heirs and assigns.

159.
Of Assignment.

AND whereas by an indenture dated the   day of   ,
18 , made between A. B. of the one part and C. D. of the other part, the premises demised by the hereinbefore-recited indenture were assigned to and the same are now vested in the said C. D. for all the residue of the term of   years created by the said indenture of lease, subject to the payment of the rent reserved by and to the performance of the covenants contained in the same indenture.

160.
Of Mesne Assignments.

AND whereas by virtue of divers mesne assignments [and acts in the law], and ultimately by an indenture dated the   day of   , 18 , made between A. B. of the one part and C. D. of the other part, the premises intended to be demised by the said indenture of lease became and are now vested in the said A. B. for all the residue of the term thereby granted, subject to the payment of the rent thereby reserved, and to the performance and observance of the covenants and provisions therein contained on the part of the lessee or assignee.

161.
Of Purchase Agreement of Leaseholds.

AND whereas the said A. B. hath contracted with the said C. D. for the sale to him of the premises demised by the said indenture of lease, subject to the payment of the rent thereby reserved, and to the observance and performance of the covenants and provisions therein contained on the part of the lessee or assignee, but free from all other incumbrances, for the sum of £   .

[N.B.—Thus, supposing you wish to prepare an assignment of a lease granted to A. B., you will first set out the names and descriptions of the parties, then insert recitals Nos. 158 and 161, and at once proceed to the witnessing part. If there have been various dealings with the property, then the recitals will be Nos. 157, 160 and 161. The indenture referred to in No. 161, being the assignment to your vendor.]

162.

Of a Mortgage.

WHEREAS by an indenture dated the   day of   , 18 , made between A. B. of the one part and C. D. of the other part, in consideration of £   paid by the said C. D. to the said A. B., he the said A. B. granted unto the said C. D. and his heirs the hereditaments, hereinafter described and intended to be hereby granted, To hold unto and to the use of the said C. D., his heirs and assigns, subject to a proviso for reconveyance of the said hereditaments on payment by the said A. B., his heirs, executors or administrators, unto the said C. D., his executors, administrators or assigns, of £   with interest for the same after the rate, on the day, and in the manner therein mentioned.

163.

Of Agreement for Sale, subject to [Incumbrances and] a Right of Re-purchase.

AND whereas the said A. B. hath contracted with the said C. D. for the purchase of the said hereditaments for the sum of £   , subject [nevertheless to the hereinbefore-recited incumbrances, and also] to a right in the said C. D. or his heirs to repurchase the said hereditaments at any time within one year from the date of these presents, upon the terms hereinafter mentioned.

164.
Of Contract for Sale of Lands, and that no Conveyance made.
AND whereas the said A. B. some time since agreed with the said D. F. for the sale to him of the said hereditaments, [so devised to the said A. B. by the said will of the said C. B. as aforesaid,] for the sum of £   , but no conveyance hath yet been executed in pursuance of such agreement.

165.
Of Sub-Contract.
AND whereas the said D. F. hath agreed with the said G. H. to give up to him the said G. H. the benefit of his said contract or bargain.

166.
Another Form of Recital of Sub-Contract.
AND whereas the said D. F. hath agreed that the said G. H. shall have the benefit of the said contract upon the terms of paying the said sum of £   to the said A. B., and the sum of £   to the said D. F.

167.
Of Agreement to make new Conveyance and to join in confirming same.
AND whereas the said A. B. hath agreed to make a new conveyance of the said premises, and the said C. D. and E. F. have agreed to join therein for the purpose of confirming and giving effect to the same.

168.

Another Recital in Confirmation Deed.

AND whereas upon a recent investigation of the title of the said A. B. to the hereditaments demised or expressed to be demised as aforesaid by the hereinbefore-recited indenture of lease, it appeared that the said indenture was not executed by the said G. S., and it also appeared that the respective titles of the said M. W. and H. S. to their said respective shares were liable to be defeated as to the said share of the said M. W. in favour of the said R H., party hereto, his heirs and assigns, if she the said M. W. should die without issue living at her death; and as to the said share of the said H. S. in favour of the said J. H., his heirs and assigns, if she the said H. S. should die without leaving issue living at her decease; and whereas, by reason of the premises, it has been deemed expedient that the title of the said A. B., his executors, administrators and assigns, to the said hereditaments and premises should be established and confirmed, and for that purpose the said G. S. and H. his wife, R. H., party hereto, and J. H. have respectively agreed, upon the request of the said A. B., to concur in these presents in manner hereinafter mentioned.

169.

Of Agreement by Persons interested in Purchase-Money to join in Conveyance.

AND whereas the said A. B. and C. his wife, and D. E. and F. his wife, being (together with the said E. G. and R. M. G. in their own respective rights, and with the said E. G. and G. B. as the personal representatives of the said R. G., deceased) interested in the said purchase-money under the trusts of the said will, have respectively agreed to join in these presents in manner hereinafter mentioned.

170.

Of Agreement by Heir to effectuate Ancestor's Contract by joining in Conveyance.

AND whereas the said A. B. hath agreed to carry into effect the said recited contract, and for that purpose to join in these presents in manner hereinafter mentioned.

171.

Of Agreement on Marriage to convey Copyholds and Leaseholds, and to pay off Mortgage out of Wife's Personalty—Husband to be entitled to Residue.

AND whereas, upon the treaty for the said intended marriage, it was agreed that the said copyhold and leasehold estates should be conveyed to the uses, upon and for the trusts, intents and purposes, and with, under and subject to the powers, provisoes, agreements and declarations hereinafter expressed or declared of or concerning the same respectively, and that the said mortgage for £   should be forthwith in the first place paid off and discharged out of the personal property of the said A. B., and that the said C. D. should, immediately upon or after the solemnization of the said intended marriage, be and become absolutely entitled in his marital right to the residue which should remain of the said personal property after payment of the said mortgage money.

172.

Of Codicils not affecting Devise of Realty.

AND whereas the said testator made several other codicils to his said will, none of which revoked or in any manner affected the devise of his real estates contained in his said will.

173.
Of no Devise of Mortgage or Trust Estates.

AND whereas the said A. B. did not in and by his said will make any devise or disposition of his legal estate in the hereditaments vested in him as a trustee or mortgagee, and such hereditaments (including the said hereditaments so mortgaged to him as aforesaid) upon his decease descended upon and became vested in the said C. D. as his eldest son and heir at law.

174.
Of Contract for Sale of Mortgage Debt.

AND whereas the said A. B. has contracted with the said C. D. to assign and convey to him the said C. D. the said principal sum of £   , so due and owing as aforesaid, upon the hereinbefore-recited security, together with all interest due or to become due for the same, and all the estate, right and interest of the said A. B. in the hereditaments comprised in the said indenture of mortgage for the sum of £   .

175.
Of Contract for Licence to use Invention.

AND whereas the said A. B. has contracted with the said C. D. for the sale to him of the licence to make, use and exercise the said invention within the said town of   for the term of   years to the intent and in manner hereinafter expressed at the price of £   .

176.
Death of Old and Appointment of New Trustees.

AND whereas the said A. B. and C. D. have departed this life, and by virtue of a power for that purpose contained in the hereinbefore-recited will of the said E. F., the said G. H. and I. K. have been appointed trustees thereof, in the stead of the said A. B. and C. D.

177.
Revocation of Appointment of Executor and Appointment of Substitute.

AND whereas the said A. B. made a codicil to his said will, such codicil being dated, &c., and thereby revoked the appointment of the said C. D. to be one of the executors and trustees of his said will, and nominated and appointed the said E. F. to be an executor and trustee thereof in the place of the said C. D.

178.
Agreement by Executor to assent to Legacy.

AND whereas the said A. B. has requested the said C. D. to join in these presents for the purpose of assenting to the said legacy of £   , so bequeathed to him the said A. B. in and by the hereinbefore in part recited will, which the said C. D. hath agreed to do in manner hereinafter mentioned.

179.
That Trust Property put up for Sale but bought in.

AND whereas the said A. B. and C. D., as such trustees as aforesaid, lately caused the hereditaments in and by the said will of the said E. F., deceased, directed to be sold to be put up for sale by public auction, but no adequate price having been bid for the same, the said hereditaments were bought in.

180.
Letters of Administration.

AND whereas the said A. B. died on, &c., leaving his personal representative, and letters of administration of the goods and chattels, rights and credits of the said A. B., on &c., granted to the said   by the   district [or principal] registry of the Court of Probate.

181.
Limited Administration.

AND whereas letters of administration of the goods and chattels, rights and credits of the said A. B., so far as relates to or concerns   were on, &c., granted to the said C. D., by the   district [*or* principal] registry of the Court of Probate.

182.
Agent.

AND whereas the said A. B. became the purchaser of the said hereditaments, as the agent and on behalf of the said C. D., as they the said A. B. and C. D. do hereby respectively declare.

183.
Appointment of New Trustees.

AND whereas by indentures dated &c., and made between, &c., they the said A. B. and C. D., in execution of the power for that purpose contained in the said hereinbefore-recited indenture of the   day of   , 18 , did appoint the said E. F. to be a trustee in the place of the said G. H. for the purposes mentioned in the said indenture.

184.
Of Tenancy by Curtesy.

AND whereas the said A. B. died on the   leaving the said B. B., her eldest son and heir at law, and on her death the said H. B. the father, as the surviving husband of the said A. B., became tenant for his life by the curtesy of England of the said hereditaments hereinafter described and intended to be hereby granted.

185.
Of Death of Mortgagee Intestate as to Mortgaged Estate.
AND whereas the said A. B. died on, &c., intestate, so far as relates to the legal estate in the said hereditaments comprised in the hereinbefore-recited mortgage, leaving the said J. B. his eldest son and heir at law.

186.
Of Death of Surviving Trustee Intestate as to Trust Estates.
AND whereas the said C. B. survived his co-trustees, the said E. D. and E. F., and afterwards died without having made any conveyance or disposition by will or otherwise of the said trust estate, or any appointment of a new trustee or trustees thereof, leaving D. B. his eldest son and heir at law.

187.
Of further Charge.
AND whereas by an indenture dated, &c., made between the said A. B. of the one part, and the said C. D. of the other part, in consideration of the said sum of £   then due to the said C. D., by virtue of the last-recited indenture, and of the further sum of £   then lent by the said C. D. to the said A. B., the hereditaments comprised in the said indenture became and now stand charged as well with the payment of the said sum of £   as of the said sum of £   with interest for the same sums respectively to the said C. D., his executors, administrators and assigns.

188.
Of further Charge by Indorsement.
AND whereas by a deed poll dated, &c., under the hand and seal of the said A. B., and indorsed on the hereinbefore-recited indenture of mortgage of the   , the hereditaments

comprised in the said indenture became chargeable with the sum of £   with interest to the said C. D., his executors, administrators or assigns.

189.
Of Transfer of Mortgage.

AND whereas by an indenture dated, &c., and made between the said A. B. of the first part, the said C. D. of the second part, and the said E. F. of the third part, in consideration of the sum of £   paid to the said A. B. by the said E. F., all that the said principal sum of £   secured by the hereinbefore in part recited indenture of mortgage, and all other monies which might thereafter become due and owing for or in respect of the said sum of £   , and all securities for the same, were assigned unto the said E. F., his executors, administrators and assigns, for his and their own use and benefit: [*If the mortgage was of leaseholds proceed thus:*] and, for the considerations aforesaid, all the premises comprised in and demised by the hereinbefore-recited indenture of lease were assigned and confirmed unto the said E. F., his executors, administrators and assigns for the residue of the said term of   years by the said lease granted, subject nevertheless to such equity or right of redemption as was then subsisting in the same premises under the hereinbefore-recited indenture of mortgage: [*If the mortgage was in fee substitute this clause for the last:*] and, for the considerations aforesaid, all the hereditaments and premises comprised in the said indenture of mortgage were granted and assured [*or* appointed, *&c., as the case may be*] to the use of the said E. F., his heirs and assigns, subject nevertheless to such equity of redemption as was then subsisting in the said hereditaments and premises by virtue of the said indenture of mortgage.

190.

Of Erection of Buildings since Conveyance.

AND whereas since the execution of the said hereinbefore in part recited indenture, the said A. B. has erected and built upon the said piece of ground therein comprised divers messuages or tenements, with suitable offices and outbuildings.

191.

Of Policy of Assurance for Life.

AND whereas by a policy of assurance under the hands of three of the directors of the   Life Assurance Society, dated &c., and numbered   the sum of £   was insured to the said A. B. payable on the death of the said C. D., if he should die within the time and in manner in the said policy of assurance expressed in that behalf, and if such premiums as therein mentioned should be duly paid at the times thereby appointed.

RELEASES.

192.

To Executors by a Residuary Legatee.

THIS INDENTURE, made the   day of   , 18 , between A. B., of &c., of the one part, and C. D., of &c., and E. F., of &c., of the other part: Whereas G. H., late of &c., deceased, by his will, dated the   day of   , 18 , bequeathed unto the said C. D. and E. F. all the residue of his personal estate whatsoever and wheresoever, upon trust, after payment thereout of a legacy of £100 to I. K., and a further legacy of £100 to L. M., for the said A. B. absolutely; and whereas the said testator died without having revoked or altered his said will, which was duly proved on or about the   day of   , 18 , in   by the said C. D. and E. F.; and whereas the whole of the residue of the personal estate of the said testator has been got in by the said C. D. and E. F., and after payment thereout of the expenses incidental to getting in the same, and the said legacies of £100 and £100, there remains in their hands the sum of £   ; and whereas the accounts of the said C. D. and E. F., showing the gross amount of the said testator's personal estate and the payments thereout, have been handed to and fully inspected by the said A. B., and he hath signed the said accounts in order to express his approbation of the same; and whereas the said C. D. and E. F. have before the execution hereof paid to the said A. B. the sum of £   being the balance appearing by the said accounts to be due to him in respect of the said testator's residuary personal estate: Now this indenture witnesseth, that, in consideration of the premises, he the said A. B. doth by these presents release and discharge the said C. D. and E. F. and each of them, and their and each of their heirs, executors and administrators, from the residue of the personal estate of the said testator, and from all trusts declared by the said recited will of and concerning the same, and from all actions, suits, cause and causes of action or suit, debts, sum and sums of money, accounts, reckonings, claims and demands whatsoever, at law and in equity, which he the said A. B. now hath, or which he, his heirs, executors or administrators, can or may at any time hereafter have or be entitled unto, against the said C. D. and E. F. or either of them, or their or either of their heirs, executors or administrators, for or by reason or on account of or in relation to the estate or effects of the said testator, or the residue thereof, or the trusts relating thereto, and contained in his said will, or for or by reason or in relation to any act, matter or thing in anywise incidental to or connected with the same; and the said A. B. doth hereby for himself, his heirs, executors and administrators, covenant with the said C. D. and E. F. and each of them, their and each of their executors and administrators, that in case the said C. D. and E. F. or either of them, their or either of their executors or administrators, shall hereafter be called upon or compelled to pay any debt or debts, sum or sums of money owing from the said G. H., deceased, and which is or are not already discharged, he the said A. B., his executors or administrators, will immediately pay or reimburse the said C. D. and E. F. and each of them, their and each of their executors and administrators, such sum or sums as aforesaid, together with all costs and expenses which they or he shall have paid, borne, incurred or become liable to on account or in consequence of the demanding or recovery of such debt or debts, sum or sums, as aforesaid, or in anywise relating thereto.

In witness, &c.

193.

Of Trusts created by Marriage Settlement of a Sum of Money.

THIS INDENTURE, made the   day of   , 18 , between A. B., of &c., of the one part, and C. D., of &c., of the other part: Whereas by an indenture dated the   day of   , 18 , and made between E. F. of the first part, G. H. of the second part, I. J. of the third part, and K. L., M. N. and O. P. (all since deceased) of the fourth part (being the settlement executed in contemplation of the marriage then intended and shortly afterwards solemnized between the said G. H. and I. J.), after reciting that the sum of £   three and a half per cent. reduced bank annuities had been transferred to and was then standing in the names of the said K. L., M. N. and O. P. in the books of the Governor and Company of the Bank of England, it was declared that the said K. L., M. N. and O. P., and the survivors and survivor of them, their or his executors and administrators, should stand possessed thereof on the trusts following, that is to say, upon trust to allow the said E. F. and his assigns to receive the dividends thereof for the term of his natural life, and from and immediately after his decease then upon trust for the said G. H. for the term of his natural life, and after his decease upon trust for the said I. J. for the term of her natural life, and after the several deceases of the said E. F., G. H. and I. J., upon trust for the child, if only one, or if more than one then all and every the children of the said G. H. and I. J. his wife equally, to be divided between them share and share alike, as tenants in common, to be vested in such of them as should be a son or sons when and as he or they should attain his or their respective ages of twenty-one years, or being daughters should attain the like age or be married, which should first happen; and it was declared that, from and after the several deceases of the said E. F., G. H. and I. J., it should be lawful for the said trustees to lay out and expend the interest, dividends and annual income of the said £   three and a half per cent. reduced bank annuities, or such part thereof as they should deem sufficient, for or towards the maintenance and education of the child or children of the said G. H. and I. J. his wife, until he or they should attain his or their respective ages of twenty-one years; and whereas there was issue of the said marriage five children, and no more, viz. A. H., B. H., C. H., D. H., and the said A. B., all of whom, except the said A. H., are now living; and whereas the said K. L. and M. N. both died in the lifetime of the said O. P.; and whereas the said O. P. died in the month of   , 18 , having first duly made his will, bearing date the   day of   , whereof he appointed the said C. D. sole executrix, who duly proved the said will in the Prerogative Court of Canterbury on the   day of   ; and whereas the said E. F., G. H. and I. J. have all died since the date and execution of the said recited indenture of settlement; and whereas during the lives of the said E. F., G. H. and I. J., and the survivor of them, the interest, dividends and annual produce of the said trust fund was duly paid to the party entitled thereto, and since the death of the said I. J., who survived the said E. F. and G. H., all and every the interest, dividends and annual produce of the said sum of £   three and a half per cent. annuities (which by operation of law have respectively become three and a half per cent. and three per cent. reduced annuities), up to and inclusive of the dividends which became due thereon on the fifth day of April last, have from time to time been duly laid out and expended by the said trustees and the survivors of them in, for and 'towards the maintenance and education of the said A. H. (since deceased), B. H., C. H., D. H. and A. B., as the said A. B. doth hereby admit and acknowledge; and whereas the said A. H. attained his majority on the   day of   , when the sum of £   , then three and a half per cent. reduced annuities, was divided into five shares or sums of £   , each like annuities, four of which, with all dividends thereon respectively accrued, have been duly applied and disposed of; the first for the benefit of the estate of the said A. H., who died on the   day of   ; the second to the said B. H., who attained his majority on the   day of   ; the third to the said C. H., who attained her majority on the   day of   ; and the fourth to the said D. H., who attained her majority on the   day of   ; and whereas all the dividends which have accrued due on the said sum of £   like annuities (being the one fifth part of the said sum of £   like annuities, to which the said A. B. hath since become entitled as after mentioned) since the fifth day of April, 184 , up to and inclusive of the fifth day of April last, have been duly applied in and towards the maintenance of the said A. B., as the said A. B. doth hereby admit and acknowledge; and whereas the said A. B. attained her age of twenty-one years on the   day of   last, and thereupon became entitled to the said sum of £   three per cent. reduced annuities; and whereas the said A. B. having requested the said C. D. to transfer to her the said sum of £   three per cent. reduced annuities, being the said one fifth part or share of and in the said sum of £   three and a half per cent. reduced annuities, to which the said A. B. became entitled as aforesaid, the said C. D. hath immediately before the execution hereof transferred the said sum of £   three per cent. reduced annuities into the name of her, the said A. B., in the books of the Governor and Company of the Bank of England, as she, the said A. B., doth hereby acknowledge and declare; and whereas the said A. B. hath agreed to execute the release hereinbefore contained: Now this indenture witnesseth, that, in consideration of the premises, she the said A. B. doth by these presents remise, release and for ever quit claim unto the said C. D., her heirs, executors, administrators' estates and effects, and the several and respective estates and effects of the said K. L., M. N. and O. P., respectively deceased, all and all manner of actions and suits, accounts, reckonings, claims and demands whatsoever, either at law or in equity, which she the said A. B., or any person or persons claiming by, from or under her, ever had, now have, or hath or can, or shall or may have, against, upon or from the said C. D., her heirs, executors, administrators' estates or effects, or the estates and effects of the said K. L., M. N. and O. P. respectively deceased, or any of them, for or by reason or on account of all and every the share, estate and interest of the said A. B. of and in the said sum of £   reduced annuities, or the interest, dividends and annual produce accrued thereon, and all other the estate and interest to which the said A. B. is entitled under the hereinbefore-recited indenture of settlement, or for or by reason or on account of any other matter, cause or thing in anywise relating to the premises.

In witness, &c.

194.

Of Charges on Real Estate.

THIS INDENTURE, made &c., between E. L., of &c., of the first part, H. L., of &c., of the second part, and J. B., of &c., and J. P. B., of &c., of the third part: Whereas C. E. P., late of &c., deceased, made her will dated &c., and thereby devised her estate at &c., called &c., with its appurtenances unto B. P., his heirs and assigns, subject to and chargeable with the payment of the sum of 2,000*l.* to the said E. L., and the like sum of 2,000*l.* to the said H. L., to whom the said testatrix gave the same legacies accordingly, and after other various devises and bequests, the said testatrix devised the residue of her real estate to the said J. B. and J. P. B., their heirs and assigns; and whereas the said testatrix died on &c., without having revoked or altered her said will, which was duly proved in the district registry at &c., on &c.; and whereas the said B. P. died in the lifetime of the said testatrix, viz., on the &c.: Now this indenture witnesseth, that the said E. L. and H. L. do hereby respectively acknowledge that they have respectively received from the said J. B. and J. P. B., the respective legacies of 2,000*l.* and 2,000*l.*, bequeathed to them as aforesaid, less the respective sums of 100*l.* and 100*l.* deducted and retained for and in respect of legacy duty; and the said E. L. and H. L., in consideration thereof, do and each of them doth hereby remise, release and for ever quit claim unto the said J. B. and J. P. B., their heirs, executors and administrators, all and singular the lands, tenements and hereditaments by the said will devised subject to the said legacies respectively, and all other the real estate of the said testatrix; to the intent that the said J. B. and J. P. B., their heirs and assigns, may henceforth stand seised thereof, freed from the said legacies respectively, and from all and all manner of actions, suits, accounts, reckonings, claims and demands whatsoever, both at law and in equity, which they the said E. L. and H. L., or either of them, or the executors or administrators of them, or of either of them, now can or may, or but for these presents hereinafter contained could or might have or demand against the said parties respectively, or the said J. B. and J. P. B., or either of them, or the heirs, executors or administrators of them, or either of them, in respect of the said legacies or either of them, or any part thereof respectively.

In witness, &c.

REQUEST BY CESTUIS QUE TRUST TO TRUSTEES TO SELL OUT STOCK FOR A MORTGAGE.

195.

To A. B. and C. D., trustees of an indenture of settlement dated the   day of   , 18 .

I, the undersigned E. H., do hereby (with the consent of

the undersigned A. H., my wife) request that so much of the 3*l.* per Cent. Consolidated Bank Annuities standing in your names as such trustees as aforesaid as will realize the sum of £   sterling may be sold, and that the said sum of £   may be advanced and lent to me, the undersigned E. H., upon security of my bond, payable on demand, with interest in the meantime at the rate of £   per cent. per annum, pursuant to the power or authority for that purpose contained in the said indenture. Dated this   day of   , 18   .

———

SETTLEMENTS.

196.

(On Marriage) of Real Estate.

THIS INDENTURE, made &c., between A. B., of &c., of the first part, C. D., of &c., of the second part, and E. F., of &c., and G. H., of &c., of the third part: Whereas the said A. B. is seised in fee simple in possession free from incumbrances of the hereditaments hereinafter mentioned, and intended to be hereby granted; and whereas a marriage has been agreed upon, and is intended to be shortly solemnized between the said A. B. and C. D., and upon the treaty for such marriage the said A. B. agreed to settle the said hereditaments to the uses, upon and for the trusts and subject to the provisions hereinafter declared concerning the same: Now this indenture witnesseth, that, in consideration of the premises, the said A. B. doth grant unto the said E. F. and G. H. and their heirs, all &c. [*set out parcels*], To hold the said hereditaments unto the said E. F. and G. H., their heirs and assigns, to the use of the said A. B., his heirs and assigns, until the solemnization of the said intended marriage; and after the solemnization thereof, to the use of the said A. B. and his assigns for his life, without impeachment of waste; and from and after his decease to the use of the said C. D., for her life for her separate use, without power of anticipation, and free from the debts, control and engagements of any husband with whom she may afterwards intermarry; and from and after the decease of the survivor of them, the said A. B. and C. D., to the use of all or such one or more exclusively of the other or others of the children of the said intended marriage, for such estates or estate, interests or interest, and if more than one in such shares, and under and subject to such charges, powers of charging and other powers, provisoes and limitations for the benefit of all, or any one or more of the said children, and in such manner as the said A. B. and C. D. shall, by any deed or deeds, with or without power of revocation and new appointment, from time to time or any time appoint, and in default of and until such appointment, and so far as no such appointment shall extend, then as the survivor of them shall in like manner, or by will from time to time, or at any time appoint; and in default of and until any such appointment, and so far as no such appointment shall extend, to the use of all and every the children of the said intended marriage, and the heirs and assigns of such children respectively, as tenants in common; and if there shall be only one such child, then to the use of such only child, his or her heirs and assigns; and in default of such issue, to the use of the said A. B., his heirs and assigns: provided always, and it is hereby declared, that it shall be lawful for the said A. B. during his life, and after his death, for the said C. D. during her life, from time to time to demise all or any of the said premises for any term not exceeding twenty-one years in possession, so that there be reserved in every such lease the best yearly rent or rents, to be incident to the immediate reversion that can be reasonably obtained without any premium, and so as there be contained in every such lease a condition for re-entry on nonpayment within a reasonable time to be therein specified of the rent or rents thereby reserved, and so that the lessee or lessees execute a counterpart thereof: provided always, and it is hereby agreed, that it shall be lawful for the said E. F. and G. H., or the survivor of them, or his heirs, or their or his assigns, but during the lifetime of a tenant for life only with his or her consent in writing, to sell the said hereditaments or any part thereof, by public auction or private contract, and subject to such conditions, and generally in such manner as to them or him shall seem desirable, and to stand possessed of the net proceeds of such purchase money, upon the same trusts as are hereinbefore declared, and in the same manner as if no such sale had taken place.

In witness, &c.

[No clause for maintenance, appointment of new trustees, or receipt clause is necessary; the Act referred at p. 97 of the "Treatise" rendering unnecessary any such clauses.]

———

197.
Marriage Settlement of Personalty.

THIS INDENTURE, made the   day of   , 18 , between A. B., of &c. [*intended husband*] of the first part, C. D., of &c. [*intended wife*] of the second part, and E. F., of &c., and G. H., of &c. [*trustees*] of the third part: Whereas the said C. D. is entitled to a sum of £1,000 3*l.* per Cent. Consolidated Bank Annuities, lately standing in her name in the books of the Governor and Company of the Bank of England; and whereas a marriage hath been agreed upon and is intended shortly to be solemnized between the said A. B. and C. D., and upon the treaty for the said marriage it was agreed that the said sum of £1,000 3*l.* per Cent. Consolidated Bank Annuities should be transferred into the names of the said E. F. and G. H., and that the said E. F. and G. H., their executors, administrators and assigns, should stand possessed of and interested in the same and the dividends and annual produce thereof, upon the trusts and subject to the provisions hereinafter declared and contained; and whereas in pursuance of the said agreement the said C. D. hath, with the consent of the said A. B., transferred the said sum of £1,000 3*l.* per Cent. Consolidated Bank Annuities into the names of the said E. F. and G. H.: Now this indenture witnesseth, that, in consideration of the said intended marriage, it is hereby agreed and declared by and between the parties to these presents, that the said E. F. and G. H., their executors, administrators and assigns, shall stand possessed of and interested in the said sum of £1,000 3*l*. per Cent. Consolidated Bank Annuities, and the dividends thereof, in trust for the said C. D., her executors, administrators and assigns, in the meantime until the solemnization of the said intended marriage, and after the solemnization thereof, upon trust that they the said E. F. and G. H., and the survivor of them, his executors or administrators, or their or his assigns, do and shall either permit and suffer the whole or any part of the said sum of £1,000 3*l*. per Cent. Consolidated Bank Annuities, to remain in its present state of investment, or do and shall at any time or times, with the consent in writing of the said A. B. and C. D. during their joint lives, and of the survivor of them during his or her life, and after the death of the survivor of them at the discretion of the said E. F. and G. H. or the survivor of them, his executors or administrators, or their or his assigns, sell, transfer and dispose of the said sum of £1,000 3*l*. per Cent. Consolidated Bank Annuities, or any part thereof, and do and shall, with such consent or at such discretion as aforesaid, invest the monies to arise by such sale, transfer or disposition, in their or his names or name, in any of the parliamentary stocks or public funds of Great Britain, or at interest upon government or real securities in England or Wales (but not in Ireland), or on the debentures or stock of any such railway, canal or other incorporated company in Great Britain as the said trustees or trustee shall think well established and sound; and shall and may from time to time, with such consent or at such discretion as aforesaid, alter, vary or transpose any such investments; and do and shall, during the joint lives of the said A. B. and C. D., pay the dividends, interest and annual proceeds of the said sum of £1,000 3*l*. per Cent. Consolidated Bank Annuities, and of the proceeds to arise by sale, transfer or disposition thereof, or of any part thereof, and of the stocks, funds and securities in or upon which the same may be invested, unto the said C. D. for her sole and separate use, independently and exclusively of the said A. B., and of his debts, control, interference and engagements, but so nevertheless that the said C. D. shall not have power to deprive herself of the benefit thereof by sale, mortgage, charge or otherwise in the way of anticipation; and the receipts of the said C. D. shall be good and effectual discharges for the said dividends, interest and annual proceeds; and from and after the death of such one of them the said A. B. and C. D. as shall first die, do and shall pay the dividends, interest and annual proceeds of the said trust monies, stocks, funds and securities unto the survivor of them during his or her life; and from and after the death of the survivor of them the said A. B. and C. D., the said E. F. and G. H., their executors, administrators and assigns, shall stand possessed of and interested in the said trust monies, stocks, funds and securities, and the interest, dividends and annual proceeds thereof, in trust for all and every or such one or more exclusively of the others or other of the children of the said C. D. in such manner generally as the said C. D. shall by any deed or deeds, writing or writings, with or without power of revocation and new appointment, or by her last will or testament or any codicil or codicils thereto, direct or appoint; and in default of any such direction or appointment, and so far as any such direction or appointment shall not extend, in trust for all and every of the children and child of the said C. D., who being sons or a son shall attain the age of twenty-one years, or being daughters or a daughter shall attain that age or marry, to be divided between or amongst such children if more than one, in equal shares, and if there shall be but one such child, the whole to be in trust for such one child: provided always, and it is hereby declared, that no child or children taking any part of the said trust monies, stocks, funds or securities under or by virtue of any direction or appointment to be made in pursuance of the power herein contained, shall have or be entitled to any further or other share of or in that part of the said trust monies, stocks, funds and securities of which no such direction or appointment shall have been made, without bringing his, her or their appointed share or shares into hotchpot and accounting for the same accordingly; and it is hereby declared, that it shall be lawful for the said E. F. and G. H.

and the survivor of them, his executors and administrators, and their or his assigns, at any time or times after the decease of the survivor of the said A. B. and C. D., or in the lifetime of them or of the survivor of them, in case they, he or she shall so direct by any writing or writings under his or her hand, to levy and raise any part or parts of the then expectant or presumptive or vested share or shares of any child or children, under the trusts hereinbefore declared, not exceeding in the whole for any such child one moiety or equal half part or share of his, her or their expectant or presumptive or vested share, and to pay and apply the same for his, her or their preferment, advancement or benefit, in such manner as the said E. F. and G. H. or the survivor of them, his executors or administrators, or their or his assigns, shall in their or his discretion think fit: provided always, and it is hereby declared, that in case there shall be no child of the said intended marriage, who being a son shall attain the age of twenty-one years, or being a daughter shall attain that age or marry, the said E. F. and G. H., their executors, administrators and assigns, shall stand and be possessed of and interested in the said trust monies, and the interest, dividends and annual produce thereof, or of so much thereof respectively as shall not have become or been applied under any of the trusts or powers herein contained, upon the trusts following, that is to say, in case the said A. B. shall die in the lifetime of the said C. D., then, from and after his death and such default or failure of children as aforesaid which shall last happen, in trust for the said C. D., her executors, administrators and assigns : but in case the said C. D. shall die in the lifetime of the said A. B., then, from and after the decease of the said A. B. and such default or failure of children as aforesaid which shall last happen, upon such trusts as the said C. D. shall, notwithstanding her coverture, by her will or any codicil or codicils thereto, direct or appoint; and in default of such direction or appointment, and so far as any such direction or appointment shall not extend, in trust for such person or persons as at the decease of the said C. D. would have become entitled thereto under the statutes for the distribution of the personal estate of intestates, in case the said C. D. had died possessed thereof intestate and without having been married, such persons, if more than one, to take as tenants in common in the shares in which they would have been entitled under the same statutes.

In witness, &c.

198.

Proviso to be inserted in Settlement of Equity of Redemption.

PROVIDED always, and it is hereby further declared and agreed, that in case the said J. P. [*intended husband*] during his life shall pay off and discharge the said principal sums secured by the hereinbefore-recited indenture of mortgage, or either of them or any part thereof, to the person or persons entitled thereto, such payment shall not be deemed or considered to entitle the said J. P. to a claim in respect thereof upon the hereditaments hereby granted, but shall merge and be extinguished in the same hereditaments for the benefit of the person or persons who shall be entitled thereto, or to the monies arising from the sale thereof, by virtue of the trusts and powers herein contained.

199.

Testimonium to Instrument executed by Attorney.

IN WITNESS whereof the said   has set his hand and seal, and   by virtue of a power of attorney enabling him in that behalf, a copy whereof is hereunto annexed, has set the hand and seal of [A.] this   day of   , 18   .

[*Note.*—A deed executed under a power of attorney should always be signed in the name of the principal, " By   , his attorney."]

Wills.

200.

Will of a Person making various Devises and Bequests, and giving the Residue of his Property to his Children.

This is the last will and testament of me, A. B., of &c. I bequeath to my wife C. B. the sum of [one hundred pounds], which I direct my executors to pay to her within three calendar months after my decease. I devise unto my son Thomas, his heirs and assigns, all that farm known by the name of "The Holly Farm," consisting of a messuage and outbuildings, and about fifty acres of land, situate at [Nettlebed], in the county of [Oxford], in the occupation of   [free from the mortgage of 1,000*l.* thereon, in favour of Thomas Jackson, which sum of 1,000*l.*, and all interest due thereon, I direct shall be paid out of my personal estate after payment of the legacies or sums of money bequeathed by this my will (*a*)]. I devise unto my son John, his heirs and assigns, all that my freehold messuage situate at and being No.   , [St. Paul's Churchyard], in the city of [London], now in the occupation of   . I bequeath unto my said wife for her absolute use and benefit all and every my household furniture, chattels and effects of every description. I bequeath unto my friend E. F., of &c., the sum of [one hundred pounds]: And as to all the residue of my real and personal estate and effects, of whatever description and wheresoever situate, I give, devise and bequeath the same unto and to the use of my said sons Thomas and John, their heirs, executors, administrators and assigns, according to the natures and tenures thereof, as tenants in common. I appoint my said sons Thomas and John, and my friend G. H., of &c., executors of this my will; and to the said G. H. I bequeath the sum of [one hundred pounds]. In witness whereof I have hereunto set my hand this   day of   , 18 .

Signed, &c.

(*a*) If the testator intends the devisee to take the farm subject to the mortgage, the words within brackets should be omitted.

201.

Will of a Person giving all his Property to his Wife, and appointing her Executrix.

THIS is the last will and testament of me, A. B., of &c. I give, devise and bequeath all my real estate of whatever description and wheresoever situate, and also all my leasehold and other personal estate and effects whatsoever and wheresoever, unto and to the use of my wife C. B., her heirs, executors, administrators and assigns, according to the nature and tenure thereof: And I appoint my said wife executrix of this my will.

In witness whereof I have hereunto set my hand this day of   , 18 .

A. B.

Signed by the said testator as his last will in the presence of us, who in his presence at his request, and in the presence of each other, have hereunto subscribed our names as witnesses.

E. F., of &c.
G. H., of &c.

[N.B.—There is no necessity in a simple will of this nature to direct the payment of debts, and funeral and testamentary expenses, as the law requires that, without any direction by the testator. It is only necessary to insert such a direction in a will when the testator intends charging any specific property with the payment of his debts.]

202.

Codicil appointing a new Trustee and Executor in the room of a deceased Trustee and Executor, and giving an additional Legacy.

THIS is a codicil to the last will and testament of me, A. B., of &c., which will bears date the   day of   , 18 : Whereas C. D., one of the trustees and executors appointed by my said will has lately died : Now I do hereby appoint E. F., of &c., to be a trustee and executor of my said will in the place of the said C. D.: And I direct that my said will shall be read and construed in the same manner, and shall have the same operation in all respects, as if the name of the said E. F. had been inserted therein instead of the name of the said C. D.: I bequeath to my servant G. H., provided she shall be in my service at the time of my decease, the sum of £   : And in all other respects I confirm my said will.

In witness whereof I have hereunto set my hand this day of   , 18 .

Signed by the said testator as a codicil to his will in the presence of us, who in his presence at his request, and in the presence of each other, have hereunto subscribed our names as witnesses.

203.

Bequest of Furniture to Wife for Life and Widowhood, with Directions as to Inventory.

I BEQUEATH all and every my household goods, furniture, effects and chattels unto my wife A. B. during her life and widowhood; and I direct my executors, as soon as practicable after my death, to cause an inventory to be taken of the same in duplicate, and for them and my said wife to sign both parts, and that one part shall be kept by my said wife and the other by my executors; and after the death or marrying again of my said wife I direct that the said household goods, furniture, effects and chattels shall fall into and become part of my residuary personal estate.

204.

Bequest to Trustees upon Trust for Daughter to her separate Use, and afterwards for her Children.

I BEQUEATH unto the said A. B. and C. D. the sum of £   , upon trust to invest the same in the public stocks or funds, or upon mortgage of real or leasehold property in England (such leaseholds not having less than fifty years of their term unexpired), or on the debentures of any such railway or other incorporated company (all calls on the shares thereof having been paid) as my said trustees or trustee shall think well established and sound, with power from time to time to vary any such investments; and I direct that my said trustees and trustee shall stand possessed of the stocks, funds or securities in or upon which the said sum of £   shall be invested, upon trust to pay the interest, dividends and annual produce thereof into the hands of my daughter   during her life for her separate use, free from the debts, control or interference of any husband, and so that she shall not have power to alien, charge or incumber the same in the way of anticipation; and after the decease of my said daughter, the said stocks, funds and securities, and the interest, dividends and annual produce thereof, shall be upon trust for all and every, or such one or more, of the children and child of my said daughter as she shall, whether covert or sole, by any deed or deeds, or by will, from time to time appoint; and in default of and subject to any such appointment, upon trust for all and every the children and child of my said daughter, who, being sons or a son, shall attain the age of twenty-one years, and being daughters or a daughter shall attain that age or marry, and if there shall be only one such child, then the whole to be in trust for such child, but so, nevertheless, that no child of my said daughter to whom or in whose favour any appointment shall have been made shall share in the unappointed part of the said trust fund, without bringing his or her appointed share into hotchpot and accounting for the same accordingly; and in case there shall be no child of my said daughter who shall take a vested interest under the foregoing trust, then I declare that the said stocks, funds and securities, and the interest, dividends and annual produce thereof, shall be in trust for   .

205.
Devise of Trust Estates.

I DEVISE all estates vested in me as mortgagee or trustee unto and to the use of the said [*trustees*], their heirs, executors, administrators and assigns respectively, subject to the equities and trusts affecting the same respectively, and, so far as I am beneficially interested as mortgagee, to be disposed of as part of my personal estate for the purposes of my will.

206.
Clause to be inserted in a Will prohibiting any Party claiming thereunder from disputing it.

AND my will further is, that if my said daughter or her husband, or any person or persons in her, his, their or any or either of their behalf, shall dispute this my will, or my competency to make the same, or if my said daughter and her husband or either of them shall refuse to confirm this my will so far as he or she can, when required by my executors or either of them so to do, or if any proceedings whatsoever shall at any time be had or taken by any person or persons whomsoever, by any possible result of which any estate or interest be in any way attainable by my said daughter or her husband, or any person or persons in their right, of larger extent or value than is intended for her by this my will, and such proceedings shall not be formally disavowed, stayed or resisted by my said daughter and her husband, to the full extent of their, her and his ability to do so, then I revoke the use or disposition hereinbefore contained for the raising and paying, during the life of my said daughter, of the yearly sum of 500*l.*, and also the use and disposition hereinbefore contained in her favour (in the event hereinbefore mentioned) of the rents of my said estates hereinbefore devised, and all other benefits hereby given, or in trust for my said daughter, or derivable by her under this my will, and in lieu thereof I give and bequeath to my said daughter the sum of £   .

[The above is a valid clause and is good in law. See *Cooke* v. *Turner* (15 M. & W. 727). The daughter in the above case was heiress at law, and if she had disputed the will it would have been a forfeiture; but a trustee under a settlement made by her was held not to create a forfeiture by disputing the will. See *Cooke* v. *Turner* (19 L. J., N. S., Ch. 81.)

But query, could not the clause be so framed as to prevent *any person* claiming a benefit or *any* account from disputing the will?]

CONVEYANCING CHARGES.

	£	s.	d.
Instructions	0	6	8

This charge is always allowed for any document, whatever its nature.

Drawing, 1s. per folio . . . . . .

This charge of 1s. per folio is allowed for all documents.

Fair copy, 4d. per folio . . . . .

This charge is always made, but will not be allowed by a taxing master unless the copy is made.

Engrossing, 8d. per folio . . . . .

This charge includes the examination of the draft with the engrossment.

Stamps (as paid) . . . .

| Attending to stamp . . . . . . | 0 | 6 | 8 |

This charge is always made, but is not allowed by a taxing master unless ad valorem duty is paid.

| Parchment, per skin . . . . . . | 0 | 5 | 0 |

	£	s.	d.

Letters, each 0 3 6
Ditto, if special 0 5 0
Perusing document, when drawn by another solicitor, per skin of 15 folios 0 5 0
   No charge is allowed for perusing any alterations made by another solicitor in a draft prepared by yourself, but all correspondence and attendances respecting such alterations are allowed.
Examining engrossment with draft, per skin of 15 folios 0 3 4
   This is only allowed when the draft is prepared by another solicitor.
Attendances, of whatever description, per hour or fractional part 0 6 8
Journeys, per day (exclusive of expenses) . . 3 3 0
   £2 : 2s. only is allowed by some of the taxing masters.
Making attested copies of documents, per folio . 0 0 6
Stamps and paper for same (as paid) . . .
Examining and attesting same, 3s. 4d., or 6s. 8d., according to length . . . . .
Attending searching for judgments . . . 0 13 4
The like, crown debts 0 13 4
The like, annuities 0 13 4
Paid 0 1 0
Attending making search at the Middlesex Registry for incumbrances 0 13 4
   Or according to the time engaged, besides the fee paid on the search and for references.
Attending reading over and attesting execution of deed 0 6 8
   This charge is allowed, irrespective of the number of persons executing the deed, if done at the same time; but for each separate attendance the same fee is allowed.

410   PRECEDENTS.

	£	s.	d.
Attending completion	0	6	8
	0	13	4
	1	1	0

Or according to circumstances.

	£	s.	d.
Instructions for case for the opinion of counsel	0	6	8
Drawing same, per sheet	0	6	8
Fair copy „	0	3	4
Fee to Mr. and clerk, with same (as paid)			
Attending him	0	6	8
Instructions for abstract	0	6	8
Drawing same, per sheet	0	6	8
Fair copy „	0	3	4
Attending examining same with deeds, per hour	0	6	8

 This charge does not include the clerk taken with you, for whose attendance 3s. 4d. per hour is allowed, but if a journey is undertaken, then the charge is made by the day, and the expenses of the journey must be added.

Perusing abstract

 The charge usually made is 6s. 8d. for every three sheets.

Fee to Mr.   and clerk, to advise on same (as paid)

	£	s.	d.
Attending him	0	6	8
Instructions for requisitions on title	0	6	8
Drawing same, per brief sheet	0	6	8
Fair copy	0	3	4
Perusing answers to requisitions on title, if short	0	6	8

Or according to length.

	£	s.	d.
Instructions for further requisitions	0	6	8
Drawing same (as before)			
Perusing requisitions on title	0	6	8

 Or according to length and the difficulty of the matter.

Drawing answers thereto

 This is regulated by the difficulty of the matter.

Fair copy of the whole, for purchaser's solicitor, per brief sheet 0 3 4

INDEX TO TREATISE.

ABSTRACT OF TITLE,
    Preparation of, 9.
    Delivery of, 9.
    Appointment to compare with deeds, 10, 27.
    At whose office examined, 10, 27.
    Additional, 14.
    How compared with deeds, 10, 27.
    Great care required in, 28.
    Perusal of, 29.
    How perused, 29.
    Counsel's opinion on, 31.
    Of copyholds, examining with copies of court roll, 69.
                should be compared with court rolls, 69.

ACKNOWLEDGMENT OF DEED,
    By married woman on purchase, 38.
    Not necessary of disentailing deed, 104.
    Executed by married women generally, 104.
    How taken in London, 105.
              in the country, 105.
    Not necessary when married woman has power of appointment, 106.
    Of assignment of married woman's reversionary interest in personalty, 35, 106.

ADMINISTRATION, Letters of. *See* PROBATE.

AGREEMENT,
    Importance of, 1.
    Cannot be departed from, 1.
    Unless all parties sui juris, 1.
    How to be prepared, 2.
    Precedents of little service, 2.
    Relating to several matters, 2.
    Frame of such a one, 2.
    Fair copy of, 2.
    Perusal of, 2.
    Engrossment of, 2.
    Appointment to exchange, 3.
    Completion, 3.
    Written, advisable in most cases, 3.
    Stamp on, under hand, 3.
            under seal, 3.
    How commenced, 3.
    Executors bound by without being named, 4.

AGREEMENT—*continued.*
 Heir not bound by unless under seal, 4.
 As to equitable interests, 4.
 Such interests ought not to rest on an agreement, 4.
 Interests of married women parties to, 5.

APPOINTMENT,
 To complete sale, 13.
     purchase, 37.
     mortgage, 46.
     lease, 59, 65.
 To uses under settlement, 91.

ASSIGNMENT FOR BENEFIT OF CREDITORS. *See* COMPOSITION DEED.

AUCTIONEER,
 Selection of, 5.
 Usually prepares particulars and plans, 5.
 Authority to receive deposit from, on completion, 13.

BILL OF SALE,
 Filing security under 17 & 18 Vict. c. 36..42.

COMPLETION,
 Of agreement, 3.
  sale, 13.
  purchase, 38.
  mortgage, 47.
 Interest until, 14.
 Search for judgments, &c. on, 37—47.

COMPOSITION DEEDS, ASSIGNMENTS FOR BENEFIT OF CREDITORS, &c.,
 Observations on, 86.
 Assignment, 86.
 Notice of execution, 86.
 Registration, 86.
 Proceeding under deed of assignment, 87.
 Composition deed, 87.
     outline of, 87.
 Inspectorship deed, 87.
      liability of trustees under, 88.
 Decisions under the Bankruptcy Act, 1861..89.
 Costs of, 90.

CONDITIONS OF SALE,
 Preparation of, 6.
 Should be settled by counsel, when, 6.
 Proof of, 6.
 Difference in practice between town and country solicitors in preparing, 7.
 What should be stated in, 7.
 Perusal of, on behalf of purchaser, 23.
 Advising intending purchaser on, 23.

CONTRACT OF SALE,
 Instructions for, 5.
 By whom prepared, 9.
 Preparation and completion of, 9.

CONTRACT OF SALE—*continued.*
    Open, 15, 20, 24.
        What title sufficient under, 15.
        Disadvantages of, to vendor, 15.
    Advising on, 20.
    Vendor's solicitor should prepare it, 9, 25.
    Perusal of, 25.
    By letters, 26.
    When letters binding, 26.
    When formal agreement to be entered into, 9, 25.

CONVEYANCE, *See* SALES and PURCHASES.
    Perusing draft, 10, 35.
    Examination of engrossment by vendor's solicitor, 13.
    Preparation of, 32.
                by counsel, when necessary, 35.
    Parties to, 32.
    Judgment creditor, when necessary party to, 33.
    Alterations in draft of, 12.
    Qualifying words in, 36.
    Re-perusal of draft by vendor's solicitor, 36.
    Engrossment of, 36.
    Should be on stamped parchment, 37.
    Appointment for completion, 13, 37.
    Completion of, 13, 38.

CO-PARTNERSHIP DEEDS,
    Observations on partnerships, 80.
    Deed always preferable, 80.
        preparation of, 81.
        engrossment of, 81.
        completion of, 81.
        custody of, 81.
    When different solicitors concerned for intended partners, 82.
    Perusal of draft, 82.
    Appointment to complete, 82.
    Stamp on deed, 83.
    Dissolution of, 83.
    Preparation of deed of dissolution, 83.
    Costs of such deed, 84.
    Dissolution by death, 84.
           by retirement, 85.
           should be advertised, 85.

COPYHOLDS,
    Observations on, 67.
    Hardship of this tenure, 68.
    Perusing abstract, 69.
    Examining with court rolls, 69.
    Inquiries to be made of steward, 69.
    Barring entail of, 70.
    Freebench, 70.
    Requisitions on title, 71.
    Copies of court roll should be called for, 71.
    Difference between purchase of, and of freehold, 72.
    Preparation of surrender, 72.
            of deed of covenant, 72.
    Surrender of, should be passed before deed of covenant executed, 73.
    Draft surrender should be submitted to steward, 73.
    Steward not obliged to depart from usual form of surrender, 73.

COPYHOLDS—*continued.*
    Engrossment of surrender, 73.
              of deed of covenant, 78.
    Appointment to complete, 73.
    Purchase of, with freeholds, 73.
    Apportionment of purchase-money, 73.
    Identity of, when purchased with freeholds, 74.
    Surrender of, 74.
    Purchaser not obliged to accept surrender by attorney, 74.
    Completion of matter, 74.
    Deputation to take surrender, 74.
    Admittance, 75.
              on mortgage of, 75.
    Entry on court rolls on satisfaction of mortgage, 75.
    Fees payable on admission to, 76.
    Identity of, cannot be required, 76.
    Fine payable on admission, 77.
    Heriots on death, 77.
    Fees may be demanded before admittance, 77.
        But not fine, 77.
    Admittance compellable by mandamus, 78.
    On purchase of by railway company, 78.
    Enfranchisement of, 78.
        Lord's title should be called for, 78.
    Compulsory enfranchisement, 79.
    Voluntary enfranchisement, proceedings on, 79.
    As to common right after enfranchisement, 80.
    On enfranchisement, judgments, &c. should be searched for, 80.
    Manor within Registry Acts, 80.
    Copyhold of manor not, 80.
    Enfranchising through medium of Copyhold Commissioners, 80.

COSTS,
    Of acknowledgment of deed by married woman, 5.
    On purchase by railway company, 17.
    Of licence to assign, 17.
    Of conveyance and mortgage by one deed, 19.
    Of proving title on open contract, 24.
    Of mortgage, 47.
    On paying off mortgage, 49.
    Of intending mortgagee when mortgage goes off, 51.
    On transfer of mortgage, 53.
    Of lease, 57, 60, 65.
    Of co-partnership deeds, 82, 83.
    On dissolution of partnership, 84, 85.
    Of petitioning creditor in bankruptcy, 90.

COVENANTS,
    By vendor, 12.
        trustee or mortgagee, 12
        owner of estate, 12.
    To insure, most usually broken, 21.
            observations and cases on, 22.
            in mortgage deeds, 46.
    Meaning of "ordinary covenants," or "usual covenants," 55.
    In leases, where no agreement, 54.
    Restrictive of assignment, 56.
    That lessor's solicitor shall prepare assignment, 57.

DEEDS. *See* ACKNOWLEDGMENT OF DEED.
    Examination of abstract with, 10, 27.

DEEDS—*continued.*
    Registration of, 38, 47, 60, 93, 122.
    Custody of co-partnership, 81.
    Composition. *See* COMPOSITION DEEDS.
              points decided upon, 89.
    Custody of, under settlement, 100.

DISCLAIMER,
    Need not be in writing, 120.
    But deed generally advisable, 120.
    Recital in deed of, 121.
              of copyhold property by trustee, 121.
                    effect of, 131.
    Who prepared by, 121.
    Costs of, 121.
    Should be registered, when, 122.
    Stamp on, 122.

DISENTAILING DEEDS, AND DEEDS EXECUTED BY MARRIED WOMEN,
    Observations on, 103.
    By tenant in tail in possession, 103.
            in remainder, 103.
    Parties to, 103, 104.
    Enrolment of, 104.
    Acknowledgment of, not necessary, 104.
    Perusal of, for tenant for life, 104.
    Acknowledgment of deed by married woman, 104.
    Practice on taking acknowledgment in town, 105.
                          in the country, 105.
    Cases where no acknowledgment required, 106.
    Passing married woman's reversionary interest in personal property, 106.

DISSOLUTION OF PARTNERSHIP. *See* CO-PARTNERSHIP DEEDS.

DISTRINGAS ON STOCK,
    Advisability of, 101.
    How placed, 101.
    How removed, 102.

ENFRANCHISEMENT. *See* COPYHOLDS.

ENROLMENT,
    Of disentailing deed, 104.

EQUITABLE INTEREST,
    Agreement relating to, 4.
    Should be carried out by deed, 4.
    Of married woman in real estate, 5, 34.

EXECUTORS,
    Bound by agreement although not named, 4.
    When entitled to release, 114.

FIRE,
    Pending completion of sale and purchase, 16, 23.

FIXTURES,
    If not attached to freehold, deed must be filed, 42.
    Secus if attached, 42.

FREEHOLD.
  When purchased with copyhold, 73.
    consideration money must be apportioned, 73.
  And copyhold must be distinguished, 74.
  When fixtures attached to, 42.

FURNITURE,
  Bill of sale of, must be registered, 44.

GRANT,
  The word does not create a warranty, 36.

HEIR,
  not bound by agreement unless named, 4.

INCOME TAX,
  When cannot be deducted, 19.

INCUMBRANCES,
  Search for on purchase, 37.
  Should be discharged before completion, 38.
  Search for on mortgage, 46.
    on enfranchisement, 80.

INSPECTORSHIP DEED,
  Observations on, 87.
  How prepared, 87.
  Contents of, 88.
  When creditors under, liable as partners, 88.

INSTRUCTIONS,
  Should be signed if no agreement, 3.
  For sale, what should be done on, 9.

INSURANCE,
  Condition as to, 21, 23. *See also* COVENANTS.

INTEREST,
  Calculation of, on completion, 14.
  Difficult question, 14.
  When payable, 16.
  Rate of, 16.
  When no time named for completion, 16.
  Any rate may be reserved under mortgage, 48.

JUDGMENT CREDITOR,
  When necessary party to conveyance, 33.
  Covenant by, 33.

JUDGMENTS,
  Should be searched for before completion of purchase, 37.
  The like, on mortgage, 46.
    enfranchisement of copyholds, 80.

LEASES,
  Observations on, 54.
  Practice on behalf of lessee, 54.
  Agreement for, must be followed, 55.
  Meaning of words " ordinary covenants" or " usual covenants," 55.
  Of agricultural property, 55.
  Covenants in, where no agreement, 55.
  When lessor's title can be required, 55.
  As to covenant restrictive of assignment, 56.

INDEX TO TREATISE. 417

LEASES—*continued*.
    Objections to such a covenant, 56.
    As to covenant that lessor's solicitor shall prepare assignment, 57.
    Validity of such a covenant, 57.
    Costs of, 57, 59.
        of plan, 57.
    Preparation of draft, 58.
    Perusal of draft, 58.
    Of mining property, 58.
        proviso for cesser of rent in, 58.
            If omitted, no relief at law, 58.
                Nor in equity, 58.
    Engrossment of, 59.
            of counterpart, 59.
    Completion of, 59.
    Registration of, when requisite and when not, 60.
    Who should register, 60.
    Practice on behalf of lessor, 60.
    Underlease, when necessary, 61.
    Preparation of agreement for, 61.
    What should be inserted in, 61.
    Completion of agreement for, 62.
    Preparation of, 63.
    Of house property, 63.
       agricultural or mining property, 63.
    By mortgagor, 63.
        Effect of, 64.
    By mortgagor and mortgagee, 64.
    Under power, 64.
    By mortgagee, 64.
    Fair copy of, 65.
    Engrossment of, 65.
            of counterpart, 65.
    Completion of, 65.
    Of copyholds, 66.
    Licence to demise should be first obtained, 66.
    Costs of licence, 66.
    Inquiries to be made as to lord's interest in manor, 66.
    Statute as to granting leases of settled property, 67.

LEGACY AND SUCCESSION DUTIES, 117.
    Practice on preparing and passing accounts, 118.
    Legacy receipts, 118.
    Annuity receipts, 118.
    Residuary accounts, 118.
    Succession accounts, 119.

LESSEE,
    Proceeding, when concerned for, 54.
    Covenants by, 55.
    Cannot compel production of lessor's title, when, 55.
    Covenant restraining assignment by, 56.
    Costs paid by, 57.
    Of mines, clause for protection of, 58.
    Registration of lease in behalf of, 60.
    Special covenants by, 61.
    Inquiries to be made by his solicitor on lease of copyholds, 66.

LESSOR,
    Title of, 55.
    His costs in regard to lease paid by lessee, when, 57.

LESSOR—*continued.*
    When holding under a lease, 61.
    Granting lease under power, 64.

LETTERS,
    When they form contract, 26.

LETTERS OF ADMINISTRATION. *See* PROBATE.

LICENCE,
    To demise copyholds, 66.
    Expense of, who pays, 66.

MARRIED WOMAN,
    Interests of, party to agreement, 5.
    Conveyance of equitable interest by, must be acknowledged, 34.
    Must acknowledge deed to which she is a party, 38.
    Deeds executed by, 104.
        Husband must join in, 105.
            When his concurrence dispensed with, 105.
                Practice in such a case, 105.
    Acknowledgment of deed by, in London, 105.
                             in country, 105.
    Filing certificate and affidavit of acknowledgment, 105.
    When seised to her separate use with power of appointment, 106.
    When no power of appointment, 106.
    Reversionary interests of, in personal estate, 106.

MIDDLESEX REGISTRY. *See* REGISTRY.

MINING PROPERTY,
    Lease of, 58.
        should provide for cesser of rent, when, 59.

MISNOMER,
    Will not avoid deed, 35.

MORTGAGEE,
    Covenants entered into by, on sale, 12.
    Additional costs on death or lunacy of, 49.
    Must pay costs if matter goes off and no agreement with mortgagor, 51.

MORTGAGES,
    Observations on, 38.
    Difference between mortgage and purchase, 39.
    Title on, 39.
    Various, 39, 40.
    Of freehold land or ground rents, 40.
        freehold houses, 40.
        copyholds, 40.
        leaseholds, 41.
        leasehold ground rents, 41.
        mills, manufactories, &c., 41.
        chattels must be filed (under Bills of Sale Act), 42.
    By trustees, 42, 44.
    Of life interests, 43.
        reversions, 43.
        policy of assurance, 43.
        furniture, stock in trade, &c., 44.
    Preparing deed, 45.
    Difference in preparation from purchase deed, 46.
    Trustee mortgagees may give power of sale, 46.

MORTGAGES—*continued.*
 Appointment to complete, 46.
 Succession duty (if any) to be cleared, 46.
 What searches should be made before completing, 47.
 Completion of, 47.
 Registering in Middlesex or Yorkshire, 47.
     under Bills of Sale Act, 47.
 Of freehold and copyhold property, 47.
 No restriction on rate of interest, 48.
 Paying off, 49.
 Perusal of reconveyance, 49.
 Costs of, 49.
 Exercise of power of sale in, 50.
 Disposal of purchase-money, 50.
 Paying into court under Trustee Relief Acts, 51.
 Costs, where intended mortgage goes off, 51.
 Powers under Trustees Relief Amendment Act, 51.
 Powers under the 23 & 24 Vict. c. 145..52.
 Transfers of, 52.
 Costs of transfer, 53.
 Disclosing title to transferee, 53.

MORTGAGOR,
 Covenants by, 46.
 Not bound to pay costs if matter goes off, unless agreement, 49.
 When dead, course as to balance in mortgagee's hands, 50.
 Trustees, statutory powers to, 52.

PARTICULARS OF SALE,
 Preparation of, 5.
 Misdescription in, may be fatal, 5.
 Proof of, 6.
 What should be stated in, 7.

PARTNERSHIP. *See* COPARTNERSHIP DEEDS.

POWER OF SALE,
 Exercise of, 50.

PROBATE OF WILL AND LETTERS OF ADMINISTRATION,
 Practice on obtaining, 115.

PURCHASE-MONEY,
 When parties beneficially interested in can be compelled to join in conveyance, 16, 17.
 When not, 17.
 From railway company, costs of investment of, 17.
 Irregularity in position of receipt for, 28.
 Received under power of sale in mortgage, 50.

PURCHASER,
 Cannot be compelled to go to a distance to examine deeds without notice, 10.
 What title he can insist on under an open contract, 15.
 Of lease cannot be compelled to take underlease, 6.

PURCHASES,
 Advising client on, 20.
 Contract by letters, 20—26.
 Under open contract, 20, 24.
 At auction, 20.
 Course of proceeding on purchase at auction, 20.

PURCHASES—*continued.*
  Of leaseholds, breach by vendor of covenant to insure, 21.
  As to insurance money in case of fire before completion, 23.
  Advising intending purchaser at auction, 23.
  Proceeding after verbal contract for, 25.
  Perusing abstract, 37.
  Comparing abstract with deeds, 27.
  Preparing requisitions on title, 29.
  When requisitions should be prepared by counsel, 31.
  Perusing answers to requisitions, 32.
  Preparing conveyance, 32.
  Parties to conveyance, 32.
    judgment creditor, 83.
    devisees in trust, 34.
    married woman, 34.
    misnomer not fatal, 35.
  Perusing alterations in draft, 35.
  When papers should be laid before counsel, 35.
  "Grant," meaning of the word, 36.
  Engrossing conveyance, 36.
  Appointment to complete, 37.
  Succession duty, proof that purchased property is free from, 37.
  Searching for judgments, &c., 37.
  Completion of, 38.
  Acknowledgment of by married woman, 38.
  Registering conveyance, 38.
  Where married woman party, deed must be acknowledged, 38.
  Of freehold and copyhold, ad valorem duty must be apportioned, 73.

RAILWAY COMPANY,
  Costs of investing purchase-money of land taken by them under compulsory powers, 17.

RECEIPT,
  For purchase-money, irregularity in position of, 28.

RECONVEYANCE,
  Prepared by mortgagor's solicitor, 49.
  Mortgagee's costs on, 49.

REGISTRATION,
  Not necessary when property in the City of London, 60.
  Of conveyance, 38.
    mortgage, 47.
    lease, 60.
    settlement, 93, 99.
    will, when necessary, 115.
      when not, 115.
    disclaimer, when necessary, 122.

REGISTRY,
  Should be searched, when, 37, 46.
  Manor is within the Acts, 80.
  Copyhold property is not, 80.
  Marriage settlement of chattels need not be registered, 99.

RELEASE,
  When it can be required by executor, 114.

RENTS,
  As to when no time fixed by contract for completion, 16.

INDEX TO TREATISE. 421

REQUISITIONS ON TITLE,
    How perused and answered, 10.
    What answers can be required by purchaser, 11.
    How prepared, 29.

SALE, BILL OF. *See* BILL OF SALE.

SALE, CONDITIONS OF. *See* CONDITIONS OF SALE.

SALE, CONTRACT OF. *See* CONTRACT OF SALE.

SALES,
    Instructions for, 5.
    By auction, 5.
    As to auctioneer, 5.
    Preparation of particulars, 5.
        Misdescription in may be fatal, 6.
    Preparation of conditions, 6.
        Great care necessary in framing, 6.
        Should be settled by counsel, when, 6.
    Proof of particulars and conditions, 6.
    Difference between town and country solicitors on, 7.
    Plan to annex to particulars, 7.
    What should be stated in particulars and conditions of, 7.
    Attending at, 8.
    Signing purchase contract, 8.
    By private contract, 9.
    Preparation of abstract of title, 9.
    Abstract to be sent, 9.
    Examination of abstract, 10.
    Answering requisitions, 10.
    Perusing draft conveyance, 10.
    Vendor's usual covenants on, 12.
    Examination of engrossment, 13.
    Appointment to complete, 13.
    Proceedings at completion, 13.
    Authority to auctioneer to pay over deposit, 13.
    Question of interest on purchase-money, 14.
    Under open contract, 15.
    Title to be furnished thereunder, 15.
    Purchaser should have benefit of vendor's insurance against fire included in contract, 16.
    Trustees or mortgagees' covenants on, 16.
    To railway companies, 17.
    Licence to assign, vendor must get, 17.
    Act to amend Law of Property, 18.
        to give Powers to Trustees and others, 18.
        to facilitate Title to Real Estate, 18.
    Mortmain Act, 18.
    Leases and Sales of Settled Estates Act, 18.
        Amendment Act, 19.
    Trustee Act, 19.
        Extension Act, 19.
    Of coal mine, purchase-money paid by instalments, 19.
    Exercise of power of sale by mortgagee, 50.

SEPARATE USE,
    Under settlement, 95.

SETTLED ESTATES,
    Leases of, power to grant, 94.
    Sale of, 102.

SETTLEMENTS,
 Remarks on, 90.
 Of real estate, 91.
 Preparation of, 91.
 Perusal of, 93.
 Engrossment of, 93.
 Registration of, 93.
 Of small estate, 93.
 Hotchpot clause, 94.
 Of personal property, 94.
  stock in the funds, 95.
 Separate use, 95.
 Maintenance and advancement clauses, 96.
 Clause enabling provision for children of second marriage, 96.
 Power to advance trust money to husband, 97.
 Trustees' receipt clause, 97.
 Power to appoint new trustees, 97.
 Vesting property in trustees under, 97.
 Of mortgage money, 98.
  bonds or promissory notes, 98.
  railway shares, &c., 98.
  household furniture, &c., 98.
  life policy, 99.
 Useful clause in, 99.
 After marriage, 99. *See* VOLUNTARY SETTLEMENT.
 Custody of title deeds, 100.
 Notice of, when necessary, 101.
 Consequence of neglect to give such notice, 101.
 Distringas on stock, 101.
  How obtained, 101.
  How removed, 102.
 Statutory power to sell real estate comprised in, 102.
 Orders under the statute, 102.

STAMP,
 On agreement under hand, 3.
  Under seal, 3.
 Disclaimer, 122.

STOCK,
 Settlement of, 95.
 Distringas on, how placed, 101.
  How removed, 102.
 In name of a deceased trustee, 116.
 Probate duty not payable thereon, 117.
 Practice to obtain exemption, 117.

SUCCESSION DUTY. *See* LEGACY AND SUCCESSION DUTY.
 Evidence of payment of should be required before completing purchase or mortgage, 37, 46.

SURRENDER. *See* COPYHOLDS.

TITLE,
 Preparing abstract of, 9.
 Delivery thereof, 9.
 Examination thereof with deeds, 27.
 Requisitions on, 29.
 Under open contract, 15, 24.
 When to commence, 15.
 "Marketable," meaning of, 15.
 Perusal of abstract of, 27.
 Counsel's opinion on, 31.
 Of lessor, 55.

TRUSTEE,
    Covenants by, 12.
    Qualifying words in conveyances by, 36.
    Mortgage to, 42, 44.
    Mortgage by, 52.
    When entitled to release, 114.

TRUSTEE RELIEF ACT,
    When money should be paid into court under, 51.

TRUST ESTATES,
    Devise of, 109.

UNDERLEASE,
    Purchaser cannot be compelled to take on sale of lease, 6.
    Preparation of, 61.

VENDOR,
    Covenants by, 12.

VOLUNTARY SETTLEMENT, 99.
    When binding, 100.
        And on whom, 100.
    Does not bind purchaser even with notice, 100.

WILLS,
    Observations on, 107.
    Taking instructions for, 107.
    Preparation of, 108.
    Should be forwarded to testator when prepared, 109.
    Devise of property in mortgage, 109.
    Devise of trust estates, 109.
    Appointment of trustees and executors, 109.
    Copyholds to be sold should not be devised, 110.
    Fair copy of, 111.
    Completion of, 111.
    Instructions to prove, 111.
    How property estimated for probate, 111.
    Debts must not be deducted, 111.
    How proved, 112.
    New law as to proving, 112.
    Advising executors before probate, 113.
    Administering estate under, 113.
    Paying legacies under, 114.
    Of real estate in register counties should be registered, 115.
    Contra of personal estate, 115.

INDEX TO THE PRECEDENTS.

ACKNOWLEDGMENT,
    Indorsed on deed to be inrolled in Chancery, 125.

ADVANCEMENT. *See* SETTLEMENT.
    Trusts for, in settlement of personalty, 400.

ADVERTISEMENT,
    For creditors under 22 & 23 Vict. c. 35..125.

AFFIDAVIT,
    Of execution of bill of sale, 126.
    Verifying notice of dissolution of partnership, 127.
    To obtain distringas on stock, 261. *See* DISTRINGAS.

AGREEMENT,
    For purchase of leaseholds, stock in trade, &c., 127.
        sale and purchase of freeholds by private contract, 131.
        sale of freeholds, 133.
        sale of a ship, 134.
        lease of a house, 136.
        underlease of garden ground, 137.
    From year to year of agricultural land, 138.
    To let a house for three years, 139.
    Under seal between a brewer and his manager, 140.
    Of reference where no action brought, 143.
        where action brought, 144.
    For a mortgage, 145.
        releasing an annuity charged on real estate, 148.

ANTICIPATION,
    Clause in settlement restraining, 395.

APPOINTMENT,
    Of gamekeeper, 150.
        money under a power, 151.
    Power to revoke, 156.
    Of new trustee, 156.
            by indorsement, 158.
    Power of, in settlement, 396, 399.

APPRENTICESHIP,
    Indenture of, 159.
        Proviso to be inserted in, if necessary, 160.

ARBITRATION,
    Clause for, in lease, 285.
            in copartnership deed, 360.

ASSENT,
    Forms of, to composition deed, 197.

ASSIGNMENT,
    Of leasehold by indorsement, 161.
                   mortgagor and mortgagee, 162.
                   separate deed, 166.
                   a mortgagee under power of sale, 168.
    Of reversionary interest in stock, 171.
       goodwill of business, 175.
       debts, 177.
    For the benefit of creditors, 180.
    Restriction as to, 288.
    Licence for, 295.

ATTORNEY,
    Testimonium to instrument executed by, 402.

ATTORNMENT,
    Of tenant, 183.

BEQUEST. *See* WILL.
    To wife for life and widowhood, 405.
        trustees for separate use of daughter, and afterwards for her children, 406.

BILL OF SALE,
    Affidavit of execution of, 126.
    Of chattels (conditional), 183.

BOND,
    From manager of brewery and his sureties, 187.
    On marriage for conditionally securing sum of money, 188.
       wife and her issue, 188.
       common money, 189.
    Defeasance to, for replacing stock, 190.

BREACHES OF COVENANT,
    waiver of, 295.

BUILDING,
    Conveyance of land for, 221.

CESSER,
    Of covenant to produce, proviso for, 220.

CESTUI QUE TRUST,
    Request by, to trustees to sell stock for mortgage, 394.

CHANCERY,
    Indorsement on deed to be inrolled in, 125.

CHARITY,
    Conveyance of charity property, 229.

CLERK OF THE PEACE,
    Conveyance by, 231.

CODICIL. *See* WILL.
    appointing new trustee and executor, 404.

INDEX TO THE PRECEDENTS. 427

COMPOSITION DEED, 191.
    Ditto, 192.
    Ditto, 193.
    Ditto, 194.
    Assent to, 197.
    Ditto, 197.

CONDITION. *See* BOND.

CONDITIONS OF SALE,
    Of freeholds in lots with unexceptionable title, 198.
    property held under an underlease, 202.
    leaseholds in lots by mortgagees, 204.
    freehold and leasehold and rent-charge, 206.
    Under decree of Court of Chancery, 209.
    Of reversionary interest in stock, 212.
    Where property is held on an underlease, 213.
    If title not marketable, 214.
    Of freehold ground rents, 214.
    Where land originally acquired by a parish, 216.

CONFIRMATION,
    Deed of, by woman after marriage, 217.

CONTRACT. *See* AGREEMENT.

CONVEYANCE,
    Of freehold by appointment and grant, with covenant to produce deeds, 218.
    land for building purposes, 221.
    freeholds in mortgage to trustees of loan society, 222.
    By mortgagee under power of sale, 225.
    Of land for burial ground under 43 Geo. 3, c. 108..226.
    freeholds and covenant to surrender copyholds, 227.
    charity property, 229.
    life interest in real estate, 230.
    By clerk of peace to trustees of settlement, 231.
    Covenant in, that infant shall execute deed at twenty-one, 234.

CONVEYANCING CHARGES, 408.

COPARTNERSHIP. *See* PARTNERSHIP.

COPYHOLDS,
    Absolute surrender of, 234.
    Deed of covenants on such surrender, 236.
    Conditional surrender of, 237.
    Deed of covenants on such surrender, 238.
    Power of attorney to surrender, 239.
    Disclaimer of, by trustees, 240.
    Deed of enfranchisement of, 241.
    Warrant to enter satisfaction on conditional surrender of, 244.
    Surrender of, to trustees of settlement, 244.

COVENANT,
    Deed of, by purchasers of building land, 245.
    as to judgment debts and indemnification, 248.
    to produce deeds, 251.
    not to contaminate river, 253.
    And proviso relating to grants of right of way, 270.
    By mortgagees against incumbrances, 224, 225.

COVENANT—*continued.*
  By mortgagees on sale of leaseholds, 164, 171.
    vendor on sale of goodwill, 176.
      on assignment of debts, 178.
    purchaser on assignment of debts, 179.
      in conveyance by vendor to produce deeds, 220.
    proviso for cesser thereof, 220.
  To pay mortgage money, 301, 304, 313, 316, 320, 327.
      mortgage money and further advances, 310.
      mortgage money to two mortgagees, 324.
    insure in mortgage of freeholds to two mortgagees, 325.
      mortgaged property, 305, 311, 314, 321.
      chattels, 186.
    keep chattels in repair, 187.
  By lessee,
    To pay rent, 273, 277, 283.
        taxes, 273, 277, 283.
      build, 277.
      repair, 273, 278, 283.
      paint outside and inside, 273, 279, 283.
      yield up in repair, 273, 278, 284.
      allow lessor to enter and view, and to repair after notice, 273, 274, 278, 280, 284.
    Not to exercise noxious trades on premises, 274, 280.
    To use premises as a private dwelling only, 284.
    Not to convert hotel for any other purpose, 274.
        conduct business so as to forfeit licence, 274.
    To use a particular sign on premises, 274, 275.
    At end of term to give up licences, 275.
    To insure, 275, 281, 283.
    Not to assign during last seven years without licence, 282.
  By lessor,
    For quiet enjoyment, 275, 284.
    To produce original lease, 285.
  By debtor in assignment for creditors, 181.
  In release by residuary legatees, 389.
  Deed of, not to issue execution on judgment against certain property, 248.
  To indemnify purchaser against judgment debt, 250.
  Deeds of, to accompany surrenders of copyholds, 236, 238.
  By purchaser of land set out for building purposes, 222.
  That infant shall execute deed at twenty-one, 234.
  Waiver of breaches of, 295.

COVENANTS FOR TITLE,
  In purchase deed, 219, 221, 228.
    conveyance of land for burial purposes, 227.
    grant subject to yearly rent-charge, 268.
    grant of rent-charge, 268.
  By vendor in assignment of leaseholds, 161, 167.
    vendor and mortgagee in ditto, 164, 165.
    purchaser in assignment of leaseholds, 162, 165, 167.
  In assignment of reversionary interest in stock, 175.
    mortgage of freeholds to building society, 301.
    mortgage of leaseholds to building society, 304.
    mortgage of leaseholds, 310, 314.
    mortgage of pecuniary legacy, 317.
    mortgage of freeholds to mortgagee, 320.
    ditto to two mortgagees, 324.
    transfer of mortgage, 337.

COVENANTS FOR TITLE—*continued.*
    In release of equity of redemption, 340.
        bill of sale, 186.
    By lord of manor on enfranchisement, 243.

CREDITORS,
    Advertisement for under 22 & 23 Vict. c. 35..125.
    Assignment for benefit of, 180.

DEBTS,
    Assignment of, 177.

DECLARATION,
    In bar of dower, 219.
    Of existence of person who had given a power of attorney, 257.
    That mortgage money advanced on joint account, 325.
        mortgaged property shall be charged with further advances, 328.
        power of sale in mortgage deed shall be applicable to further advance, 329.
    Of trusts in settlement of personalty, 398.
    Statutory, conclusion of, 257.
    Of the existence of a person who had given a power of attorney at the time of the attorney exercising the power, 257.

DEED,
    Composition, 191, 192, 193, 194.
    Of covenant, 245, 248, 251, 253.
    Disentailing, 259.
    Instructions for executing, 271.

DEVISE,
    Of trust estates, 407. *See* WILL.

DISCLAIMER,
    Of copyholds by trustee, 240. *See* COPYHOLDS.
    Of trusts under will, 257.
    Ditto (short form), 259.

DISENTAILING DEED,
    By tenant in tail, with consent of protector, 259.

DISSOLUTION,
    Of partnership, deed of, 362.
        notice of, 365.
        affidavit verifying notice, 127.

DISTRESS,
    power of, in mortgage, 302, 305.

DISTRINGAS ON STOCK,
    Affidavit to obtain, 261.
    Notice to bank, 262.

DOWER,
    Declaration in bar of, in conveyance, 219.

ENFRANCHISEMENT. *See* COPYHOLDS.
    Deed of, 241.

EQUITY OF REDEMPTION,
    Release of, 340.
    Proviso to be inserted in settlement of, 402.

EXCEPTION. *See* LEASE.
    Of mines, 276.
    Out of lease of water from a well, 286.

EXECUTION,
    Of deed, instructions for, 271.

FIRE,
    Clause in lease suspending rent after, 286.

FREEHOLDS,
    Agreement for sale and purchase of, 131.
    Ditto, 133.

FURNITURE. *See* WILL.
    Bequest of, with directions as to inventory, 405.

FURTHER CHARGE. *See* MORTGAGE.
    By new deed, 326.
        indorsement, 328.

GAMEKEEPER,
    Appointment of, 150.

GOODWILL,
    Of business, assignment of, 176.

GRANT,
    In fee of a plot of land subject to rent-charge, 263.
    Of a yearly rent-charge, 267.
        right of way in surrender of copyholds, 235.
        common rights on enfranchisement, 242.
        a right of road, 268.
        special right of road to railway, 269.
    Covenants and proviso relating to the said grants, 270.

HABENDUM,
    In conveyance to uses, 219.
        in fee, 221.
        by mortgagee, 225.
        of land for churchyard, 227.
        to trustees of settlement, 233.
    grant subject to yearly rent-charge, 264.
    assignment of leaseholds by indorsement, 161.
        by separate deed, 167.
        by mortgagor and mortgagee, 16?.
        by mortgagee, 177.
        of reversionary interest in stock, 174.
        of goodwill, 176.
    mortgage of freeholds to building society, 299.
        leaseholds to building society, 303.
        leaseholds, 308, 312.
        pecuniary legacy, 315.
        freeholds to two mortgagees, 322.
    re-conveyance, 330.
    re-assignment, 332.
    transfer of mortgage debt, 333.
        premises, 333.
    transfer of mortgage, with concurrence of mortgagor, 335.
        and further advance, 339.
    release of equity of redemption, 340.
    bill of sale, 184.
    lease, 272, 276, 282.
    deed of enfranchisement, 242.
    assignment for benefit of creditors, 180.
    disentailing deed, 261.

HOTCHPOT CLAUSE, 399. *See* SETTLEMENT.
INDEMNITY,
    Covenant of, against judgment debt, 250.
INFANT,
    Covenant for execution of deed by, at twenty-one, 234.
INSTRUCTIONS,
    For execution of deed, 271.
INSURANCE,
    Covenants for, 186, 275, 281, 283, 305, 311, 314, 321, 325.
JUDGMENT DEBTS,
    Deed of covenant as to, 248.
LEASE,
    Of public house and premises, 272.
        land for building purposes, 276.
        a house, 282.
    Covenant to produce in an underlease, 285.
    Arbitration clause in, 285.
    Clause in, suspending rent during fire, 286.
    Exception from, of water from well, 286.
    Licence by lessor to permit sale by auction on premises, 287.
    Notice to quit premises, 288.
    Clause in, restricting assignment of, but not to be unreasonably withheld, 288.
    Proviso for determining by either party, 289.
            requiring lessee to give up any part of demised premises on notice, 290.
            in mining lease for reduction of rent in case faults met with, 291.
            authorizing lessor to dispose of part of demised land on allowing abatement or expending money received, 292.
    Notice to lessee to abate nuisance, 293.
    Surrender of, 294.
    Waiver of breaches of covenant, 295.
    Licence to assign, 295.
    Power in settlement to grant, 396.
LEGACY,
    Mortgage of, 315.
LESSEE,
    Covenants by. *See* COVENANT.
LESSOR,
    Covenants by. *See* COVENANT.
LICENCE,
    By lessor to permit sale by auction on premises, 287.
        to assign, 295.
LIMITATIONS,
    To uses to bar dower, 219.
    In fee, 221, 224, 225, 228, 230.
        conveyance subject to yearly rent-charge, 264.
MANAGER,
    Of brewery, bond from, 187.
MARRIAGE,
    Bond on, to secure money on wife and children, 188.
    Confirmation of deed by woman, after, 217.
    Settlements in contemplation of, 395, 397.

432   INDEX TO THE PRECEDENTS.

MEMORIAL,
    Of lease, 296.
        conveyance, 296.
        assignment, 297.
        mortgage, 298.
    Indorsement on, where deed and memorial executed in the country, 298.
    Of an endorsed deed, 298.

MINING LEASE,
    Clause in, suspending rent on fault found, 291.

MORTGAGE,
    Agreement for, 145.
    Of copyholds. *See* COPYHOLDS.
        freeholds to building society, 299.
        leaseholds to building society, 302.
    Separate form of power of distress by mortgagor, 306.
    Another form of ditto, 306.
    Of leaseholds for a sum certain and further advances, 307.
        for a sum certain, 311.
    a pecuniary legacy, 315.
    Notice thereof, 317.
    Of freeholds to one mortgagee, 318.
        to two mortgagees, 322.
    Further charge, 326.
        by indorsement, 328.
    Reconveyance of freeholds, 329.
    Re-assignment of leaseholds, 331.
    Transfer of, to trustees of marriage settlement, 332.
        with concurrence of mortgagor, 334.
        with further advance, 338.
    Release of equity of redemption by indorsement, 340.
    Proviso that mortgagor, being a solicitor, shall have his costs, 341.
        for mortgage money to remain for a term certain, 341.
    Of chattels. *See* BILL OF SALE.
    Form of receipt to be indorsed on where no reconveyance taken, 342.
    Notice of sale by mortgagee, 342.
    Form of undertaking to pay mortgagee's costs to be taken before investigation of title, 342.
    Release by mortgagee in fee of part of mortgaged hereditaments, 343.

MORTGAGEE,
    Covenants by. *See* COVENANT.

NOTICE,
    Of mortgage, 317.
    To Bank of England of distringas on stock, 262.
    To quit when commencement of tenancy uncertain, 288.
    Of mortgagee's intention to exercise power of sale, 342.
    To quit from landlord to tenant, 344.
        from tenant to landlord, 344.
        and for double rent, 345.
    To railway company claiming compensation as occupier, 345.
        owner, 347.
    By mortgagee to tenant to pay rent to him, 348.
    By second mortgagee to first, 349.

PARTITION,
    Deed of, by tenants in common, 350.

RE-ASSIGNMENT,
    Of mortgaged leaseholds, 331.
RECEIPT,
    To be indorsed on mortgage where no reconveyance taken, 342.
RECITALS,
    Of conveyance to uses, 218.
        seisin in fee and contract of sale, 221.
        seisin in fee and mortgage for term, 222.
        amount due under mortgage, 330, 331, 333, 334, 338.
    That churchyard too small for parishioners, 226.
            piece of land convenient to be added thereto, and desire to vest same in vicar, 226.
    Of contract for sale of leaseholds, 161, 164, 166.
        mortgage, 163, 169, 222.
        will, 171, 230.
            death of testator and probate of will, 173.
            sale of property under will and investment of proceeds, 173.
            sale by auction of reversionary interest, 173.
    That vendor had carried on business, &c., in assignment of goodwill, 176.
    Of contract for sale of goodwill, 176.
    That vendor had carried on business in assignment of debts, 177.
    Of contract for sale of debts, 177.
                        copyholds, 236.
        absolute surrender, 236.
        conditional surrender, 238.
        right to shares in mortgage to building society, 302.
        money due and agreement to secure same by mortgage, 307.
        agreement for advance by two mortgagees, 322.
        money due under mortgage, 326, 328, 333, 334, 338, 340, 343.
        agreement for further advance, 307, 326, 328, 339.
                for reconveyance, 330.
                for re-assignment, 331.
                to transfer to trustees of settlement, 333.
                to transfer, 335.
                to pay off prior mortgage, and advance further sum, 339.
                for sale of equity of redemption, 340.
        seisin in fee of manor, 241.
                by copyhold tenant, 241.
        agreement to enfranchise, 241.
        ownership of money in the funds, 315.
        intended marriage, 395, 397.
        transfer of property to trustees of settlement, 397.
        agreement to assign for benefit of creditors, 180.
                to accept composition from debtor, 191, 192, 193, 194.
                to give bond, 187, 189.
        obligee having employed obligor, and of agreement to give bond for fidelity, 187.
        intended marriage and agreement to give bond, 188.
        agreement to sell stock and advance proceeds, 190.
        sale of stock and advance of proceeds, 190.
        agreement to replace same stock, 190.
        intention to leave England, and desire to appoint attorney, 371.
        will in disclaimer, 257, 259.
            probate thereof, 258.
    That disclaiming trustee has never acted, 258, 259.
    In disclaimer of copyhold that no one admitted, and of desire to disclaim, 240.
    In release, of will, death of testator, and probate, 388.
    That residue of personal estate got in, 388.

INDEX TO THE PRECEDENTS. 435

RECITALS—*continued.*
  Of inspection and approval of accounts, 389.
    marriage settlement of real estate, 395.
                  of personalty, 397.
    will in appointment thereunder, 151.
    that no appointment executed, 154.
    desire to execute appointment, 154.
    settlement in disentailing deed, 260.
  That tenant in tail eldest son, and desire to bar entail, 260.
    protector had agreed to consent, 260.
  Of ownership of land, and of same having been set out for building purposes, 245.
    judgment, 248.
    assignment of judgment debt, 248.
    agreement for covenant to produce deeds, 251.
    one copartner having carried on trade, 350.
    agreement for partnership, 350.
  That stock should be taken as part of copartnership capital, 351.
  Of payment of succession duty, 376.
    seisin in fee, 376.
    agreement for purchase, 376.
    contract for sale, 219, 377.
    lease, 377.
    conveyance to uses to bar dower, 377.
    assignment, 378.
    mesne assignments, 378.
    purchase agreement of leaseholds, 371.
    mortgage, 379.
    agreement of sale with right of repurchase, 379.
    contract for sale of lands, and that no conveyance made, 380.
    sub-contract, 380.
    ditto (another form), 380.
    agreement to make new conveyance and to join in confirming same, 380.
  In confirmation deed, 381.
  Of agreement by persons interested in purchase money to join in conveyance, 381.
    agreement by heir to effectuate ancestor's contract by joining in conveyance, 382.
    agreement on marriage to convey copyholds and leaseholds, and to pay off mortgage, 382.
    codicils not affecting devise of realty, 382.
    no devise of mortgage or trust estates, 383.
    contract for sale of mortgage debt, 383.
    contract for licence to use invention, 383.
    death of old and appointment of new trustees, 383.
    revocation of appointment of executor and appointment of substitute, 384.
    agreement by executor to assent to legacy, 384.
  That trust property put up for sale but bought in, 384.
  Of grant of administration, 384.
    limited administration, 385.
    purchase by agent, 385.
    appointment of new trustees, 385.
    tenancy by curtesy, 385.
    death of mortgagee intestate as to mortgaged estate, 386.
    death of surviving trustee intestate as to trust estates, 386.
    further charge, 386.
          by indorsement, 386.
    transfer of mortgage, 387.
    erection of buildings since conveyance, 388.
    policy of assurance for life, 388.

RECONVEYANCE,
    Of mortgaged freeholds, 329.

REDEMPTION,
    Release of equity of, 340.
    Proviso for. *See* MORTGAGE.

REFERENCE,
    Agreement for, where no action brought, 143.
                        where action brought, 144.

REGISTRATION. *See* MEMORIAL.

RELEASE,
    Of equity of redemption, 340.
    To debtor by creditors in assignment, 182.
    Undertaking by creditors to execute, 191, 193.
    By creditors in composition deed, 196.
    To executors by residuary legatee, 389.
    Of trusts of money created by marriage settlement, 390.
        charges on real estate, 393.

RENT,
    Reservation of. *See* RESERVATION.

RENT-CHARGE,
    Grant of land subject to, 263.
    Grant of, 267.

REQUEST,
    By cestui que trust to trustees to sell out stock for mortgage, 394.

RESERVATION,
    Of rent in lease, 272, 277, 282.

REVERSIONARY INTEREST,
    In stock, assignment of, 171.

RIVER,
    Deed of covenant not to contaminate, 253.

SALE,
    Conditions of. *See* CONDITIONS OF SALE.
    Power of, in mortgage of freeholds to building society, 300.
                        of leaseholds to building society, 303.
                        of leaseholds, 309, 313.
                        of pecuniary legacy, 316.
                        of freeholds to one mortgagee, 319.
                            to two mortgagees, 323.
                        to apply to further charge, 327.
        in transfer of mortgage, 335.
        in mortgage of chattels, 185.
        in settlement, 396.
    Notice of, under power in mortgage, 342.
    Licence by lessor to permit on demised premises, 287.

SATISFACTION,
    warrant to enter, 244. *See* COPYHOLDS.

SETTLEMENT,
    Of real estate on marriage, 395.
        personalty on marriage, 397.
        equity of redemption, proviso to be inserted in, 402.
    Power of appointment in, 396, 399.

STATUTORY DECLARATION,
    Conclusion of, 257.

STOCK,
    Assignment of reversionary interest in, 171.
    Affidavit to obtain distringas on, 261.
    Notice to bank, 262.

SURRENDER. *See* COPYHOLDS.
    Of lease by indorsement, 294.

TENANT,
    Attornment of, 183.

TENANT IN TAIL. *See* DISENTAILING DEED.

TENANTS IN COMMON,
    Deed of partition by, 349.

TESTIMONIUM,
    To instrument executed by attorney, 402.

TITLE,
    Covenants for. *See* COVENANTS FOR TITLE.

TITLE DEEDS,
    Covenants to produce, 220, 251.

TRANSFER,
    Of mortgage to trustees of settlement, 332.
              with concurrence of mortgagor, 334.
              with further advance, 338.

TRUSTEE,
    Disclaimer by, of devised copyholds, 240.
    Appointment of new, 156.
              by indorsement, 158.

TRUST ESTATES,
    Devise of, 407.

TRUSTS,
    Disclaimer of, under will, 240, 257, 259.
    Declaration of, in marriage settlement of personalty, 398.
    For wife's separate use, 395, 398.
        children, 396, 399.
        next of kin in default of issue, 401.
    In assignment for benefit of creditors, 181.
        will for daughter's separate use, 406.

UNDERLEASE,
    Of garden ground, agreement for, 137.

UNDERTAKING,
    To pay intending mortgagee's costs, 341. *See* MORTGAGE.

USES,
    In settlement of real estate, 396.

VENDOR,
    Covenants by. *See* COVENANT—COVENANTS FOR TITLE.

WAIVER,
    By lessor of breaches of covenants, 295.

WARRANT,
    To enter satisfaction, 244. *See* COPYHOLDS.

WATER,
    Exception of, from lease, 286.

WELL,
    Exception of water from, 286.

WILL,
    Of a person making various devises and bequests, and giving the residue of his property to his children, 403.
    Giving every thing to wife and appointing her executrix, 404.
    Codicil to appointing new trustee and executor, and bequeathing additional legacy, 404.
    Bequest of furniture to wife, 405.
    Trusts in, for daughter's separate use, 406.
    Devise of trust estate in, 407.
    Clause prohibiting any claimant thereunder from disputing it, 407.
    Disclaimer of trust under, 240, 257, 259.

WITNESSING PART,
    In conveyance by appointment, 219.
            by grant, 221.
            by vendor and mortgagees, 223.
            by mortgagee, 225.
            of land to add to churchyard, 226.
            of freeholds, and covenant to surrender copyholds, 228.
    Conveyancing charges, 408.

LONDON:
PRINTED BY C. ROWORTH AND SONS,
BELL YARD, TEMPLE BAR.

Smith's (Josiah W.) Manual of Equity Jurisprudence.—
A Manual of Equity Jurisprudence founded on the Works of Story, Spence, and other writers, and on the subsequent cases; comprising the Fundamental Principles and the Points of Equity usually occurring in General Practice. By JOSIAH SMITH, B.C.L., one of Her Majesty's Counsel, Judge of County Courts. Ninth Edition. In 12mo. 1868. Price 12s. cloth.

Chitty's Archbold's Practice of the Court of Queen's Bench.
In Personal Actions and Ejectment, including the Practice of the Courts of Common Pleas and Exchequer. A New and Improved Edition (the Twelfth). By SAMUEL PRENTICE, Esq., Barrister-at-Law. In 2 vols. royal 12mo. 1866. Price 2l. 12s. 6d. cloth.

    Mr. Baron Martin, in *Andrews* v. *Saunderson*, thus speaks of this work:—"There is an admirable book—Mr. Prentice's Edition of Chitty's Archbold's Practice—a most useful book—one of the best books ever written; and the law is there stated in accordance with, &c. &c."

Chitty's Forms of Practical Proceedings in the Courts of
Queen's Bench, Common Pleas, and Exchequer of Pleas. With Notes and Observations thereon. A New and Enlarged Edition (the Tenth). By THOMAS CHITTY, Esq. In Royal 12mo. 1866. Price 1l. 11s. 6d. cloth.

Thring's Joint Stock Companies.—The Law and Practice
of Joint Stock and other Public Companies: including the Statutes, with Notes, and the Forms required in Making, Administering, and Winding-up a Company. With a Supplement containing the Companies Act, 1867, and Notes of recent Decisions. By HENRY THRING, M.A., of the Inner Temple, Esq., Barrister-at-Law: Parliamentary Counsel to the Home Office. Second Edition. 12mo. 1868. Price 18s. cloth.
(The Supplement may be had separately, price 2s. sewed.)

Cooke on Inclosures.—The Acts for Facilitating the
Inclosure of Commons in England and Wales; with a Treatise on the Law of Rights of Commons in reference to these Acts, &c. With Forms, as settled by the Inclosure Commissioners. By G. WINGROVE COOKE, Esq., Barrister-at-Law. Fourth Edition. 12mo. 1864. Price 16s. cloth.

Stephen's Principles of Pleading.—Seventh Edition. By
F. F. PINDER, Esq., Barrister-at-Law. 8vo. 1866. Price 16s. cloth.

Smith's Mercantile Law.—Seventh Edition. By G. M.
DOWDESWELL, Esq. Royal 8vo. 1865. Price 1l. 16s. cloth.

Roscoe's Nisi Prius.—A Digest of the Law of Evidence
on the Trial of Actions at Nisi Prius. Eleventh Edition. By WILLIAM MILLS, M.A., of the Inner Temple, Barrister-at-Law, and WILLIAM MARKBY, M.A., of the Inner Temple, Barrister-at-Law. Royal 12mo. 1866. Price 1l. 11s. 6d. cloth.

Levi's Commercial Law.—International Commercial Law.
Being the Principles of Mercantile Law of the following and other Countries, viz.:—England, Scotland, Ireland, British India, British Colonies. By LEONE LEVI, Esq., F.S.A., F.S.S., of Lincoln's-Inn, Barrister-at-Law, Professor of the Principles and Practice of Commerce at King's College, London, &c. In 2 vols. royal 8vo. Price 35s. cloth, lettered.

Pritchard's Admiralty Digest.—Second Edition. By
R. A. PRITCHARD, D.C.L., and W. T. PRITCHARD. With Notes of Cases from French Maritime Law, by ALGERNON JONES, in 2 vols. Royal 8vo. 1865. Price 3l. cloth.

Morgan and Davey's Chancery Costs.—A Treatise on Costs
in Chancery. By GEORGE OSBORNE MORGAN, M.A., and HORACE DAVEY, M.A., Barristers-at-Law. With an Appendix, containing Forms and Precedents of Bills of Costs. In 8vo. 1865. Price 1l. 1s. cloth.

Griffith's Law and Practice in Bankruptcy; with an
Appendix of Statutes, Orders, Forms, and Fees. Partly founded on the eleventh edition of Archbold's Treatise. By WILLIAM DOWNES GRIFFITH, Esq., assisted by C. A. HOLMES, Esq., Barristers-at-Law. In 2 vols. royal 8vo. 1867. Price 2l. 10s. cloth.

www.ingramcontent.com/pod-product-compliance
Lightning Source LLC
Chambersburg PA
CBHW031959300426
44117CB00008B/830